FABLE SCHOLARSHIP

WITHDRAWN

GARLAND FOLKLORE BIBLIOGRAPHIES
(General Editor: Alan Dundes)
Vol. 8

GARLAND REFERENCE LIBRARY
OF THE HUMANITIES
Vol. 367

Garland Folklore Bibliographies

General Editor
Alan Dundes
University of California, Berkeley

FABLE SCHOLARSHIP
An Annotated Bibliography

Pack Carnes

GARLAND PUBLISHING, INC. • NEW YORK & LONDON
1985

Library of Congress Cataloging in Publication Data

Carnes, Pack, 1939–
  Fable scholarship.

  (Garland folklore bibliographies ; vol. 8) (Garland
reference library of the humanities ; vol. 367)
  Includes indexes.
  1. Fables—History and criticism—Bibliography.
I. Title. II. Series: Garland folklore bibliographies ;
v. 8. III. Series: Garland reference library of the
humanities ; v 367.
Z5896.C37 1985   [PN980]   016.3982   82-48494
ISBN 0-8240-9229-5 (alk. paper)

Printed on acid-free, 250-year-life paper
Manufactured in the United States of America

For
Roland "Jimmy" Baader
and Ute, Rio, Miriam and Danny

CONTENTS

EDITOR'S PREFACE

The Garland Folklore Bibliographies are intended to provide ready access to the folklore scholarship of a particular country or area or to the scholarship devoted to a specific folklore genre or theme. The annotations are designed to be informative and evaluative so that prospective readers may have some idea of the nature and worth of the bibliographical items listed. No bibliography is ever complete and all bibliographies are doomed to become obsolete almost immediately upon publication as new monographs and articles appear. Still, there is no substitute for a comprehensive, intelligently annotated bibliography for anyone desiring to discover what has been written on a topic under investigation.

Fable is one of the most fascinating subgenres of folktale. Generally speaking, it is a short narrative, single episode, typically with *dramatis personae* consisting of animals and plants. Occasionally the characters are humans or objects. Fable is intended to be understood metaphorically rather than literally, and almost invariably it includes an explicit moral or didactic message.

According to this definition, in theory nearly any animal tale told anywhere in the world might qualify as a fable. But the conventions of folklore scholarship have decreed, somewhat ethnocentrically, that the fable is a largely literary form, confined to the Indo-European and Semitic world. Most of the great compilations of fables bear the marks of literary style even though the story-line may have originally stemmed from oral sources. To the extent that the fable is deemed, rightly or wrongly, a *literary* narrative genre, it is not presumed to flourish among peoples without a written language. Consequently, it is rare for scholars to speak of American Indian fables or Australian aboriginal fables—except where fable is used indiscriminately as a vague syn-

onym for folktale. Given this bias in fable scholarship, anyone
undertaking a bibliographical survey of fable research is more or
less bound by consensus to restrict the coverage to the Aesopic
tradition and comparable materials in India and the Near East.
It may well be that future generations of fable scholars will reject
this somewhat arbitrary restriction of the genre, but the history
of fable studies to date does reveal a fairly consistent emphasis
upon literary texts.

The gamut of fable scholarship runs from classics through
medieval literature right up to contemporary fabulists. The bibliography of this scholarship therefore requires linguistic exper-
tise far beyond the skills of conventional folklorists. Fortunately,
Professor Pack Carnes of the University of Arizona possesses the
requisite reading knowledge of numerous critical languages. In
addition to his fluency in German, Japanese and Danish, he is
able to read Latin, Greek, French, Dutch, and Chinese among
other languages.

Pack Carnes began his formal education in Germany and
France, with summers in Denmark. After attending high school
in the United States, he enrolled in Wabash College in Indiana,
earning a B.A. in German in 1962. After a year of graduate work
in German and Classics at UCLA plus a similar year of study at
Albert-Ludwigs-Universität in Freiburg i. Br., he served as As-
sistant Professor of English and Latin at Toyo Eiwa College and
Tokyo Joshi Daigaku in Japan from 1965–1969. During that
time, he wrote numerous textbooks on modern conversational
Japanese as well as textbooks to teach English to native speakers
of Japanese. In that same period, he spent summers as director
of the Summer Institute for teachers of foreign languages for
the Ministry of Education of Japan. Returning to UCLA, he
completed his M.A. in German in 1970, and his Ph.D. in Germanic Languages and Literatures in 1973. After a year at Lawrence University and three years at the University of Cincinnati,
Professor Carnes joined the department of German at the University of Arizona in 1976.

Professor Carnes has written a number of articles on the fable
and several on the joke. His professional interest in these genres
may be attributed in part to his remarkable talents as a racon-
teur. Members of the American Folklore Society who have had

the good fortune and pleasure to be present for Professor Carnes' delivery of his papers can vouch for his extraordinary performances which include an incredible ability to assume various linguistic accents and dialects, a further tribute to his unusual competence in languages. All scholars interested in the fable will have cause to be grateful to Professor Carnes for the great care he has lavished in assembling this marvelous annotated bibliography of fable scholarship. The helpful annotations plus the various indices succeed admirably in making the complex world of fable studies accessible to beginner and sophisticated scholar alike.

Alan Dundes, Editor
Garland Folklore Bibliography Series

INTRODUCTION

One of the most difficult tasks involved in the writing of a bibliography is exactly this part: writing the introduction. This section is very important in a bibliography, for here the limitations and the scope of the work that follows are set out and defended.

The time limits are roughly the past one hundred years. There are very few works before the 1880's, and 1982 is only partially done. The rough edges are on the side of more, rather than less, especially in the case of certain fundamental works that are still profitably read.

The subject matter limitations are far more difficult. There is no agreement among the authors of the works that follow upon the concept of fable, save in the most general terms, and it follows that many more write of "fables" meaning something akin to, but not the same as, the general term as represented here. The "fable" in this bibliography is generally assumed to comfortably fit under the rubric "Aesopic," although that, too, is rather widely interpreted. The base line, as it were, is Aesopica as found in the monumental *Aesopica* by Ben Edwin Perry. This work contains 725 separate motifs, the *Vita Aesopi* and a large number of classical witnesses to Aesop. Materials concentrating upon these elements are the core, but I have often ventured into other traditions: the Sumerian materials and *Panchatantra* on one end of the scale and the modern fabulists (Thurber, Arntzen, Schnurre, Monterroso, and the like) on the other. The center of gravity however is set, four-square, on the traditional corpus of Aesopica. Numerous exceptions have been made to admit works on Aesopic-like fables, and all works dealing with materials for which the claim of "Aesopic" has been made have been included.

Numerous problems of selection remain. The question of an author's relationship to Aesopica is one. La Fontaine is a prime example. La Fontaine wrote and rewrote Aesopic fables. As a fabulist of the first water, he clearly is to be included in this work. Yet La Fontaine is as popular with critics as he was with his public, and a complete bibliography of La Fontaine would fill a number of volumes of this size. Decisions clearly have to be made, and the general guideline that was followed here involves the specifics of fable study. Only those works that were specifically directed toward La Fontaine's fables or fable theory or La Fontaine's position in the history of fable writing were included. General treatments of La Fontaine were usually excluded, as they can be found in any La Fontaine bibliography. The same principles apply to Chaucer, Henryson, Lessing, and the dozens of other fabulists whose work is discussed in the entries that follow. Nevertheless, the works listed in the index under those fabulists' names will provide a relatively complete guide to the research on these materials.

Another question is that of textual investigations. The problem of textual criticism is of great importance to the classicist, while remaining somewhat tedious, often hopelessly redundant, to others. Much of this material is superceded, as often by time and style as by new scholarship, for there is fashion in research, too. My decisions here are to include all that seemed relevant and to exclude only such items as a now half-century-old polemic on the accentuation of a diphthong. That has meant the removal of some 200 to 300 entries, but all the points covered in those articles and notes are discussed in newer works and do not, in any case, lead to significant discussions of the Aesopica involved.

The apparatus provided is meant to be of the greatest use possible. Redundancy here is intentional. There are three indices covering subject matter, with most of the major subjects listed together with names of co-authors not easily found in the alphabetical listing by first authors. The fables discussed are given an index by Perry number wherever applicable; those fables not found in Perry are listed in the subject index. Perry numbers cover all the fables in the classical corpus, and those most likely to be found in Medieval and Renaissance fable writers. Most of the fables of the modern fabulists are covered by these numbers insofar as they have treated traditional themes and motifs. Perry numbers in the commentary are listed as P followed by a number. This is generally followed by an English version of the Greek or Latin title given by Perry, as, e.g., P15 "Fox and Grapes."

The third index is a listing of Tale Types together with a listing of Motif-Index numbers. The first of these is from Antti Aarne and Stith Thompson, *The Types of the Folktale* (Helsinki: Academia Scientarum Fennica, 1964), no. 184 in the Folklore Fellows Communications. The tale types are signaled in the commentary by A-T, followed by a number. The Thompson Motif Index numbers refer to the six-volume work by Stith Thompson, *Motif-Index of Folk-Literature* (Bloomington, Indiana: Indiana University Press, 1955). These are signalled by TMI followed by the motif number. Thus the fable mentioned above would most likely be listed in the commentary as P15 "Fox and the Grapes" (A-T 59; TMI J871) and be indexed under these numbers.

There are also "internal indices." At the end of a number of entries, a reference will be given to other works that supercede the work to which it is attached, offer another point of view, or develop the ideas with a different emphasis.

This bibliography is a personal one. It is an essay in the original meaning of that term, in the sense of trying to do something that has not been done before. It is a bibliography of scholarship, of secondary materials concerned with the Aesopic fable—and all of the words in that definition have had to be reevaluated. In that sense, it is intensely personal. But in another sense it is far from my own. I have had a great deal of help.

I am greatly in debt all round. The help afforded me by the libraries that have been constantly hounded for materials and copies of this and that and editions of this or that text—often on the slimmest of evidence and the most incomplete of references—is amazing. The staffs of the Newberry, Yale, Berkeley, UCLA, Cincinnati, Illinois, and many other libraries have my most respectful thanks. The staff of the University of Arizona library is especially to be thanked. In particular, the immediate constituents of the Inter-Library Loan Service in the University of Arizona library: Gloria Alvillar-Ritter and Denise Shomon, Colleen Carmean, Mina Parish, and a number of others, who have worked so hard for hundreds of requests. It is very difficult to overstress not only the forthcoming attitude expressed by these people, but the utter impossibility of having completed this work without their help. To Mrs. Ingrid Scott Hillebrand and Miss Lori Wiggins I owe an enormous debt for preparing the manuscript from an illegible multi-colored blur.

Finally, Alan Dundes, the General Editor of this series. There is some of him in this as there is in all of the bibliographies of this series. Without Alan, there would be none of this. That is the formal part; the personal part is more important. Men such as Alan come around only once or twice in a generation. Men with foresight and vigor matched only by their industry and acumen are rare indeed, and we are all enriched by their presence.

Pack Carnes
University of Arizona

Fable Scholarship

1. Achelis, Thomas Otto. "Aesope Tragedian." *Archiv für das Studium der neueren Sprachen und Literaturen*, 131 (1913), 435-437.

   Attempts to clear up confusion (more imagined than real) of Aesop the fabulist with an actor named Aesop at Rome during time of Cicero, pointing out the lack of connection between the fable and tragedy.

2. ————. "Aesopus Graecus per Laurentium Vallensen Traductus Erfurdiae 1500." *Münchener Museum für Philologie des Mittelalters und der Renaissance*, 2 (1913-1914), 222-229.

   Description of a manuscript of Lorenzo Valla's 33-fable translation handwritten into a leather-bound composite volume from the beginning of the sixteenth century and found in the University Library in Jena. The fables are handwritten on four blank pages at the end beginning "Aesopus grecus per Laurentiā Vallensē traductus incipit feliciter," then prologue, then four pages pasted in with fables no. 1 to the beginning of no. 24. The manuscript seems closer to the Erfurt printed version of 1500, as the Venice versions show a different ordering of the fables.

3. ————. "Die Aesopusübersetzung des Lorenzo Valla." *Münchener Museum für Philologie des Mittelalters und der Renaissance*, 2 (1913-1914), 239-278.

   Catalogue of the various editions of Lorenzo Valla's 33-fable translation from the Greek to Latin dated roughly 1438. Printed versions from 1495 (Venice) reflect the manuscript order and are related to the Accursiana tradition. These are compared to the Erfurt printed versions. Influence of Valla upon later translations and listings of some forty editions, omitting however Sebastian Brant's expanded edition of Steinhöwel's *Esopus*.
   See: Finch, "The Greek Source of Lorenzo Valla's Translation of Aesop's Fables" and Galli, "First Humanistic Translations of Aesop."

4. ————. "Zu den äsopischen Fabeln des Dati und Corraro." *Rheinisches Museum für Philologie*, NF 70 (1915), 380-388.

Various notes on the forty-fable collection of Leonardo
Dati described here as Augustan. Corraro's fables are
dated between 1429 and 1431 and relationships established
among the Renaissance Italian fable translation-collec-
tions.
See: Berrigan, *Fabulae Aesopicae* for an edition of
these translations, and Galli, "First Humanistic Translations of Aesop."

5. ————. "Die lateinischen Äsophandschriften der Vaticana
und Laurentiana." *Münchener Museum für Philologie des
Mittelalters und der Renaissance*, 3 (1915-1918), 216-
225.

Reports on twenty-eight manuscripts in the Vatican
Library, ten of which are shown to be of the Gualtherus
Anglicus (Walther of England) cycle and six of the Rinuccio
d'Arezzo translation, two of the Valla translation and
one each of the "Omnibonus leonicenus" and Gregorius Corraro and Gabriel Faernus traditions.

6. ————. "Die Fabeln des Rimicius in Steinhöwels Aesop."
*Beiträge zur Geschichte der deutschen Sprache und
Literatur*, 42 (1917), 315-330.

Discussion of the order of the seventeen fables from the
100-fable translation-collection of Rinuccio d'Arezzo found
in Heinrich Steinhöwel's *Esopus* of 1476/77. Steinhöwel
followed Rinuccio for sixteen and then added a later fable
to make up seventeen, matching the seventeen "extravagantes
antique" in the book preceding the Rinuccio fables. Notes
on the uses of the fables and close studies of the borrowing and various textual problems. Full indices to the
Greek text of Halm.

7. ————. "Antike Läusefabel." *Berliner Philologische
Wochenschrift*, 37 (1917), 61-63.

Answer to Thomas Brit (*Preussische Jahrbücher*, 164, p.
273) to the effect that the louse is not known in the
corpus of Aesop proper but that a louse fable (P471 "The
Lice and the Farmer"; TMI J2101.6.) is known from Appian
through the collection of Joachim Camerarius.

8. ————. "Zu Lessings Aufsatz Romulus und Rimicius."
*Archiv für das Studium der neueren Sprachen und Litera-
turen*, 139 (1919), 137-148.

An analysis of Lessing's attempt to disentangle the
confusion between the Romulus tradition, the medieval

prose fable tradition, and the so-called Rimicius fables. The latter are named in fact from a corrupted form of the name Rinuccio, called "Rimicius" in the *Esopus* of Heinrich Steinhöwel and later collections dependent upon that collection. Extensive discussion of the manuscripts and texts in Wolfenbüttel which Lessing used.

9. ————. "De falso credita fabularum Babrii conversione Latina." *Philologus*, 76 (1920), 113-126.

The fables P15 "The Fox and the Grapes" (A-T 59; TMT J871) and P155 "Wolf and the Lamb" (A-T 111A; U31) as found in Steinhöwel's collection of 1476/77 do not come directly from the "Romulus" or the medieval prose tradition as had been thought but appear to come from the translations from the Greek, in particular, from the Rinuccio translation of one hundred fables. Steinhöwel took seventeen fables from that translation for a section later in his work. Good indices.

10. ————. "De fontibus, quibus Christianus Petrui filius Lundensis ecclesiae canonicus in Aesopi vita fabulisque convertendis usus sit." *Nordisk Tidsskrift for Filologi*, 4 (1922), 1-14.

Christian Pedersen's 1556 edition of Aesop follows the German translation-collection of Steinhöwel (1476-77). The German version was certainly used as opposed to the Latin. Parallel texts of the Danish and German versions. See: Bengt Holbek, *Aesops levned og fabler*, for edition and exhaustive commentary.

11. ————. "Die Fabel Doligami." *Rheinisches Museum für Philologie*, 73 (1920-1924), 102-123.

Extensive investigation with regard to the identity of the person named in the cryptic phrase "... und mer etlich der fabel aviani *ach doligami* ..." in the preface to Heinrich Steinhöwel's *Esopus* of 1476/77. The phrase appears to have been puzzling to most sixteenth-century editors as well, as the phrase drops out in most later editions. The suggestion is made that the name might be a corruption of Politiani.

12. ————. "Die Adresse der Epistula Aesopi." *Münchener Museum für Philologie des Mittelalters und der Renaissance*, 4 (1924), 119-121.

The medieval Romulus prose fable tradition contains a letter with a prescript that assumes Aesop's authorship:

"Magistro Rufo Aesopus salutem," which is here amended
to read: "Magistro Rufo Aesopus," the "salutem" considered a later addition.

13. ————. "Die Fabeln Avians in Steinhöwel's Aesop."
     *Münchener Museum für Philologie des Mittelalters und
     der Renaissance*, 4 (1924), 195-221.

     Lengthy discussion of the twenty-seven fables from the
     Avianus collection that Steinhöwel chose and translated
     for his 1476/77 Ulm edition. Textual problems as well
     as the choice of fables are discussed with an analysis
     of those fabular motifs in Avianus, which had already
     appeared in early sections of Steinhöwel's collection.
     Tables of concordance and keys to Halm. Extensively dis-
     cussed are P70 "The Oak and the Reed" (A-T 28C; TMI J832),
     and P525 "Bald Man and the Fly" (TMI J2102.3).
     See: Carnes, "Heinrich Steinhöwel's *Esopus* and the
     Corpus of Aesopica in Sixteenth-Century Germany," and
     Duff, *Avianus*.

14. ————. "O si tacuisses." *Philologus*, 74 (1918), 470-
     472.

     The famous proverbial expression is attributed to
     Boethius, but is also found in P124 "Fox and the Crow,"
     Phaedrus I, 13 (A-T 57; TMI K334.1) in the version given
     by Odo de Ceritona (see Hervieux 2, 654) in additional
     material given under the title "contra venam gloriam."

15. ————. "Die Hundert äsopischen Fabeln des Rinucci da
     Castiglione." *Philologus*, 83 (1928), 55-88.

     Description and evaluation of the one hundred fable
     collection of Rinuccio (1448), with listings of the fables
     in an attempt to establish the manuscript tradition and
     the order in which Rinuccio worked. The source seems to
     have been a collection of the Vindobonensis group but one
     that might well have contained only one hundred fables
     (such as, e.g., the cod. Laur. 57).

16. ————. "Heinrich Eckert von Homberchs Ausgabe von Lorenzo
     Vallas Aesop und der Codex Urb. Lat. 886." *Münchener
     Museum für Philologie des Mittelalters und der Renaissance*,
     5 (1928-1931), 202-209.

     Deals with the problem of the order of the thirty-three
     fables in the Valla collection by comparing the order in
     the earlier printed works, especially the Erfurt and Jena
     editions and the Antwerp/Delft edition printed in 1498 by

Heinrich Eckert von Homberch, to the order found in the manuscript tradition, represented by the manuscripts related to Codex Urb. Lat. 886 of the Vatican.

17. Adams, F.B. "The Codex Pithoeanus of Phaedrus." *The Horn Book Magazine* (June, 1956), 260-266.

Popular account of the history of the fable from Greek times to the present occasioned by the purchase of the ninth-century Pithoeanus codex of Phaedrus by the Pierpont Morgan Library from the Marquis de Rosanbo. The final note is a comparison of various versions of P124 "Fox and the Crow" (A-T 57; TMI K334.1) from the Greek prose tradition through James Thurber.

18. Ader, Dorothea, and Axel Kress. "Ein Fabeltext als Gegenstand textlinguistischer Beschreibung in der Sekundarstufe I." *Der Deutschunterricht*, 29: 6 (1977), 7-21.

Extended discussion of language codes in the didactic elements of the fable, using in particular an Asian version of P149 "The Lion's Share" (A-T 51; TMI J811.1). Verbal codes and specific communicative codes are illustrated; verbal codes say one thing, communicative codes, being formulaic, mean quite another.

19. Adolf, Helen. "The Ass and the Harp." *Speculum*, 25 (1950), 49-57.

The "Ass of Boethius" is well represented in both the iconography and the literature of the Middle Ages and earlier, with examples from ancient Egypt and Babylonia as well as medieval Germany. Adolf finds a connection between *Asinus Lyras* (P542 "The Ass and the Lyre"; TMI J512.4) and the elements of *Ignorantia*.

20. Adrados, Francisco Rodriguez. *Estudios sobre el lexico de los fabulas esopicas.* Salamanca: Colegio trilingue de la Universidad, 1948. 285 pp.

Investigation into the language of the fable of the Greek Prose collection in the Vindobonesis, the Accursiana, and the Varia traditions. Extensive detail, well-indexed.

21. ———. "El Papiro Rylands 493 y la tradicion fabulistica antigua." *Emerita*, 20 (1954), 337-388.

Description and discussion of the fable collection text represented in Papyrus Rylands 493 which appears to be of

the family that is the oldest of which we are aware, the
Augustana. Reconstruction of this text might allow us a
view of the state of the collection in the first century
A.D.

22. ————. "El tema del águila, de épica Acadia a Esquilo."
     Emerita, 32 (1964), 267-282.

     Discussion of the Archilochus fable P1 "Eagle and the
     Fox" (TMI K2295) with a number of Near Eastern parallels,
     centering upon its evolution in archaic Greek forms.
     A number of Homeric similies are discussed and common
     traits cited.

23. ————. "El tema del león en el Agamenón de Esquilo
     717-749." *Emerita*, 33 (1965), 1-5.

     The idea of Helen compared to a lion cub is taken from
     the fables, with the lion as predator. This theme is
     traced through the fables and Aeschylus; Helen is com-
     pared to the "evil" of the lion with traditional motifs
     used to illustrate the theme, especially P142 "Old Lion
     and the Fox" (TMI J644.1), P143 "Lion and the Bull"
     (Babrius 97), P336 "Sick Lion, Fox and Stag" (A-T 50; TMI
     K402.3, K813).
     See: Perry, "Fable."

24. ————. "El tema del torrente en la literatura griega
     arcaica y clasica." *Emerita*, 33 (1965), 7-14.

     Discusses the possibility that Theognis and Sophocles
     might have been influenced by P133 "The Dog with the
     Meat and his Shadow" (A-T 34A; TMI J1791) and P70 "Oak
     and Reed" (A-T 298C; TMI J1791 and J832).

25. ————. "La tradición fabulistica griega y sus modelos
     métricos." *Emerita*, 37 (1969), 235-315 and 38 (1970),
     1-52.

     Extensive discussion centering upon concept that the
     present form of the Greek prose tradition, the Vindobonesis,
     the Augustana and the Accursiana collections are the re-
     sult of re-writing in prose of choliambic fables, traces
     of which verses can still be seen. The present collections
     are formed by a series of re-formations, contaminated
     with an "original" which was extant as late as the ninth
     century. The metrics are used to determine relationships
     among the various manuscript traditions. The argument
     concludes with an investigation of the Babrian fables.

26. ————. "Desiderata en la investigación de la fábula
esópica." *Actas del v. congreso español de estudios
clasicos.* Madrid: Publ. de la Soc. Españ. de estudios
clasicos, 1978, pp. 215-235.

Addresses problems, primarily textual, with the corpus
and the transmission of the Aesopic fable. Suggests
major courses of research and various tools.

27. ————. "Prolegómenos al estudio de la fábula en época
helenística." *Emerita,* 46 (1978), 1-81.

A reconstructed history of the Hellenistic fable collections from Demetrius of Phalerum to those extant today.
The fables from the Cynics and the prosified fables of
the later Hellenistic period are highlighted, with the
stoic and other moralizing tendencies as well as versification demonstrated to be illustrative of the fundamental
changes involved in using the fables as a pedagogical
tool.

28. ————. "Elementos cinicos en las 'Vidas' de Esops y
secundo y en el 'Diálogo' de Alejandro y los gimnoso-
fistas." *Homenaje al Eleuterio Elorduy, con ocasión de
su 80 anversario.* Ed. Rocamora Vallas. Bilbao: Universidad de Deusto, 1978, pp. 309-328.

Traces elements of the writings of the Cynics through
the Aesopic material.

29. ————. "Hechos generales y hechos griegos en los origen
de la satira y la critica." *Homenaje a Julio Caro
Baroja.* Ed. Antonio Carreira et al. Madrid: Centro
de Investigaciones Sociologicas, 1978, pp. 43-63.

Deals with the Aesopic tradition, in particular with the
Vita Aesopi in the last section (pp. 61-63), with the
character Aesop as *pharmakos.*
See: Adrados, "The Life of Aesop."

30. ————. "The Life of Aesop and the Origin of the Novel
in Antiquity." *Quaderni Urbinati di cultura classica,*
30 (1979), 93-112.

A thoroughgoing discussion of the *Vita Aesopi* as a pre-
cursor to the modern novel. Aesop is a story of an Anti-
Hero, a comedy in which the slave can ridicule his master.
Rodriguez Adrados dissects the *Vita* and finds part re-
modelled on analogy of Ahikar although differences between
the two are considerable. He finds a distinct Greek layer

of material in the "oriental" framework, especially the
Greek theme of the unjust death. This death and its ex-
piation by the Delphians is seen, following Wiechers
(q.v.), as an aetiology of the death of the *pharmakos*.
Aesop functions within many aspects of the original
fertility cycle of the pharmakos, with the added feature
of wisdom. This merging of traditions, together with a
sprinkling of fables, becomes the new creation of the
comic-realistic novel.

31. ────. "La fábula de la golondrina de Grecia a India
     y la Edad Media." *Emerita*, 48 (1980), 185-208.

     A study of P39 "Wise swallow and the Birds" (also P447,
     P437A and P614; A-T 233D; TMI J652.2) emphasizing its
     changes from the putative Demetrius of Phalerum form
     through the Augustana and P. Rylands 495 and Yale 1158
     versions of Babrius, Phaedrus and even Indian forms.
     Some suggestions with regard to the evolution and dis-
     persion of this and similar fables; textual criticism of
     a number of forms.
     See: Perry, "Demetrius of Phalerum."

32. ────. *Historia de la fábula greco-latina. I: Intro-
     ducción y de los orígenes a la edad helenística.* 2 vols.
     Madrid: Editorial de la Universidad Complutense, 1979
     [1980]. 727 pp.

     These two large volumes form the first part, the pre-
     Roman section, of a proposed history of the Graeco-Roman
     fable by one of the most prolific scholars of the day.
     The corpus of classical fables (more than 500) is dis-
     cussed from Sumerian analogues to the modern day, with
     emphasis upon the reconstruction of the Hellenistic col-
     lections and an investigation of the fable in the Middle
     Ages. These volumes begin this investigation with an
     attempt to reconstruct the collection of Demetrius of
     Phalerum, which forms an important turning point in the
     history of the form. The operative definition of the
     fable depends to a great extent upon the nature of the
     forms in this collection. Extensive discussion of the
     structure, metrics, content and language of the Greek
     fable, as well as a lengthy discussion of the *Vita Aesopi*.
     Complete indices planned for the second part.

33. Ages, Arnold. "Voltaire and La Fontaine: The Use of the
     Fables in the Correspondence." *Revue de l'Université
     d'Ottawa*, 39 (1969), 577-85.

Voltaire's use of images and allusions from La Fontaine's fables appear with such frequency that they
assume the role of a leitmotif, to heighten irony or to
strengthen an argument. Extensive discussion of P15
"The Fox and the Grapes" (A-T 59; TM1 J871), P60 "Old
Man and Death" (cf. TMI C11), P70 "Oak and Reed" (A-T
298C; TM1 J832), and P426 "Fox and the Crane" (A-T 60;
TM1 J1565.1).

34. D'Agostino, Vittorio. "Fedro poeta e favolista per le
    scuole." *Per lo studio degli autori latini.* Torino,
    1936, pp. 97-105. First in *Gymnasium* 3 (1934), 3-11.

    Interesting characterization of Phaedrus' life and
    works, demonstrating his breaking out of the "Aesopian
    format"; stressing the personal intrusions into the col-
    lection and commenting upon the increasing bitterness
    found there. Phaedrus' past and future usefulness as
    school texts is underscored.

35. Ahrens, Hermann. *Die Fabel vom Löwen und der Maus in der
    Weltliteratur.* Dissertation, Rostock, 1920.

    Traces the history of P150 "Lion and the Mouse" (A-T 75;
    TMI B371.1) throughout world literature from its earliest
    mention through the eighteenth century. Indian versions
    are covered first, with the earliest clear evidence for
    the motif dating from the fifth century A.D. although
    this is clearly reflective of a much older tradition.
    The Greek versions are simpler than the Indian, with the
    Pseudo-Dositheus apparently the oldest of these forms.
    Discusses the fabular motif through the Middle Ages and
    deals with the manuscript tradition as well as the literary
    stemma of the motif in the Romulus versions. The six-
    teenth-century versions all derive from Steinhöwel in
    Germany; in France the most independent version before
    La Fontaine is that of Clément Marot (1597).

36. Albertini, Virgil. "A Study of James Thurber's Fables."
    The Northwest Missouri State College Studies, 30: 2
    (1966), 3-15.

    Suggests curiously that Thurber follows the Aesopic
    tradition more closely than any other fabulist. Uses
    P426 "Fox and the Crane" (A-T 60; TMI J1565) to contrast
    with Thurber's "Moth and Star," to demonstrate Thurber's
    dependence upon the classical fable. Notes the irony and
    humor in Thurber although does not allow verbal humor or
    human actors in the classical forms. Recognizes the

political satire in Thurber's fables, as well as the con-
stant male-female conflict.
See: Jochum, "Die Fabeln James Thurbers."

37. Alewell, Karl. *Über das rhetorische Paradeigma: Theorie,
    Beispielsammlungen, Verwendung in der römischen Litera-
    tur der Kaiserzeit.* Dissertation, Kiel, 1913.

    The rhetorical use of fables (as well as similies and
    parables and other rhetorical devices) is discussed with
    particular regard to Aristotle, who lists fables in that
    class of rhetorical features listed as paradeigma.
    See: Perry, "Fable."

38. Alfonsi, L. "Parva moralia in Fedro." *Latomus*, 23
    (1964), 21-29.

    Connections are made between the poetic motifs of
    Phaedrus and a significant body of philosophical thought
    which enhances the appreciation of the poet.

39. Alsino, J. "Elementos esópicos en el cuento popular
    neogriego." *Actas de v. congreso español de estudios
    clasicos.* Madrid: Publ. de la Soc. Españ. de Estudios
    Clasicos, 1978, pp. 237-241.

    A short discussion of various Aesopic motifs found in
    modern Greek folktales and stories.

40. Alster, Bendt. *Studies in Sumerian Proverbs.* Copenhagen
    Studies in Assyriology, volume 3. Copenhagen: Akademisk
    Forlag, 1975.

    Deals with a selected group of Sumerian proverbs
    studied through an understanding of the individual words
    which is in turn based upon their function in the struc-
    tures in which they are found. Structural analysis of
    proverbs includes a number of fables or fabular motifs
    and the relationships found between fables and proverbs
    are alluded to.

41. Althaus, Hans Peter. *Die Cambridger Löwenfabel von 1382:
    Untersuchung und Edition eines defectiven Textes.*
    Berlin: de Gruyter, 1971, 238 pp.

    Extensive discussion of the textual tradition and a
    graphological analysis of the so-called "lion fable" in
    the T.S. 10, K22 (University Library, Cambridge). In-
    cludes an edition and exhaustive bibliography as well as
    a glossary to the terminology used.

42. Alverdes, Paul. *Rabe, Fuchs und Löwe: Fabeln der Welt.*
    Munich: Ehrenwirth, 1965, pp. 383-386. Also "Nachwort"
    published in *Das Nashorn als Erzieher: Fabeln der Welt.*
    Munich: Deutscher Taschenbuch Verlag, 1967, pp. 157-
    159.

    Popular, cursory overview of the history and the nature
    of the fable from Aesop and earlier, through the modern
    day, corresponding to the range of the collection which
    forms the main body of the work. Excellent selection
    and bibliographic notes.

43. Amory, Fredric. "Skaufalabalkur; its Author and its
    Sources." *Scandinavian Studies*, 47 (1975), 293-310.

    Discusses the literary relationship among late Icelandic
    beast epics and the continental beast epics and fables.
    The comic *Skaufalabalkur* and the *Skitharima* are well in-
    troduced although described as fables without definition
    of that term. Relationships to the *Fabula de Aegro
    Leone* and the *Ecbasis Cuisdam Captivi* and *Ysengrimus* and
    ultimately to the *Roman de Renart* are pointed out. P585
    "Sick Lion, Fox and Bear" (TMI B240.4) is the dominant
    motif with a complicated tradition of continental fabula-
    tion. Well-argued as well as the scanty evidence allows.

44. Anders, Heinrich. "Randglossen zu 'Shakespeare's Belesen-
    heit.'" *Jahrbuch der deutschen Shakespeare Gesellschaft*,
    62 (1926), pp. 158-162.

    Phaedrus IV, 10 (P266 "The Two Wallets"), apparently in
    the original Latin, is responsible for the allusion to
    the wallet in Shakespeare's *Troilus and Cressida* (III, 3,
    145) and also for the similar allusions to wallets in the
    Faerie Queen.

45. Anger, Alfred. "Herders Fabeltheorien." *Die Fabel:
    Theorie, Geschichte und Rezeption einer Gattung.* Ed.
    Peter Hasubek. Berlin: Erich Schmidt, 1982, 134-145.

    Outline and discussion of the fable theories of Johann
    Gottfried Herder, after a discussion of the lack of at-
    tention paid to those ideas in contrast to the great
    scholarly interest afforded to Lessing and other eighteenth-
    century theorists. Herder's interest in the fable is ex-
    tensive and comprehensive but not much appeared in his
    lifetime and what did appear was not easily accessible,
    being diffused throughout his writings. Anger details
    Herder's theoretical writings with particular emphasis
    upon contrasts with those of Lessing. Sees an important

change from the 1768 writings and the essay of 1787.
Herder proceeded from Lessing in his earlier writings
on the fable, but his later works no longer depend upon
other theories. He asks six questions of the Aesopic
fable in order to establish the concept of the form.
These ideas range from the use of animals in the fable
to the differences between the parable (and the example)
and the fable.

46. Anonymous (Lecture collective). "Avez-vous lu 'la cigale
     et la fourmi'?" *Europe*, 515 (1972), 132-146.

     Consists of opinions from various sources: Jean-Jacques
     Rousseau, René Jasinski, Jean Pierre Collinet and others,
     on their reading of La Fontaine's version of P373 "Cicada
     and the Ant" (A-T 280; TMI J711.1), the first fable in
     the La Fontaine collection, with the point of demonstrating
     that it is not enough to read; one must know how to read.

47. Archibald, Herbert Thompson. "The Fables in Archilochus,
     Herodotus, Livy and Horace." *Transactions of the
     American Philological Association*, 33 (1902), 80-90.

     Four types of literary uses of the fable are discussed:
     Herodotus uses the fable in a manner approaching the
     popular narrative; Livy as a rhetorical device; Archi-
     lochus uses the fable as invective; and Horace makes the
     humor inherent in the fable a means to an ethical and
     directly satirical end. Extensive discussion of P1 "Eagle
     and Fox" (TMI K2295), P4 "Hawk and Nightingale" (TMI
     J321.1), P130 "Belly and Members" (A-T 293; TMI J461.1)
     and P352 "Country Mouse and City Mouse" (A-T 112; TMI
     J211.1).

48. ————. "The Fable in Horace." *Transactions of the
     American Philological Association*, 41 (1910), 14-19.

     The ten fables found in Horace are discussed after a
     brief overview of the fable in classical literature.
     P93 "Serpent and the File" (TMI J552.3), P101 "Borrowed
     Feathers" (A-T 244; TMI J951.2), P124 "Fox and Crow"
     (A-T 57; TMI K334.1), P142 "Fox and Old Lion" (A-T 50A;
     TMI J644.1), P188 "Ass in Lion's Skin" (A-T 214B; TMI
     J951.3), P352 "Country Mouse and City Mouse" (A-T 112;
     TMI J211.1), P376 "Frog and Cow" (A-T 277A; TMI K643.1),
     P520 "Mountain in Labor" (TMI U114).

49. ————. *The Fable as a Stylistic Test in Classical
     Greek Literature*. Baltimore: Furst, 1912. 79 pp.

Discussion of the origin of the fable and its relationship to other genres, with an investigation of the
Greek fable throughout Greek literature, ranging from
its use in the epic to its function in philosophic texts.

50. Arens, J.C. "Fables van Babrius en Abstemius bij Revius."
    Neophilologus, 45 (1961), 333-336.

    Discussion of a number of fables found in Revius,
    among which are Babrius 42, P328 "Dog at the Banquet"
    (TMI J874). Two fables from Abstemius are compared to
    Revius' versions.

51. Arndt, Karl. "'De gallo et iaspide': Ein Fabelmotif bei
    Frans Synders." *Aachener Kunstblätter*, 40 (1971),
    186-193.

    Detailed, lucid description of Frans Synders' *Hahn und
    Edelstein* in context as painting and as a literary motif,
    depicting P503 "Cockerel and the Pearl" (TMI J1061.1),
    the fable that stood at the head of most medieval fable
    collections (eponymous, for example, to Ulrich Boner's
    Edelstein). The painting, once attributed to Rubens,
    was completed before 1620 and represents a breach with
    the fable illustration tradition that preceded it. Arndt
    tends toward an interpretation of the painting in line
    with the medieval and sixteenth-century use to which the
    fable was put, that is, the fable was given to describe
    those who do not in fact understand the fables, the
    "pearls" of the collection. So, too, says Arndt, did
    Frans Synder wish to defend his work.

52. Arthur, Marilyn B. "The Tortoise and the Mirror: Erinna
    PSI 1090." *Classical World*, 74 (1980), 53-65.

    Brief mention of the tortoise in P106 "Zeus and the
    Turtle" (TMI A2231.1.4--Why the turtle carries his house
    with him) and P230 "Turtle takes lessons from the Eagle"
    (TMI J657.2, cf. K1041; A-T 225A) in a discussion of the
    tortoise figure in the hexameters of Erinna. The turtle
    had an important set of symbolic meanings for the Greeks,
    in this case, both positive and negative. The two fables
    demonstrate the paradoxical nature of the turtle to re-
    main home (P106) and yet with a desire to fly (P230).

53. Austin, Herbert D. "The Origin and Greek Versions of
    the Strange Feathers Fable." *Studies in Honor of A.
    Marshall Eliott*. 2 vols. Baltimore: The Johns Hop-
    kins University Press [1912]. 1, 305-327.

Extensive discussion of P101 "Borrowed Plumage" (A-T
244; TMI J951.2) in literature; actually a complex of
similar fables clustered about a central motif when considered from the point of view of the main actor, the
jackdaw. The complex extends to P2 "Eagle, Jackdaw and
Shepherd" (TMI H2413.3), P123 "Jackdaw and Crows" and
P219 "Jackdaw and Pigeons" (both TMI J951.2), P126 "Jackdaw and Fox" (TMI J2066.2), P131 "Runaway Jackdaws"
(TMI U255.2), P294 "Crane and Peacock" (TMI J242.5).
In this complex the vanity of the daw is the motivation
for his actions, generally a masquerade. The assembly
of birds (rather than a single adversary or none at all)
and the use of various types of feathers appear to be of
medieval origin; the Romulus fables almost always have a
large bird rather than a daw. Babrius 72 is the most
popular Greek version; Phaedrus' version seems to be a
contamination of motifs although this ultimately proved
to be the most popular. Motif-complex is then discussed
in later Greek forms and the early prose tradition.

54. Avery, Myrtilla. "Miniatures of the Fables of Bidpai
     and of the Life of Aesop in the Pierpont Morgan Library."
     The Art Bulletin, 23 (1941), 103-116.

     Extensive and detailed study of the illustrations to
     the *Kalilah and Dimnah* and the *Vita Aesopi* in the late
     tenth century manuscript (M397). The fables had been
     edited by Husselmann (q.v.). The illustrations are
     similar to South Italian miniatures. Discusses illustra-
     tion mechanics.

55. Awouma, Joseph-Marie. *Contes et Fables du Cameroun:
     Initiation à la Littérature orale*. Yaounde: Editions
     Clé, 1976.

     Short collection of some twenty texts and cursory
     discussion of their status as oral literature.

56. Axelson, Bertil. "Die zweite Senkung im jambischen
     Senar des Phaedrus." *Vetenkaps-Societeten i Lund*,
     Årsbok (1949), 45-68.

     Exhaustive discussion of the position of the accentua-
     tion in the metrics of Phaedrus' fables.

57. Badstüber, Hubert. *Die deutsche Fabel von ihrer ersten
     Anfängen bis auf die Gegenwart*. Vienna: Gerold, 1924.
     48 pp.

     Historical overview of the fable in Germany from its
     beginning in the seventh century with the Franks to the

present. Badstüber decries most contemporary scholarship on the fable, suggesting that there is no satire nor necessarily any didactic purpose to the fable, as it is more closely connected with the epic. Contains a highly opinionated survey of fabulists from "Aesop" and Phaedrus through Emanuel Fröhlich and Hermann Rollett. Badstüber explains the decline of the fable in modern times as the result of the increase in industrialization and a corresponding alienation of the "folk" who husbanded their animals. Although professing to be a comprehensive survey, the work contains a large number of errors and omissions.

See: Leibfried, *Fable*.

58. Baist, Gottfried. "Der dankbare Löwe." *Romanische Forschungen*, 29 (1910), 317-319.

A short historical overview of P563 and P563A "Thankful Lion" (A-T 156; TMI B381), the most famous reflex of which is Androcles and the lion, much changed from the original versions. The thorn in the paw of the lion is a snake in at least one eleventh century version; the lion is an elephant in others. Baist claims a "Tiererlebnis" lies at the heart of the Androcles story, not a parable or Märchen.

See: Arthur Gilchrist Brodeur, "The Fable of the Grateful Lion" and "Androcles and the Lion."

59. Baker, Howard. "A Portrait of Aesop." *Sewanee Review*, 78 (1969), 557-590.

An enlightened discussion of the difficulties with the *Vita Aesopi* and the portrait of Aesop that emerge from both the literary tradition and the iconography. Baker touches upon the fables in their historical context and treats P142 "Old Lion and Fox" (A-T 50A; TMI B240.4) and P543 "Widow of Epheseus" (A-T 1510; TMI K2213.1) and especially P3 "Dung Beetle and the Eagle" (TMI L315.7) in relationship to Aristophanes' *Peace* and Erasmus' *Adagia*.

60. Baldi, Agnello. "Tracce del mit di Etana in Archiloco ed Esopo." *Aevum*, 35 (1961), 381-384.

Note on the survival of traces of a Babylonian myth in both Archilocus and in Aesop.

61. Baldwin, T.W. "Lower Grammar School: Shakespere's Construction: *Aesop*." *William Shakespere's Small Latine*

and Lesse Greeke. 2 vols. Urbana: University of
Illinois Press, 1944. Vol. 1, pp. 607-640.

The Latin curriculum is examined in detail as part of
the wider problem of Shakespeare's education and the
types of education during the Elizabethan era in general.
The Grammar, the *Sententiae Pueriles* and Cato are discussed, the Aesop, pp. 607-640. Aesop was the next subject "for construction" after Cato, done in the second
form but usually continued into the third. In all these
cases, the emphasis was upon the moral and various interpretations of the fables as well as the Latin to be
gained from their memorization. That this was indeed
the standard mode of education throughout Europe during
the sixteenth century is clear from Erasmus, Luther,
Brinsley, and others. Baldwin then details Shakespeare's
moral use of the fable, noting the previous work done in
the field. Shakespeare's use of some ten or eleven fables
(some in somewhat obscure allusions) cannot have come
from the Greek nor apparently from the Caxton or Henryson
English versions but must have come from some Latin version, most likely one of the editions of Joachim Camerarius. Baldwin lists all direct quotations and allusions
to Aesopica found in the works of Shakespeare as well as
a number of possible ones and finds an analogue in
Camerarius for most of them. The moral applications
seem to parallel those in Camerarius very well. There
are also possible allusions to Phaedrus although these
are not clearly seen as directly attributable to the
Roman poet. Comprehensive survey of previous research.
See: Yoder, *Animal Analogy in Shakespeare*.

62.   Barie, Paul. "Menenius Agrippa erzählt eine politische
      Fabel." *Der altsprachliche Unterricht*, 13:4 (1970),
      50-77.

This article is concerned with a linguistic and "ideological" investigation of P130 "Stomach and Feet"
(A-T 293; TMI J461.1) as reportedly told by Patrician
Menenius Agrippa in the year 494 B.C. This political
fable was used then to convince the population of Rome
to rally. The fable is investigated from the point of
view of its symbolization (modern examples are used), of
its ideology (also with modern examples), and as a Latin
text, for use in schools as such with criticism and
analysis.

63.   Barner, Wilfried, et al. "Arbeitbereich IV: Lehrdichtung
      und poetische Eigenart (Fabeln und Laokoon)." *Lessing:*

Epoche--Werke--Wirkung. Munich: Beck, 1975, pp. 189-202.

As part of an introduction to a wide selection of Lessing's works, this section on the fable begins with an overview (with bibliography on the fable and Lessing's *Abhandlungen*). The fable is then treated as a fashionable literary genre in the eighteenth century; then narrowed to Lessing's specific concern for the form. Focus is upon Lessing's definition of the fable and his attitudes toward the fable, his views of the form as something between poetry and philosophy, and call for the return to the original brevity of the Aesopic fable.

64. Barnett, Lionel. "Introduction." *Hitopadesa: The Book of Counsel.* Translated by Francis Johnson. London: Chapman and Hall, 1928. 201 pp.

Brief history of the Hitopadeśa, demonstrating its complex relationship to the Pañchatantra. Textual notes to the tradition and notes critical to the translation.

65. Barrick, Mac E. "Sameniego's Fables: An Index of Antecedents." *Kentucky Romance Quarterly*, 23 (1976), 409-420.

Building upon the fact that the fable thrives when didacticism is considered a primary function of literature, Barrick finds it no accident that Spain's greatest fabulists, Tomas de Iriate and Felix Maria de Samaniego, flourished when Neoclassicism was the dominant literary style. The fables are indexed and keyed to standard collections; tentative conclusions indicate as many as 64 are similar to La Fontaine, some 20 linked to John Gay; fewer than 15 of the 157 fables are completely original with Samaniego.

66. Bartelink, G.J.M. "Een thema uit de fabelliteratuur en het dierenepos in de Middeleeuwen." *Lampas. Tijdschrift voor Nederlandse classici*, 10 (1977), 283-301.

Wide-ranging discussion of the influence of Aesopica upon the animal epic of the Middle Ages.

67. Bassan, Fernande. "La Fontaine, heritier d'Esope et de Pilpay." *Comparative Literature Studies*, 7 (1970), 161-178.

La Fontaine's sources discussed, particularly those sources for the later books of fables among which some twenty fables are seen as coming from Pilpai (*Kalila and Dimna*, *Bidpai*, etc.). Discussion also upon the "non-oriental" fables in the later books. Fables not keyed to standard collections.

68. Bastin, Julia. *Recueil général des Isopets*. 2 vols. Paris: Librairie ancienne Honoré Champion, 1929-1930.

Introduction (vol. 1) describes the textual history of the *Isopets*, with traditional fable history. Annotated French texts of *Isopets I* and *II* and the *Isopet de Chartres*; Latin of *Novus Aesopus*.

69. ————. "Quelques Notes sur Julien Macho et son Esop." *Mélanges de linguistique romane et de philologie offerts à M. Maurice Delbouille*. 2 vols. Gembloux (Belgium): J. Ducolot, 1964. 2, 45-47.

The Augustinian Julien Macho of Lyon was a translator of wide-ranging interests, from mystic works to his Aesopic translations. The *Esop* was translated from the Latin side of the bilingual compilation of Heinrich Steinhöwel and was published in Lyon in 1480. Four incunabula editions, 1480, 1484, 1486, amd 1499, all Lyon, are listed.

70. Batany, Jean. "Renardie et asnerie: La Fontaine et la tradition médiévale." *Europe*, 515 (1972), 62-73.

A well-grounded discussion of La Fontaine in the light of his possible and potential medievalisms. La Fontaine's ideas concerning animal behavior and symbolization show medieval traits of the type of the Isengrimus and the Renart tradition, yet numerous avenues of further research, demonstrating the complexity of La Fontaine's archaisms, are indicated.

71. Batereau, Otto. *Die Tiere in der mittelhochdeutschen Literatur*. Dissertation, Leipzig, 1909. 69 pp.

An extensive catalogue of the animals to be found in German Literature (and much that is not so much literature) during the Middle High German period. The fables are discussed, and relationships among the various animals, listed by animal rather than by text, are discussed from a number of points of view: in fables but also in proverbs, in an allegorical sense, and so on. No index but animals arranged by groups and alphabetically within the groups.

72. Bauer, Gerhard. "Der Burger als Schaf und als Scherer: Sozialkritik, politisches Bewusstsein und ökonomische Lage in Lessings Fabeln." *Euphorion*, 67 (1973), 24-51.

     Intriguing socio-historical interpretation of the Lessing fable and of Lessing the fabulist. Lessing's fables are not critical observations but moral dicta; still Lessing is typical for his age in the declining years of Absolutism, which Lessing criticized and in the times of accelerating industrialism and capitalism which he did not understand. Special concern is given to Lessing's fables as compared to Phaedrus.

73. Baum, Paul Franklin. "The Fable of Belling the Cat." *Modern Language Notes*, 34 (1919), 462-470.

     An exhaustive historical survey of P613 "Belling the Cat" (A-T 110; TMI J671.1) from *Kalilah and Dimna*, apparently the earliest known, but not always with this collection, through the fifteenth century. The earliest version known in the West seems to have been Odo of Cheriton. Baum lists the Old French and other medieval versions and focuses upon six fourteenth-century versions in an attempt to define the relationships to the fable as found in *Piers Plowman*. The suggestion is made that the Plowman poet may have known the fable in either manuscript form (from, possibly, Odo's *Fabulae*), or from oral tradition. Extensive lists of versions of the fable are followed by examples of proverbial phrases derived from the fable from the fourteenth century through the sixteenth century.

74. ———. "The Mare and the Wolf." *Modern Language Notes*, 37 (1926), 350-53.

     Chaucer's Miller's mare and wolf are seen as a conflation of "Lion and Horse" (cf. P187) and P693 "Fox and Mule" (A-T 47; TMI K566, K1955).

75. Baum, Richard. *Recherches sur les oeuvres attribuées à Marie de France*. Heidelberg: C. Winter, 1969. 241 pp.

     A report on the research concerning the *lais*, the fables, and other works attributed to Marie de France. Extended discussion of the fable: stages of research in its historical development, theories concerning the instigation for the writing of the fables, relationships between the fable and various other types of writing, report on the manuscript tradition. The collection as

a whole is the main concern: the fables are not individually discussed. Extensive bibliography.

76. Bauman, Richard. "The Folktale and Oral Tradition in the
    Fables of Robert Henryson." *Fabula*, 6 (1963), 108-124.
    [Rewrite and condensation of M.A. Thesis in Folklore
    at Indiana University, 1962 with same title, 67 pp.]

    An interesting and important attempt to relate Robert
    Henryson's "Moral Fables of Aesop" to the oral tradition
    and to the *exempla* tradition. Incorrectly identifies
    Heinrich Steinhöwel's German and Latin edition/collection
    as a Flemish collection, but properly emphasizes the
    need for postulating oral sources; fables keyed to A-T
    numbers.
    See: Denton Fox, *The Poems of Robert Henryson.*

77. Baumann, Sally. "The Individual in the Fables of La
    Fontaine." Dissertation, University of Chicago, 1976.

    La Fontaine's fables show an increased importance of
    the narrative at the expense of the moral, which does
    not adequately express the implications of the story line
    as a complex, self-contained drama. The opposition in
    the fable story is usually between two individuals, but
    the fables also contain the individual's relation to his
    environment, particularly to the state. Relationship to
    the state involves the "court cycle" fables and various
    aspects of the establishment of an ethical code. Dis-
    cussion of the narrator's relationship to his narration,
    which gives aid to the idea that the fables, taken to-
    gether, possess a certain coherent logic.

78. Becher, Wilhelm. "Eine Aesopische Fabel auf einem
    römischen Grabstein." *Neue Jahrbücher für klassische
    Philologie*, 11 (1903), 74-75.

    Refers to the report by Borman and Bennedorff (q.v.)
    on a marble gravestone found near Florence with reference
    to P426 "Fox and Stork" (A-T 60; TMI J1565.1). Feels
    Bennedorff is reading too much into the contrasting
    names mentioned in the text. The stone is likely to
    have been for a family.

79. Beck, Hans-Georg. *Geschichte der byzantinischen Volks-
    literatur.* Byzantinisches Handbuch im Rahmen des
    Handbuchs der Altertumswissenschaft, Zweiter Teil,
    Dritter Band. Munich: Beck, 1971.

    Discussion of the medieval Greek tradition of Aesop's
    life and fables, the Byzantine *Aesopos* especially the

G version of the vita in the tripartite working of the vita Aesopi. No definitive versions of the fables are found in the Byzantine tradition, but there are traces of large collections formed during this era or carried through this era. These are the Augustana known from roughly the tenth century, best known in Monac. 564 from the thirteenth century but most likely datable as early as the third century and the Accursiana, associated with the monk Maximo Planudes, indicated by Beck as a possible compiler of this "typical Byzantine collection of fables." The so-called Syntipas fables are traceable to a Syrian version of the Aesopic fables traveling under the name of Iosip, having been translated into Greek (presumably by Andreopulos).

See: Perry, *Text Tradition*, and Perry, "Fabularum quae syntipae nomine inscribitur," pp. 511-550 in Perry, *Aesopica*.

80. Becker, Josef. "Grille und Ameise: Zum Verständnis von zwei Fabelfiguren." *Der Deutschunterricht*, 12: 4 (1960), 111-114.

This article uses P373 "Cicada and the Ant" (A-T 280A; TMI J7111.1) to illustrate techniques in producing fables in the school with already well-known and traditional fable figures; the leading idea being that the familiar characters do not strain the child's ability to form fables.

81. Bedrick, Theodore. "The Prose Adaptations of Avianus." Dissertation, University of Illinois, Urbana, 1940.

The medieval rewritings and prose paraphrases of Avianus during the Middle Ages are discussed. The use of Avianus in schools as a medium for the instruction of Latin is highlighted.

82. Belli, Marco. *Magie e pregivdizi in Fedro.* Venice: Cordella, 1895. 29 pp.

Discusses the traces of magic and superstition in Phaedrus II, 3, P64 "Wrong Remedy for Dog Bite" (TMI J2108), in which the throwing of the blood-drenched bread is seen as a charm. Aesop says that the man ought not to allow other dogs to see the bread or they might feel that their guilt is being rewarded.

83. Bellosta, Marie-Christine. "La Vie d'Esope le Phygien
     de La Fontaine ou les ruses de la vérité." *Revue
     d'Histoire Littéraire de la France*, 79 (1979), 3–13.

     Discussion of the reasons for the inclusion of *Vita
     Aesopi* in the La Fontaine collection. Concludes the
     romance is treated like a fable and serves as the first
     element in the collection.

84. Bender, Ernst. "Lessing: Der Hamster und die Ameise:
     Zur Behandlung in Sexta." *Der Deutschunterricht*, 7: 5
     (1955), 64–68.

     Presentation of Lessing's fable of the Hamster and
     the Ants for practical use in the sixth forms in school,
     approached from a structural and an interpretative
     manner.

85. Bercovitch, Sacvan. "Clerical Satire in the 'Vox and
     the Wolf.'" *Journal of English and German Philology*,
     65 (1966), 287–294.

     Finds a serious clerical satire disguised in the clever
     stratagem of the Vox and the Wolf, the sole representative
     before the time of Chaucer of tales from the Roman de
     Renard. The satire is a protest directed against those
     clerics who perverted their offices toward mundane ends,
     in the form of P593 "Fox and Wolf in the Well" (A–T 32;
     TMI K1961 and K2010).

86. Berger, Arnold Erich. *Lied-, Spruch- und Fabeldichtung
     im Dienst der Reformation*. Deutsche Literatur in
     Entwicklungsreihen. Reihe Reformation, vol. 4. Leip-
     zig: Reclam, 1938.

     Introduction and notes contain a short overview on the
     frequency and extent of fables and fable collections in
     early sixteenth-century Germany, as introductory back-
     ground materials to the fables selected for inclusion
     in the text. Leaves generally unanswered basic questions
     concerning the actual rhetorical, aesthetic, and peda-
     gogical uses to which the fables were put during this
     time, especially by Martin Luther.
         See: Both, "Luther und die Fabel"; Vander Meulen, "Erasmus
     Alberus."

87. Berner, Josef. *Fable in Unterricht: Unterrichtsbeispiele
     für Hauptschulen und die Unterstufe allgemeinbildener
     höherer Schulen*. Vienna: Österreichischer Bundes-
     verlag, 1979. Deutsche Sprache und Literatur im Unter-
     richt, no. 5. 72 pp.

A comprehensive treatment of the use of the fable in middle-school pedagogy, beginning with a discussion of the range, structure, characters of the form, as well as the origin, historical context, and the reception of the fable in and out of a school context. Uses P384 "Mouse and Frog" (A-T 278; TMI J681.1) to demonstrate the introductory materials and numerous classical and modern motifs, each with a suggested plan for use in class, for graded materials from the fifth through the eighth school year.

88. Berrigan, Joseph R. "The Libellus Fabellarum of Gregorio Correr." *Manuscripta*, 19 (1975), 131-138.

Deals with the then unpublished 53-fable collection of Gregorio Correr (later published with a translation into English by Berrigan, see 89). Describes in detail the Codex Marcianus Latinus xii 155 (= 3953) which seems to have been Correr's master copy. Details those fables which were not previously treated by Finch (q.v.).

89. ———. *Fabulae aesopicae Hermolai Barbari et Gregorii Curarii*. Lawrence, Kansas: Coronado Press, 1977.

Provides texts and translations for two of the very earliest Italian Renaissance translations of fables. The first is the translation/collection of Ermolae Barbaro consisting of thirty-three fables completed in 1422, years before Lorenzo Valla translated the same thirty-three fables. This is followed by Correr's work, more a selection of original creations than squarely in the tradition of the Aesopic fable. Berrigan has previously discussed, however, *loci* for many of the motifs in the collection in his article on the *Libellus Fabellarum* of Correr. No notes, no indices; fables not keyed to standard editions.

90. ———. "The Latin Aesop of Ermolae Barbaro." *Manuscripta*, 22 (1978), 141-148.

A survey of the contents and the history of Barbaro's fable translation and collection as preserved in the British Museum manuscript 33782. The text is the same used by Valla and was provided by his mentor Guarino. Excellent overview of Humanistic fable collection/translations and their relationships.

91. Bertini, Ferrucio. *In monaco Ademarro e de sua reraccolta de favole fedriane*. Geneva: Tilgher, 1975. 233 pp.

A study of the fables of Ademar de Chabannes (988–
1034) especially in the Vossianus latinus 8, 15 containing 67 Ademar fables. Reviews research on the life of
Ademar and his relationship to Phaedrus and the *Romulus*.

92. ———. "Un perduto manoscritto de fedro fonte della
      favole medievali di Ademaro." *Helikon*, 15–16 (1975–
      1976), 390–400.

      Critical notes to Phaedrus I, nos. 3, 11, and 22 on
      the basis of his work with Ademar and the Codex Pithoeanus,
      which is described in detail. The versions in the
      Pithoeanus are given priority over all others.

93. ———. "Fortuna medievale ed umanistica nella favola
      dell'asino e del cinghiale (Phaedrus I, 29)." *Lettera-
      ture comparate. Problemi e metodo: Studi in onore di
      E. Paratore*. Bologna: Putron, 1981, pp. 1063–1073.

      Notes on various responses to P484 "Ass insults the
      Boar" (TMI J411.1) during the Middle Ages and the Renais-
      sance.

94. Bertlosao, Stella J. "A Origen de fabula." *Revista de
      Historia* (San Paulo), 42 (1971), 175–182.

      The apparent origin of the fable (not defined) is to
      be sought in India although the textual transmission
      reasons for that conclusion are not clear.

95. Bertschinger, Josef. *Volkstümliche Elemente in der
      Sprache des Phaedrus*. Bern: Beck, 1920.

      An attempt to identify specific national (i.e., Greek)
      elements in the Latin of Phaedrus.

96. Beyer, Jürgen. *Schwank und Moral: Untersuchungen zum
      altfranzösischen Fabliaux und verwandten Formen*. Heidel-
      berg: Carl Winter, 1969.

      In the context of the Fabliaux in general, two chapters
      deal with the fable; the first is on Marie de France;
      the second on Petrus Alfonsus. Beyer discusses the
      nine "Schwankfabeln" in the Anglo-Norman collection and
      then deals with the fable in more general terms, in order
      to come to grips with the *Schwank* as a changed form when
      in a fable collection and also the other way around.
      Excellent discussion of the process involved when essen-
      tially amoral material is mixed with didactic materials.

97. ————. "The Morality of the Amoral." *The Humor of the Fabliaux*. Ed. Thomas D. Cooke and Benjamin Honeycutt. University of Missouri Press, 1974, pp. 15-42.

Essentially a summary of the longer works (see above), dealing with the *Schwank* and its relationship to, among other forms, the fable.

98. Beyerle, Marianne. "La Fontaines Fabel 'Le Serpent et la lime' im Vergleich zu ihrer Vorlagen." *Archiv für das Studium der neueren Sprachen und Literaturen*, 199 (1962), 167-173.

Two potential sources for La Fontaine's fable: P93 "Viper and the File" (TMI J552.3) which seems to be nearer to La Fontaine in situation and P59 "Weasel and File" (also TMI J552.3), closer to La Fontaine in its moral. Discussion of La Fontaine's use of sources and his attitudes toward his materials.

99. Biard, Jean-Dominique. *The Style of La Fontaine's Fables*. Oxford: Blackwell, 1966. French Translation: *Le Style des fables de La Fontaine*. Paris: Nizet, 1970. [First Dissertation, University of London]

General survey of previous work on La Fontaine's stylistics, then exhaustive investigation of particulars after establishing how important considerations of style were to La Fontaine, whose preoccupation with the fable was based essentially upon aesthetic grounds. Key concepts of grace, conciseness, beauty, and subtlety and selective imitation are keys to La Fontaine's style. His language is investigated in regard to vocabulary, use of archaisms, neologisms, proverbs and the like as well as narrator, intrusions and humor in the texts. La Fontaine's originality is seen to be in the tone and in the style, not in the invention of material. Good bibliography.

100. Bieber, Dora. *Studien zur Geschichte der Fabel in den ersten Jahren der Kaiserzeit*. Dissertation, Munich, 1905. 58 pp.

From a widely diversified set of sources, the author distills a definition of the fable as a fictive story the purpose of which is to express a warning by representing a general (and generalized) truth. The fable often compresses, often expands its generalized statement so as to appear to be a miniature art form. The author then collects such evidence as still exists in

an attempt to determine the nature of the fable collections which lie at the basis for the paraphrases of
Phaedrus and Babrius that appeared in the Middle Ages;
deciding upon a book in prose that carried the name of
Aesop with Aesop as a narrator. This book is assumed
to be that from which Plutarch and Phaedrus as well as
Horace worked. The *Vita Aesopi* is closely associated
with it. No evidence is, however, forthcoming to support
these speculations.

101. Bihler, Heinrich. "Zur Gestalt mittelalterlicher latein-
      ischer, französischer und spanischer Fassung der Fabel
      vom Fuchs und Raben." *Medium Aevum Romanicum: Fest-
      schrift für Hans Rheinfelder*. Ed. Heinrich Bihler and
      Alfred Noyer-Weidner. Munich: Max Huber, 1963, 21–48.

      Well-balanced discussion of the medieval versions of
      P124 "Fox and the Crow" (A-T 57; TMI K334.1) beginning
      with the *Romulus Nilanti* and Marie de France and con-
      trasting the allegorical content of the first with the
      moralizing versions of the second together with the
      satirical form of Juan Ruiz. Numerous other versions
      are brought to bear upon the discussion.

102. Birch, Cordelia Margret. *Traditions of the Life of
      Aesop*. Dissertation, Washington University, 1955.
      239 pp.

      An evaluation of the main traditions of the *Vita
      Esopi*: the three Greek versions and the singular Latin
      Lollinianus 26. Concludes that the so-called P1 is
      better "morally," grammatically and stylistically and
      that the text tradition demonstrates that although no
      one manuscript depends upon any other similarities
      clearly show all of them descend from a common archetype.

103. Birt, Thedor. *Das antike Buchwesen in seinem Verhältnis
      zur Litteratur*. Berlin: Wilhelm Hertz, 1882.

      The Phaedrine fables are discussed in this work as an
      example of the origins of the classical shape and nature
      of the "book" (pp. 385–95, et passim), the scope of which
      is categorized by the number of verses. The result of
      this verse counting leads Birt to assume that more than
      half of the text of Phaedrus is missing. He adds further
      evidence from the Prologue as found in the Perotti
      Appendix and then a not-very-convincing argument con-
      cerning the political intrigues in which Phaedrus was
      involved. Discussion of Phaedrus IV, 7 (with a few lines
      of Aesop on the stage), in which the "fable" is discussed
      in terms of its "triadic" structure.

104. Bissondayal, B. "La Fontaine's Debt to the East." *Contemporary Review*, 1118 (Feb. 1959), 126-128.

An account of La Fontaine's familiarity with the "East," here virtually exclusively India, and more specifically, the fables of "Pilpay." These fables seemed to have been most admired by La Fontaine, who preferred them to those of his own medieval tradition.

105. Bitschofscky, R. "Zu den Fabeln des Romulus." *Wiener Studien*, 32 (1910), 261-271.

Cautious comments upon Thiele's Romulus edition of 1910 (q.v.), generally of a text-critical nature. Many emendations are suggested to the Romulus text on the basis of classical readings and the Phaedrine fables.

106. Blake, N.F. "Reynard the Fox in England." *Aspects of the Medieval Animal Epic*. Louvain: Louvain University Press, 1975, pp. 53-65.

Surveys recent attempts to establish the *Roman de Renart* in England prior to its printing in the late fifteenth century. Reopens the question of whether the "Vox and the Wolf" was in fact dependent upon the Reynard tradition. This work, which contains P593 "Fox and the Wolf in the Well" (A-T 32; TMI K1961) and an unsuccessful fox in a Chanticler episode (cf. P597) does not seem to be closely related to the continental *Roman de Renart* and in fact is more likely to have been constructed from the fable tradition. Blake's conclusions are based upon stylistic considerations as well, the brevity, introduction of the animals without names, and the like are all characteristic of fables. Suggests that the same might be true of "A Song on the Times" (early fourteenth century) and the "Nun's Priest's Tale" of Chaucer, leaving the field clear for the idea that the *Roman de Renart* was first introduced into England in 1481.

107. Blaser, Robert-Henri. *Ulrich Boner: Un Fabulist suisse de xiv*[e] *siècle*. Mulhouse: Baly, 1949. 305 pp.

After a biographical sketch of Boner, Blaser discusses his sources, Latin and German, direct and indirect. Each fable is then analyzed in a comparative study, divided into the fables of the prologue, the Aesopic fables, the Avianus fables, and the fables of the epilogue. The third section is a theoretical investigation of the nature of the fable and how it might fit into the moral systems of Boner's times and earlier. The

moral doctrine of William of Conches is then compared
to that of Boner. Excellent bibliography.

108. Blavier-Paquot, Simone. *La Fontaine: Vues sur l'art du
     moraliste dans les fables de 1668.* Paris: Les Belles
     Lettres, 1961. 168 pp.

     Studies the early fables with the point of demon-
     strating the aesthetic role of the moral within the
     structure of the fable. La Fontaine's techniques of
     fabulation are demonstrated in his handling of the
     morals; the structure of the morals gives insight into
     an understanding of the process of composition.

109. ————. "La Concepción de la Fábula en La Fontaine."
     Revista de Literatura (Madrid), 51-52 (1964), 97-108.

     Illuminating essay on La Fontaine's understanding of
     the fable and other related terms contrasted with
     eighteenth-century theory. Much of his idea of the
     fable was inherited together with his material.

110. ————. "Et même les fables de La Fontaine." *Missions
     et demarches de la critique: Mélanges offerts au Pro-
     fessor J.A. Vier.* Paris: Klincksieck, 1973, pp. 747-
     53.

     The phrase in the title comes from Georges Pompidou
     who classified the fables of La Fontaine as fundamental
     to elementary schooling as orthography and mathematics.
     This article surveys the popularity and the uses of the
     La Fontaine fables in France. The opinion of various
     writers and thinkers on La Fontaine are examined; the
     fables are finally put into the context of French
     classical literature.

111. Blondheim, D.S. "A Note on the Sources of Marie de
     France." *Modern Language Notes*, 23 (1908), 201-202.

     Discusses P567 "Nightingale and the Hawk" (TMI U31.2)
     and its relationship to the *Romulus Metricus*.

112. Bloomfield, Maurice. "The Fable of the Crow and the
     Palm: A Psychic Motif in Hindu Fiction." *American
     Journal of Philology*, 40 (1919), 1-36.

     This article deals with a now-lost "Hindu" fable
     which now appears in literature only in the truncated
     form: "pertaining to the crow and palm tree." The
     fable has the crow alighting on a palm tree just as

the tree is about to fall, making it appear that the
crow causes the tree to fall. This is apparently an
important "psychic" motif in Hindu fiction. A number
of other fables in the same category are discussed,
and literary parallels from a wide range of Indian
literature are listed.

113. Bloomfield, Morton W. "The Wisdom of the Nun's Priest's
     Tale." *Chaucerian Problems and Perspectives: Studies
     in Honor of Paul E. Beichner*. Notre Dame: Notre Dame
     University Press, 1979. 264 pp., pp. 70-82.

     The Nun's Priest's Tale belongs to the genre of the
     fable and is related to the beast epic. Bloomfield
     discusses the idea of fable proper and demonstrates
     that the fable pattern is quite clear in the Nun's
     Priest's Tale although Chaucer has taken a simple form
     and has dramatically increased its complexity. One is
     left puzzled as to its point, and that is very unlike
     a fable; this is an extraordinary degree of enrichment,
     resulting in the two morals, rare indeed in the fable
     but characteristic of Chaucer. The tale is then com-
     pared to Henryson's treatment of the same motif and to
     the material as developed in the beast epic. Bloom-
     field concludes that it is a fable that has become a
     type of non-fable and then finally, as one returns to
     the moral, a kind of super-fable in which the wisdom of
     humility is taught. Excellent summary of previous re-
     search.

114. Blumenfeldt, Albert. *Die echten Tier- und Pflanzenfabeln
     des Strickers*. Dissertation, Berlin, 1916. 54 pp.
     (Partial printing and abstract).

     The literary development of Der Stricker, the south
     Frankish fable writer, is outlined. Part One discusses
     Der Stricker's animal and plant fables, manuscript
     tradition (including two fables which had remained un-
     published by Blumenfeldt's day), and the unity of the
     collection. Part Two investigates the style and tech-
     niques of the Stricker fable. The epimythic moral is
     given the most weight. The final sections deal with
     the "ethics" of the fable collection, compared to that
     expressed in other works by the same author.

115. Blunt, A.F. "Poussin and Aesop." *Journal of the Wart-
     burg and Courtland Institute*, 29 (1966), 436-437.

     Discusses a drawing by Poussin in the Louvre (Pl. 72a;
     Louvre no. 32451) as a depiction of Aesop's P91 "Donkey

and the Little Dog" (A-T 214; TMI J2413.1). Poussin
also illustrated P35 "Satyr and the Peasant" (A-T 1342;
TMI J1837) apparently an analogy to an engraving in the
Fabulae Centrum by Gabrielis Faernus (1563).

116. Bødker, Laurits. *Indian Animal Tales: A Preliminary
      Survey*. Helsinki: Academia Scientiarum Fennica, 1957.
      = FFC 170.

      An attempt to systematize the Indian Animal Tales
      available in the Danish archives and some additional
      materials, including many fables. Types are arbitrarily
      assigned by function and TMI numbers are given wherever
      applicable. Among the fable works indexed are the
      Panchatantra and some of the *Jatakas*.

117. Bolkestein, H. "Fabula Aesopica apun Plutarchum Qu.
      Conv. I, 614 E restituta." *Mnemosyne*, 4th Series,
      4 (1951), 304-307.

      Attempts a reconstruction of the fragmentary form of
      P426 "Fox and Crane" (A-T 60; TMI J1565.1) as found in
      Plutarch's *Quaestiones convivales*.

118. Bolte, Johannes. "Der Streit der Glieder mit dem
      Magen." *Andrea Guarnas Bellum Grammaticale und seine
      Nachahmungen*. Berlin: A. Hoffmann, 1908.

      Attributes the pseudo-Ovidian poem xcii with its
      treatment of P130 "Stomach and Feet" to an anonymous
      humanist before 1500; the edition of the text from a
      Köln edition dated about 1520.

119. Bone, Gavin. "The Sources of Henryson's 'Fox, Wolf and
      Cadger.'" *Review of English Studies*, 10 (1934), 319-
      320.

      Suggests that the source is a reference in Caxton's
      Reynard, chapter four.
      See: Fox, *The Poems of Robert Henryson*.

120. Boretsky, M.I. "Das Problem des Names des römischen
      Fabeldichters Avian." *Pytanna klasysnoji filolohiji:
      Questions de philologie classique*, 14 (1977), 83-90. [In
      Ukrainian, with summaries in German and Russian.]

      Avianus is confirmed as the proper name of the fourth-
      century fable-poet, the carrier of the Babrian tradition,
      very popular during the Middle Ages. Fairly extensive
      analysis of the arguments for and against the name and

reasons for the many variants of the name found in the manuscript tradition. Good bibliography.

121. ———. "Essay on the Utilization of a Lexical System for the Comparative Analysis of the Fables of Avianus and Babrius." *Pytanna klasysnoji Filolohiji: Questions de philologie classique*, 15 (1978), 55-78. [In Russian, with summaries in German and English.]

Comparative study of the use of various differing terms within specific semantic categories results in a very specific close relationship between the two poets. There can be no doubt of the influence of Babrius on Avianus, the author concludes although the exact nature of this influence is not yet definable.

122. ———. "The Artistic Universe and Lexical Frequency in Poetic Works (on the example of the Classical Literary Fable)." *Izvestija AN SSR, Ser. litoratury i Jazyka*, 37: 5 (1978), 453-461.

An attempt to reconstruct the social and artistic milieu for the classical fabulists: Phaedrus, Babrius, and Avianus by means of lexical frequency counts.

123. ———, and A.A. Kronik. "Opyt analiza nekotorkh storon sotsial'no-psikhologicheskoy atmosphery antichnoy literaturnoy basni." *Vesnik Drevnej Istorii*, 145 (1978), 157-168.

This article attempts to describe and evaluate the interpersonal relationships in the fables of Phaedrus, Babrius, and Avianus by means of a close analysis of the nouns used in the fables which describe or otherwise contain information about the nature of various relationships. A clear idea of the social-psychological atmosphere of each poet is determined by a construct of nine types of relationships among which the lexical items are distributed. The authors suggest that this work is potentially important for research in other problems connected with these fabulists.

124. Borman, E., and O. Bennedorff. "Eine Aesopische Fabel auf einem römischen Grabstein." *Jahresheft des österreichischen Archäologischen Institutes in Wien*, 5 (1902), 1-13.

Report on a gravestone from the area around Florence with a description of the stone and a meaning for the cryptic inscription. Bennedorff adds archeological notes. The 1.48-meter-high marble stone contains an illustrated truncated text related to P426 "Fox and Stork" (A-T 60; TMI J1565.1). See: Wilhelm Becher, "Eini Aesopische Fabel."

125. Bornecque, Pierre. "Thèmes et organization des Fables." *Europe*, 515 (1972), 39-52.

Sees the fables of La Fontaine as 26 themes, analyzed from 73 fables and the organization of the twelve books as a combination of themes and theme-bundles.

126. ———. *La Fontaine: Fabuliste*. 2nd ed. Paris: Société d'édition d'enseignement supérieur, 1975. 363 pp.

Illustrated broad picture of La Fontaine the fabulist. Treats La Fontaine and his socio-historical milieu, introduces the La Fontaine fable, and reviews various theories of the fable during the seventeenth century. An extensive analysis of the fable is followed by a discussion of the politics of La Fontaine and of his aesthetics. Excellent bibliography.

127. Borthwick, E.K. "A 'Femme Fatale' in Asclepiades." *Classical Review*, 81 (1967), 250-254.

In passing, notes a reference to P176 "Man who warmed a Snake" (A-T 155; TMI W154.2) in Asclepiades A. P. v. 162.

128. ———. "Two Textual Problems in Euripides' *Antiope*, fr. 188." *Classical Quarterly*, 17 (1967), 41-47.

Sees the debate of Amphion and Zethus as an example of P373 "Cicada and the Ant" (A-T 280a; TMI J711).

129. ———. "Beetle, Bell, a Goldfinch and Weasel in Aristophanes' *Peace*." *Classical Review*, 82 (1968), 134-139.

Attempts to make sense of *Pax*, 1077-1079 in part by relating the apparent non sequiturs to proverbs and fables, in particular P50 "Weasel and Aphrodite" (TMI J1908.2), P107 "Zeus and the Fox" (TMI A2231.1.4) and perhaps P613 "Belling the Cat" (A-T 110; TMI J671.1).

130. Bosch, Rafael, and Ronald Cere. *Los Fabulistas y su sentido histórico*. New York: Collección Iberia, 1969.

Concentrates especially upon Iriate and Samaniego in a survey of the Iberian fabulists from a socio-historical point of view. Excellent bibliography.

131. Boswell, Jackson Campbell. "Samson's Bosom Snake." *Milton Quarterly*, 8:3 (1974), 77-80.

    Discusses Milton's use of P176 "Man who warmed a Snake" (A-T 155; TMI W154.2) in *Samson Agonistes*. Reviews the motif as common in the Renaissance, with reflexes in Spenser and Lodge and others.
    See: Le Compte, "Samson's Bosom Snake Again."

132. Both, Wolf von. "Luther und die Fabel." Dissertation, Breslau, 1927. 53 pp.

    Attempts to systematize the dozens of uses of the fable by Luther, the allusions, citations, parodies and the actual fable collection begun by Luther. Luther's fable activity is characterized as a natural consequence of his time. The individual fables Luther knew and used are listed with most of their occurrences keyed to the Weimar edition of Luther's works. Luther's pedagogical ideas with regard to the fable are investigated as well as his rhetorical use of the genre. The fable collection is introduced by an investigation of Luther's attitude toward the fables as expressed in the Introduction to the posthumously published collection. Fables are keyed to the 1476/77 Steinhöwel collection where applicable, but not indexed to any modern standard.
    See: Carnes, "Heinrich Steinhöwel."

133. Bourguignon, Jean. "Quelques archaismes dans les fables de La Fontaine." *Verba et Vocabula. Ernst Gamillscheg zum 80. Geburtstag.* Ed. Helmut Stimm and Julius Wilhelm. Munich: Fink, 1968, pp. 81-95.

    This article deals with La Fontaine's often-noted penchant for archaisms. In the fables, this is done for great effect; they are not artificial, nor is the language a pastiche. La Fontaine seems to love older words, but he deals with them as would an artist not a theoretical historian. Numerous examples make these points clear.

134. Bowra, C.M. "Fox and Hedgehog." *Classical Quarterly*, 34 (1940), 26-29.

    Attempts to explain a cryptic iambic trimeter, quoted by Zenobius by using fables. The contrast between the fox and the hedgehog is not clear, but in certain specific fables, such as P427 "Fox and the Hedgehog," known from Aristotle, certain characteristics of these animals are made clear. More relevant seems to be P1 "Eagle and the Fox" where the fox is the victim, seemingly

closer to other fables in Archilochus. More generally,
the fox takes on certain characteristics from the overall point of view of foxes in the fables. Archilochus
seems to compare himself to the fox and his opponent
to the hedgehog.

135. Branan, Elisabeth Marie Girod. "Indépendance, rêve,
      sommeil et solitude dans les *Fables* et les *Contes*
      de Jean de La Fontaine." Dissertation, Tulane, 1976.

      The interrelated themes of independence, reverie,
      dreaming and solitude have often been noted in the
      works of La Fontaine. This study undertakes a sys-
      tematic investigation of these types of escape in two
      genres of literature: the *Fables* and the *Contes*. Deals
      with the 1668 edition and compares this with what are
      apparently other forms of escape in the edition of 1678.

136. Brandt, W. *Der Schwank und die Fabel bei Abraham a*
      Sancta Clara. Dissertation, Munster, 1923.

      Overview of the use of the fable and other monoepi-
      sodic forms in Abraham a Sancta Clara (1644-1709). The
      short form for him is a rhetorical device for use in
      sermons and therefore there is no question of retention
      of anything of the traditional form of the fable.

137. Braune, Wilhelm. *Die Fabeln des Erasmus Alberus: Ab-*
      druck der Ausgabe von 1550. Neudrucke deutscher
      Literaturwerk des 16. und 17. Jahrhunderts, nos.
      104-107. Halle: Niemeyer, 1892.

      Edition of Erasmus Alberus' *Buch von der Tugend und*
      Weisheit, the 49-fable collection in the 1550 edition.
      Excellent introduction with source studies and a critical
      assessment of the fable in sixteenth century.
      See: Carnes, "Heinrich Steinhöwel" and Vander Meulen,
      "The Fables of Erasmus Alberus."

138. Bräuning-Oktavio, Hermann. "*Neue Fabeln und Gedichte*
      Johann H. Mercks." *Goethe,* 23 (1961), 336-351.

      The 73 fables of Johann H. Merck are contained in
      handwritten sheets in Darmstadt of which only one third
      have been printed. Bräuning-Oktavio here introduces the
      fables of Merck and edits fourteen of them—some quite
      Aesopic in character, most not.

139. Bray, Bernand. "Avatar et fonctions du je d'auteur
      dans les Fables de La Fontaine." *Travaux de linguis-*

tique et de Littérature (Strasbourg), 13:2 (1975), 303-322.

First-person narrative, narrator intrusion, and the author as character are particularly delicate problems in literature. The expressions used by La Fontaine in these circumstances are the subject of this well-argued essay, which surveys those passages where the poet is compared to other fabulists; where he refers to himself in the Preface as in the fables in a number of ways. La Fontaine's use of "je" is clearly original and to a certain extent enigmatic.

140. Breivega, Ola. *"Vos et tu* dans les Fables de Marie de France." *Actes du 6e Congrès des Romantistes Scandinaves, Upsal 11-15 août 1975.* Ed. Lennart Carlsson. (AUUSRU no. 18). Stockholm: Almqvist & Wiksell, 1977 274 pp., pp. 31-40.

Of the 102 fables attributed to Marie de France some 34 contain dialogues which use the pronouns *vos* and *tu.* Establishment of certain "hierarchies" within the closed universe of these 34 fables is accomplished by the use of these pronouns, and this, in turn, is reflective of the human condition.

141. Briegel-Florig, Waltraud. *Geschichte der Fabelforschung in Deutschland.* Dissertation, Freiburg in Breisgau, 1965. 307 pp.

Survey of fable studies, especially theories on the nature of the fable, in Germany from the Middle Ages through the Reformation and Renaissance and the Baroque to the modern day. Deals with the word "fable" and general theories of the fable emphasizing the special favor shown the genre in the eighteenth century and its association with the rise of Philology on the one hand and Folklore on the other. A short history of the positivistic collections of philological works ends with a thoroughgoing analysis of Petsch and Kayser, all with an eye toward highlighting the widely divergent views of the genre. Excellent use of research and excellent bibliography.

142. Briner, Eduard. *Die Verskunst der Fabeln und Erzählungen Hagedorns.* Dissertation, Zurich, 1920. 100 pp.

Hagedorn's fables, especially the verse forms in the fables are discussed, first as inspired by La Fontaine's "vers irreguliers." Hagedorn's antecedents in fable

writing: Hunold, Brockes, Mayer, Wilkins as translators,
and especially William Triller's collection of original
fables (1737) are discussed to illuminate the accomplishment of Hagedorn, whose fable collection appeared in
1738. Briner investigates each verse form used by
Hagedorn and ends with an attempt to evaluate the meaning and function of Hagedorn's narrative verse forms.

143. Brockelmann, Carl. "Fabeln und Tiermärchen in der
      älteren arabischen Literatur." *Islamica*, 2 (1926),
      96-128.

      Begins with foreign influences upon the *Amtal lugman
      al Hakim* and *Kalila and Dimna*, the two most important
      fable collections of Arabic literature; important uses
      of the fable in earlier literature are pointed out.
      Pays special attention to P53 "The Farmer's Sons" (TMI
      J1021) and P15 "Fox and the Grapes" (A-T 59; TMI J871);
      P149 "Lion, Ass and Fox in the Hunt" (A-T 51; TMI J811.1.1)
      very well-known in Arabic literature from at least
      1000 A.D. Also discusses in P155 "Wolf and Lamb" (A-T
      111A; TMI U31); P137 "Gnat and Bull (Elephant)" (A-T 281;
      TMI J953.10); P193 "Fowler and the Lark" (TMI K730.1);
      and P372 "Three Bulls and a Lion" (TMI J10-2). Many
      others mentioned suggest that a number of Arabic fables
      might preserve a version that is closer to the Greek
      forms than the modern preserved Western version; or the
      earliest known version of a fable well known in the
      west, such as P613 "Belling the cat" (A-T 110; TMI J671.1)
      known in Arabic literature from as early as 750 A.D.

144. Brodeur, Arthur Gilchrist. "Androcles and the Lion."
      The Charles Mills Gayley Anniversary Papers. Berkeley:
      University of California Press, 1922, pp. 197-213.

      Traces P563 and P563A "Lion and Shepherd" and "Andro-
      cles and the Lion" (A-T 156; TMI B381) from the *Noctes
      Atticae* (book V, chapter xiv) of Aulus Gellius, who
      attributed the work to Apion the Egyptian. Seen here
      as having a historical event as its source and needing
      therefore no "folklore" source. The externals adorning
      the motif are the *fabula ficta* of the "genuine, if per-
      verted" genius of Apion the Egyptian.

145. ———. "The Fable of the Grateful Lion." *PMLA*,
      39 (1924), 485-524.

      Builds upon Brodeur's earlier work in which the Andro-
      cles story P563 (A-T 156; TMI B381) is described as an

historical event elaborated upon by Apion the Egyptian. This article suggests the further development of Apion's story through the Middle Ages, until it reaches its ultimate development in Chrétien's *Yvain*, and attempts to reconcile the very strong differences between the two. Indian tales and a long catalogue of medieval fables and parts of epics are brought in in an attempt to make the connections. The *Gulfier* legend is related but rejected as a source, and Brodeur decides upon an oral version, not recorded. The literary traditions do not bear upon the tradition until after the Renaissance. The article ends with a discussion of all the variants of the Man (knight) and Lion (serpent) motifs Brodeur is able to muster.

146. Bronnen, Arnolt. *Aisopos: Sieben Berichte aus Hellas. Der antike Aesopus-Roman, neu übersetzt und nach den dokumentarischen Quellen.* Hamburg: Rowohlt, 1956. 388 pp.

   A new translation of the *Vita Aesopi* with annotations that identify localities, personages, etc., mentioned in text.

147. Brotherson, Gorden. "How Aesop Fared in Nahuatl." *Arcadia*, 7 (1972), 37-43.

   Descriptions of the sixteenth-century translation of "Aesop" into Nahuatl, the language of the Aztec Empire. Discussion centers upon the 47 fables and the accommodations made to adapt the motifs to the new language and culture. The translator is unknown, but the suggestion is made that he may have been the Franciscan Barbardino de Sahagun.

148. Brown, William N. *The Panchatantra in Modern Indian Folklore.* Dissertation, The Johns Hopkins University, 1916. Reprinted in *Journal of the American Oriental Society*, 39 (1919), 1-54.

   Compares various motifs from Book 1 of the Panchatantra to similar motifs found in oral sources as recorded in very uneven modern collections of Indian folktales with very mixed results.

149. Brucker, Charles. "La conception du récit dans le fable ésopique en langue vulgaire: de Marie de France à Steinhöwel." *Actes du Colloque des 27, 28 et 29 Avril 1979: Le Récit Bref au Moyen Age.* Amiens: Université de Picardie, 1980, pp. 387-427.

This essay approaches the fable from the point of
view of the narrative as opposed to the moral. The
narrative is most clearly seen in those places where it
is not interrupted by dialogue and therefore those
fables with dialogue are excluded. Brucker sees a
somewhat paradoxical conciseness in the vulgar fable
when compared to the medieval Latin forms, and a specific logical connection between the narrative and the
moral, even though the versions in French, Spanish and
German are generally longer than the Latin. The fables
of Marie de France are examined in detail and mention
is made of the narratives in the *Ysopet de Lyon*, the
Ysopet-Avionnet, the *Contes moralisés* of Nicole Bozon,
the fables of Gerhard von Minden and those of Heinrich
Steinhöwel as well as of the *Libro de los Gatos*.

150.   Brunner-Traut, Emma. "Tiermärchen im alten Ägypten."
        Universitas, 10 (1955), 1071-1078.

        Egypt has yielded a large number of ostraka upon which
        are sometimes found illustrations. Brunner-Traut sees
        traces of various Märchen and fable motifs in some of
        these illustrations, although none of them is clearly
        identifiable as any of the motifs listed for them. She
        finds illustrations reminiscent of the battle of the
        mice and cats found, naturally, in the fables. One
        illustration shows a dancing kid with a fox playing a
        pipe. This does seem to be illustrative of P97 "Goat
        and Wolf as Musician" (TMI K551.3.2), but without a
        text, there is no way to be certain. The article sug-
        gests that these ostraka contain our earliest known
        versions of these and other fables.

151.   ————. *Altägyptische Tiergeschichte und Fabel: Gestalt
        und Strahlkraft*. 2nd enlarged and revised edition.
        Darmstadt: Wissenschaftliche Buchgesellschaft, 1968.
        First in *Saeculum*, 10 (1959), 124-185.

        A general survey of animals and representations of
        animals in Old Egyptian sources: papyri, inscriptions,
        sculpture, and the like. Special attention is given to
        the conflict between the mice and the cats, but many
        other motifs are touched upon as well. Reconstruction
        for a number of narratives is attempted on evidence of
        iconography and *sententiae*-like inscriptions as well as
        from more substantial materials. Suggests Egyptian
        primacy for a number of fabular motifs and proposes
        Egyptian sources for some Greek fables. Excellent dis-
        cussion of previous research. Numerous illustrations.

152. ────. "Erzählsituation und Erzählfigur in ägyptischem Erzählgut." *Fabula*, 22 (1981), 74-78.

Egyptian materials imply a special set of conditions. The civilization that created these materials is gone, and the materials themselves are fragmentary. The role of the narrator and the materials narrated are not easily definitively reestablished. A number of fables are mentioned or alluded to as integral to a number of texts, i.a., the *Tefnut* lion-goddess cyclical narration contains a number of fables and fabular motifs, including P150 "Lion and Mouse" (TMI B371.1) and other similar episodes.

153. Brush, Murray Peabody. *The Isopo Laurenziano, edited with Notes and an Introduction*. Dissertation, Johns Hopkins, 1898. iii and 187 pp.

An edition of the *Isopo Laurenziano*, a collection of forty-six fables written in the latter half of the fourteenth century, known in a single manuscript contained in the Laurentian library. An extensive introduction deals with the interrelationships of the complex of Italian fable collections, with a description of the manuscripts and of those collections deriving from Marie de France and those derived from the collection of Walter of England and of fables corresponding to these collections. The *Isopo Laurenziano* is shown to be descended from the collection of Marie de France. The edition continues with extensive notes and a bibliography.

154. ────. "Ysopet III of Paris." *PMLA*, 24 (1909), 495-546.

Begins with an overview of the history of the Walter of England collection, the ancestor of the Ysopet. Sources and questions of authorship are discussed and then its derivatives in Europe and especially in France are listed. The manuscript containing the Ysopet III (BN, no. 983, fonds français) is described and the collection proper evaluated. A comparative table lists correspondences in other collections. An edition of the text follows.

155. ────. "Esopo Zuccarino." *Studies in Honor of A. Marshall Elliott*, Vol. 1. Baltimore: The Johns Hopkins Press, 1911, pp. 375-422.

An edition of the Italian translation of the "Gualterus" Aesop compiled in 1462 or somewhat earlier by Accio Zucco,

containing 64 fables, all in sonnets. The collection
is contained in a single manuscript (BM, Additional
10389) and in some sixteen printed editions. The collection and its versification is discussed in detail
and a complete edition follows.

156. Buchanan, Milton A. "Sebastian Mey's Fabulario." *Modern
      Language Notes*, 21 (1906), 167-171, 201-205.

      The now extremely rare Sebastian Mey's Fabulario was
      published at Valencia in 1613. Many of the prose stories
      and fables are from the Romulus tradition and from
      Avianus. Buchanan summarizes all the stories, generally
      facetiae, and some of the fables although thirty-three
      fables are omitted. Descriptions of the collection and
      bibliographical and sources notes are provided.

157. Buehler, W. "On Some Mss of the Athens Recension of
      the Greek Paroemiographers." *Studies in Greek Litera-
      ture and Paleography in Honor of A. Turyn*. Ed. J.L.
      Heller. Urbana: University of Illinois Press, 1974.
      624 pp., pp. 410-435.

      A description and classification of eight manuscripts
      of the collections of proverbs that were published to-
      gether with the 1505 edition of Aesop and the Adages of
      Erasmus. Detailed evaluation of the Athous recension
      and other witnesses to that collection of proverbs.
      See: Perry, *Aesopica*.

158. Bürger, Karl. "Epilogische Volkswitze in den Fabelsamm-
      lungen." *Hermes*, 27 (1892), 359-362.

      Treats Babrius 60, i.e., P167 "The Fly" (TMI J861.3)
      as an "epilogical joke."

159. Bürger, Peter. "La Fontaines Fabeln." *Renaissance und
      Barock*, II. Vol. 10 of Neues Handbuch des Literatur-
      wissenschaft. Frankfurt: Athenaion, 1972, pp. 316-
      327.

      Discusses a few important modern theories of La Fon-
      taine's fable activity (Clarac, Spitzer, Couton, and
      others). Suggests that in order to come to grips with
      the real accomplishment of the La Fontaine fable, one
      needs to appreciate that La Fontaine was dealing with
      a genre that had no social position at all, as poetics,
      but which was very popular as a didactic form. The
      accomplishment is the poetic fable. The techniques with
      which this is accomplished are discussed at length. The

results of this blend are a fable capable of a wide
variety of interpretations as well as a wide-ranging
selection of themes handled in the fables. Bürger then
deals with the problem of animals in the fables and the
effect of the fables upon the public which received
them. The use of a "lower" literary form allowed La
Fontaine the chance to use speech patterns and expressions that were for all practical purposes "banned"
from higher torms of literature.

160. Burrow, J.A. "Henryson: *The Preaching of the Swallow.*"
Essays in Criticism, 25 (1975), 25-37.

Identifies the major theme of the fable as prudence,
and this provides a key to the understanding of the
structure of the fable.
See: Fox, "Henryson's Fables," *ELM*, esp. 349-355.

161. Burton, Thomas Roghaar. "The Animal Lore and Fable
Tradition in John Dryden's *The Hind and the Panther.*"
Dissertation, University of Washington, 1967. 217 pp.

Describes Dryden's extensive borrowing from fable
tradition and animal lore as having been done with care;
the work contains fables and attempts the structure of
a fable, which is not entirely successful.

162. Bush, George E. "The Fable in the English Periodical,
1660-1800." Dissertation, St. John's University,
1965. 192 pp.

Describes the common attributes of the fable and the
periodical from the late seventeenth century through the
eighteenth, and suggests that fables were chosen by
periodical editors because they fitted the tastes of
the time. Exhaustive examination of the two centuries
of periodicals with a synoptic discussion of the fables
as found there. Lists of fables in appendix.

163. Cajkanović, M. *Srpske narodne pripovetke.* Belgrade,
1929.

The fable is essentially a literary genre that developed from the beast epic. The fable is unlike the
beast epic in that it is not designed to entertain and
is charged with a decided satirical emphasis. Thus the
fable is to be considered essentially a literary creation
and not a folklore category. That is why the fabular
motifs have difficulty, says Cajkanović, in staying in
the total tradition; there is always a tendency to either

become attached to the beast epic or to find literary
expression as a (literary) fable.

164. Callahan, Virginia W. "Ramifications of the Nut-Tree
     Fable." *Acta Conventus Neo-Latini Turonensis.* Ed.
     Jean-Claude Margolin. Vol. 1. Paris: Librairie
     Philosophique J. Vrin, 1980, pp. 197-204.

     Deals with the literary history of a *topos*, that of
     a nut-tree being cudgeled in order that the fruit might
     be reached. The motif is discussed in terms of P250
     "The Nut Tree" (TMI W154.6). Some who used the
     motif, indeed used the fable, include Ovid, Leonardo
     da Vinci, and Erasmus.

165. Cameron, Alan. "Macrobius, Avienus and Avianus."
     Classical Quarterly, N.S. 17 (1967), 385-399.

     Dating Avianus is aided by Claudian's *De bello gil-
     donico* (398): Theodosius identified with Macrobius.
     Cameron suggests that Avianus used a Latin translation
     of Babrius (by Julius Titianus), which solves many prob-
     lems. Contains a good survey of the cluster of prob-
     lems of Avianus' name and concludes that the proper
     form is Avienus.
     See: Küppers, *Die Fabeln Avianus.*

166. Campbell, Lily. "The Lost Play of *Aesop's Crow.*" *Modern
     Language Notes*, 49 (1934), 454-457.

     Notes evidence of a now-lost play of George Ferrers
     which was, says Campbell, a play in the mood of the
     court of Edward VI in the year 1552. The play apparently
     used motifs from P123 "Jackdaw and Crow," P129 "Jackdaw
     and Pigeons," and P472 "Vainglorious Jackdaw and the
     Peacock" (TMI J951.2).

167. Camurati, Mireya. *La Fábula en Hispanoamérica.* Mexico:
     Universidad Nacional Autónoma de México, 1978. 369 pp.

     This volume covers the fable activity of all of Latin
     America. Begins with an attempt to come to grips with
     a definition of the fable from both theoretical con-
     siderations as well as empirical evidence from a number
     of ancient and modern fable collections. The specifics
     of the Hispanic-American fable are discussed: the de-
     velopment of a specific Latin American fable with a
     specific vocabulary and with different subjects and
     unique functions. Part of this history is the indigenous
     fable, which, strictly speaking, Camurati adds, ought to

be excluded because it is found in native languages,
not in Spanish. It is nevertheless treated in the work.
The special social and political fable that developed
in Latin America is discussed with numerous examples
of specific events for which fables were composed. The
main section of the work is a series of short sections
on fabulists and their fables arranged by countries,
listed alphabetically by country from Argentina (with
nine fabulists evaluated) to Venezuela (with five fabulists) followed by a section on the indigenous fable
(Nahuatl, Incan, Maya, and many others). The second
part of the work is an anthology of selected fables.
Excellent bibliography of primary sources.

168. Canby, Henry Seidel. "The English Fabliau." *PMLA*, 21
(1906), 200-214.

Discusses the relationship between fabliau and fable.
The fabliau is clearly for entertainment but shares
with the fable a reflection upon the human condition.
The fable points up a moral, however, and in contrast,
the author of the fabliau is seldom if ever very
serious. The two forms have many points in common,
both originating from an observation upon human nature.
See: Jürgen Beyer, "Schwank und Moral."

169. Cancik, Hubert. "Phaedrus." *Römische Literatur*. Ed.
Manfred Fuhrmann. Vol. 3 of Neues Handbuch der
Literaturwissenschaft. Frankfurt: Athenaion, 1974,
pp. 271-274.

Deals with the idea raised by Phaedrus that the fable
is a form suited to, if not invented by, the slave.
Aesop was a slave, so, too, was Phaedrus. The slave
needs to say things obliquely, as the fable does. This
approach is found also in the body of the Phaedrus fables
themselves. Well-argued discussion of Phaedrus within
the broader scope of Roman poetry: the didactic pathos,
the verse forms, the tone of the fable--all this--make
the fable Phaedrus' own form, a form which he uses to
describe not the idyllic world of "might makes right,"
the bitter sharpness of the world of "might makes right,"
the world of the Wolf and the Lamb at the stream in the
Phaedrus I, 1; P155 "Wolf and the Lamb" (A-T 111A; TMI
U31).

170. Carey, Fredrick Mason. "The Vatican Fragment of
Phaedrus." *Transactions of the Philological Association*, 57 (1916), 96-106.

A discussion of the codex Reginensis latinus 1616, of which the second part is a ninth century compilation containing a fragment of Phaedrus with fables from book 1 (nos. 11, 12, 13, 17, 18, 19, 20 and 21). The fragment came from the scriptorium of Fleury.

171. Carnes, Pack. "Heinrich Steinhöwel's Esopus and the Corpus of Aesopica in Sixteenth-Century Germany." Dissertation, University of California at Los Angeles, 1973.

Survey of the fable in Germany through the end of the sixteenth century. Description of the Steinhöwel collection/translation as a pivotal collection, at once at the end of the medieval tradition and the beginning of modern fable editing. Influence of Steinhöwel upon generations of fable collections is discussed. Contains a compendium of all fabular motifs in German, indexing all German and most Latin collections of the sixteenth century, keyed to Perry's *Aesopica* and various motif-indices.

172. ————. "The Fable Joke." *Southwest Folklore*, 5: 4 (1981), 1-11.

Illustrates the partial displacement of the traditional fable in contemporary narrative situations by the joke or the fable joke, a joke designed to masquerade as a fable, often complete with epimythium. This is accomplished by the use of jokes in the traditional rhetorical niche of the fable and is facilitated in part by the nature of the fable itself: a tendency toward humor and a structure that is essentially the same as the joke.

173. Carratello, U. "Marziale conio Rufo e Fedro." *Giornale Italiano di Filologia*, 17 (1964), 122-148.

It is to the Platonic dialogue that Martial is alluding in his epigram III, 20, not to the fabulist Phaedrus.

174. Cassell, Anthony K. "The Crow of the Fable and the Corbaccio: A Suggestion for the Title." *Modern Language Notes*, 85 (1970), 83-91.

Suggests that Boccaccio had the crow of P129 "Jackdaw and the Crows" or P472 "Vain Jackdaw" in mind (both TMI J951.2) for the title. Cassell reviews the literature on the subject and then suggests the Phaedrine fable or more likely medieval versions of the fable. He refers to the Babrian version (no. 72, called here

curiously "the original Greek") and to numerous other
forms of the fable. The relationship between *Il Corbaccio*
and the fable is more easily shown in the subsidiary aspects: admonition against cosmetics and artificial adorn-
ment in general, stressing the sin of altering nature's
work. Cassell then documents and stresses the wide-
spread familiarity with the fable throughout Western
European History.

175. Castaigne, Eusèbe Joseph. *Trois fabulistes: Ésope,*
      Phèdre et La Fontaine. Etude bibliographique et
      littéraire. Paris: A. Picard, 1889. 29 pp.

      A study of Causeret's *Trois Fabulists* (q.v.) describing
      the man and the work in glowing terms. Argues slightly
      with Causeret's spending so much effort on Phaedrus but
      is generally highly complimentary.

176. Causeret, Charles. *De Phaedri sermone grammaticae ob-*
      servationes. Paris: Garnier, 1886. 111 pp.

      Reviews previous work in overview. The main body of
      the monograph consists of various grammatical and
      lexical studies. Rare vocabulary elements are discussed
      in connection with their use in other authors; then
      various grammatical categories, especially Phaedrus'
      use of cases, tenses, and moods. The conclusion is
      drawn: there is nothing grammatically wrong or strange
      in the fables of Phaedrus that is not also found in
      other works of the same general period. Causeret then
      gives a history of the criticism on the Phaedrine
      (Perotti) Appendix.

177. ———. *Trois fabulists: Ésope--Phèdre--La Fontaine.*
      Paris: Gédalge jeune, 1889. 216 pp.

      Deals with the attitudes and treatment of fabular
      motifs by the three fabulists in the title. "Aesop"
      stands for the Greek Prose tradition; Phaedrus, the dry
      concise poet, represents the next stage of development
      that reaches its zenith in La Fontaine. Finds a broad
      range of differences in the treatment of the same motifs,
      especially in the characterizations. For Phaedrus the
      animals, for example, are not treated as literary
      products with care for their identities in strong con-
      trast to those of La Fontaine. The morals are straight-
      forward and harsh; those of La Fontaine more subtle.

178. Chambry, Émile. "Une édition critique des fables

ésopiques." *Bulletin de l'Association Guillaume
Budé*, 10 (1926), 25-35.

Decries the previous lack of a truly philologically
sound and integrated edition of the fables within the
Aesopic tradition as a defense of his own. Discusses
the huge number of manuscripts containing fables--many
not yet edited or collated--in four classes and a fifth,
a "mixed" class. The number of fables in any given
manuscript of this formidable number is quite variable;
the difficulties for the editor are overwhelming.

179.   ———. "À propos d'Esope." *Supplément critique au Bul-
        letin de l'Association Guillaume Budé*, 1 (1929), 179-
        187.

An answer to Hausrath's criticism of Chambry's 1925-
27 edition of Aesop. Hausrath had proclaimed Chambry's
edition a step backwards from Halm; Chambry tries to
defend his textual emendations and apparatus.

180.   Chapman, Hugh. "La Cometa, A Political Fable by Andrès
        Bello." *Hispanic Review*, 12 (1944), 338-344.

Citing the political fable as being within the
scope of the genre from its beginnings, Chapman describes
the political situation that led to the writing of this,
the first of Bello's four fables. Andrès Bello left
England in 1829 to go to Chile. His ideas on the political
turmoil of the time were expressed in fables, in part
inspired by fables of Iriarte and Florian, in particular, Iriarte's fable "El volatin y su maestro," and
Florian's "Danseur de corde et le balancier," both of
which teach the importance of rules of law despite the
accompanying loss of freedom. The influence is more
clearly seen in the original title of Bello's fable
which had the subtitle Volatin. Chapman analyses both
the Spanish and the French sources and compares them to
the various versions of *La Cometa*.

181.   Charitonides, Ch. "In Fabulas Aesopicas." *Mnemosyne*,
        43 (1915), 225-226.

Critical notes to the Greek fables of the Halm edition.

182.   ———. "Paratereseis eis tous Aisopeious mythous."
        Platon, 1 (1949), 185-200.

Critical notes to the edition of August Hausrath with

a wide-ranging list of explications of various passages and suggested emendations.

183. ————. "Kritika." *Platon*, 4 (1952), 101-114.

Critical notes to *Aesopica: Greek and Latin Texts* by Ben Edwin Perry and to various fables from the Augustana recension.

184. Chatelain, Émile. "Un nouveau document sur le codex Remensis de Phèdre." *Revue de Philologie*, 11 (1887), 81-88.

The investigator of the codex Remensis of Phaedrus which was burned in 1774 had always before been limited to three auxiliary sources: the J. Sirmond notes made on the margin of a copy of the Pithou manuscript as a comparison to that witness; to the notes of Gude who visited the libraries of France and recorded the variants; and to the comparison study done by Dom Vincent made in 1769. It was possible to reconstruct the manuscript with the aid of these sources; well enough indeed that Hervieux was able to present a complete description of this manuscript which is equal in value to the study of the Phaedrine text to the Pithou. Chatelein has discovered three paper leaves upon which the Jesuit Denys Roche had written a number of variant readings from the Remensis. There follows a printing of the various readings from all five books of Phaedrus.

185. Chauveau, François. *Vignettes des Fables de La Fontaine (1668)*. Ed. J.D. Baird. Exeter: Exeter University Press, 1977. 119 pp.

Contemporary engravings designed for the fables of La Fontaine. Extensive introduction (32 pages).

186. Chefneux, Hélène. "Les fables dans la tapisserie de Bayeux." *Romania*, 60 (1934), 1-35 and 153-194.

The Bayeux tapistry's fable embroidery is used to prove that the *Livre d'Alfred* did in fact exist. Chefneux begins with a careful description of each illustration (reproduced in the text) and its identification with a fable from the Marie de France collection. All are found within that and the Romulus traditions. Reviews all principal editions of the fables before the end of the thirteenth century and displays the results of the study on a table of concordances. The second part begins with a review of theories concerning the

putative fable collection of King Alfred. Extensive
analysis leads Chefneux to the conclusion that the fables
of the tapestry and those of Marie de France are from
the same source and suggests the collection is attributed
to Alfred.

187. Cheney, David Raymond. "Animals in 'A Midsummer Night's
      Dream.'" Dissertation, State University of Iowa,
      1955.

      Illustrates sixteenth-century animal "connotations"
      by an examination of the animals in Shakespeare's play.
      Shakespeare's probable sources of material and tradition
      are discussed and the uses to which the animals are put
      follow. Allegorical uses are suggested and a call for
      a dictionary of animal meanings and symbols is issued.

188. Chesnutt, Michael. "The Grateful Animals and the Un-
      grateful Man." *Fabula*, 21 (1980), 24-55.

      A remarkably complete discussion of the motif, found
      usually in fabular form, of the grateful animals (A-T
      160) from the Middle Ages to early modern times. The
      motif is found, inter alia, in Gower's *Confessio amantis*,
      and the *Gesta Romanorum*, but Chesnutt follows the traces
      of the motif from the *Kalila and Dimna* tradition to the
      Novus Aesopus of Baldo, where the fable is no. 19 and
      is derived ultimately from the eighth-century Arabic tra-
      dition. Chesnutt then describes the history of the *Novus
      Aesopus* and the *Buch der Weisheit der alten Weisen*. His
      conclusions include: the *Kalila and Dimna* contained the
      old "oriental" form of the motif which was translated
      into Greek and circulated in Southern Italy or Sicily
      perhaps in the 12th century. The Anglo-French variants
      are all based upon a common source, perhaps *Kalila and
      Dimna* with Baldo. The motif may have been brought to
      England directly from Italy or Sicily. Ends with early
      modern forms of the fable. Excellent review of previous
      research.

189. Chesterton, G.K. "Aesop." *G.K.C. as M.C.: Being a
      Collection of Thirty-Seven Introductions*. Agincourt:
      Methuen, 1929, 83-89, often reprinted.

      Attempts to explain the use of animals in the fable
      by suggesting that there can be no good fables with
      human beings as actors; all actors must be impersonal.
      The fable must not allow for what Balzac called the
      "revolt of the sheep." The immortal justification of

the fable is: we cannot teach truth without turning men into chessmen.

190. Chevalier, Maxime. "Pour les sources des fables d'Hartzenbusch." *Bulletin Hispanique*, 81 (1979), 303-310.

Investigates some of the Spanish sources of the fables of Juan Eugenio Hartzenbusch, including Lope de Vega, Calderon, and others. A number of the fables are attributed to oral tradition, especially fable 74 "La esposa modela" (A-T 1354; TMI J217.0.1).

191. Chitimia, Ion C. "L'Évolution du types de la fable Ésopique dans les littératures européennes." *Actes du VIe Congrès de l'Association Internationale de Littérature Comparée*. Ed. Michel Cadot, et al. Stuttgart: Bieber, 1975, 597-600.

Surprisingly simplistic survey of the Aesopic fable in Europe. Discusses types and various collections from antiquity through La Fontaine and Lessing. The European forms were also strongly influenced by the *Panchantantra*, especially through the Arabic of the *Kalila and Dimna*. The Renaissance returned to the "authentic Aesopic" forms, concise and in prose, aided in this by the invention and spread of printing.

192. ———. "L'Évolution de la fable en tant que structure et art littéraires." *Zagadnienia Rodzajow Literackich*, 15: 2 (1972) [1975], 29-35.

Superficial treatment of the changes in form and type of the fable in Europe. The type called the Aesopic is brief and has a tendency toward a moral. This is the specific form in classical antiquity. This is traced through its changes in the Middle Ages as it becomes longer and more diffuse, a progression which continued until the Renaissance, which saw a return to the short prose fable. The Indian fable mixed with the European prose versions as demonstrated by the use of Bidpai by La Fontaine. Ends with modern Rumanian versions.

193. Christensen, Arthur. *Motif et Thème: Plan d'un dictionnaire des motifs de contes populaires, de légendes et de fables*. Folklore Fellows Communications, no. 59. Helsinki: Academia Scientiarum Fennica, 1925. 52 pp.

An attempt to offer a dictionary of motifs indexed

by general theme (Temperance, Intelligence, Stupidity
and the like); more concerned with the embodiment of
a certain trait expressed in the motif than other
features of content as, e.g., in Aarne-Thompson. Many
of these features are keyed to the fables in the *Panchatantra* and especially to the fables of La Fontaine.

194. Christes, Johannes. "Reflexe erlebter Unfreiheit in
      den Sentenzen des Publilius Syrus und den Fabeln des
      Phaedrus." *Hermes*, 107 (1979), 199-220.

      Investigates the idea of slavery, especially as ex-
      pressed by those who have experienced it as Publilius
      Syrus and Phaedrus did. Phaedrus apparently was not
      unsatisfied with his circumstances, indeed seemed proud
      of his once having belonged to the *familia Caesaris*.
      But Christes sees a disillusion from the earlier fables
      mentioning slavery, P269 "Wild Boar, Horse, and Hunter"
      (Phaedrus IV, 4; TMI K192), P1 "Fox and Eagle" (Phaedrus
      I, 28; TMI K2295, L315.3) and P476 "Ass to Old Shepherd"
      (Phaedrus, I, 15; TMI U151) in those written after his
      trouble with Sejanus.

195. Christoffersson, H. *Studia de fontibus fabularum Bab-
      rianarum.* Lund, 1904.

      Deals with various problems concerning research on
      Babrius the man and especially the sources of his
      fables. Various theories on the composition techniques
      of Babrius' work are analyzed, including an extended
      discussion of the meaning of the apparent prologue to
      a second book, where Babrius seems to be saying that
      he "sings for a second time." Now superseded by
      Crusius, Hausrath, Perry, and Vaio.
      See: Perry, *Babrius and Phaedrus*.

196. Cioranescu, A. "Sobre Iriarte, La Fontaine y fabulis-
      tas en general." *T. de Iriarte, Fábulas literarias.*
      Santa Cruz de Tenerife, 1951, 1-12. Reprinted in the
      author's *Estudios de literatura española y comparada.*
      La Lagua, 1954, 197-204.

      A comparative study of Iriarte and La Fontaine, with
      emphasis upon the influence of the latter upon the
      former. Includes a cursory survey of fable activity
      in Iriarte's time.

197. Clarac, Pierre. *La Fontaine, l'homme et l'oeuvre.*
      Paris: Boivin, 1947. 200 pp. Rprt. 1959.

Clarac considers the key to the work of the fabulist
to lie in the person but insists that the evidence must
be re-examined by each reader. In addition to a full-
range appreciation of La Fontaine and his works, the
Fables are given careful and well-argued notes. The
bibliography is annotated and includes a detailed
chronological table.

198. Clark, Eugene F. "The Fable *Frosch und Maus* as found
      in Luther and Hans Sachs." *Journal of English and
      German Philology*, 13 (1914), 51-59.

      Investigates the possibility that Luther might have
      been influenced by Hans Sachs in his version of P384
      "Frog and Mouse" (A-T 278; MI J681.1). The argument
      hinges upon the use of an unusual proverb by both Sachs
      and Luther, the Luther fable appearing two years after
      the Sachs version. Clark suggests that Luther knew
      Sachs' "Frosch und Maus" in addition to Steinhöwel.

199. Clark, George. "Henryson and Aesop: The Fable Trans-
      formed." *English Literary History*, 43 (1976), 1-18.

      Demonstration of the transformation of the fables in
      Henryson's *Moral Fables*; especially the "Preaching of
      the Swallows," P437 "Owl and the Birds," P39 "The Wise
      Swallow" (A-T 233C; TMI J652.2, J621.1) and "Cock and
      the Jasp," P503 "Cockerel and the Pearl" (TMI J1061.1)
      accomplished by great emphasis upon certain aspects of
      time and space. Henryson's Aesopian stories thus
      "outgrow" the artistic and intellectual limitations of
      their traditional form. The transformation causes a
      great deepening in contrast to the cold and indifferent
      Aesopian attitude.

200. Clark, Ismael. *La Fábula. Sus elementos históricos,
      literarios, sociales y populares y mi intromisión en
      ella*. Dissertation, Havana: Academia Nacional de
      Artes y letras, 1936.

      Historical overview of the fable begins with an
      analysis of the word "fable" and rehearses the history
      of the form from its putative beginnings in India and
      its arrival in Greece through the *Jatakas* and the Roman
      fable, all the while comparing the ancient forms with
      Samaniego, other modern fabulists, and modern Spanish
      translations of the classical motifs. The medieval
      beast epic, especially Renart in its Germanic reflexes,
      is discussed, followed by a few modern fabulists: La
      Fontaine, Gay and Samaniego.

201. Clark, John Abbot. "Ade's Fables in Slang: An Apprecia-
      tion." *The South Atlantic Quarterly*, 46 (Oct. 1947),
      537-544.

      Discusses the lack of interest in George Ade's fables
      and pseudo-fables of his day. Analyzes Ade's purpose
      in writing the fables and explains his idea of form,
      keeping the classical form but in modern language (thus,
      "in slang"). The Indiana humorist is shown to be a
      satirist and social critic but, above all, a genuine
      realist.

202. Clark, R.C. "'Die Clag von Wolff eim hage,' A 15th
      Century Manuscript." *Modern Language Notes*, 82
      (1967), 421-427.

      Mention is made of a fragmentary manuscript containing
      four poems, the first of which "an Aesopian dialogue"
      between a young and an old Lion (P706 "Lion's son learns
      about Man"), related to Hans Sachs: "Der jung frech
      leb," in a miscellany of poems in German (ms 14 of the
      University of Pennsylvania Library). Bulk of the
      article on the second poem, "Die clag von Wolff eim
      hage."

203. Clarke, Dorothy Clotelle. "On Iriarte's Versification."
      PMLA, 67 (1952), 411-419.

      On Iriarte's syllable-count meter used in his fables,
      discusses his standard versification and accentuation.
      The nine-syllable line is probably Italianate in origin
      and the decasyllable as well as the eleven-syllable
      lines show Iriarte's originality although Iriarte used
      independent lines of all lengths from four to fourteen
      syllables. Rhyme schemes are also touched upon.

204. Clayborne, Dorothy Hite, and Chauncey Edgar Finch.
      "The Fable of Aesop in *Libro de buen amor* de Juan Ruiz."
      Classical Journal, 62 (1967), 306-308.

      The primary source of the twenty-two fables in the
      Libro de buen amor is the Walter of England collection,
      but two fables, clearly in the Aesopic tradition, are
      not in the Walter collection: P149 "Lion, Ass and Fox"
      (TMI J811.4) and P276 "Wounded Eagle" (TMI U161).
      Ruiz most likely drew upon classical sources, probably
      Greek. The first of these is slightly changed, the
      second virtually identical to the Greek forms.

205. Clement, Paul A. "Moralia 614 E." *American Journal of Philology*, 66 (1945), 192-196.

     Deals with the lacuna at the beginning of Plutarch's version of P426 "Fox and Crane Entertain Each Other" (A-T 60; TMI J1565.1). From what is known of the fable, it seems clear that notions of *hunger* and *entertainment* need to be supplied, suggests Clement.

206. Coenen, Hans Georg. "Zur Deutbarkeit von Fabeln." *Linguistische Berichte*, 41 (1976), 15-21.

     Attempts to identify and delineate those conditions which are normally observed in the interpretation of a fable. Insofar as an interpretation of a fable is a special case of text processing, one might look at the restricted conditions which control the process of fable interpretation as "text processing rules" which are genre specific for the fable. The fable is structurally of two parts, the *récit* and the *moralité*, demonstrated by examples from La Fontaine; the first occurs in a specifically fictive world; the *moralité* is a datum in the "real" world.

207. Coenen-Mennemeier, Brigitta. "Fabeln bei La Fontaine und Anouilh." *Praxis des neusprachlichen Unterrichts*, 18 (1971), 12-20.

     On fundamental differences of technique and poetic style in the fables of La Fontaine and Jean Anouilh.

208. Collart, P. "Deux papyrus des Publicazioni della società italiana." *Revue de philclogie* (1919), 36-46.

     On fragments discovered that contain two portions of the *Vita Aesopi* with similarities to the Westermann text. A connection is made with the school of the Sophists.

209. Collinet, Jean-Pierre. "La Fable neo-latine avant et après La Fontaine." *Acta Conventus: Neo-Latini Amstelodomensis: Proceedings of the Second International Congress of Neo-Latin Studies*, ed. P. Tuynman, G.C. Kuiper and E. Kessler. Munich: Fink, 1979, pp. 244-257.

     Calls for a comprehensive study of the neo-Latin fable in France; discusses the influence of the neo-Latin fable on La Fontaine's forms, noting that during

the sixteenth century in France, the flourishing of
fables was in the vernacular. The mid-century edition
of Phaedrus and its influence, as well as Latin versions of various fabular materials, such as Renard and
the *culex* cycle are evaluated. Notes to the article
contain a good bibliography relating to rhetorical and
literary materials during the seventeenth century.

210. Collins, William Lucas. *La Fontaine and Other French
      Fabulists*. Edinburgh: Blackwood, 1882. 176 pp.

      Contains a biographical sketch of La Fontaine followed
      by a commentary on his fables with an emphasis upon
      stylistic considerations. Short background discussions
      of earlier fabulists and the Reynard cycle and brief
      mention of later fabulists and La Fontaine's influence
      upon them.

211. Colson, F.H. "Phaedrus and Quintilian I.9.2." *Classical
      Review*, 33 (1919), 59-61.

      Takes issue with Postgate's assertion that Quintillian
      was speaking of Phaedrus in his mention of fables used
      in school instruction. Colson infers that Quintillian
      was not speaking of Phaedrus or Babrius and that
      neither was used in schools. No Phaedrine quotation is
      found in the extant "grammatici" and "rhetores." This
      is not, he feels, consistent with his use as a school
      text.

212. Colton, Robert E. "The Story of the Widow of Ephesus
      in Petronius and La Fontaine." *Classical Journal*, 71
      (1975), 35-52.

      Extensive account of the motif of the Widow of
      Ephesus, P543 "Widow and Soldier" (A-T 1510; TMI K2213.1),
      comparing the prose version of Petronius with La Fon-
      taine's tale (1, 10). La Fontaine's version is more
      refined: he eschews, for example, the rough and prurient
      language of the soldier. La Fontaine strives to improve
      upon Petronius' story, enriches the material, and omits
      unpleasant details.

213. Concato, Salvatore. *Fedro Studio*. Bologna: Nicola
      Zanichelli, 1884. 32 pp.

      Deals with the life and works of Phaedrus and covers
      all the literature to date superficially. The relation-
      ship of Phaedrus to Babrius is investigated. Places
      the birthplace of Phaedrus in Greece, which is clearly

not correct; cites but apparently does not use the work
of Hervieux on the Latin fabulists.

214. Cons, Louis. "A Neolithic Saying and an Aesop's Fable."
     American Journal of Archaeology, 28 (1924), 276-277.

     Finds in P173 "Hermes and the Woodcutter" (TMI Q3.1),
     especially in a variant recorded by Halm, no. 398b,
     echoes of the neolithic pattern of discovering axe-
     heads in a river and suggests that the line "It is not
     every time that the river brings axes," might be a
     prehistoric proverb.

215. Conti, Augusto. "Le favole di Fedro." *La Rassegna
     nazionale, publicazione mensile*, 12 (1883), 741-761.

     Extensive discussion of the Phaedrus translation by
     Giuseppe Rigutini (Firenze: Sansoni, 1883) during which
     Conti provides a roughly systematic interpretation of
     a number of Phaedrine fables.

216. Cordemann, Margarete. *Der Umschung der Kunst zwischen
     der ersten und zweiten Fabelsammlung La Fontaines*.
     Dissertation, Munich, 1917.

     Stresses differences to be seen between the two edi-
     tions and sees an evolution of the type as well as of
     the poet's poetics between the two collections.

217. Couprie, Alain. "Autour du thème de la cour dans la
     Fables de La Fontaine: Problèmes méthodologiques."
     L'Information Littéraire, 32 (1980), 54-57.

     Investigates the theme of the heart in the fables of
     La Fontaine after a review of the opposing schools of
     La Fontaine criticism: those concerned with aesthetics
     and those concentrating upon content. A thematic study
     is justified through the fables themselves but clearly
     must be concerned with aesthetics. The theme of the
     heart is discussed in terms of the texts and in its
     historical context.

218. Couton, Georges. "La Source d'une fable de La Fon-
     taine (X,9)." *Revue de la histoire Littéraire de la
     France*, 52 (1952), 314-315.

     Argues that La Fontaine was unlikely to have read the
     three disparate sources that have been postulated for
     "Le Berger et le roi" (X, 9). Suggests "Le six voyages
     de J.B. Tavernier."

219.   ——————. *La Poétique de La Fontaine. Deux Études: La
        Fontaine et l'art des emblèmes; Du pensum aux fables.*
        Paris: Presses Universitaires de France, 1957. 38 pp.

        Couton maintains in the first study that emblems have
        left an important trace in the fables of La Fontaine.
        Arguing essentially from Aliciati, the emblem contained
        a moral commentary and thus the historical explanation
        of a number of passages in the *Fables*. The second study
        concerns the school curriculum in seventeenth-century
        France, the study of fables and rhetoric which La Fon-
        taine combines in his work.

220.   ——————. *La Politique de La Fontaine.* Paris: Les Belles
        Lettres, 1959. 153 pp.

        Allegorical interpretation of La Fontaine in particular
        and of seventeenth-century French literature in general
        is used to illuminate La Fontaine's views on foreign
        policy. Finds criticism of royalism and much else.
        Much is left as speculation (tied to a reading of
        Machiavelli, for example), but a few conclusions based
        upon the poet's less ambiguous sections seem worthwhile.

221.   ——————. *La Fontaine: Fables choisies mises en vers.
        Introduction, notes et relevé de variantes.* Paris:
        Garnier, 1962. xxxvii and 576 pp.

        Lengthy introduction discusses the relationship be-
        tween La Fontaine's *Fables* and the emblems of the six-
        teenth and seventeenth century. A survey of the fable
        in France is followed by a general introduction to the
        fable. Very extensive notes and thirty-two illustra-
        tions.

222.   ——————. "Le livre épicurien des Fables: Essai de lec-
        ture du livre xiii." *Travaux de linguistique et de
        littérature Publiés par le Centre de Philologie et de
        Littérature Romanes de l'Université de Strasbourg*,
        13: 2 (1975), 283-290.

        Investigates the division of La Fontaine's *Fables*
        into books. Without a doubt this is done in imitation
        of Phaedrus. Uses Book Seven of the second edition
        fable by fable to establish that each book contains a
        similar form of construction, the division of fables
        corresponds somewhat to theme and attitude.

223.   Coville, Alice Perkins. "The Usefullness of Fables and
        Folklore in Teaching Kindness and Consideration."

Home Progress, 4 (1915), cols. 1169–1173.

Finds fables (not clearly explained or defined) as positive tools in teaching children. The lessons to be derived from the fables (and other tales) are important, but these forms are also valuable as exercises of the imagination.

224. Cox, R. Mcrritt. "The Literary Maturation of Thomas de Iriarte." *Romance Notes*, 13 (1971), 117–123.

Three works are important in the study of Thomás de Iriarte: his translation of Horace's *Poetics*, an essay entitled "Donde las dan las toman," and "La Musica." These works established Iriarte and he was able to build upon them to produce his best-known work: *Fábulas literarias*.

225. Coyle, Lee. "The Fabulous Fabulist." *George Ade*. New York: Twayne, 1964, pp. 40–48.

Evaluates George Ade's *Fables in Slang*, in which Ade retained the form of the classical fable and some of its stilted manner but wrote them in highly colloquial language. Deals with Ade's characters, all of whom are typical Americans. Coyle describes the success of the fables, as he discusses the themes and conventions Ade establishes.

226. Crane, Thomas F. *The Exempla or Illustrative Stories from the Sermones Vulgares of Jacques de Vitry*. Publications of the Folk-Lore Society, no. 26. London, 1890.

Contains informative materials upon the nature of the *exempla* found in the extensive collection, which contains a number of fables as well as other didactic tales.

227. Craven, T.C. "Studies in the Style of Phaedrus." Dissertation, McMaster University, Hamilton, Ontario, 1973.

Analysis, essentially mathematical, of Phaedrus' meter and language. Study of verse-endings confirms received order of the fable, and notice is made of an increasing use of Greek loan-words. Phaedrus may have had a preference for the seven-verse poem.

228. Crowne, David K. "A Date for the Composition of Henryson's Fables." *Journal of English and German Philology*,

61 (1962), 583-590.

A not entirely successful attempt to date the *Fables*;
two are "not before 1484" on the basis of correspondences
in Caxton.

229. Crusius, Otto. "De babrii aetate." *Leipziger Studien
      zur klassischen Philologie*, 2 (1879), 127-248.

Classical study of Babrius. Discusses the nationality,
dates, metrics, and languages of Babrius. Babrius is
a Roman name, well-attested in Latin inscriptions but
unknown as a Greek name. On the basis of the decidedly
Italianate character of Babrius' choliambic meter Babrius is certain to have been a Roman, writing in Greece,
although not necessarily at Rome or even in Italy. Extensive discussion of the metrics, which deserve to be
treated in the history of the Latin, not Greek, meter.

230. ————. "Studien zu Babrios und den Aisopeia." *Jahr-
      bücher für classische Philologie*, 133 (1883), 225-
      249.

Discusses the manuscript tradition of Babrius and his
relationship to the corpus of Aesopica and proverbs.
Various notes to specific fables.

231. ————. "Die Betonung des Choliambius." *Philologus*,
      53 (1884), 216-227.

Concerned with the nature and the position of the
stress in the last dipod in Babrian Choliambics.

232. ————. "Babrius 95.106." *Philologus*, 53 (1884), 227.

Notes to Babrius 95 (P336 "Sick Lion, Fox and Stag,"
TMI K402.3, K813) and 106 (P337 "Lion, Fox and Ape,"
TMI W128.2). The first is told for the sake of the
narration, not for the moral, and is therefore less a
fable than a novelle; much the same is true of Babrius
106.

233. ————. "Die Fabeln des Babrius auf Wachstafeln aus
      Palmyra." *Philologus*, 53 (1884), 228-253.

A detailed analysis of the wax tablets found in the
ruins of Palmyra (destroyed in 272 or 273 A.D.). These
tablets, found by the Dutch Naval officer van Assendelft (therefore "Tabulae ceratae Assendelftianae") contain fourteen fables, some in choliambics and of Babrian
origin. The fables are written from memory: the be-

ginnings are better remembered than the middle sections, but these school texts preserve evidence for the Babrian version of P358 "Ass in the Lion's Skin" (A-T 214; TMI J512, J951.1) in which the ass is recognized by dropping the skin instead of being betrayed by his braying (P188. TMI J951.1). This has survived in Avianus--clearly paraphrases of Babrius--but the original is known only in this paraphrase.

234. ————. "The Fables of Avianus (Ellis)." *Jahrbücher für classische Philologie*, 139 (1889), 641-656.

Very comprehensive review of Ellis' Oxford edition of Avianus. Crusius praises Ellis although he suggests that Ellis might have spent more time with the manuscripts and should have provided an overview on the comparative relationship between Avianus and Babrius. Crusius sees an intermediary of Titian's Latin prose paraphrase between Avianus and Babrius. Long list of emendations, corrections.

235. ————. "Babriana." *Rheinisches Museum*, 46 (1891), 318-320.

Various notes to Babrius fables as edited by Rutherford. Suggests emendations and corrections to the notes of Rutherford's edition.

236. ————. "Über eine alte Tierfabel." *Rheinisches Museum*, 49 (1894), 229-308.

Deals primarily with P50 "Weasel as Bride" (TMI J1908.2; Babrius 32 "Weasel and Aphrodite") in Lucian, in Gregory of Nyssa and in other fabulists as well as a wide-ranging number of proverbial expressions.

237. ————. "Zu den alten Fabeldichtern." *Philologus*, 54 (1895), 474-488.

Treated Avianus and his dates and the "apologi" fables. The paraphrase of Avianus, for which Heidenhain had claimed a more complete text had been used, is demonstrated to be a relatively simple paraphrase of Avianus from a text that was basically the same as our received text. Therefore we can learn little to help the Avianus tradition itself. Ends with a number of notes for the Avianus fables.

238. ————. *Babrii Fabulae Aesopeae*. Leipzig: Teubner, 1897.

Most complete edition of Babrius. Long introduction
covers history of text and the Roman nationality of
Babrius. Exhaustive treatment of the Babrius meter
and index of lexical items. Edition contains all known
recovered Babrian fables in prose paraphrase, some
still disputed.

239. ———. "Apologus." *Realencyclopädie der classischen
Altertumwissenschaft*. Stuttgart: Druckenmüller, 1895,
2, 167-170.

Discusses the term "apologue" in all its applications:
the Aesopic fable fits as a sub-category in some instances. Apologue seems to have meant "narration," in
both a poetic and a rhetorical sense.

240. ———. "Avianus." *Realencyclopädie der classischen
Altertumswissenschaft*. Stuttgart: Druckenmüller,
1895, 4, 2373-2378.

Various theories of the time and person of Avianus
are discussed, including an extensive review of the
ideas of Ellis and Cannegieter. The 42-fable Avianus
collection is described in terms of its relationship to
Babrius, followed by a summary of the life of the collection and its diffusion.

241. ———. "Babrios." *Realencyclopädie der classischen
Altertumswissenschaft*. Stuttgart: Druckenmüller,
1895, 4, 2655-2667.

Reviews texts and literature, the name and the
nationality of Babrius (best evidence implies Roman,
before the third century A.D.). The fable collection
is described (no clear idea of original form of the
collection) as are all sources, language, metrics and
style. Lists virtually a complete set of parallels to
classical literature including paremiological materials.
The final section deals with the influence of the Babrian
fables and their textual history.

242. ———. "Aus der Geschichte der Fabel." Introduction
to *Das Buch der Fabeln*. Ed. C.H. Kleukens. Leipzig:
Insel, 1913. 61 pp.

Survey of the nature and history of the fable from
Homer to the modern day with an interesting discussion
of the characters. Individual fables dealt with include the Phaedrine and Hesiod fables. The Physiologus
as well as the beast epic materials in the Middle Ages

are introduced as is the fable activity of the Humanists and the Reformers. La Fontaine is counted as a high-point of fable activity; modern fabulists discussed include Henrik Ibsen and even Nietzsche.

243. Curdy, A.E. "The Versions of the Fable of the Peacock and Juno." *Studies in Honor of A. Marshall Elliott.* Vol. 1. Baltimore: The Johns Hopkins Press, 1911, pp. 329-346.

This article contains an examination of P509 "Peacock complains to Juno about his Voice" (TMI W128.4) from Phaedrus (3. 18) to Caxton. Curdy compares the various versions by "motifs" in order to determine the relationships of the medieval forms to the fable. The summary indicates that there are a number of branching traditions, most of which leave no successors; the Phaedrine and the Steinhöwel versions have numerous descendants.

244. Cutts, John P. "An Anterior Analogue of La Fontaine's *La Cigale et la fourmi.*" *Revue de littérature comparée*, 36 (1962), 252-258.

Suggests William Byrd's *Psalmes, Songs and Sonnets,* 1611, as an analogue to La Fontaine's treatment of P373 "Cicada and the Ant" (A-T 280; TMI J711.1); with the important consideration, however, that the least important influence upon La Fontaine is the textual borrowing. What is important is how the material is handled: La Fontaine is apparently the first to focus attention upon the grasshopper.

245. Czerniatowicz, Janina. "Romans Grecki w Polsce doby odrodzenia." *Eos*, 54 (1964), 315-328.

Discussion of Greek literature--especially the Romance--brought to Poland by the Humanists of the fifteenth century. The *Vita Aesopi* and the fable collection of Heinrich Steinhöwel (Ulm 1476/77) are discussed extensively.

246. Dadone, Margherita. "Appunti sulla fortuna di Fedro. I. Fedro e Seneca." *Rivista di studia classica*, 2 (1954), 3-12.

Survey of Phaedrus studies, followed by a summary of certain passages from Phaedrus used by Seneca. A number of similar turns of phrase found in both poets.

247. ————. "Appunto sulla fortuna di Fedro. II. Fedro e

Persio: III. Fedro et Marziale." *Revista di Studi
Classici*, 2 (1954), 79-86.

Demonstrates the possibility that Persius and Martial
knew Phaedrus. The first of these is tenuous; the
second probable.

248.   Dahlberg, C. "Chaucer's Cock and Fox." *Journal of
English and German Philology*, 53 (1954), 277-290.

Accepts Donovan's argument for the relationship between Cock and Fox in the Nun's Priest's Tale. Presents
analogues for Chaucer's Chauntecleer episodes: a thirteenth-century development of the Roman de Renart with
Rousiel or Rousian as the Fox (cf. P597). The second
is an early fourteenth-century poem "Li Dis d'Enteude-
ment" which also offers a name similar to Russell, a
necessary key to identify Daun Russell as heretic. This
is in line with a long tradition of equating the fox
with corrupting influence in the church.

249.   Dain, A. "Un recueil byzantine des fables de Babrios,
Parisinus suppl. Gr. 1245." *Actes du ix*[e] *Congrès
International d'Études Byzantines à Thessalonique I.*
Hellenica Supplement, 9 (1958), 101-111.

Notes on the Bibliothèque Nationale manuscript found
in the Near East by Minoides Mynas which contains 65
fables. Specifically deals with the copy made by
Mynas and another, containing 62 fables, copied from
this manuscript and now in the British Museum.

250.   ————. "Sur deux recueils de Babrios trouvés par
Minoide Mynas." *Bulletin de l'Association Guillaume
Budé*, 4th Series, 1 (1960), 113-121.

Notes on copies of manuscripts of Babrius found by
Minoides Mynas in the mid-nineteenth century. The
first contains 123 fables of Babrius in 40 folios from
the eleventh century (Paris. suppl. 748). The other is
the Paris. suppl. 1245 with 65 fables. Recounts the
history of the manuscripts and their importance.

251.   Daly, Lloyd William. *Aesop without Morals*. New York:
Thomas Yoseloff, 1961.

An edition of the fables and the life of Aesop in
English with morals considered unnecessary by the trans-
lator. The texts are those found in Ben Edwin Perry's
Aesopica and the fables in the collection are from the

Greek prose fables, for which translations have been either nonexistent or difficult to come by. As Perry had at that time also promised a translation of the Babrius and the Phaedrus fables (in the Loeb series), Daly does not translate these but provides a translation for the *Vita Aesopi*, the first known translation. Excellent short introduction to the life and the fables.

252.   ———. "Hesiod's Fable." *Transactions of the American Philological Association*, 92 (1961), 45-51.

An attempt to understand the fable in Hesiod's *Works and Days* (lines 203-211) P4 "Hawk and Nightingale" (TMI J321.1) in its context to illuminate the moral of the fable, which is found later on in the poem, in particular, lines 274-84. Here the thought is expressed that there is no justice among the fish and beasts and winged birds, but there is justice for men. Hesiod then intends the fable as an illustration of the ruthless exercise of might.

253.   ———. "Aesop and Brito." *Classical Studies Presented to Ben Edwin Perry by His Students and Colleagues at the University of Illinois*, 1924-1960. Illinois Studies in Language and Literature, no. 58. Urbana, Ill.: University of Illinois Press, 1969, pp. 6-14.

Describes a treatise written ostensibly to explain and characterize various Greek words in Latin, a work which demonstrates the general state of Greek knowledge at the time. Compiled by a certain Guillemus Brito of the University of Paris in the thirteenth century, the Mss contain eight lines which are a reference to the *Vita Aesopi*, specifically the episode with the figs.

254.   Danner, G. Richard. "Individualism in La Fontaine's 'Le Loup et le Chien.'" *Kentucky Romance Quarterly*, 24 (1977), 185-190.

Well-argued call for multi-dimensional interpretation of texts, in particular for La Fontaine I, 5 "Le Loup et le chien," P346 "Wolf and the Well-Fed Dog" (A-T 201; TMI L451.3). The full meaning of the fable as presented in La Fontaine is not necessarily the simplistic praise of liberty that is generally associated with this fable in La Fontaine and elsewhere, as that emphasizes only the wolf's point of view. What is perfectly natural for the wolf may not in fact be so for the dog, who never claims to desire the type of freedom represented by the

wolf. A repeated emphasis upon the theme of being
satisfied with one's state is discovered. La Fontaine
has left out an expressed moral here. This implies
ambiguity; a call for us to read these works without
preconceived notions of their meaning.

255.   ————. "La Fontaine's Ironic Vision in the Fables."
       The French Review, 50 (1977), 562-571.

Defines irony as a conflict between what seems to be
real and that which is real in context, containing
a real or pretended awareness of that conflict and a
response--often comic--on the part of the observer. La
Fontaine's ironic mode analysed in specific fables and
suggested as present in all the fables. Calls for a
systematic study of irony in La Fontaine.

256.   Dargan, E.P. "Cock and Fox: A Critical Study of the
       History and Sources of the Medieval Fable." *Modern
       Philology*, 4 (1906-07), 1-27.

The roughly fifteen versions of P124 (A-T 57; TMI
K334.1) from the ca. 750 Rheims ms to the Caxton version
of 1484 are covered. Dozens of versions are discussed
in the elaborate charts in order to discuss the nature
of their relationships. Dargan does this by the comparative study of what he calls *Leitmotives*. Through
this complicated procedure he discovers a "cheese story"
and a "wolf story" which conflate and then separate again
to form the Phaedrus paraphrase and the Alfred fables
which in turn form the Marie branch, the Renart branch
and the Romulus branch (which in turn become Steinhöwel,
Machault, and Caxton). All of which seems to forget
that the fable is purely Phaedrine (Book 1, 13).

257.   Daub, Adam. "Zu den biographia des Suidas." *Jahrbücher
       für classischen Philologie*, 27 (1881), 241-245.

Varied comments on the *biographika* regarding Aesop
and others: the putative birthdate is given here as in
the 40th Olympiad; Aesop flourished in the 52nd Olympiad.
Discusses various interpretations and uses of the
biographika.

258.   Daube, David. "Counting." *Mnemosyne*, 30 (1977), 176-
       178.

Erotic enumeration is introduced. Daube then compares
the parallels between an episode in the *Vita Aesopi* and
an anecdote in Balzac's *Contes Drolatiques*. In both,

the wife of Aesop's master, Xanthus, has promised him
his liberty (in other versions a shirt) if Aesop can
make love to her ten times. Aesop succeeds nine times
and barely misses the tenth. He insists that he essentially accomplished his task and ought to be compen-
sated. An orally circulated version is postulated for
the Balzac account not in most of the early modern
printed versions of the *Vita*.

259. ————. *Ancient Hebrew Fables: The Inaugural Lecture
of the Oxford Centre for Postgraduate Hebrew Studies,
Delivered in Corpus Christi College 17 May 1973*.
Oxford: Oxford University Press, 1973. 32 pp.

Stresses underlying political meaning of fables and
frequent need of allegory. Three fables from the Old
Testament and six from the Rabbis of the roughly three
dozen fables in the Talmud and Midrash. After a rather
restrictive definition of the fable, Daube chooses six
fables which seem unique.

260. Davidson, Linda. "The Use of *blanchete* in Juan Ruiz's
Fable of the Ass and the Lap-Dog." *Romance Philology*,
33 (1979), 154-160.

Questions why Ruiz would use "blanchete (branchete)"
(probable meaning: small, white dog). Uses Greek,
Latin, and English natural histories to determine that
the lap dog also indicated a small hunting animal with
a double meaning extended to the sexual hunt.

261. ————. "The Medieval Zoo of Juan Ruiz: A Study of
Animal Imagery in the *Libro de Buen Amor*." Dissertation, Indiana University, 1980. 551 pp.

The more than 550 references to animals in the *Libro
de Buen Amor* are organized according to the poetic
functions they fulfill with two general categories:
figurative use of an animal, and use of an animal as a
character in the work proper. The latter function is
the primary area under which the fables are discussed.
The final section is a glossary of the animal appear-
ances, with literary and historical overviews of each
animal presented.

262. Davies, M. "Aeschylus and the Fable." *Hermes*, 109
(1981), 248-251.

A note on Martin West's suggestion concerning the
relationship of Aeschylus and the fable. Davies suggests

the similarities between Aeschylus Ag. 48 ff./104 ff.
and Archilochus' epode are essentially illusory.

263.   Davis, James Herbert. "An Attractive Education: The
       Fables and the *Dialogues des morts*." *Fénelon*. Boston:
       Twayne, 1979, 53-63.

       Discusses the fables as fairy tales, romances, and
       true fables. The fables are characterized as "incisive-
       ly didactic and indisputably pedagogical." The sixteen
       animal fables are provided with epimythia with a variety
       of themes, a few having political overtones. Fénelon
       does not sacrifice his morals for considerations of
       style, most likely never having intended the fables
       for publication. He is, nevertheless, to be counted
       among the few contributors to seventeenth-century
       children's literature. This monograph covers all of
       Fénelon's life and works and includes a selective bib-
       liography.

264.   Dawson, Warren R. "The Mouse in Fable and Folklore."
       Folk-Lore, 36 (1925), 227-248.

       Ascribes the origin of the Aesopic fables to Egypt on
       the evidence of P130 "Stomach and Feet" (A-T 293;
       TMI J461.1) and P150 "Lion and Mouse" (A-T 75; TMI
       B371.1). Alludes to P384 "Mouse and Frog" (A-T 78;
       TMI J681.1), P520 "Mountain in Labor" (TMI U114), P352
       "Country Mouse and Town Mouse" (A-T 112; TMI J211.1),
       P79 "Cat and Mice" (TMI K2061.9) and others. Includes
       variants of other fables in which the mouse replaces
       more common actors. The mouse in Bidpai as well as
       Egyptian literature and the Old Testament is discussed,
       followed by brief mention of Gilgamesh, Aristotle,
       Pliny, and the medieval beastiaries. Mice in legends
       and custom end the work.

265.   De Boor, Helmut. "Über Fabel und Bîspel." *Sitzungs-
       berichte der Bayerischen Akademie der Wissenschaften*,
       Phil.-hist. Klasse, 1966, fasc. 1. 40 pp.

       Deals with the concepts of *bîspel* and *fabel* as literary
       genres during the Middle Ages. The discussion revolves
       around whether or not the diffuse term "bîspel" desig-
       nates a genre. Begins by determining if the Middle
       Ages had a concept of genre, which is answered in the
       affirmative. *Fabel* was and remained a foreign word for
       the German Middle Ages. Investigates various uses of
       "bîspel," from sermons through the Physiologus and Der
       Stricker. Results indicate that *bîspel* did not indicate

a literary genre specifically, rather a rhetorical feature which might show up in a literary treatment.

266. Defourny, Michel. "Panchatantra et pensée brahmanique."
*Proceedings of the Third International Beast Epic,
Fable and Fabliau Colloquium, Münster 1979.* Ed. Jan
Goossens and Timothy Sodmann. Köln: Böhlau Verlag,
1981, 95-101.

Argues that the Indian fable, such as found in the
Panchatantra, the *Mahabharata* or the Buddhist *Jakatas*,
is deeply rooted in the animal reality of the land,
animals being an integral part of Indian life and
mythology, part of the very idea of reincarnation, and
as such part of Brahmanistic world view. Defourny investigates fables from the *Panchatantra*, especially
"Lion, Crow, Jackal and Camel" (I, xii) which demonstrates
the Indian idea of social hierarchy. Other fables and
myths are mentioned.

267. Delassault, Geneviève. "Le Maître de Sacy et La Fontaine: traducteurs de Phèdre." *Revue des Sciences
Humaines*, 68 (1952), 281-294.

Overview of the sixteenth-century humanistic concern
with the fable, especially Nevelet and Faerne and their
Latin texts, Giles Corrozet and Guillaume Haudent in
their verse translations, all with regard to the rediscovery of Phaedrus. Deals with *Les Fables de Phèdre*
translated into French in 1647 and traces the history
of the Phaedrine fable in France up to the 1668 edition
of La Fontaine's fables. Most of the fables in this
edition are from Phaedrus, and La Fontaine's treatment
of the Roman poet is compared to that of his contemporaries.

268. Delcroix, Maurice. "L'Oiseleur, l'autour, et l'alouette:
Analyse." *Cahiers de l'Association Internationale
des Etudes Françaises*, 26 (1974), 143-158.

A structural, semiotic--in Delcroix's term a *textual*--
analysis of La Fontaine's "Fowler, Hawk and Lark" (VI,
15; TMI J681.1). His analytic methodology is to give
a complete accounting of the complex organization of
the relationships within a text and of their linear
progression in a language as ordinary as possible.
The minute analysis yields a wealth of information;
much of it is applicable to other texts.

269. Della Corte, Francesco. "Phaedriana." *Rivista di Filologia*, 17 (1939), 136-144.

Reviews what is known of the life of Phaedrus, placing
his date of birth as 15 B.C. His status as a former
slave is affirmed as are the putative difficulties under
Sejanus. Everything concerning his life is extrapolated
from hints in his fables.

270. ————. *Moralita della favola*. Genoa: Romano Ed. Mod.,
1945. 13 pp.

Historical overview of the fable, placing the origin
of the form in India and describing its Greek roots.
The Latin fable is outlined with Phaedrus and his contemporaries. The moral of the fable is contrasted with
the narrative, with the moral seen as a reflection of
its own time. Phaedrus captures his era exactly. Brief
mention made of La Fontaine and Lessing.

271. ————. "Tre papiri favolistici latini." *Atti dell'xi
Congresso Internazionale di Papirologia, Milano 2-8
settembre 1965*. Milan: Università di Milano, 1966,
542-550.

Critical notes to three papyri in the *Corpus papyrorum
Latinarum* containing P133 "Dog with Meat and his Shadow"
(A-T 34; TMI J1791.4), P284 "Man and Lion Traveling
together" (TMI J1454), P158 "Wolf and Old Woman Nurse"
(TMI J2066.5), P283 "Fire-Bearing Fox" (TMI J2101.1,
K2351.1.1), and some smaller fragments of others.

272. ————. "Punti di vista su la favola esopica." *Annali
della Facoltà di Magistero dell'Università di Palermo*,
4 (1971-1972), 1-30. Also *Opuscula*, 4, 117-146.

Varied and wide-ranging notes on the history of the
fable, on the Indian origin of the fable, on the relationship of mythology, onomastics, proverb study,
the animal epic, the bestiaries, to the fable, and the
idea of a literary versus a folklore fable.

273. De Lorenzi, Attilio. *Fedro*. Florence: La Nuova Italia,
1955.

Very comprehensive review of Phaedrus' life and works.
Begins with the life and best-evidence guesses concerning the dates of the poet and his fables. Phaedrus'
relationships with the emperor and other poets are determined as well as can be gleaned from the evidence
of the fable collection itself. The special case of
the third book and its prologue and epilogue are given
separate treatment to determine the value of the apparent

allusions to living persons. The transmission of the
fables and the Perotti appendix as well as the paraphrases are described. A roughly five-page "essential
bibliography" is the result of all this, followed by
an appended discussion of the silence of Quintillian
and the mentioning of Phaedrus by Martial.

274. Descoeudres, Jean-Paul. "Vom listenreichen Igel."
Antike Kunst, 14 (1971), 145-147 and 16 (1973), 89.

Describes in great detail a fragmentary piece of
ceramic (illustrated), with a picture of a dog-like
animal with carefully drawn teeth and an indefinite
object to the right, which Descoeudres identifies as a
hedgehog. Discusses this fragment with Hesiod's *Work
and Days* and concludes that the scene is most reminis-
cent of P675 "Wolf and Hedgehog," known from the cod.
Bruellensis 536.

275. Desmed, R. "Une traduction latine des "Fables" de La
Fontaine." *Latomus*, 23 (1964), 86-93.

Desmed describes a very early Latin translation of
the first three books of La Fontaine's *Fables* by Jean-
Baptiste Giraud (1701-1776), on example of P36 "Evil
Wit" (La Fontaine, IV, 19).

276. Diebler, Arthur Richard. *Henrisones Fabeldichtungen*.
Dissertation, Leipzig, 1885. Printed: Halle/Salle:
Erhardt Karras, 1885. 88 pp.

A commentary on Henryson's sources, now for the most
part reviewed and superseded by Jamieson and Fox
(q.v.).

277. Diels, Hermann. "Altorientalische Fabeln in griechischen
Gewande." *Internationale Wochenschrift für Kunst und
Wissenschaft*, 4 (1910), 993-1002.

Diels is occupied in this essay especially with P439
"Laurel and Olive" (TMI J411.7), a fragment of Callimachus. He combines the statement of the Greek that
the fable is Lydian and Babrius' statement that invention of the fable is to be found in Syria and combines
all this with the fact that the old Aramaic *Ahikar* shows
a similar quarrel and concludes that the fable had its
origin in Babylonia.
See: Eric Ebeling, *Die Babylonische Fabel*.

278. Diestel, Gustaf. *Bausteine zur Geschichte der deutschen Fabel.* Program, Dresden, 1871. 82 pp.

A historical overview of the development of the German fable through the eighteenth century with particular emphasis upon Gellert's fable activity. Lessing is treated superficially. Grimm's theory of an Indo-European "Tiersage," parts of which are still found in the beast epic and the fable is given a great deal of attention. Diestel takes no stand but seems to imply favor for this idea in discussing "Aesop." Attempts definition of the fable but confused in widely-roaming investigations on the origin and nature of the form.

279. Dieterle, J. *Die beiden Perioden von Lessings Fabeldichtung.* Program, Leipzig, 1912. 48 pp.

Discusses the verse and prose fables of Lessing in an attempt to discover Lessing's theoretical distinction between the forms. Uses versions of fables from various fabulists to highlight the Lessing forms and to demonstrate his freeing himself from the verse-fable tradition of La Fontaine. Uses the morals as the proper starting point for an investigation of the prose fable, which he claims is Lessing's primary form.

280. Dithmar, Reinhard. "Die humoristische Fabel im Unterricht." *Die Schulwarte*, 5 (1969), 19-25.

On the usefulness of the modern humorous fable and its function in elementary education.

281. ———. "Fuchs und Rabe--bei Aesop, La Fontaine und Lessing." *Unterricht Heute*, 21: 10 (1970), 472-476.

Suggests the use of P124 "Fox and Crow" (A-T 57; TMI K334.1) for use in the seventh to the ninth school year, as a comparison of different fables with same motif is not only possible but a source of enjoyment. Analyzes the Aesop fable with "Situation, *actio, reactio*, and result." The La Fontaine fable is then compared to the Aesopic form and the Lessing version to both.

282. ———. "Parabolische Rede--Sprachform des kritischen Denkens." *Die Schulwarte*, 8 (1970), 44-54.

The fable is useful in teaching when considered a specific form of critical thought from the point of view of parabolic speech. Fable as form is discussed in terms of the parable and the example.

283. ————. "Existenz- und Gesellschaftskritik in der Fabel von Äsop bis Brecht." *Die Schulwarte*, 11 (1971), 1-9.

The specific "moment" of the fable is social criticism, yet the form remains essentially unpolitical. Various forms from Aesop through modern fable and parable writers are examined. The types of social criticism are variable, but the function remains.

284. ————. *Die Fabel: Geschichte--Struktur--Didaktik*. Paderborn: Schöningh, 1971 (3rd. ed., 1974).

A comprehensive treatment of the fable from three general categories: a historical section which deals with the classical fable, the "oriental" fable (Indian), and the medieval German fable and the fable in Germany from the Reformation through the modern period. James Thurber is treated at the end together with the most important modern German fabulists. The "Systematic" section with the imagery: allegory, simile, parable, and the like then proceeds to the construction of the fable as well as the effects of the form. The final section is a survey of the use of the fable in pedagogical situations with a short history of the use of the fable in schools from its beginnings to the modern day. Several specific studies of the usefulness of the fables in the school are presented, including creation of fables, comparative fable studies, and games.

285. ————. "Das unpolitische Verständnis der Fabel in der Literaturdidaktik." *Blätter für den Deutschlehrer*, 4 (1971), 110-119.

Dithmar maintains in this essay that one of the most important tasks of modern German pedagogy is to bring the pupil to the concept and the practice of critical thinking. The fable serves this function.

286. ————. "Nachwort." *Fabeln aus drei Jahrtausenden*. Zurich: Manesse, 1976, pp. 217-235.

Cursory overview of the history of the fable and fable theory. Concisely but carefully traces the fable from rhetorical beginnings (explaining therein the textual tradition in part).

287. ————. *Fabeln, Parabeln und Gleichnisse: Beispiele didaktischer Literatur*. Munich: Deutscher Taschenbuch Verlag, 1977. 368 pp.

A wide-ranging collection of fables and other didactic short forms from the Old Testament and the Judaic simile through the Indian and Greco-Roman fable to the medieval and modern fable and parable. The European fable of the seventeenth and eighteenth centuries is given over one hundred pages, and a significant number of examples from the moderns are included from Edwin Hoernle to James Thurber, Wolfdietrich Schnurre, and Helmut Arntzen. The collection is provided with an extensive introduction of the fable and parable forms and function with mention and comparison to other short didactic pieces. The copious notes contain bio-bibliographical information on each fabulist.

288. Dobrian, Walter A. "Hacia una nueva apreciación de Samaniego." *Explicación de Textos Literarios*, 1 (1972), 119-123.

Short overview of Felix Samaniego's fabular activity with a discussion of the influence of La Fontaine and Samaniego's relationship to Iriarte. A number of examples of Samaniego's style are discussed.

289. Doderer, Klaus. "Über das 'betriegen' zur Wahrheit: Die Fabelbearbeitungen Martin Luthers." *Wirkendes Wort*, 14 (1964), 379-388.

A short review of the literature on Luther's fables followed by an incisive discussion of the idea of fable as expressed by Luther in the prologue to his fable collection, focusing upon the fable as a vehicle for transmission of "warheit," with an excursus into the precise meanings of these terms. The felicitous phrase "betriegen zur warheit" becomes the essential element of his concept of the fable. The epimythium for Luther is proverbial and more the wisdom of the folk than an absolute truth; for Luther the fables serve to teach true human relationships in society.

290. ————. *Fabeln: Formen, Figuren, Lehren*. Zurich: Atlantis Verlag, 1970. 338 pp.

This study covers the ideas of fable from nearly every point of view. The entire complex of "fable" is approached from considerations of form, characterization, length, as well as historical viewpoints, and society's reception to the fable. Specific fable interpretations are balanced by an overview of theoretical systems describing large sections of fable activity.

Four fables: "Aesop's" P30 "The Shipwrecked Man" (TMI J1034); Martin Luther's unique version of P149 "Lion, Ass, and Fox" (A-T 51; TMI J811.1); Lessing's "Oak and Pig;" and Kafka's "Mouse in the Trap," are given extensive informative interpretations. Excellent selection of fables chosen for examples; good bibliography and illustrations.

291. Donovan, M.J. "The *Moralite* of the Nun's Priest's Sermon." *Journal of English and Germanic Philology*, 52 (1953), 498-538.

Chaucer's tale is seen to be a sermon on alertness to moral obligation; the key is the identification of Chauntecleer (as any holy man) and of Daun Russell. The roles of the cock and the fox throughout medieval literature are investigated; in Chauntecleer, we see that even the alert can fail. No specific source is suggested.
See: Dahlberg, "Chaucer's Cock and Fox."

292. Donti, Lamberto. "Discorso sulla illustrazioni dell' Esopo di 1485 e sulla Passio xilografica." *Bibliofilia*, 50 (1948), 53-107.

A very thorough discussion of the 1485 Aesop's illustrations including reproductions of twenty of the cuts. The printing history is reviewed together with a fixing of the illustrations in their tradition.

293. Donzelli, Giuseppina. "Una versione Menippea della *Aisopou Prasis?*" *Rivista di Filologia e di Istruzione Classica*, 88 (1960), 225-276.

Discusses the *Vita Aesopi*, especially the death of Aesop at the hands of the Delphians, in the Westermann and in the G (edited by Perry) versions, with special attention to its relationship to the school of the Cynics, more particularly to Menippus of Gadara, also a slave, and the authors of the *Diogenous prasis*. The cynics are connected to the Aesopic traditions from early on; and the affinities of Menippus' work to the Aesop romance suggest he may have been inspired by an earlier version.

294. Dorjahn, A.P. "On Phaedrus I, 10." *Classical Journal*, 32 (1937), 560-562.

Note on P474 "Wolf and Fox before Judge Ape" (TMI B270) with reference to Rigaltius' and Lessing's criticism of

the fable; suggests that a study of legal antiquities
might offer a deeper understanding of life and literature.

295. Dorson, R.M. "King Beast of the Forest Meets Man."
     Southern Folklore Quarterly, 18 (1954), 119-128.

     Prints sixteen oral versions, with an introduction,
     of P706 "Lion's Son learns about Man" (A-T 157; TMI
     J22.1) collected in Michigan. The lion appears in four
     of the versions, other animals appear more frequently
     in the versions collected, all from the New World.

296. Doyle, Charles Clay. "On the Neglected Sources of Some
     Epigrams by Thomas More." *Moreana*, 46 (1975), 5-10.

     Demonstrates Thomas More's Epigram 206 "De chirugo et
     anu" to be a versified rendering of Rinuccio d'Arezzo's
     fable "De muliere et medico," P57 "Old Woman and
     Thieving Physician" (TMI J1169.1). It is suggested that
     More may have known the fable in the form of Odo of
     Cheriton's version which is known to have circulated
     in manuscript form during his day. More's epigram 43
     "Aliud in astrologum uxoris impudicae maritum" and
     other epigrams are compared to fabular motifs with sug-
     gested relationships.

297. ————. "The Background of More's Epigrams." *Moreana*,
     55 (1977), 61-64.

     In this short essay, Doyle continues his investigation
     of the Aesopic connection in More's epigrams. An earlier
     version of P57 "Old Woman and Thieving Physician" (TMI
     J1169.1) which lies at the basis of epigram 206 "De
     chirugo et anu" can be found in the *Mensa Philosophia*
     (1475). P702 "Dog in the Manger" (TMI W156) and P133
     "Dog with Meat and his Shadow" (A-T 34; TMI J179.4)
     are also discussed as possible starting points for
     other epigrams.

298. Draak, Maartjie. "Is Ondank 'S Werelds Loon?" *Neo-
     philologus*, 30 (1946), 129-138.

     Builds upon Krohn and McKenzie in the study of the
     fabular complex P176 "Man who Warmed a Snake" (A-T 155;
     TMI W154.2) and P640, P640A "Soldier and Serpent,"
     or "Dragon and Peasant" (A-T 155; TMI J1172.3, W154.2.1)
     and demonstrates a complexity beyond that seen by Krohn.
     Emphasis is upon the European versions.

299. Draheim, H. "Bericht über die Litteratur zu Phaedrus
     und der römischen Fabeldichtung für das Jahr 1888."
     *Jahresbericht über die Fortschritte der klassischen
     Altertumswissenschaft*, 69 (1889), 107-121. Part of
     a continuing series: On 1889, 68 (1891), 210-225;
     1892-1894, 84 (1896), 235-258; 1895-1898, 101 (1899),
     142-147; 1899-1905, 126 (1905), 149-158; 1904-1908,
     143 (1909), 55-62; 1909-1919, 204 (1920), 195-203.

     A fairly comprehensive, though highly selective,
     survey of the main points of the literature on Phaedrus,
     and, much less complete, on Avianus and the medieval
     Latin fable tradition; generally in Germany and Western
     Europe. American, British, and Eastern European scholar-
     ship is only touched upon. Especially valuable for edi-
     tions, glossaries, and school texts.
          See: Heydenreich, "Bericht" and Port, "Griechische und
     Römische Fabel."

300. ———. "De Phaedri senario." *Jahrbücher für classische
     Philologie*, 139 (1889), 129.

     Draheim notes that in no case is the penultimate
     syllable of a polysyllabic word line in the second, third,
     or sixth thesis. This is roughly similar to the law of
     diplody in Terence.

301. ———. "De Aviani elegis." *Jahrbücher für classische
     Philologie*, 143 (1891), 509-511.

     Various notes on the verse forms of Avianus' fables
     as reconstructed in part from the corrupt received
     forms.

302. ———. *Aesopus latinus*. Program, Berlin, 1893.

     An edition of the so-called Anonymous Neveleti, called
     here the "Aesopus latinus," since "Aesopus" is in the
     transmitted title and *latinus* would make the necessary
     distinction from the Greek prose tradition. The text
     is based upon the codex Erl. 849 now in the University
     Library in Munich. Extensive critical apparatus.

303. Dressel, Johann Paul Rich. *Zur Geschichte der Fabel, I:
     Die aesopische Fabel bei den Greichen*. Program,
     Berlin, 1876. 30 pp.

     A historical overview of the Greek fable up to Bab-
     rius. Wide-ranging knowledge of literature is brought
     to bear on the subject, but Dressel's idea that Phaedrus

and subsequent collectors had no firm or particular
idea of the fable as a form has been demonstrated to
be in error.

304. Driberg, J.H. "Aesop." *Spectator*, 148 (1932), 857.

A short, rather curious, evaluation of Aesop the man
and his fables on the occasion of the publication of
the Gregynog edition of Caxton's *Aesop*. Driberg strangely
derives Aesop from "Aethiop" and confuses the Indian
tradition with the Greek, insisting upon an African
origin for it all.

305. Duchemin, Jacqueline. "Recherche sur un thème aris-
      tophanien et ses sources religieuses." *Études
      classiques*, 25 (1957), 273-295.

Suggests, in passing, a connection with P3 "Eagle and
Beetle" (TMI L315.7), used in *Peace* by Aristophanes, with
a Babylonian poetic myth and a large number of other analogues.

306. ————. "Aspects pastoraux de la poésie homérique:
      les comparisons dans l'Iliade." *Revue des Études
      Grecques*, 73 (1960), 362-415.

Lists and evaluates important analogues in the Homeric
canon to various pastoral subjects and in *Aesopica*, both
in the fables and in the proverbial phrases attributed
to Aesop. A number of these are fairly precise matches
and contain occasionally some moral overtones as well.

307. Duda, Helen. "Animal Nature in the Aesopic Fables."
      Dissertation, University of Illinois at Urbana-
      Champaign, 1948.

Attempts to describe the characterization given animals
in the fables in terms of the natural characteristics
of the animals and in deviations from those features.

308. Duff, John Wight. "Phaedrus." *A Literary History of
      Rome in the Silver Age*. London: Routledge, 1927, pp.
      133-154.

Discusses the life and fables of Phaedrus (as well as
the fables in the "Appendix"); his relationship to the
Greek tradition and that portion of his work specifically
Roman. Phaedrus the moralist is contrasted with Phaedrus
the literary artist, and a discussion of his influence
upon Roman style and art as well as upon modern fable

writers such as La Fontaine and Krylov follows. A
brief explanation of his meter ends the chapter.

309. ————. *Roman Satire: Its Outlook on Social Life.*
Berkeley: University of California Press, 1936.

The fable is considered a genre allied to that of
satire. A chapter on Phaedrus ("Phaedrus and Persius")
traces the development of the Phaedrine fable, using
the material to characterize Phaedrus the man. Dates
and style are discussed in relationship to individual
fables.

310. Dunston, J. "The Romulus-Pliny from St. Bénigne's Abbey
at Dijon Recovered in Mss. Burney 59 and Hamilton 517."
Scriptorum, 7 (1953), 210-218.

The ms. Burney 59 of the British Library, the first
with the text of the medieval Romulus paraphrase of the
Phaedrine fables, together with Hamilton 517 of Berlin,
are described in detail as the St. Bénigne from which
is derived the "G" (ms. Gud. Lat. 182 of the Herzog
August Library of Wolfenbüttel) and which forms the
basis for the editions of Romulus by Oesterley and
Thiele. Both of these early editions contain inaccuracies,
not realizing the importance of ms. Burney 59. The history of the manuscript from the abbey library to the
British Museum is speculated upon but no conclusions
are drawn.

311. Dwyer, Eugene. "The Fowler and the Asp: Literary vs.
Generic Illustration in Roman Art." *American Journal
of Archaeology*, 82 (1978), 400-404.

This article discusses portrayals of P115 "Fowler and
Asp" (TMI N335.1) as found on marble disks (oscilla)
from Pompeii and other sources. These are used to
further clarify other similar scenes from the fifth
century and later. General discussion of the relationships between Aesopic fable iconography and more general
representation of bird-catching suggests that the basis
for the scenes might be the fabular manuscript tradition, although no known extant manuscript provides an
example. Excellent illustrations.

312. Eames, Marian. "John Ogilby and His Aesop." *Bulletin
of the New York Public Library*, 65: 2 (1961), 73-88.

Sketch of Ogilby's career especially as a translator
and adaptor of Aesop with details of edition of *Aesop*

(1651, 1664) and illustrations from crude beginnings
to Hollar's work. Some may be Barlow's.

313. Eberling, Erich. *Die babylonische Fabel und ihre*
Bedeutung für die Literaturgeschichte. Mitteilungen
der altorientalischen Gesellschaft, 2, 2. Eduard
Pfeiffer, 1927. 53 pp.

The findings containing fabular motifs among the surviving tablets are scarce but often remarkable. Eberling
gives versions of P439 "Laurel and Olive" (TMI J411.7)
in two cuneiform tablets from the Berlin Museum, with
such a remarkable agreement to the Callimachus fable
that Babylonian origin for the motif is suggested. Mention is made of other fragments and jokes and proverbs
as well. Some examples seem to be precursors of other
Greek fables.

314. Edgerton, Franklin. *The Panchatantra Reconstructed: An*
Attempt to Establish the Lost Original Sanskrit Text
of the Most Famous of Indian Story-Collections on the
Basis of the Principal of Extant Versions. 2 vols.
American Oriental Society Series, nos. 2 and 3. New
Haven: American Oriental Society, 1924.

Volume one contains a reconstructed Sanskrit edition
with full apparatus. Volume 2 is an historical discussion of the literary tradition of the *Panchatantra*,
in four relatively independent strands: 1) the *Tan-*
trakhyayika and its descendants, 2) the so-called
Southern Panchatantra including the *Hitopadésa*, 3) the
Bhrathatha versions and 4) the Pahlavi versions. There
is extensive explanation of methodology and a translation of the Sanskrit text.

315. Edler, Otto. *Darstellung und Kritik der Ansicht Lessings*
über das Wesen der Fabel. Program: Herford, 1980.
23 pp.

A paraphrase of Lessing's *Abhandlungen zur Fabel* with
the curious idea that Lessing wrote his own fables in
accord with his definition of the genre. Ends with
summaries of nineteenth-century views on Lessing's ideas
on the origin of the fable.

316. Edlund, I.E.M. "Meaningful or Meaningless? Animal
Symbolism in Greek Vase-Painting." *Mededelingen van*
het Nederlandsch historisch Instituut te Rome, 42
(1980), 31-35.

Far from being simple decorative adornments to the ceramic art forms, the presence of a number of animals on Greek vases appears to demonstrate, among other things, a particular form of symbolism found in the Aesopic fables.

317. Edwards, Bateman. "An Aesopic Allusion in the Roman d'Alexander." *Studies in Honor of Frederick William Shipley*. Washington University Studies in Language and Literature, no. 14. St. Louis: Washington University Press, 1942, 95-99.

Edwards studies P129 "Jackdaw and the Pigeons" (A-T 244; TMI J951.2) with its relationship to P101 "Borrowed Feathers," but with the added motif of looking for food. The motif and its moral are alluded to in the *Roman d'Alexander*, Branch IV, stanza 47, which mentions both the food and the moral against avarice. Links between the Greek prose tradition and the French Romance cannot be determined, however. The earliest known translation of this fable is in the Lorenzo Valla collection of 1438.

318. Eggert, Gerhard. "Die Tierfabel als politisches Instrument." *Geist der Zeit: Wesen und Gestalt der Völker*, 19 (1941), 634-643.

The rhetorical use of the fable and the *Märchen* in political circumstances is demonstrated, especially in Nazi propaganda.

319. Eichhorn, Karl. *Mitteldeutsche Fabeln, zum ersten Mal herausgegeben*. Program, Meiningen, 1896, 1897, 1898. 29 pp., 61 pp., and 29 pp.

The three parts of this study published over three years, contain a description of the Leipzig manuscript 1279 and the medieval German fables found there. The language and the place of origin of the manuscript are discussed in the first part, with part two being an annotated edition of the fables. The last part is a source study with no surprises as all the fables are within the medieval Romulus and Avianus traditions.

320. ————. *Untersuchungen über die von Pfeiffer im 7. Band von Haupts Zeitschrift herausgegebenen Fabeln*. Program, Meiningen, 1899. 24 pp.

Eichhorn continues his detailed study of the history of the fable with the Pfeiffer fables, beginning with

the compiler of the collection, characterized from
passages in the fables, as is the date, set at around
1220. This is followed by a lengthy discussion of the
language and metrics of the collection and a source
study for each fable.

321.   Eichner, Siglinde. *Die Prosafabel Lessings in seiner*
       Theorie und Dichtung: Ein Beitrag zur Ästhetik des
       18. Jahrhunderts. Bonn: Bouvier, 1974. 480 pp.

       Very comprehensive discussion of Lessing in relation-
       ship to the "aesthetics" of the fables in the eighteenth
       century. Wolff, Leibnitz, and Baumgartner's philosophical
       theses are investigated together with the theoretical
       fable writings of Herder and Grimm. The Lessing fable
       is compared to classical forms, especially Phaedrus,
       and then to Lessing's own theories of literature. The
       idea of the fable as a sociological category in literary
       studies runs through the study. Eichner also presents
       a survey of the highpoints of Lessing fable research
       with complete presentations of most of the major con-
       tributors to Lessing interpretations, making the work
       a major contribution to Lessing fable bibliography.

322.   Einhorn, Jürgen Weinhard. "Der Bilderschmuck der Hand-
       schriften und Drucke zu Ulrich von Pottenstein 'Buch
       der natürlichen Weisheit.'" *Verbum und Signum.* *I:*
       Beiträge zur mediävistischen Bedeutungsforschung.
       Ed. H. Fromm, et al. Munich: Beck, 1975, 389-424.

       The "Buch der natürlichen Weisheit" is known in two
       editions, of which the shorter is known to have been
       done by Ulrich von Pottenstein around the year 1415.
       Einhorn presents the manuscript tradition and details
       the illustrations.

323.   Ejges, Iosip. "K voprosu ob evoljucii basni kak zanra."
       Russkii iazyk v sovetskoi skole, 1 (1931), 19-29.

       Ejges presents the problems involved in the study of
       the evolution of the fable as a literary genre. The
       concept of the fable as a coherent genre, as a consistent
       line in literary history, is approached but without
       significant results. To consider the long history of
       the fable as an unchanging form is to run into a series
       of unsolvable problems.

324.   Ellenberger, Bengt. *The Latin Element in the Vocabulary*
       of the Earlier Makars Henryson and Dunbar. Lund Studies
       in English, no. 51. Lund: Printab, 1977. 163 pp.

Finds that the *Moral Fables* of Henryson contain a high percentage of Latinisms: in the prologue and in the "moralities" 2.6 times the average, which he attributes to Henryson's vocation and to the writing of "Allegory" in general. The fables proper on the other hand, are relatively low and even then, surprisingly, only "brutall beistis irrationall" occasionally use Latinisms heavily, not the narrator.

325. Ellinger, Georg. "Über Lichtwers Fabeln: mit einer vergleichenden Betrachtung der Fabeln Gleims und Pfeffels." *Zeitschrift für deutsche Philologie*, 17 (1885), 314-340.

Ellinger decries the lack of a comprehensive history of the fable in the eighteenth century and then attempts to trace the progress of the fable in Germany after Gellert towards what he sees as the special practiced "Fabelton." Most of the points made are stylistic in nature, with comparisons with these and other fabulists, especially Lessing and La Fontaine. Conclusions include the idea that Lichtwer's fables are on a different level from Gellert's; Gleim, who is independent from Gellert and the general nature of the eighteenth century German fable, constructed for a while a brief, epigrammatic style; Pfeffel helped cause the fable to break out of its constraints.

326. ————. *Über Gellerts Fabeln und Erzählungen.* Program, Berlin, 1895.

Sets up the development of a particular style to be seen in the fables and the stories of Gellert. The fables in particular are characterized by meter, the long relative clause that seems invariable at the beginning of the narrative, the common use of parenthetic ideas, the moral expressed with great latitude either as an epimythium or as a specific sort of moral poem serving as a promythium.

327. Elliot, Charles. "Sparth, Glebard and Bowranbane." *Notes and Queries*, 9 (1962), 86-87.

An attempt to identify three animals named from the "The Trial of the Fox."

328. Ellis, Robinson. *The Fables of Avianus.* Oxford: Clarendon Press, 1887. 151 pp.

Extensive discussion of biographical details of Avianus, of his syntax and prosody. Dates Avianus'

collection to "before 385" and describes his fables as
Latin versions of Babrius. The textual tradition is
carefully followed with complete apparatus. Ellis
suggests that Avianus must have been quite a young man
when he published his fables. The second section, on
the prosody of Avianus, is centered upon a discussion
of how far the metrical "mistakes" and inaccuracies are
to be attributed to the poet himself. He discards a
few verses as unlikely to be from Phaedrus. His treatment of the syntax is a well-researched discussion of
the peculiarities of Avianus' "rude Latin." Final section is on the manuscript tradition.

329. ———. *The Fables of Phaedrus. An Inaugural Lecture.*
      London: Frowde, 1894. 36 pp.

      Phaedrus was born in Macedonia as a slave and freed
      by Augustus. Books one and two were published in the
      reign of Tiberius, attacked by Sejanus to whom allusion
      is made in fable 1, 6; book three was written to allevi-
      ate his distress and generally contains only Aesopic
      fables, with only one story of his own; book four is
      given over to myths and other stories; five contains
      only ten fables—Ellis is, therefore, convinced that a
      number of fables have been lost in transmission between
      the fourth and the ninth or early tenth century (the
      date of the Pithoeanus ms.). Well-documented discussion
      of the manuscript tradition followed by an indictment
      of the fables in the "Appendix" as imitations. Phaedrus'
      style is characterized as succinct, simple, witty, and
      artistic. Contains appendices on Lessing and Christopher
      Wace's emendations of Phaedrus.

330. ———. "Crusius' *Babrius*." *Classical Review*, 12 (1898),
      119-121.

      A review of Crusius' *Babrii Fabulae Aesopeae* with
      numerous suggestions and emendations.

331. Emmrich, Karl. "Gottlieb Konrad Pfeffel als Fabel-
      dichter: Ein Beitrag zur Geschichte der Fabel im 18.
      Jahrhundert." *Weimarer Beiträge*, 3 (1957), 19-49.

      Emmerich compares Gottlieb Konrad Pfeffel (1726-1809)
      to earlier fabulists Gellert and Lessing and sees
      Pfeffel's orientation to the French as essentially
      correct as against the feudal social order.
      See: Rölleke, "Die deutsche Fabeldichtung."

332. ———. "Vorwort." *Der Wolf und das Pferd: Deutsche Tierfabeln des 18. Jahrhunderts*. Darmstadt: Wissenschaftliche Buchgesellschaft, 1960, pp. 5-24.

Both the introduction and the text selection of this roughly 200-item collection are heavily weighted toward the social-critical fable, prose and verse, of the eighteenth century. Many of the fabulists represented here are virtually unknown and are reprinted here for the first time: Bock, Burman, Kazner and Willamov, and many others. Emmerich represents the fable of the Enlightenment as essentially moral-didactic but with a definite radicalization after the middle of the century toward a specifically social critic form. Gellert and Lichtwer are of the moral-didactic type; Lessing and Herder represent the turning point, and Pfeffel, Kazner, Fischer and others represent the "radicalization." The essential points of difference can be seen in the use of the animals; earlier, they symbolized human characteristics such as Strength by the lion. Later the animals represented classes and offices such as despots and tyrants.

333. Eschbach, Maria. *Die Fabel in moderen Deutschunterricht*. Paderborn: Schöningh, 1972. 80 pp.

Eschbach begins this compact monograph with a concise analysis of the genre problem of the fable together with a short history of the form. Pedagogical functions comprise the bulk of the work, with a good review of the literature on this limited topic and a step-by-step evaluation of the uses of the fable in various grade levels. The fable is viewed as a tool and as a text in language teaching and the relationship to modern generations of school children to the fable and the text, which is followed by extensive notes and a good bibliography.

334. Esser, Albert. "Eine augenärztliche Fabel des Aesop." *Klinisches Monatsblatt für Augenheilkunde*, 77 (1926), 553-554.

Note on P57 "Old Woman and Thieving Physician" (TMI J1169.1) together with translation.

335. ———. "Die ärztlichen Fabeln des Aesop." *Münchener medizinische Wochenschrift*, 74 (1927), 73-76.

Notes on and translations of various fables concerning physicians, including P57 "Woman and Thieving Physician"

(TMI J1169.1), and P170 "Physician and Sick Man" in all
of which the physician is invariably pictured in a bad
light. Esser concludes from this that Aesop was against
physicians.

336. Evans, Bergen. "George Ade: Rustic Humorist." *The
      American Mercury*, 70 (1950), 321-329.

      A celebration of the Indiana humorist and his style
      with mention of his "Fables in Slang," describing their
      effectiveness and popularity.

337. Ewald, Dieter. *Die moderne französische Fabel: Struktur
      und Geschichte*. Dissertation, Munster, 1975. Also:
      Die moderne französische Fabel. Rheinfelder: Schäuble,
      1977.

      A well-written dissertation turned monograph promoting
      the interesting idea that the modern fable is a genre
      which is especially suitable for offering certain critical
      insights into sociological and philosophical questions
      as well as for dealing with a number of literary prob-
      lems. The structure of the fable is analyzed and com-
      pared with other short forms. This is followed by a
      historical overview and a discussion of the La Fontaine
      fable. A number of modern fabulists (Franc-Nohain,
      Richard and Leclerc) are compared to La Fontaine. The
      remainder of the study examines individual problems with
      individual fabulists (Duhamel, Bernier, Closuit, Apol-
      linaire, Anouilh and Ponge), and ends with the immediate
      consequence of this type of a study upon the idea of a
      fable genre.

338. ————. "Gattungstheorie im Fremdspracheunterricht der
      Sekundarstufe, II: Am Beispiel der französischen
      Fabel." *Neusprachliche Mittelungen aus Wissenschaft
      und Praxis*, 33 (1980), 204-211.

      Genre theory in secondary education, especially as re-
      gards foreign language training, is discussed with ex-
      amples of the usefulness of teaching fables in French
      classes.

339. Ewert, Maximillian Ferdinand. *Über die Fabel der Rabe
      und des Fuches*. Dissertation, Rostock, 1892, and
      Berlin: C. Vogt, 1894. 124 pp.

      Detailed examination of Phaedrus 1, 13; Babrius 77;
      P124 "Fox and the Crow" (A-T 57; TMI K334.1), followed
      through the corpus of European Literature, with the

text reproduced in each case. Mixed results, no conclusions drawn other than the obvious popularity of
the motif.

340. Fechter, Werner. "Die Zitate aus der antiken Dichtung
in der 'Ecbasis Captivi.'" *Der altsprachliche Unterricht*, 12: 4 (1969), 5-30.

Discusses the structure of the *Ecbasis captivi* in
terms of an "Aussenfabel" and an "Innenfabel," the
latter being P258 "Sick Lion, Wolf and Fox" (TMI K961)
which is geographically located in the poem near Bor-
deaux. The fable is also made more "realistic" in that
reference is made to the feudal system on the one hand
and to the Benedictine Order on the other. The last
three-fourths of the essay concerns the author and the
sources of his direct citations.

341. Festa, N. "Su la favola di Fedro." *Rendiconti della
Classe di Scienze morali, storiche e filologiche
dell'Accademia dei Lincei* (1924), 39-54.

Focuses upon the polemic that Phaedrus directs toward
his detractors especially that found in the prologue.

342. Field, Nora Rooche. "Arthur Golding's *A Morall Fabletalke: An Annotated Edition*." Dissertation, Columbia,
1979. 384 pp.

Golding's *Morall Fabletalke* is a translation of 125
Aesopic fables from Arnold Freitag's *Mythologia Ethica*,
here introduced by a description of the manuscript and
a review of Golding's life and works. This is followed
by an historical survey of the Aesopic fable, especially
the classical fable and the fable in the Renaissance.
The history of English fable collections, including a
section on translations, positions Golding in his
historical and literary context. The actual translation
is investigated with regard to purpose and to selection.
The methodology of the translation from the Latin is
for the most part confined to the notes. Contains a
bibliography.

343. Finch, Chauncey E. "The Alphabetical Notes in Rinuccio's
Translation of Aesop's *Fables*." *Medievalia et Humanistica*, 11 (1957), 90-93.

A short essay on the notes in *Vat. Ottobon. lat.* 2112
(f. 59r-76r) arguing that these alphabetical notes
designate the transition points for fables beginning

with each of the letters indicated. Argues against
Lockwood who dismisses these notes as the addition of
a scribe.

344.   ————. "Two Manuscripts of Rinuccio's *Vita Aesopi*."
        Classical Bulletin, 33 (1957), 10.

A note describing Vat. Lat. 5129, one of two manuscripts not described by either Lockwood or Perry, and
Vat. Russ. 1124, not listed by either. The first is
undated and has numerous omissions; the second is
dated 1487 and has the dedicatory letters and *Vita*,
but not the fables.

345.   ————. "The Greek Source of Lorenzo Valla's Transla-
        tion of Aesop's Fables." *Classical Philology*, 55
        (1960), 118-120.

After a review of Achelis' research, Finch refines
the choice of source manuscripts for Lorenzo Valla's
33-fable collection down to two (both collated by
Chambry): Ambrosians 91 of the fifteenth century, containing 33 fables; and Lat. Pal. Gr. 122 of the sixteenth
century which contains 32 fables of the Accursiana class.
These seem to have had a common ancestor (the "missing
fable" in the second lost in mutilation). Both have
the fables in the same order and are identical to Valla's
fables. Valla himself suggested that his manuscript had
only 33 fables. Neither could have been the direct
source; Finch suggests a common ancestor of the two
to be the putative source.

346.   ————. "The Morgan Manuscript of Phaedrus." *American
        Journel of Philology*, 92 (1971), 301-307.

Finch describes here his investigation of the ninth-
century *Codex Pithoeanus* (now Pierpont Morgan Library
ms. 906) and his comparison of that manuscript with
Ulysse Robert's 1893 edition of P. Finch confirms
almost all of Robert's work, describes the now different
numbering system, the script, and the single significant
error made by Robert.

347.   ————. "Notes on the Fragment of Phaedrus in Reg. Lat.
        1616." *Classical Philology*, 66 (1971), 190-191.

A brief re-evaluation of the D manuscript of Phaedrus,
the Vat. Reg. Lat. 1616, dating from the ninth or tenth
century. Builds upon the study by Carey, corrects two
errors made by Carey and by Brenot and gives further
information concerning the titles of the fables.

348. ————. "The Fables of Aesop in Urb. Gr. 135." *Transactions of the American Philological Association*, 103 (1972), 127-132.

Discussion of the fables found in the Vat. Urb. 135, the Mp manuscript of the Greek prose tradition. A comparison of the manuscripts used in Chambry's edition shows that this manuscript has been overlooked and is generally more reliable than others in the *codices mixti* class. Fables are keyed to the Chambry edition.

349. ————. "The Renaissance Adaptation of Aesop's Fables by Gregorius Corrarius." *Classical Bulletin*, 49 (1973), 44-48.

The two sets of fables translated in the school of Vittorino are those of Ognibene da Lonigo and of Gregorio Correr. Ognibene translated his collection first, and afterwards, Correr translated his fifty-nine fables. Discusses the adaptations of the Correr fables, in dealing with eleven fables from the collection.
See: Berrigan, "The Libellus Fabellarum of Gregorio Correr" and Berrigan, *Fabulae Aesopicae*.

350. ————. "Aesopica in Codex Pal. Lat. 1378." *Transactions of the American Philological Society*, 108 (1978), 55-67.

Codex Vat. Pal. Lat. 1378 contains letters from a certain Franco de Amelia in which are found eight fables. The letters seem to date from around the middle of the fifteenth century. Some of the fables seem to have been composed by the letter-writer, but also included are versions of P325 "Lark and the Farmer" (A-T 93; TMI J1031), P693 "Unlucky Wolf, Fox and Mule" (A-T 47 C and 47 E; TMI J1608, K551.18); and P721, "Father, Son and Donkey," from Poggio (A-T 1215; TMI J1041.2). Texts of the fables are appended.

351. Fischel, W.A. "Aesop's Paradox: The Classical Critique of Democratic Decision Processes." *Journal of Political Economics*, 80 (1972), 208-212.

Uses P721 "Father, Son and Donkey," from Poggio (*Facetiae*, no. 100; A-T 1215; TMI J1041.2), to demonstrate democratic decision processes. Most democratic decisions are inconsistent and order-bound. The moral for the extended economic fable reads: "When there are externalities to private consumption and even though there are no costs to market transactions and a simple majority

decision is acceptable, it is sometimes just as well
solely to look after one's own."

352. Fischer, Adolf. *Das Verhältnis der Fabeln des Phaedrus
     zur äsopischen Fabelsammlung.* Program, Klosteneuburg,
     1905. 34 pp.

     An evaluation of the fables included in the Phaedrus
     collection in comparison with the putative corpus of
     fables available in the Greek prose tradition as repre-
     sented in the collection (no longer extant) of Demetrius
     of Phalerum. Many of the earlier fables seem to have
     Greek analogues; those from books two and three seem to
     have progressively fewer Greek versions. Many of the
     fables in books four and five are Roman in origin and
     some appear to be roughly contemporary with Phaedrus.

353. Fischer, Albert. *Kritische Darstellung der Lessingchen
     Lehre von der Fabel.* Dissertation, Halle, 1891.
     Printed as *Lessings Fabelabhandlungen, Kritische Dar-
     stellung.* Berlin: Trautwetter, 1892.

     Stresses Lessing's clear separation of the fable from
     those forms, such as the epic and the drama, that are
     not didactic in nature. As long as the fable is con-
     sidered a poetic genre, Lessing could not give any
     credence to the independent value of poetic activity,
     and the *Abhandlungen zur Fabel* means for Fischer the
     decisive break, without which there would have been no
     Laocoon and no *Hamburgische Dramaturgie*. Lessing's
     fable activity also strongly influenced his work with
     the drama.

354. Fisichella, R. "Appunti per un saggio su Fedro." *Or-
     pheus*, 23 (1976), 3-31.

     This essay is concerned almost exclusively with per-
     sonal observations on the poet himself with such in-
     formation as can be gleaned from the fables. The ar-
     tistic elements of the collection of fables are touched
     on during the course of the reconstruction of the poet's
     political problems.

355. Flinn, John. *Le Roman de Renart dans la littérature
     française et dans les littératures étrangères au
     moyen âge.* Toronto: University of Toronto Press,
     1963. 732 pp.

     This comprehensive study of the Roman de Renart deals
     with the numerous problems of the animal epic, including

the very complicated issue of the relationship of the
Renart tradition to *Aesopica*. Chapter eleven discusses
the fables of Odo of Cheriton, John of Sheppy, Nicole
Bozon, Juan Ruiz and the *Libro de buen amor*, Jacques
de Vitry, and Etienne de Bourbon. Three fable collections, the Munich Romulus, the Bern Romulus, and the
confused tradition of the seventeen *fabulae extravagantes*, known essentially from their inclusion in the
Esopus of Heinrich Steinhöwel, are investigated. Flinn
concludes that the *extravagantes* appear to offer
variants to different episodes of the *Roman de Renart*
but suggests that the direction of borrowing might well
be *Renart* to fables.

356. Fochi, Adrian. "Motive esopice in folklorul românesc."
     Revista de Etnografie si Folclor, 26 (1981), 15–34.

     The renowned Rumanian folklorist investigates the
     problem of traces of Aesopica (nineteen complete fables
     and a number of Aesopic proverbs) found in traditional
     materials, much in the oral tradition. This latter
     fact suggests that Aesopica is more readily carried in
     orally transmitted form than had been previously thought.

357. Fohrer, G. "Fabel." *Die Religion in Geschichte und
     Gegenwart.* 3rd ed. Tübingen, 1958. Vol. 2, cols.
     853–854.

     Short and economical overview of the fable, excellently
     written, though beginning with the curious idea that
     there was a "Volksbuch" of Aesopic fables circulating
     in the sixth century B.C. Good review of the fables
     found in the Old and New Testaments and the earliest
     forms of the fable to be found in the Ancient Near East.

358. Ford, G.B. "An Interpretation of the Fable of the Hawk
     and Nightingale in Hesiod's *Works and Days*." *Orpheus*,
     12 (1965), 3–9.

     Discusses P4 "Hawk and Nightingale" (TMI J321.1); the
     first appearance of the fable in Greek.

359. Förster, Richard. "Lessing und Reiskes zu Aesop."
     Rheinisches Museum für Philologie, 50 (1895), 66–89.

     The first part is a description of an eighty-page
     manuscript from the University Library in Breslau
     (IV. Qu. 104b) which is clearly the "Augsburg manuscript"
     mentioned in Lessing's essay: "Romulus and Rimicius,"
     as having been sent to him by Madame Reiske. Contains

numerous notes in Lessing's hand on pagination, on
sources and various other comments. The second part
of this article is a description of a copy made by
Madame Reiske of a manuscript of the *Vita Aesopi*.

360. ———. "Lessings Anmerkungen zu den Fabeln des Aesops."
      Zeitschrift für vergleichende Literaturgeschichte,
      N.F. 8 (1895), 87-126.

      An edition with commentary of the notes Lessing made
      to the copy made by Madame Reiske of the Codex Augus-
      tanus described in his article "Lessing and Reiskes zu
      Aesop."

361. Foureman, Ariadna. "'Mérite' and Morality in Books IX
      and XII of La Fontaine's *Fables*." *Modern Language
      Quarterly*, 24 (1963), 197-296.

      La Fontaine is not describing his characters as worthy
      of esteem, in effect denying them "mérite" by exempting
      them from the accepted code of behavior. There is also
      no "morality" as a "set of rules."

362. Fowler, Harold North. "On Some Greek Inscribed Wax
      Tablets." Abstract in *Proceedings of the American
      Philological Association*, 24 (1893), xliv.

      Fowler describes seven wax tablets with Babrian fables
      bought in Palmyra in 1881, and suggests that the variant
      readings are due to the fact that the writer was unable
      to appreciate quantitative meter.
      See: Hesseling, "On Waxen Tablets."

363. Fox, Denton. "Henryson's Fables." *English Literary
      History*, 39 (1962), 337-356.

      Deals with two of Henryson's fables to demonstrate
      Henryson's poetic methodology and to show that the
      moralitas are integral parts of the fables. P503
      "Cockeral and Pearl," Henryson's "Cock and the Jasp"
      (TMI J1061.1) is used as an example of Henryson's
      operation on several levels. P39 "Wise Swallow,"
      Henryson's "Preaching of the Swallow" (A-T 233C; TMI
      J652.2) is analyzed to demonstrate that it forms an
      integrated allegory.

364. ———. "Henryson and Caxton." *Journal of English
      and Germanic Philology*, 67 (1968), 586-593.

      Argues that Henryson need not have known or used

Caxton's *Aesop*, based upon the French translation of
the German/Latin of Heinrich Steinhöwel, or Caxton's
Reynard.

365. ————. "A Scoto-Danish Stanza: Wyatt, Henryson and
the Two Mice." *Notes and Queries*, 18 [216] (1971),
203-207.

Discusses Wyatt's satire "My mothers maydes" together
with Henryson's fable of version of P352 "Country and
City Mouse" (TMI J211.1). The two are similar in making
the mice sisters. An early sixteenth-century manuscript
with a phonetic transcription in Danish orthography
contains the first stanza of a Scots song with this
fable. Fox suggests that Wyatt and Henryson might have
known that song and argues that it is unlikely that
Wyatt knew Henryson.

366. ————, ed. *The Poems of Robert Henryson*. Oxford:
Clarendon Press, 1981. cxxiii + 596 pp.

Contains the text of Henryson's fables together with
his other major works, the *Testament of Cressid* and
Orpheus and Eurydice and the short poems. The Introduction contains a concise survey of the literature on
sources, textual criticism and other problems, demonstrating a deep understanding of Henryson and the fable
in the Middle Ages. Henryson is shown as being dependent upon Gualterus Anglicus for at least seven of
his fables: "The Fox, Wolf and Husbandman," from the
Disciplina clericalis, contains at least two fables:
P669 "Fox and Shadow of the Moon" (A-T 34; TMI J1791.3)
and P593 "Fox and Wolf in the Well" (A-T 32; TMI K651).
P562A "The Cock and the Fox" (A-T 6; cf. 61A, TMI
K561.1 and K721) is derived with some assurance from
Chaucer's "Nun's Priest's Tale." Considers Caxton not
to have been an important source. Contains texts of
the fables, commentary with variant readings and parallels; the fables, wherever possible, are keyed to Perry
and the Aarne-Thompson types. Good bibliographical
references in the text, a list of works frequently
cited, and a glossary.

367. Fradejas, José. "Varias versiones más de la fábula de
la lechera." *Cuadernos para Investigación de la Lit.
Hispanica*, 1 (1978), 21-30.

Traces more versions of the fable of the "Milkmaid
with the Pot of Milk" who dreams of all the money to be

made from the milk will buy. The milk spills and the
dreams are dashed (La Fontaine VII, 10 "La Laitière et
le pot au lait," A-T 1430; TMI J2061.2). The fable is
traced from Indian origins through various sorts of
Spanish literature.

368. Fraenkel, Eduard. "Zur Form der *ainoi*." *Rheinisches
      Museum für Philologie*, 73.

      Notes to the *ainoi* in Sophocles, Aristophanes and
      others and its relationship to the gnomic sentence and
      the fable. Sees a strong connection between the *ainos*
      and the fable, more precisely to the epimythium and
      with the introduction of decisive action into the fable.
      See: Perry, "Fable."

369. François, Carlo. "Le Chat des *Fables* de La Fontaine."
      Romance Notes, 12 (1971), 370-376.

      The cat is the only animal that La Fontaine does not
      treat sympathetically. La Fontaine deals with cats in
      twelve fables and pictures them as evil, frequently
      comparing them to the devil.

370. Franke, Carl. "Die Abweichungen der Reinschrift von
      dem Concept in Luthers Fabeln." *Beiträge zur Geschichte
      der deutschen Sprache und Literatur*, 40 (1914), 395-
      411.

      A microscopic investigation of the fair copy version
      and the sketches for the first seven fables by Martin
      Luther. These are then compared to Luther's source
      (Heinrich Steinhöwel's *Esopus*), and Franke concludes
      that Luther was concerned more with overall content
      rather than any language consideration, with the intent
      to bring out the moral more clearly whenever possible.

371. ————. "Die Tempusformen in Luthers Fabeln und in
      deren lateinischer und deutscher Quelle." *Beiträge
      zur Geschichte der deutschen Sprache und Literatur*,
      41 (1915), 481-489.

      Franke presents a linguistic analysis of Luther's
      fables with a comparison to Steinhöwel's German and
      Latin original and compares Luther's translation tech-
      niques to those of Steinhöwel. The only significant
      difference is a preference for the historical present
      by Luther.

372. Franzow, G. "Zu den demotischen Fabel von Geier und der
     Katze." *Zeitschrift für ägyptische Sprache und
     Altertumskunde*, 66 (1931), 46–49.

     A note on the story of the Vulture and the Cat told
     by Thoth, reduced to a secular tale but with an emphasis
     upon the moral content. The story is related to the
     Etana myth and ultimately to P395 "Serpent and Eagle"
     (TMI B521.1, N332.3).

373. Frazer, James George. "Medieval Latin Fabulists." *The
     Academy*, 653 (1884), 300–301. Reprinted in *Creation
     and Evolution in Primitive Cosmogonies*, 1935, and New
     York: Books for Libraries Press, 1967, 35–43.

     A general review of the Phaedrus tradition and its
     prose or "Romulus" reflexes in the Middle Ages on the
     occasion of the publication of the first two volumes
     of Hervieux's *Les fabulistes latins*.

374. Frey, Winfried. "Tierdichtung im 16. Jahrhundert:
     Luthers *Fabeln aus Esopo* und Erasmus Alberus' *Buch
     von der Tugend und Weissheit*." *Einführung in die
     deutsche Literatur des 12. bis 16. Jahrhunderts*. With
     Walter Raitz, Dieter Seitz. Opladen: Westdeutscher
     Verlag, 1981, 165–189.

     Describes the situation of *Tierdichtung* in general and
     focuses first upon fable literature in the fifteenth
     and sixteenth centuries and then upon two fable collec-
     tions during the Reformation era: Luther's thirteen-
     fable collection and Erasmus Alberus' *Buch von der Tugend
     und Weissheit*. Luther's translation/collection is
     characterized as a series of examples for error, sin,
     and vice: a medieval viewpoint. Luther does not use
     the collection for theological controversy or for the
     promotion of his Protestant theology but for practical
     ethics. This contrasts strongly with the typical picture
     of Luther the fabulist. Luther's concise style replete
     with proverbs is contrasted with that of Erasmus Alberus,
     whose collection seems at first to parallel that of
     Luther but which demonstrates remarkable differences.
     Not only in the greatly expanded narrative style but
     also in the intent of the collection as a whole are
     those differences clear. Alberus' work becomes a weapon
     specifically against monks, the practice of indulgences,
     and the papacy. With a bibliography.

375. Friedland, Louis. "Spenser as a Fabulist." *Shakespeare*

Association Bulletin, 12 (1937), 85-108, 133-154, 197-207.

Extensive investigation of Spenser's fable activity, beginning with a history of the fable in England up to Spenser, and a comprehensive study of the fable and its use by "E.K." in *The Shepheardes Calendar*. Nine fables are identified in the Calendar, which Friedland considers proper as the genre of the Aesopic fable belonged by right to the pastoral. The third section considers the fables found in Spenser's minor poems, with the conclusion that Spenser had free recourse to the Aesopic collections, in English and Latin, but not for his epic poetry. The *Faerie Queene* seems to be completely without fabular motifs.

376.   ———.   "Spenser's Fable of 'The Oake and the Brere.'" *The Shakespeare Association Bulletin*, 16 (1941), 52-57.

An answer to Rosenzweig (q.v.) with regard to a postulated passage in Ascham's *Scholemaster* in reference to the fable in Spenser's February Eclogue. Friedland believes Rosenzweig's methods are outdated and argues against imitation in a situation when the rhetorical device used is so prevalent. Ends with a series of points with regard to the use of the fable in the schools during the Renaissance.

377.   Friederici, Hans.   "Die Tierfabel als operatives Genre." *Weimarer Beiträge*, 11 (1965), 930-951.

This essay surveys fable literature by presenting a few of its developmental stages in the light of the then-prevailing social relationships. The fable is an "operative" genre because it can cause a consciousness-changing effect upon the reader; it is contrasted to other "operative" genres by its use of animals to represent human traits.

378.   Friedman, John Block.   "Henryson, the Friar and the *Confessio Reynardi*." *Journal of English and Germanic Philology*, 66 (1967), 550-561.

P628 "Wolf Hearing Confession of Fox" (TMI U11.1.1) in Henryson's version was influenced by antimendicant tracts and is itself a "confessio Reynardi" as well as an argument against the mendicant orders. The fable, though a traditional medium for satire, had been rarely used for particular attacks. Friedman considers Henryson's *Moral Fables* the finest Aesop of the Middle Ages.

379. Friend, Albert C. "Master Odo of Cheriton." *Speculum*, 23 (1948), 641-658.

Survey of materials concerning the life and works of Odo of Cheriton (ca. 1180 to ca. 1246). His fables are described as models for preachers, many of which were translated from the vernacular into Latin. Detailed account of his life and career. The fables, the "Narrationes," are dated after 1224, partly because of references to Spain (and his well-documented just completed trip to Spain) and partly on stylistic considerations.

380. ————. "The Tale of the Captive Bird and the Traveler: Nequam, Berechiah, and Chaucer's *Squire's Tale*." *Medievalia et Humanistica*, N.S. 1 (1970), 57-65.

Chaucer's *Squire's Tale* ends with the falcon grieving for its mate. The story may have come from Alexander Nequam's *De Naturis rerum* or perhaps from Berechiah ha Nakdan's *Fox Fables*, no. 71. The ultimate source is probably a Middle East version known to Berechiah.

381. Fries, C. "De Androcles leone." *Wochenschrift für klassische Philologie*, 32 (1915), 1150.

On P563 "Lion and Shepherd," P563A "Androcles and the Lion" (A-T 156; TMI B381) from Aulus Gellius, *Noctes Atticae*, V, 14, known also in the prose paraphrases of Phaedrus.

382. Fritelli, Ugo. *Lorenzo Pignotti, Favolista: Contributo alla storia della favola in Italia*. Florence: Barbèra, 1901. 81 pp.

Lorenzo Pignotti (1739-1812) used various sources for his fable collection. From England he used John Gay's fables and the additions to that collection by Edward Moore; from Germany, Gellert and Lessing. Pignotti also knew many La Fontaine fables.

383. ————. *Favolisti Toscani: Con introduzione e note*. Florence: Vallecchi, 1930.

Editions of the fables of Tommaso Crudeli, Lorenzo Pignotti, and Luigi Flacchi (called "Clasio"); introduction contains an historical and literary overview and includes parallels and influences to the fables from earlier sources, especially Lessing and La Fontaine.

384. Früchtel, Ludwig. "Zur Aesopfabel des Kallimachos." *Gymnasium*, 57 (1950), 1, 123-124.

Notes to Hausrath's article on the same fable in the
same journal. Früchtel suggests that Zeus had two
reasons to take speech away from the swans: their re-
quest for immortality and the complaint of the foxes
concerning the injustice of Zeus.

385. Fuchs, Eduard. "Die Herkunft der Geschichten und
      Beispiele in Thomas Murner's *Geuchmat*." *Euphorion*,
      24 (1922), 741-758.

Medieval Aesopica is a relatively common source for
compilations such as this. In particular specific borrowings from Steinhöwel and Albertus are listed.

386. Fuchs, Max. *Die Fabel von der Krähe, der sich mit fremden
      Federn schmücht, betrachtet in ihren verschiedenen
      Gestaltungen in der abendländischen Literatur.* Disser-
      tation, Berlin, 1886. Published Berlin: Schade, 1886.
      46 pp.

Discusses a complex of fables, P101 "Jackdaw in Borrowed Plumage," P123 "Jackdaw and the Crows," P129 "Jackdaw and the Pigeons" (all A-T 244; TMI J951.2), and
P472 "Vainglorious Jackdaw and the Peacock" (A-T 244A;
TMI J512) in various manifestations throughout general
literature. Three Greek forms are treated as two distinct forms and the Latin version is only brought into
the discussion as a medieval form. The forms in European
literature are given in Latin, German, French, and
Italian examples through the medieval period, the sixteenth century up to Lessing, noting the change in birds
and in intent of the fable.

387. Fuhrmann, Manfred. "Über kleine Gattungen als Gegen-
      stand der Anfangslektüre." *Der altsprachliche
      Unterricht*, 18: 5 (1975), 25-43.

Excellent discussion of the short forms as genre begins
the wider discussion of their use. The traditional
dichotomy between the so-called didactic and entertaining
classes of short forms is called into question. Structure as a determinant is clear in certain forms, less
precise in others. After a discussion of the Aristotelian
theory of short forms, a section is given over to the
fable, in which it is analyzed by function, by structure,
and by the mutability of the motifs involved, with examples from Phaedrus, Lessing, and Thurber.

388. Fumagalli, Carlo. *Phaedri Augusti liberti fabulae*

Aesopiae con note Italiane. Verona: Tedeschi, 1891.
83 pp.

Edition with running commentary of the fables of
Phaedrus. Rehearses earlier research and brings nothing
new to the study of the fables.

389. Gabbard, Gregory Norman, "The Animal Human Double Context in the Beast Fables and Beast Tales of Chaucer
and Henryson." Dissertation, University of Texas at
Austin, 1968. 236 pp.

Provides a survey of both fable and beast epic and
isolates "double-contextual diction" instances arising
from the tension created between human characteristics
and a non-human context. This is most highly developed
in the beast epic (culminating in Reynard) and in the
fable, the more so in the former in that it is more
complex and deals with an entire range of animals;
the fable on the other hand working in context
with very few. Heavy use of the "double context" found
in "Vox and Wolf," Chaucer's "Nun's Priest's Tale," and
Henryson's *Moral Fables*. Chaucer and Henryson are shown
to be quite different in their use of this double-context.
Chaucer likes to transfer literary phrases from the
human continuum and anatomical details from the animal,
whereas Henryson is more likely to use a double-contextual
pun, with one meaning in the human world and yet another
in the animal context.

390. Gaide, Françoise. *Avianus: Fables.* Paris: Les Belles
Lettres, 1980. 149 pp.

Gaide's edition of the Avianus fables establishes his
text upon Ellis, Duff, Guaglianone and Herrman (although
he disavows Avianus' authorship of the *Querolus*). In
the extensive introduction, Gaide reviews the research
on Avianus and concludes: the name is Avianus, not
Avienus; the fables were composed at the beginning of
the fifth century and were dedicated to Macrobius Ambrosius Theodosius. All the fables generally ascribed
to Avianus seem to Gaide to be genuine as do the promythia
and epimythia, which have often been called into question. The source for the fables is given as the Latin
translation of Babrius by Titianus, and Gaide decides
that Avianus did not know Babrius in the original.
Avianus did however use Phaedrus. Listings of manuscripts are not entirely complete; good bibliography.

391. Gallet, Jill M. "La Fontaine's *Fables*: Their Moral
      Structure." Dissertation, City University of New York,
      1976. 171 pp.

      Gallet suggests that there is a structure in the
      Fables to be seen by analyzing the arrangement of moral
      themes. The fables are grouped and are considered to
      be parts of an overall aesthetic unity disguised by the
      poet's presentation.

392. Galli, Roberta. "The First Humanistic Translations of
      Aesop." Dissertation, University of Illinois at
      Urbana-Champaign, 1978. 318 pp.

      Critical editions of the fable translations of three
      of the six extant Renaissance Italian Humanists: Guarino
      of Verona, Hermolaus Barbaro, and Lorenzo Valla, all
      from the Greek. Begins with a history of the Aesopic
      fable from its origins to the end of the Renaissance.
      Full bibliographical notes and bibliographical apparatus
      as well as a source study, demonstrating that the three
      collections come from three different texts although
      all from the same class of manuscripts. Good bibliog-
      raphy on humanism and the Renaissance.

393. Gardner, Bellamy. "Old Illustrations of Aesop's Fables."
      Apollo, 33 (1941), 91-93.

      Five illustrations of Aesopic fables from five sources
      ranging from the Bayeux Tapestry to Francis Barlow's
      fable illustrations (1687), together with a very nearly
      incomprehensible text that has no relationship to the
      illustrations at all.

394. Gardner, John, and Lennis Dunlap. "The Fable." *The
      Forms of Fiction*. New York: Random House, 1962, 25-27.

      The fable is discussed (under "short forms") as one
      of the oldest forms of fiction known. The structure
      and content of the fable are described, with its didac-
      tic element stressed. The parable is characterized as
      being realistic in its attitudes and moralistic in pur-
      pose but not cynical or ironic, and its meaning need not
      be immediately apparent as it is in the fable. The
      modern fable often combines elements of both of these
      forms.

395. Gasparov, M.L. "Social'yne motivy antichnoi literatur-
      noi basni." *Vestnik drevnej istorii*, 82 (1962), 48-
      66.

A discussion of social themes as found in the fables
of Phaedrus, Babrius, and Avianus.

396. ———. "Stil Phedra i Babriya." *Jazuk i stil antichnytch*
pisatelei (Leningrad), 1966, 46-54.

Gasparov maintains that the traditional idea of a unified fabular style is no longer tenable: this is con-
sistently denied by statistical means. He demonstrates
the differing forms that separate the style of Phaedrus
from that of Babrius: Phaedrus' style is concise,
closed-in; Babrius's style is open and expansive;
Phaedrus is abstract, Babrius more concrete; Phaedrus
is subjective and Babrius is objective. Phaedrus' language is dry, and logically clear while Babrius is light
and natural. These specifics can be observed in other
aspects of the poets' works as well.

397. ———. "Dve traditsii v legende ob Ezope." *Vestnik*
drevnei istorii, 100 (1967), 158-166.

The Aesop Romance is known from two sources: the *Vita*
Aesopi (the oldest version dated from between the second
century B.C. and the second century A.D.) and a series
of *testimonia* (See: Perry, *Aesopica*) which are somewhat
earlier, dating from the fifth century B.C. The two
traditions are decidedly different, and the pictures of
Aesop that emerge are totally at variance with each
other. Analysis leads Gasparov to believe that there
were two traditions in the life of Aesop, the popular
tradition, which stresses the motifs of social protest,
as preserved in the *Vita Aesopi*, and a second, more
learned tradition which glosses over the elements of
social protest and revolution in the *testimonia*.

398. ———. "Sjuzet i idiologija v ezopouskich basnjach."
Vestnik drevnei istorii, 105 (1968), 116-126.

There were both conservative and revolutionary elements in the "demos" of the seventh and sixth centuries
B.C. The conservative elements show up in the Aesopic
fables themselves; the revolutionary elements are preserved in the *Life of Aesop*. The epimythia of the
fables show that the world is ruled by evil, and that
fortune is fickle, thus everyone ought to look out for
himself. Gasparov concludes that these ideas--practi-
cism, individualism, scepticism--have become part of the
typical ideology in European literature from the time
of Hesiod to our own.

399.   ————. *Antichnaja literaturnija basnja.* Moscow:
       Nauka, 1971.

       The fable in the classical world is surveyed with
       special attention paid to Babrius and Phaedrus. The
       differing styles of the Macedonian poet who wrote in
       Latin and the Roman who wrote in Greek are discussed
       in detail. The Latin is subjective and in blocks; the
       Greek is factual and natural. The idea of a unified
       literary genre in the classical world is dismissed.

400.   Gassner, Josef. *Der Einfluss des Burkhard Waldis auf
       die Fabeldichtung Gellerts.* Program, Klagenfurt,
       1909. 19 pp.

       Source study in both material and style, as Gassner
       traces the influence he senses of Burkhard Waldis' 400-
       fable collection on eighteenth-century fabulists, es-
       pecially Gellert. Waldis may have influenced Gellert
       to write fables, but Gassner's arguments for further
       influence are unconvincing.

401.   Gatti, P. "Le favole del monaco Ademaro e la tradizione
       manoscritta del corpus fedriano." *Sandalion*, 2 (1979),
       247-256.

       Of the sixty-seven fables that make up the edition
       of Ademar, nineteen appear to have come directly from
       Phaedrus--all from Book I. Nineteen others come from
       the prose paraphrases of the recensio Gallicana of
       Romulus. Some of the other twenty-seven might be, or
       contain material from, original fables of Phaedrus, but
       we have no direct tradition for them. Gatti suggests
       that Ademar had a manuscript with only the first book
       of fables at his disposal.

402.   Gebhard, Walter. "Zum Missverständnis zwischen der
       Fabel und ihrer Theorie." *Deutsche Vierteljahrschrift
       für Litteraturwissenschaft und Geistesgeschichte*, 48
       (1974), 122-153.

       This complicated and compelling essay attempts to
       come to grips with the disparity between the fable as
       a form and the theories, especially those of Leibfried
       and Dithmar (q.v.), constructed to elucidate the genre.
       The incongruity between the fable and the theory is
       seen as caused by the ambiguity of "Bildteil" and
       "Sachteil."

403.   Geiger, Eugen. *Hans Sachs als Dichter in seinen Fabeln*

und Schwänken. Program, Burgdorf (Switzerland): 1908. 53 pp.

Investigates Sachs' achievement in terms of a comparison of his compositions with his sources. This results in a stylistic analysis of Hans Sachs' point of view with regard to his material and a statement of his attitudes towards narrative.

404. Geissler, F. "Die islandischen Handschriften des Buches der Beispiele der alten Weisen." *Fabula*, 5 (1962), 15-17.

Suggests reasons for identifying the 1578 Anton von Pforr edition as the source of the Icelandic translation. Overview of the textual history of the Icelandic manuscript included.

405. Gehlhar, James Norman. "A Stylistic Analysis of the Development of Literary Persian and Turkish as Seen in Versions of *Kalila wa-Dimna*, the Fables of Bidpai." Dissertation, University of Edinburgh, 1977. 452 pp.

A comparison study of stylistic elements in four Persian and four Turkish prose versions of the *Kalila wa-Dimna*, the fables of Bidpay, in order to define the influence of Persian over the Turkish. An edition of a hitherto unknown Persian translation is appended; the oldest known version of *Kalila wa-Dimna* in any Islamic language, including Arabic.

406. Génot, C.H. "La cigale et la fourmi: Illustration des Fables de La Fontaine." *Gazette des Beaux-Artes*, Ser. 6, 95 (1980), 71-76.

Ever since the earliest editions, La Fontaine's fables have always been illustrated, often by the best artists. The illustrator is also a reader and interpreter. Génot treats La Fontaine's "La Cigale et la Fourmi," P373 "Cicade and the Ant" (A-T 280A; TMI J711.1), suggesting that La Fontaine drew no moral from the fable, but properly and interestingly demonstrating how the illustrators not only did concentrate on a moral, but how they differed among themselves.

407. Gerke, Robert Stephan. "Studies in the Tradition and Morality of Henryson's Fables." Dissertation, University of Notre Dame, 1968. 364 pp.

Gerke maintains that the moralizations are often not

irrelevant, as has been often stated with regard to
Henryson's fables. They are in fact thematically or-
ganic to the narrations. He describes the fables as
allegories, using materials from the scriptures and
various traditional and theological materials extensively. Demonstrates that the specific moralizations add
to the scope and breadth of the narration.

408. Germain, Gabriel. "La Fontaine et les fabulistes
      espagnols." *Revue de littérature comparée*, 12 (1932),
      312-329.

Discusses the process of "afrancesados" during the
eighteenth century with regard to the assimilation of
the French models for fables, in particular La Fontaine
and his influence upon the literary fable in Spanish
literature of the eighteenth century, on Iriarte and
Samaniego but also Don Bernardo Maria de Calzada, Don
Miguel Garcia Asensio, Josef Ibanez, and many others.
Various editions and translations of La Fontaine are
also discussed.

409. Getzlaff, Erich. *Questiones Babriana et Pseudo-Dosi-*
      theanae. Dissertation, Marburg, 1907.

This dissertation connects the *Hermeneumata* of (pseudo-)
Dositheus with Babrius. Although Babrius cannot be
dated with certainty, it is clear that the third century A.D. is the latest that he can be placed, and since
the *Hermeneumata* belongs to the beginning of the fourth
century, the great similarity between some of Dositheus'
Greek sources and Babrius seems to speak for a dependance
upon Babrius, but only for nos. 8, 10, 12, 16, 17,
whereas five others stand obviously closer to the fables
of the Romulus collection. Nos. 16 and 17 seem to
speak of a "Babrius latinus." Since Romulus is later
than the *Hermeneumata*, Dositheus' source for these fables
must be a "Romulus vetus."

410. Giradoux, Jean. *Les cinq tentations de La Fontaine*.
      Paris: Grasset, 1938. 293 pp.

Five lectures on the life of La Fontaine in terms of
"temptations," i.e., life-style, women, way of the world,
literary temptations, and the temptations of scepticism
and of religion. In all of this the art of the fables
highlighted particularly the role of the morals in the
fables.

411. Giurdanella-Fusci, Giuseppe. *Babrio: Le sue favole e il loro rapporto con le esopiane e con quelle di Fedro e di Aviano.* Modica: Carlo Papa, 1910. ii and 143 pp.

Investigates the sources of Babrius and his relationship to Aesopic tradition. Babrius' connection to Phaedrus and to Avianus is outlined. Now superseded by Perry and Küppers, q.v.

412. Glendinning, Nigel. "El asno cargado de reliquias en los desastres de la guerra." *Archivo Español de Arte*, 35 (1962), 221-230.

Glendinning sees reflections of P182 "Ass Carrying an Image of God" (TMI J953.4) in Goya's *Desastres de la Guerra* as, for example, in Samaniego's version in his fourth book, no. 8, which is quoted. Illustrated.

413. Godenne, René. "Une imitation oubliée des 'Animaux malades de la peste' par Eustache Le Nobel: Le 'Conte du passager, et du lion, du renard, et de l'ane.'" *Romance Notes*, 15 (1973), 118-122.

Eustache Le Noble (fl. ca. 1685) wrote fables, but both he and his works are forgotten. In his *Les Promenades de M. Le Noble* Godenne found a version of La Fontaine's "Les Animaux malades de la peste" (VII, 1), P628 and P628A "Lion hearing the Confessions of the Fox and the Ass" (U11.1.1). Textual analysis of the Le Noble version and comparison with La Fontaine, suggesting Le Noble chose the fable to comment upon the court.

414. Gohin, Ferdinand. *L'Art de La Fontaine dans ses fables.* Paris: Garnier, 1929. 299 pp.

A lengthy discussion of La Fontaine's style by one of his major editors, with particular emphasis upon the language. La Fontaine's change of perspective of the characters is made clear as individual fabular motifs are perceived in an historical viewpoint.

415. Goldschmidt, Adolph. *An Early Manuscript of Avianus and Related Manuscripts.* Princeton, New Jersey: Princeton University Press, 1947. (63 pp., xxxii plates. Studies on Manuscript Illumination, no. 1.)

A study of a Carolingian manuscript (Ms. lat. nouv. acq. 1132 in the BN) used as the basis for the study of various illumination techniques for fables from the

fifth through the fifteenth centuries. The manuscript
itself is described in detail: 40 folios, written in
Carolingian miniscule, with a seventeenth- or eighteenth-
century binding, unknown earlier history. Full illustrations in facsimile and Goldschmidt has added headings
to facilitate study with comparisons drawn from various
illuminated manuscripts and the Bayeux Tapestry.

416. Goldsmith, Sadie. "The Place of the Fable in Moral
      Education." Dissertation, New York University, 1936.
      183 pp.

      Begins as an attempt to determine the influence of
      the fable upon the moral judgment of the child by means
      of a questionnaire from which data were tabulated. An
      experiment with eleven fables showed, however, no ap-
      preciable influence on the improvement of the moral
      judgment of the child. No relationship was established
      between intelligence and better understanding of the
      fable and moral judgment. Contrary to original premises
      the whole body of fables does not have equal value for
      use in moral instruction. Bibliography.

417. Goldstein, Abraham. "Meaning and Structure in Robert
      Henryson's *Morall Fabillis*." Dissertation, University
      of Toronto, 1980.

      An understanding of Henryson's *Morall Fabilis* is based
      upon recognition that the fables are based upon the
      world, which Henryson sees as literature. In particular
      the fables and the Book of Creation are related, and
      this connection is reaffirmed throughout. This world
      makes an unequivocal distinction between right and wrong
      and is a manual of instruction for man, teaching by con-
      tent and by stylistic devices, as the structure of the
      work as a whole has a meaning to be found in the clear
      division between Aesopic fables and the "Reynardian"
      fables.

418. Gombel, Heinrich. *Die Fabel vom Magen und den Gliedern
      in der Weltliteratur.* Beiheft zur Zeitschrift für
      romanische Philologie, 80. Halle/Salle: Neimeyer,
      1934. 217 pp.

      This monograph is an extensive collection of variants
      of and allusions to P130 "Stomach and Feet" (A-T 293;
      TMI J461.1) throughout world literature, with special
      emphasis upon Romance materials. He begins with Egyptian
      forms and then discusses the origin of the fable (does

not decide between Asian and Greek originality) and the
relationship of the earlier forms to classical and
medieval versions. The fable in the "eastern Aesopic"
tradition is followed by the fable in modern times.
Does not use most of the research available to him.
No index.

419. Gomez, César. *Antología de Fábulas*. Barcelona: Editorial Labor, 1969. 918 pp.

An extensive anthology of the fable in Spanish with
an impressive introduction covering the entire range
of materials from the Middle Ages through modern times
from the entire Spanish-speaking world. Especially
valuable are the "notas biograficas" on each of the
hundreds of fabulists represented.

420. Gomez, Isabel Mateo. "Fábulas, refranes y emblemas en
las sillerías de coro goticas españolas." *Archivo Español de Arte*, 49 (1976), 145-160.

Gomez finds representations of four fables: P696
"Wolf and Ass" (TMI K1022.2), P164 "Mendicant Priests,"
P392 "Sick Donkey and Wolf Physician" (TMI J512.5),
and P15 "Fox and the Grapes" (A-T 59; TMI J871), on
Spanish Gothic-style carved choir-stalls in Toledo,
Zamora, and Rodrigo.

421. Gomperz, Theodor. "Zu Phaedrus Fab. (I, 1, 8)." *Jahrbuch für klassische Philologie*, 135 (1887), 557.

Textual note to Phaedrus I, 5, to emend a corrupt
reading.

422. Gopen, George David. "The Moral Fables of Aesop the
Phrygian by Robert Henryson: An Annotated Translation." Dissertation, Harvard University, 1975.

Translates Henryson's fable collection into modern
English with annotations essentially linguistic in subject. Introduction and limited bibliography.

423. Gordon, Edmund I. "'Aesopic' Animal Tales from Sumer."
[abstract]. *American Journal of Archaeology*, 61
(1957), 188.

Questions the invention by "Aesop" of the literary
genre of the fable as he demonstrates that at least two
of the "classical" fables have been traced to earlier
Mesopotamian sources. Gordon then describes his collec-

tion of proverbs and fables later published in the
Journal of Cuneiform Studies.

424. ———. "Sumerian Proverbs: 'Collection IV.'" *Journal
of the American Oriental Society,* 77 (1957), 67-79.

A number of fabular motifs are represented in this
collection printed with translations and annotations
to analogues from other Sumerian material as well as
much else. The collection apparently contains as many
as 62 proverbs or proverbial types which include for
Gordon the parable, the anecdote, the adage, and a
number of other short forms.

425. ———. "Sumerian Animal Proverbs and Fables." *Journal
of Cuneiform Studies,* 12 (1958), 1-21 and 43-75.

A collection of Sumerian "wisdom literature," in total
some 125 texts, of which nearly forty are fables or near-
fables. Many clearly demonstrate what has come to be
known as "classical" fable structure with a narrative
followed by a short epimythic structure. Some others
are in the form of extended dialogues. The interrelation-
ship of the proverb and the fable, as well as the extreme
age of both, are well illustrated.

426. ———. "A New Look at the Wisdom of Sumer and Akkad."
Bibliotheca Orientalis, 17:3-4 (1960), 122-152.

Reviews the collections and literature on Sumerian
and Akkadian "Wisdom Literature." The collections are
described in detail and sample translations are offered.
The collections include proverbs, riddles, parables,
folk tales of a more general nature, as well as fables.
Extensive bibliographical materials, and guide to the
Sumerian, Akkadian, and Akkadian-Hittite collections.

427. ———. "Animals as Represented in the Sumerian Proverbs
and Fables: A Preliminary Study." *Drevnii Mir* [Mos-
cow], 1962, 226-249.

Surveys the extensive Sumerian "Wisdom Literature,"
concentrating upon some 300 pieces that refer to animals,
especially to dogs. Many of the texts are fables, but
proverbs, adages, riddles, and gnomic sentences of all
sorts are represented. Discusses the close relationship of these forms with particular reference to the
similarity of the proverb and the fable. Translations
and very extensive annotations with bibliographical
references are provided.

428. Gorski, Konstantin. *Die Fabel vom Löwenantheil in ihrer geschichtlichen Entwicklung*. Dissertation, Berlin, 1888. 81 pp.

Gives an overview of the varied forms in which P149 and P339 both "Lion's Share" (A-T 51; TMI B240.4; J811.1; U30) appear first in the Greek and Latin versions and then in literature down to the nineteenth century. The two versions are carefully separated. The Latin fable is traced from Phaedrus through Romulus and then through modern times with versions by French, Italian, and German authors. Although the exact genealogy lineage is often obscure, the general scheme is clearly illustrated.

429. Gottheil, Richard J.H. "An Unknown Hebrew Version of the Sayings of Aesop." *Hebrew Union College Annual*, 5 (1928), 314-352.

An edition of the Hebrew translation of an Italian work containing 355 sayings and entitled *Aderet Eliyahu*, attributed to "Aesop of Phrygia." The texts of both the Italian and the Hebrew are given.

430. Gottschick, Reinhold. "Über die Benutzung Avians durch Boner." *Zeitschrift für deutsche Philologie*, 7 (1876), 237-243.

Discusses the twenty-two Avianus fables in Boner to demonstrate that, in opposition to Schönbach, Boner did not depend upon the prose paraphrases, the *Apologi Aviani*, rather used the fables in the received form.

431. ————. *Über die Zeitfolge in der Abfassung von Boners Fabeln und über die Anordnung derselben*. Dissertation. Published Halle: Pierer, 1879. 32 pp.

A discussion, based in part upon Gottschick's ideas concerning Boner's sources, bearing upon the order in which Boner composed his fables. The fact that the Romulus and Avianus fables precede the non-fabular *Schwänke* leads him to believe these were added later. The collection is dated as early fourteenth century, and the date of the earliest edition of the *Gesta Romanorum* is in some doubt as a result.

432. ————. "Quellen zu einigen Fabeln Boners." *Zeitschrift für deutsche Philologie*, 11 (1880), 324-336.

Gottschick investigates sources for four Boner fables: 48, 94, 95, and 98 in the Pfeiffer edition, with parallels

in Paulus Diaconus, Vincent of Beauvais and various Latin
poems. Reviews his and Schönbach's previous source
studies and adds a multitude of new potential sources
for Boner.

433. ————. *Über Boners Fabeln.* Program, Charlottenburg,
     1886. 32 pp.

     A survey of the research on Boner's fables to date,
     especially the source studies and the linguistic inves-
     tigations: dialect and metric studies. A large number
     of parallels and sources are indicated.

434. ————. "Über die Quellen zu Boners Edelstein." Pro-
     gram, Charlottenburg, 1895. Published Berlin: Trowit-
     zach, 13 pp.

     Lists sources, essentially Romulus and Avianus, for
     Boner's fables. Extensive analysis of minutiae attempting
     to pinpoint a multitude of sources for the collection.
     Refers to Lessing for the Avianus fables. Finds sources
     for four in the *Gesta Romanorum* which might lead to re-
     evaluation of the dating of that work.

435. ————. *Boner und seine lateinischen Vorlagen.* Program,
     Charlottenburg, 1901. 39 pp.

     Discusses Boner's relationship to the medieval Latin
     fable collections: the Romulus paraphrases of Phaedrus
     and the "Anonymous," as well as a number of possible
     sources from rhetorical uses of the fable.

436. Gottwald, Heinrich. *Lessings Fabel als Kunstwerk.*
     Dissertation, Bonn, 1949. iii + 87 pp.

     Begins with Lessing's statement that his own fables
     might not match his theoretical statements. Gottwald
     interprets this to be a declaration of the one-sidedness
     of his theoretical works and does not use those works
     in his own analysis, choosing instead to discuss
     Lessing's fables under compositional elements: action,
     pointe, etc., but without structural considerations.
     The second part on Lessing's language is essentially a
     collection of examples; discussing the brevity of the
     fables as an artifact of his theories rather than the
     result of stylistic principles.

437. Götze, Alfred. "Luthers Fabeldichtung." *The Germanic
     Review*, 5 (1930), 127-131.

Superficial discussion of Luther's fable activity;
mistakes Luther's "Deutscher Aesop" as the Sebastian
Brandt expanded version of the Steinhöwel translation
(much more likely to have been the German-Latin version
of Steinhöwel). Gives dates and little more.

438. Gough, M. "The Monastery of Eski Gümüs. Second Preliminary Report." *Archaeological Survey*, 15 (1965),
157-164.

Reports on the discovery of a rock-cut chamber above
the narthax in the monastery. Included within are a
number of paintings with a selection of Aesopic fables.

439. Gourmont, Remy de. "La vie des animaux et la morale
dans les Fables de La Fontaine." *Mercure de France*,
200 (Oct. 15, 1905), 510-523; 201 (Nov. 1, 1905),
24-39.

Well-written essay on La Fontaine's language and
"poetic license," in particular with regard to the por-
trayal of animal characters. Comparisons are drawn
from the natural order of things (and La Fontaine's
knowledge of the natural world) as distinct from the
fabular realm. Treats animals in previous literary
tradition and ends with conclusions on the essential
non-moral aspects of the natural world vs. the (human)
moral framework of the fable.

440. Graham, Albert Edwin. "John Gay's Fables, Edited with
an Introduction on the Fable as an Eighteenth Century
Literary Genre." Dissertation, Princeton University,
1960. 507 pp.

This dissertation is an edition of John Gay's *Fables*,
based upon all the editions published during his lifetime. The introduction traces the history and the
poetics of the fable in England up to Gay. The development of the fable is discussed as a progression from
essentially pedagogical uses through its rise as a
literary form, the latter idea aided by the eighteenth-
century concern for satirical forms. John Gay's particular circumstances and milieux are used to determine
influences which brought him to the writings of the
Fables.

441. Grawi, Erna. *Die Fabel vom Baum und dem Schilfrohr in
der Weltliteratur*. Dissertation, Rostock, 1918.
201 pp.

P70 "Oak and Reed" (A-T 298C; TMI J832) is the subject of Grawi's study which begins with a short investigation into the nature of the fable, and then a discussion of the Indian and Greek forms of the fable
(*Mababharata* and Babrius). The Near Eastern tradition
is presented and this is followed by Avianus and dozens
of versions from the medieval collections. Her conclusions include: there were two distinct versions of this
plant fable, with various plants substituting with each
tradition, some representing the weaker plant, others
the stronger. The morals were changed as well, and these
range from the purely practical to the ethical problems
of beauty and usefulness. Trees are grouped under
various categories according to their use in the fable.
Index but no bibliography or list of fables discussed.

442. Gray, Douglas. *Robert Henryson*. Leiden: J. Brill,
     1979. 283 pp.

     A general survey of the life and works of Robert
Henryson, with an extensive discussion of the *Morall
Fabilis* as well as his other major works and short
poems. The fables make up the bulk of the book, in a
highly successful attempt to demonstrate that Henryson's
collection is an important and a uniquely original one
in the history of the fable up to his time. Presents
the fable in its historical context and analyzes the
use of animals in fables from earliest times through
the Middle Ages. The Romulus and Avianus traditions
are followed through to Henryson and the use of fables
as rhetorical devices is outlined. Excellent bibliographical references.

443. Grebel, Alexander. *Darstellung und Kritik von Lessings
     Fabeltheorie*. Dissertation, Jena, 1876. 27 pp.

     Herder's influence upon Lessing, Grimm's criticism of
Lessing's theories, and the defense of Lessing by
Gervinus are the major focal points of the beginnings
of Grebel's *Darstellung*. His *Kritik* is more or less
limited to Lessing's "error" in assigning the right to
be classified as "Aesopic" and to the suggestion that
Lessing's definition of the fable must be wrong as it
implies moral regulation.

444. Grenier, A. "Phèdre." *Revue de Philologie*, 28 (1904),
     198-201.

     Two suggestions to the texts of Phaedrus IV, 19 "Canes

legatos miserunt ad Iovem," and IV, 26 "Poeta," P517 and
P522.

445. Grimm, Jürgen. "Le pouvoir des fables: Ein Beitrag zur
Ästhetik der La Fontainischen Fabel." *Zeitschrift
für Französische Sprache und Literatur*, 80 (1970),
28–43.

Grimm considers "Le pouvoir des fables," published as
the fourth fable in the eighth book in the 1678 edition,
one of the most important fables for the understanding
of La Fontaine. The fable can be dated relatively pre-
cisely. The fable is carefully analyzed, with the
fable divided into two equally long sections and a
final "Moralité." The keynotes are to be found in the
ambiguous title and in La Fontaine's views on the rhetorical function of the fable. Suggests that the fable
might also well be used as an instrument to influence
actual political events.

446. ———. "Interpretationsmodelle zu La Fontaines Fabel
'le chêne et le roseau.'" *Die Neueren Sprachen*, 23
(1974), 144-145.

This article contains a series of critical notes to
interpretations of La Fontaine I, 22 "Le chêne et le
roseau," P70 "Oak and the Reed" (A-T 298C; TMI J832)
by Karl Vossler, R. Bray, Th. Spoerri, and R. Jasinski.
Grimm uses these notes to introduce a specific view of
La Fontaine research which might provide an instruc-
tional unit for teaching on the higher levels of elementary school. The interpretations are investigated
chronologically so as to afford some insight into both
the historical and the ideological implications of the
various points of view.

447. ———. *La Fontaines Fabeln*. Erträge der Forschung,
no. 57. Darmstadt: Wissenschaftliche Buchgesellschaft,
1976. x + 119 pp.

This very valuable monograph outlines La Fontaine
research and gives the results of new studies on the
Fables. He begins with a reaction of La Fontaine's
contemporaries to his fables, and proceeds to modern
research, surveying the fields of the aesthetic-oriented
interpretations and the content-oriented theoretical
writings quite extensively, usually with a certain
amount of polemic, and all in all provides an excellent
introduction to the state of La Fontaine studies together

with pointing out work yet to be done. Excellent thematically arranged bibliography.

448. ――――. "La Fontaine--Être de papier? Von den Unzulänglichkeiten einer sich absolut setzenden strukturalistischen Narrativistik." *Zeitschrift für französische Sprache und Literatur*, 88 (1978), 97-121.

Deals with H. Lindner's writings, specifically Lindner's review essay of Grimm's *Erträge der Forschung* volume, and with a strictly structural study of La Fontaine as opposed to Grimm's own approach. Grimm presents arguments for a sociological-historical interpretation; Lindner proceeds from the point of view of structural studies and tools gained from New Criticism, with emphasis upon the text itself. Grimm argues, for example, for the understanding of the social-critical traditions of Aesop, and deals with Lindner's objections. The specific points that Lindner attacks are handled, and numerous points are added to solidify the arguments Grimm previously made. Ends with an attack on strictly text-oriented methodology and the question of jargon.
See: Lindner, "Vers le Vrai La Fontaine?" and "Historisch-strukturalische Literaturwissenschaft versus historisch-soziologische Essayistik."

449. Griset, Emanuele. *Per la cronologia ed il significato delle favole di Fedro*. Torino: Bona, 1925. 13 pp.

Deals with the problematic dating of Phaedrus. The especially difficult third book depends upon the prologue and epilogue. Griset concludes books one and two must have taken place before the death of Sejanus, Seneca's quotations do not help to date Phaedrus. Phaedrus must have been published by Sejanus who must have assumed incorrectly that a certain fable was aimed at him. Book three must be placed before 31. Best guess for Phaedrus' birthyear: 25 B.C.

450. Grubmüller, Klaus. "Deutsche Tierschwänke im xiii. Jahrhundert. Aussätze zur Typenbildung in der Tradition des 'Reinhard Fuchs.'" *Werk--Typ--Situation: Festschrift Hugo-Kuhn*. Ed. I. Glier et al. Stuttgart, 1969, pp. 99-117.

Grubmüller begins with the premise that the fable (and a number of other short forms) are without definition,

at least as to the extent of the limits the terms might
have. After a discussion of the applicability of this
and other terms to the world of medieval studies, Grubmüller suggests a way toward reconstruction of literary
units within the scope of medieval literature. This
leads to a discussion of the *Märe* and the fables within
the label of Reynard studies with an extensive investigation of the nature of the *Tierschwank* by type and
function but without a firm categorization of that form
of narration. Grubmüller does not give up the idea of
a "Tierschwank" entirely, however, as he suggests that
the motifs and construction components are there and
were used in various combinations.

451. ————. "Elemente einer literarischen Gebrauchssitua-
tion: Zur Rezeption der aesopischen Fabel im 15. Jahrhundert." *Würzbürger Prosastudien II*. Ed. by Peter
Kestig. Medium Aevum—Philologische Studien, No. 31.
Munich: Fink, 1975, pp. 139-159.

A fascinating attempt to describe the consequences of
insights gained by understanding literary texts (here
Munich cgm 3974, the St. Emmeran Boner) as actional,
the way the literary tradition is used. This involves
pre-knowledge of both "reality" and the particular
"situation."

452. ————. *Meister Esopus: Untersuchungen zu Geschichte
und Funktion der Fabel im Mittelalter*. Munich: Artemis,
1977. 473 pp.

A detailed and competent history of the fable and its
position in the Middle Ages. Grubmüller begins with an
analysis of the scope of the terms *fabel, bîspel, Mare
Schwank*, and a number of others which not only overlap
each other but which run across the boundaries of other
standards, such as didactic literature or allegorical
literature in general. A precise definition might be
obtainable and useful for one short era, but a precise
definition of the general term is likely to remain a
desideratum. Grubmüller begins with the reception of
the classical fable in medieval context and then proceeds to the vernacular German fable, suggesting that
the first of these, the classical fable, has a demon-
strable continuity but that no such linear relationship
can be drawn for the vernacular fable. All the medieval
fabulists are discussed in detail and the moral attitudes
of all are compared; Grubmüller concludes that the moral
framework of the medieval fable is in accord with the

morality of the society in which it is expressed. Excellent bibliography of primary sources as well as of
scholarship in the field.

453. ————. "Semantik der Fabel." *Third International*
      Beast Epic, Fable and Fabliau Colloquium, Münster,
      1979 Proceedings. Ed. Jan Goossens and Timothy Sod-
      mann. Vienna: Böhlau Verlag, 1981, 111-134.

      One of the most important aspects of the fable con-
      cerns the concept of lexical consistency. This prin-
      ciple is constantly under attack in the case of the
      fable, since the actors, who are characterized as non-
      human, carry out human actions. P155 "Wolf and Lamb"
      (A-T 111A; TMI U31) is used to demonstrate that, in
      spite of this ambiguity, there is virtually no meta-
      phorical connection. A lack of peripheral semantic
      markers insures this: the animal characters are given
      additional markers, but these are invariably external
      and are never truly internalized. Such processes assure
      that the character will not be accepted as an individual
      but will remain a simple carrier of action. From the
      Steinhöwel version of the Wolf and the Lamb with a
      certain limited amount of anthropomorphism to the modern
      Arntzen version whose lamb learns from having read about
      himself, Grubmüller investigates the fable as running up
      against rules which delineate the actions and character-
      istics of various animals on the one hand and those
      which describe humans on the other.

454. Grumel, U. "Une fable d'Esope dans Photius: Les *trios*
      grappes." Annuaire de l'Institut de Philologie et
      d'Histoire orientales et slaves, 11 (1951), 129-132.

      A paraphrase of P15 "Fox and Grapes" (A-T 59; TMI
      J954.2) in a letter of Photius which is not in Migne
      but which is highly likely to be authentic.

455. Guaglianone, Antonio. "Il codex Perottinus Nap. IV F54."
      Giornale Italiano di Filologia. Rivista trimestrale
      di cultura, 1 (1948), 125-128; 243-249.

      A description of Nap. IV F 54, an autograph of Perotti,
      who combined the fables of Phaedrus and Avianus.

456. ————. "Gli Epimythia di Aviano." *Atti dell'Accademia*
      Pontaniana, N.S. 5 (1956), 353-377.

      An edition of the epimythia of Avianus with extensive
      commentary and notes in an attempt to determine their
      authenticity.

457. ———. "Phaedriana." *Giornale Italiano di Filologia*, 9 (1956), 349-350.

Text critical notes to 10, 39; 3, 13; 17, 3 and to 22, 4, and 17, 15, in the appendix.

458. ———. "Quaedam de Cod. Nap. IV F54 seu de Perotinno qui fertur quaestiones." *Rivista di Filologia e di Istruzione Classica*, 34 (1956), 279-283.

In the appendix to the Phaedrine fables established by Perotti, a number of fables might be "restored" by the simple expedient of changing the order of words. Perotti was not always aware of the rhythm of the senarian verse.

459. ———. "Alcuni codici illustrati e parziali di Aviano." *Giornale Italiano di Filologia*, 10 (1957), 225-229.

A note on the relationships among the Bruxelles 11193, BM Add. 33781, and Parisinus Lat. 1594 manuscripts of Avianus.

460. ———. "Due note filologiche." *Atti dell'Accademia Pontaniana*, N.S. 7 (1957), 231-241.

Concerns the value of the collation particular to the *codex Neap.* IV. F. 58, by Jacob Phillippe D'Orville in 1727, for the text of Phaedrus.

461. ———. "La tradizione manoscritta di Aviano." *Rendiconti della Accademia di Archeologia, Lettere e Belle Arti di Napoli*, 32 (1957), 1-30.

This essay begins with a survey of the direct tradition and the quoted and paraphrased tradition of Avianus' fables and therewith establishes the existence of two separate recensions of the fables. These two traditions, however, show a tendency to recombine in the late Middle Ages. Guaglianone provides a list of the known manuscripts in two categories, according to the recension to which they belong.

462. ———. "De Phaedri Fabula iv, 24 quaestiuncula." *Rivista di Filologia e di Istruzione Classica*, 35 (1957), 253-255.

The third verse seems defective and the epimythium and promythium have been transferred.

463. ———. "Fedro e il suo senario." *Rivista di Studi Classici*, 16 (1968), 91-104.

Phaedrus' choice of meter is in part a reaction
against the poetics of the Augustan Age, partly because
this meter had been the vehicle for gnomic poetry, but
also because it is suited to more natural expression,
particularly with regard to his characters. Extensive
analysis of the effectiveness of Phaedrus' meter with
numerous examples.

464. ———. "Commento alla favola iv, 5 (poeta) e alle
      altre favole giudiziarie di Fedro." *Annali della
      Facoltà di Lettere e Filosofia, Università di Macerata*,
      3/4 (1970-1971), 437-452.

      An investigation of the judicial elements, particularly
      the indicated debates within the Phaedrine fables, with
      the view toward indicating their probable influence
      upon the genre of the controversy dialogue.

465. Gual Garcia, Carlos. "El prestigio del Zorro." *Emerita*,
      38 (1970), 417-431.

      Discusses the idea that in certain fables the common-
      place, pragmatic morals of the fable are opposed to the
      idealistic ethics of the aristocratic society and that
      these oppose the fable on both philosophical as well as
      the practical levels. Begins with an historical overview
      of the fable, particularly the fox fable, in ancient
      Greek literature, with emphasis upon P605 "Fox with
      Many Tricks and the Cat with only One" (A-T 105; TMI
      J1662) and a number of other fox fables. Thoroughgoing
      review of the literature in classical and literary
      studies to Reinhard Fuchs.

466. ———. "Sobre *pithekixo*, hacer el mono." *Emerita*, 40
      (1972), 453-460.

      The standard features attached to the monkey in Greek
      literature seem to be derived from the characterization
      the animal receives in the fable. The article brings
      numerous examples of varying metaphors and descriptive
      passages from the entire range of Greek literature and
      relates them to the fabular uses.

467. ———. "La fábula esópica: estructura e ideologia de
      un género popular." *Estudios ofrecidos a Emilio
      Alaros Llorach*. I. Oviedo: Publicaciones de la
      Universidad de Oviedo, 1976, 309-322.

      This article traces the history of the fable and its
      popularity from Archilochus together with the popularity

of the *Vita Aesopi*. Investigates the distance between the fable and the popular tale and analyzes the form and the classes of society to which it becomes attached.

468. ————. "Historia y ética de la fábula esópica." *Actas del v congreso español de estudios classicos*. Madrid: Publi. de la Soc. españ. de estudios classicos, 1978. 856 pp., pp. 177 208.

An extensive evaluation of the history of the Greek fable through various authors and from various standpoints. The fable maintains a certain specific distance when studied for ethical content in the context of the classical Greek literature in which it is generally found.

469. ————. "Acevca de las fábulas griegas como género literario." *Fábulas de Esopo, Vida de Esopo, Fábulas de Babrio*. Madrid: Editorial Gredor, 1978, pp. /-26.

This article serves as the introduction to a very complete collection of the corpus of Greek fables and attempts to establish the place of the form as a literary genre.

470. Guarino, A. "La società col leone." *Labeo: Rasseyna di Diritto romano*, 18 (1972), 72-77.

Guarino uses Phaedrus I, 5, his version of P339 "Lion and Ass, Partners in the Hunt" (A-T 51; TMI J811.1.1) to describe the limits of intelligence in Phaedrus and suggests that this is clearly what Martial is alluding to in using the term "improbus" in describing the fabulist.

471. Guiton, Margret. *La Fontaine: Poet and Counterpoet*. New Brunswick, New Jersey: Rutgers University Press, 1961. 196 pp.

This general introduction to the *Fables* of La Fontaine begins with an incisive and interesting investigation of P124 "Fox and Crow" (A-T 57; TMI K334.1). Chapter two is an interesting analysis of La Fontaine's language, especially his choice of meter. In the third chapter La Fontaine is characterized as assuming the roles of a willing but unenthusiastic poet and of a satirist of his society, the social comedy. The human comedy in his characters, especially his bumpkin and, above all others, the wolf, in which the premise of using the wolf as a symbol of cruelty is attacked ends the chapter.

The fourth chapter is a celebration of La Fontaine's
language. The French is translated and an index is provided.

472. Gumbrecht, Hans U. "Fabeln und literaturwissenschaft-
      liches Erkenntnisinteresse. Vorschläge zum Umgang
      mit dem *Esope* der Marie de France in hermeneutischer
      Absicht." *Marie de France: Äsop.* Ed. and translated
      by Hans Gumbrecht. Munich: Fink, 1973, pp. 17-52.

      This essay serves as an introduction to Gumbrecht's
      annotated translation of the *Fables* of Marie de France.
      In addition to an introduction to the fables and person
      of Marie, Gumbrecht evaluates various editions of the
      fables and provides an interesting listing for the
      fables according to the type of action or main theme:
      strong/weak, worthy/unworthy, and the like. The epi-
      mythic expressions of class criticism are reflective
      of Marie de France's intent in writing the fables.
      See: Henderson, "'Of Heigh or Lough Estat.'"

473. Gupta, R.D. "Indian Parallels of the Fox Story." *As-
      pects of the Medieval Animal Epic. Proceedings of
      the International Conference, Louvain, May 15-17, 1972.*
      Ed. E. Romauts. Louvain: Louvain University Press,
      1975, 241-249.

      Gupta demonstrates Indian parallels, mainly from the
      Jatakas and the *Panchatantra*, to the Fox stories. In-
      cludes a discussion of animal stories with various
      didactic elements and compares the European fox with
      the Indian jackal, showing a gradual development of the
      cunning of the latter. Parallels in structure are ɑʾso
      demonstrated.

474. Guter, Josef. "Fünfhundert Jahre Fabelillustrationen."
      Antiquariat, 22 (1972), 25-31, 41-47, 89-93.

      The three parts of this essay provide a cursory ovɛr-
      view of fable illustration since the invention of
      printing.
      See: John McKendry, *Five Centuries of Illustrated
      Fables.*

475. Guyaux, André, and Dominique Vertin. "La Fontaine dans
      ses fables." *Papers on Seventeenth Century Litera-
      ture*, 12 (1979-1980), 191-212.

      This article deals with the problem of author/narrator
      intrusions into the fables. These seem to have a par-

ticular relationship with the morals and are therefore
to be connected to the concept of the genre. Special
attention is paid to an analysis of "Les deux pigeons"
(IX, 2).
See: Gilles Emilio de la Fontaine, *La Fontaine dans
ses Fables*.

476. Haas, Gerhard. "Märchen, Sage, Schwank, Legende, Fabel
und Volksbuch als Kinder- und Jugendliteratur."
*Kinder- und Jugendliteratur: Zur Typologie und Funktion
einer literarischen Gattung*. Ed. Gerhard Haas. Stuttgart: Reclam, 1974, 144-177.

The fable and the other forms mentioned are among the
oldest literary cultural forms preserved for us. These
texts had been traditionally intended for adults, but a
shift in emphasis toward children is traced, particularly in the case of the *Märchen*. Each form is discussed.
The fable was aimed at adults because of its rational
nature but not exclusively so as can be seen in a long
school tradition. The history of the fable as literature for children is traced through the modern day.

477. Haas, Rudolph. "Einfache Formen der Interpretationen
bei der Interpretationen einfacher Formen: Rätsel,
Nursery Rhymes, Fabeln." *Theorie und Praxis der
Interpretation. Modellanalysen englischer und
amerikanischer Texte*. Berlin: Schmidt, 1971, pp.
84-117.

Building upon a discussion of Jolles' *Einfache Formen*,
Haas delineates a structural equivalence of the charm,
the riddle and the fable, and proceeds to the riddle,
the nursery rhyme, and the fable. The fable in English
is outlined in its many forms from Chaucer through
Thurber. The Aesopic fable type is presented, and Haas
ends with a well-argued interpretation of two of Thurber's fables: "The Unicorn in the Garden" and "The
Shrike and the Chipmunks."

478. Hadjioannou, K. "Some Linguistic Comments on the Text
of At's *Vita* of Aesop published by B.E. Perry."
Byzantinische Zeitschrift, 62 (1969), 1-4.

In answer to the final portion of Ben Edwin Perry's
"Some Addenda ...," Hadjioannou concludes that the
Vita Aesopi in the At codex is a typical medieval Greek
text and not Cypriotic nor did it pass through a
Cypriote intermediary. Adds a number of corrections
and emendations.

479. Haga, Akira. "Resshingu ni okeru Fabel no imi." *Sprache und Kultur* (Osaka), 3 (1967), 10-14.

Notes to Lessing's concept of the fable.

480. Haig, Stirling. "La Fontaine's 'Le loup et le chien' as a Pedagogical Instrument." *French Review*, 42 (1969), 701-705.

Haig presents a metrical analysis of La Fontaine's version of P346 "Wolf and the Well-Fed Dog" (A-T 201; TMI L451.3), demonstrating the meanings inherent in the verse forms, to justify teaching the alexandrine and the octosyllable to students of French.

481. Haillant, Marguerite. "Explication de Texte: le chat, la belette et le petit lapin." *L'Information Littéraire*, 25 (1973), 93-98.

Haillant analyzes "Le chat, la belette et le petit lapin" (La Fontaine, Book VII, 16) which comes ultimately from Bidpai. The fable is presented as a "véritable petit tragédie" by setting, by cast of characters, and by a three-act division of the action. The text is used to demonstrate Haillant's ideas of La Fontaine as a lawyer, as a psychologist, and as an artist.

482. Hale, Clarence Benjamin. *The Text Tradition of the Aesopic Fables Belonging to the So-Called Augustana Recensions.* Dissertation, University of Illinois at Urbana, 1941.

A survey of the manuscript tradition of Recension I, the "parent stock" upon which at least three later fable recensions were based, named from the codex Monacensis 564 (once at Augsburg) containing some 231 fables.
See: Perry, *Aesopica.*

483. Hale, David George. "Intestine Sedition: The Fable of the Belly." *Comparative Literature Studies*, 5 (1968), 377-388.

Treats P130 "Stomach and Feet" (A-T 293; TMI 4661.1) from antiquity through the nineteenth century, including the popularity of the fable in Shakespeare, Milton and through the Restoration. Discusses the political uses within the literary functions to which the fable has been put.

484. ————. "William Barret's *The Fables of Aesop*." *Papers of the Bibliographical Society of America*, 64 (1970), 283-294.

Begins with a short overview of the status of the fable in Britain in the sixteenth and seventeenth centuries to focus upon William Barret's 1639 *The Fables of Aesop*, the first illustrated translation in English verse. Describes the collection which was reprinted for over a century in spite of competition from Ogilby's and L'Estrange's Aesops. Barret's translation is not apparently based upon any single known version, but follows Martin van Dorp's monumental Latin compilation. The illustrations are in the same tradition as those in Giles Corrozet (1952) by Bernard Salomon.

485. ————. *The Body Politic: A Political Metaphor in Renaissance English Literature*. The Hague: Mouton, 1971.

This monograph, originally a dissertation at Duke University, covers the metaphor of the body as society, including especially P130 "Stomach and Feet" (A-T 293; TMI 4661.1), from classical times through the Renaissance with extensive examples drawn from all periods and areas. Special attention is paid to Thomas More, Shakespeare, and the Elizabethan dramatists (especially the telling of the fable in *Coriolanus*). The motif and related metaphors are traced through Bacon and Milton to its eventual decline in the seventeenth century. Bibliography and index.

486. ————. "Aesop in Renaissance England." *Library*, 27 (1972), 116-125.

Hale establishes the presence of Aesopic motifs everywhere in Renaissance English literature and provides a short historical overview of the position of fabular literature through the Middle Ages. The function of the fables in schools and as rhetorical devices is presented as an introduction to the discussion of the editions and translations. John Ogilby's collection is given special attention at the end.

487. ————. "Robert Burton's Aesop." *Notes and Queries*, 22 (1975), 542.

A note on Robert Burton's use of Aesop in *The Anatomy of Melancholy*, with listings of over twenty fables which he quotes (or misquotes).

488. ————. "Another Source for Spenser's Oak and Briar."
     Notes and Queries, 27 (1980), 301.

     Builds upon Friedland's study and adds Petrinus Crini-
     tus' version of the "Pine and the Gourd" in the De honesta
     disciplina (Florence, 1504), which was translated into
     English in 1585 by William Bullokar.

489. Hall, Hugh Gaston. "Contamination in a Fable by La Fon-
     taine (I, 3)." Papers on French Seventeenth-Century
     Literature, 11 (1979), 91-106.

     This article deals with La Fontaine's blending of
     sources, Horace and Terence (Phormio) for his "La Grenouille
     qui peut se faire aussi grosse que le boeuf," P376 "Toad
     puffing herself to equal an Ox" (A-T 277; TMI J955.1).

490. Haller, Adolf. "Pestalozzis Fabeln." Die Ernte:
     Schweizer Jahrbuch, 22 (1941), 152-166.

     A general introduction to Johann Heinrich Pestalozzi's
     fables, as found in his 1797 Figuren zu meinem ABC-Buch,
     with a chronology of composition tied to the author's
     "geistige Haltung" together with a cursory stylistic
     analysis and an evaluation of the fables by Pestalozzi's
     contemporaries. Contains numerous examples but not in-
     dexed or keyed to any standard collection.

491. Halliday, William Reginald. Indo-European Folk-Tales
     and Greek Legends. Cambridge: Cambridge University
     Press, 1933. 158 pp.

     A survey of Greek folktales and legends together with
     some myths and incidental references to a number of
     fables and to Aesop. The Aesop Romance is discussed in
     some detail and the use of a number of fables in Greek
     literature is analyzed. Halliday suggests that a number
     of fabular motifs are to be attributed to the Far East,
     in particular, India, and that these are of great an-
     tiquity. He insists upon the originality of many of
     the Greek motifs but recommends that a common source
     in the Middle East is the more probable for both the
     Indian and Greek stories.

492. Handwerk, Hugo. Studien über Gellerts Fabelstil. Dis-
     sertation, Marburg, 1891.

     Handwerk attempts to show significant stylistic connec-
     tions between Gellert's earlier fables, published for
     his own amusement, and those in his more serious "Fabeln

und Erzählungen."
   See: Schlingmann, *Gellert: Eine literarhistorische Revision.*

493. ————. *Gellerts älteste Fabeln.* 2 parts. Program, Marburg, 1904 and 1907.

   Discusses extensively the 1756 collection of fables and tales published by C.F. Gellert more or less against his will. The collection, entitled *Sammlung vermischte Schriften*, contained twenty-two fables and other pieces and was later incorporated into the second part of *Gellert's Fabeln und Erzählungen.*

494. Hanlet, Camille. *Initiation aux Fables de La Fontaine.* Brussels: Office de Publicité, 1943.

   A general introduction to the fables of La Fontaine, based upon an historical approach.

495. ————. "Phèdre, le fabuliste latin." *Les Etudes Classiques*, 12 (1944), 317-324.

   Begins with a general review of what is known of Phaedrus' life and suggests, on the strength of allusions Hanlet reads in various fables, further elements of Phaedrus' artistic career and events in his personal relationships. Many of these are strained; e.g., in Phaedrus III, 6 "Mucca et mula," his version of P498 "Fly and Mule" (TMI J953.19), Hanlet confidently identifies the mule with Phaedrus himself and the fly with Eutychus, his patron, to whom he had dedicated his Book III.

496. ————. *Le premier maître de français: Jean de La Fontaine: Etude littérale et littéraire de 30 fables comparées avec leurs sources.* 4th ed. Liège: Dessian, 1958.

   Nineteen fables of "Aesop," of Phaedrus, and of Avianus are the subject of comparative studies with the corresponding analogues in the collection of La Fontaine.

497. Haque, Abu Saeed Zaharal. "On the *Panchatantra*." *Mississippi Folklore Register*, 3: 3 (1969), 73-84.

   General introduction to the *Panchatantra*, with a cursory survey of the dating of the work, a description of the framing technique in the five books, and paraphrases of a few tales. Brings nothing new.

498. Harkort, Fritz. "Tiervolkerzählung." *Fabula*, 9 (1967),
      87-99. Also in *Volkserzählungsgattungen und -formen*,
      1. Teil (under the title "Tiergeschichten"). Also
      "Tiergeschichten in der Volksüberlieferung." Ed. Ute
      Schwab. *Das Tier in der Dichtung* (q.v.), pp. 12-54.

      Introduction to the complex of problems of "Tier-
      geschichten" as part of the even larger complex of
      "Volkerzählung." Various theories of the "Tiergeschichte,"
      as fable, as epic, and as folktale are investigated;
      anthropomorphism is the leading common characteristic
      of these forms. The didactic element of the fable is
      foreign to the "Tiervolkserzählung" and is the most im-
      portant single difference, although earlier fables did
      not have an explicit moral. Large number of fables dis-
      cussed, especially P15 "Fox and Grapes" (A-T 59; TMI
      J871) called curiously "Vom Fuchs und der Maus (!)" and
      P24 "Fox with the Swollen Belly" (A-T 41; TMI K1022.1).
      Harkort concludes: the animal tale grows from observa-
      tions in nature and is very old; the anthropomorphism
      occurred when man felt himself animistically connected
      to the natural world. The beginnings of fable-making
      used these materials, later metaphorically, and from
      that came the "Kunstfabel" or the literary genre of
      fables.

499. Harms, Wolfgang. "Daniel Wilhelm Trillers Aufassung
      von der Fabel im Titelblatt und in Rahmentext seiner
      'Neuen Aesopischen Fabeln' von 1740." *Text und Bild:
      Aspekte des Zusammenwirkens zweier Künste in Mittel-
      alter und früher Neuzeit*. Ed. Christel Meier und Uwe
      Ruberg. Wiesbaden: Reichert, 1980, 732-746.

      Sees something of a fable theory in the frame texts
      and in the title page of Daniel Wilhelm Triller's "Neue
      äsopischen Fabeln" published in Hamburg in 1740. This
      is expressed as an attitude defensive to his own concept
      of the fable against his critics, particularly Johann
      Breitinger. Triller's choice of topics and characters
      as well as fabular style is shown to have been conditioned
      by this posture.

500. Harris, Richard L. "The Lion-Knight Legend in Iceland
      and the Valþjófsstaðir Door." *Viator: Medieval and
      Renaissance Studies*, 1 (1970), 125-145.

      The Lion-Knight motif, known in many versions in the
      Middle Ages, is discussed relative to the carvings on
      the door from Valþjófsstaðir. The motif is described

in its later chivalric epic forms as an off-shoot of
its Aesopic form: P563 "Lion and Shepherd" (A-T 156;
TMI B381).

501. Harry, Phillip Warner. *A Comparative Study of the
      Aesopic Fables in Nicole Bozon*. Dissertation, Johns
      Hopkins University, 1905. Published by the University
      of Cincinnati, 1905.

      An examination of the use of the Aesopic fables by
      the exempla writer Nicole Bozon. The sources for his
      fables were the Romulus collection (Phaedrus was un-
      known to him) and Avianus.

502. Hartel, W.V. "Phaedrus I, 16 v. 1." *Wiener Studien*, 6
      (1884), 158.

      Suggests textual emendations to a line of Phaedrus.

503. ————. "Analecta Phaedriana." *Wiener Studien*, 7
      (1885), 140-158.

      Wide-ranging emendations and commentary on the con-
      jectures and textual emendations of others (specifically
      those of L. Müller) on the Phaedrine fables including
      Perotti's appendix.

504. Harth, Dietrich. "Christian Wolffs Begründung des
      Exempel- und Fabelgebrauchs im Rahmen der Praktischen
      Philosophie." *Deutsche Vierteljahrschrift*, 52 (1978),
      43-67.

      This illuminating essay describes Wolff's concept of
      the fable as essentially a rhetorical device. Both the
      fable and exemplum are to be used to describe what has
      already been deduced. Analyzes Wolff's somewhat dif-
      ficult terminology. A fable becomes "clear" when it
      is expressed as a unit in the Lessing sense of the
      word: i.e., when it makes a single moral concept clear.
      The moral content of the fable in Wolff's concept is its
      function and there are somewhat contrasting uses for
      the fable and the exemplum. A different and, in a cer-
      tain sense, a deeper effect is ascribed to the fable.
      Wolff's ideas are discussed with reference to his con-
      temporaries and the article ends with his importance to
      eighteenth-century fable theory.

505. Harth, Phillip. "The Satirical Purpose of *The Fable of
      Bees*." *18th Century Studies* (Davis, California), 2
      (1969), 321-340.

Describes the genesis and growth of Mandeville's
Fable of the Bees from early verse translations of some
of La Fontaine's fables to the satirical final form of
1724. The satire is not to be understood by premising
an artificial unity (as Mandeville's editor Kaye does).

506. Hartman, J.J. *De Phaedri fabulis commentatio.* Leip-
      zig: Harrassowitz, 1890. 124 pp.

This extensive commentary on Phaedrus and his fables
begins with a survey of previous commentary, negatively
critical of Bentley, highly praising L. Müller with a
view toward providing a historical evaluation of the
poet. Chapter one is on the birth and nationality of
the poet: he was not a Greek, and came early to Rome.
Chapter two deals with Phaedrus' limited views of the
fable and his mixing of anecdotes with the fables,
later on allegories as well. Chapter three consists of
an investigation of individual fables in an attempt to
demonstrate how poor Phaedrus' style is. The medieval
Romulus is described as better than Phaedrus in part;
Chapter four is essentially a critique of the Phaedrine
promythia and epimythia; Chapter five returns to a
criticism of Bentley, and Chapter six discusses the
difficulties of Phaedrus' style, all very subjective.
No indices.

507. ———. "Varia ad varios." *Mnemosyne*, 48 (1920), 108.

Notes on Phaedrus' eighth fable, P156 "Wolf and Crane"
(A-T 76; TMI W154.3), especially on his language and
style.

508. Hassauer-Roos, Friederike J. "Die Fabeln Florians,
      Nivernais' und Vitallis': Überlegungen zum Funktions-
      potential der Gattung in Frankreich zwischen 1789
      und 1799." *Third International Beast Epic, Fable and
      Fabliau Colloquium, Münster 1979: Proceedings.* Ed. Jan
      Goossens and Timothy Sodmann. Vienna: Böhlau, 1981,
      135-159.

This interesting essay attempts a socio-historical
and "functional-historical" interpretation of three
fable collections from the time of the French Revolution:
the *Fables* of Jean Pierre Claris de Florian (1792);
Fables of Louis Jules Mancini-Mazarini, Duke of Niver-
nais (1796); and the *Fables* of Antoine Vitallis (1794).
Only Florian stands out among these and among an army
of eighteenth century fabulists in France all standing

in the shadow of La Fontaine. The fables discussed
are perhaps not the subject of aesthetic-oriented
literary treatments, but they may be discussed as socio-
historical documents. When discussed in terms of the
continuity of the Enlightenment fable, Hassauer-Roos
suggests that the latter term needs refining. Of the
fables investigated within the context of the French
Revolution, Florian emerges as the most complex, Niver-
nais as emphasizing one aspect of Florian, Vitallis yet
another. Appends texts from all three fabulists.

509. Hasubek, Peter. "Einleitung," and "Grenzfall der Fabel:
     Fiktion und Wirklichkeit in den Fabeln des Erasmus
     Alberus." *Die Fabel: Theorie, Geschichte und Rezeption
     einer Gattung.* Ed. Peter Hasubek. Berlin: Schmidt,
     1982, 7-12; 43-58.

     The general introduction to this valuable collection
     of essays begins with a statement outlining some of
     the problems connected with modern research on the
     fable. The essay on Erasmus Alberus notes the general
     lack of attention paid to Alberus, even by Lessing,
     though his fables were frequently reprinted in the six-
     teenth century. Emphasis is upon Alberus' criticism of
     his times, his locale description, and the form and
     function of the epimythium. The fictive nature of the
     narrative is to be seen against the reality of the
     author's additions. The localization of the action of
     the fable is quite atypical but important in his context.
     His pedagogical intent is clear but different in form
     from the fables of his contemporaries and later fabulists.

510. Hausrath, August. "Untersuchungen zur Überlieferung
     der äsopischen Fabeln." 21st supplement volume for
     the *Jahrbücher für Philologie und Pädagogik*. Leipzig:
     Teubner, 1894.

     A complete investigation of the broad view of the
     corpus of *Aesopic* by one of the greatest fable scholars
     of all time. Hausrath deals with theoretical considera-
     tions based upon a projected edition of the complete
     corpus of Aesopic fables, which he feels would demon-
     strate the influence of the Roman fable. The Augustan
     recension would be shown to be independent of the Babrian
     tradition and would be nearer to the genuine "Aesopic"
     tradition. A systematic editing of the corpus would
     further allow a reevaluation of the fabular tradition
     of the Middle Ages. Hausrath demonstrates that the
     Accursiana recension of 1479 does not represent the re-
     daction of Planudes.

511. ———. "Das Problem der äsopischen Fabel." *Neue Jahr-bücher für das klassische Altertum*, 1 (1898), 305-322.

Does not enter the problem of the ultimate origin and home of the fables, but Aesop is assigned the date of 600 B.C. and is thus a contemporary of Sappho according to Herodotus.

512. ———. "Die Aesopstudien des Maximus Planudes." *Byzantische Zeitschrift*, 10 (1901), 91-105.

Hausrath calls attention to a glossed edition of the Accursiana fables in col. Borbonicus 118 in Naples, relating Planudes to that recension. Planudes is not the author of the recension nor of the life of Aesop associated with his name.

513. ———. "Kalámous eis mechos suvapsai, suntheinai." *Berliner Philologische Wochenschrift*, 48 (1907), 1532-1533.

Finds Aesopic allusions to reeds for blow-pipes for fowling in P115 "Fowler and the Asp" (TMI N335.1) in the Halm version (no. 171) and in P235 "Ant and Dove" (TMI B362). The connection is identification of the *kalamos* with the lime-twig.

514. ———. "Fabel." *Realencyclopädie der klassischen Altertumswissenschaft*. Vol. 12 (1909), cols. 1704-1736.

Begins with the word fable and its related genre-designates as used by various classical authors. The second section deals with Aesop and the tradition of the Aesop-romance, followed by the "Aesopic fable" and other fable categories. The fourth section deals with the originality of the Greek fable, in which Hausrath presents earlier arguments for the primacy of India or Egypt over Greece in the development of some of the fables but with the conclusion that both India and Greece have claims to certain motifs. Section five is concerned with the fable after Aesop; especially Demetrius of Phalerum and the putative collection behind the Augustana recension and following recensions.

515. ———. "Veselin Cajkanovic: Über den Titel einer aramäischen Bearbeitung der äsopischen Fabeln." *Berliner Philologische Wochenschrift*, 25 (1911), 768.

Deals with the Aramaic translation of Syntipas' fables,

occasionally considered the original of the Aesopic
fables. Cajkanovic demonstrates that Aesop is the
sophos mentioned, and Hausrath confirms this belief.

516. ————. "Achiqar und Aesop: das Verhältnis der orientalischen zur griechische Fabeldichtung." *Sitzungs-
berichte der Heidelberger Akademie. Philos.-histor.
Klasse*, Jahrgang 1918, Heft 2. Heidelberg: Winter,
1918. 42 pp.

A wide-ranging demonstration that despite all examples to the contrary and admitting a number of motifs
from other sources, the general originality of the
Greek fable is not to be doubted.

517. ————. "Kleinigkeiten zur jonischen Volkserzählung
I." *Cimbria: Beiträge zur Geschichte, Altertumskunde,
Kunst und Erziehungslehre*. Dortmund: Ruhfus, 1926,
49-52.

Hausrath reaffirms his thesis with regard to the
originality of the Greek fable stated in his essay
"Achiqar und Aesop," in response to objections raised.
Numerous fabular motifs are clearly original to the
Orient, but Hausrath stands by the primacy of Greece
for some narratives.

518. ————. "Zur Arbeitsweise des Phädrus." *Hermes*, 71
(1936), 70-103.

Consists of a large number of observations and interpretations on Phaedrus (including a very thorough
review of the literature on Phaedrus) in an attempt to
determine the actual quality of Phaedrus' accomplishments.
Hausrath claims that only an unprejudiced investigation
of the method of working of Phaedrus will serve not an
aesthetic evaluation. Hausrath divides his work into
three sections, Phaedrus' rhetoric, Phaedrus the student
of popular philosophy and the independent story-teller.
With a penetrating study of Phaedrus' fables as rhetorical works, Hausrath views attempts to find real political
events in the fables with scepticism. Phaedrus is only
marginally a satirical writer.

519. ————. "Germanische Märchenmotive in griechischen
Tierfabeln. Ein Beitrag des Reinhart Fuchs." *Neue
Jahrbücher der Wissenschaften*, 13 (1937), 139-150.

Discusses the tendencies of a number of researchers
to assume that the fables in a modern edition are all

of equal age. Many of the fables in the corpus of
Aesopica in earlier editions of the corpus in fact date
as late as the ninth century, and Hausrath presents a
number of fables which are, in fact, influenced by
Northern European sources; P258 "Sick Lion, Wolf and
Fox" (A-T 50; TMI K961), P252 "Dog, Rooster and Fox"
(TMI K579.8). These are both products of Byzantine
rhetorical schools and yet show some Germanic charac-
teristics. The Byzantine rhetors were aware of Germanic
"Tiermärchen" no later than the sixth century.

520. ———. "Phaedrus." *Realencyclopädie der klassischen
      Altertumswissenschaft*. Vol. 19, 2 (1938), cols. 1475-
      1505. Also printed separately, apparently 1937.

Begins with the poet and his dates: Hausrath places
Phaedrus as flourishing between 15 and 50 A.D. Dating
the poet from the ordering of the books, which have
come down to us in fragmentary form and in some disarray,
is not safe. Covers sources, language, metrics, text-
tradition, editions, and influence on other fabulists.
The second section deals with the Phaedrus paraphrases
through the Middle Ages; the third returns to the
classical fable through Avianus in the fourth century.
The fourth section discusses the fables in the Byzantine
Rhetorical schools of the ninth through the twelfth
centuries and ends with the classical fable as found
in the medieval tradition.

521. ———. *Corpus Fabularum Aesopicarum*. 2 vols. Leip-
      zig: Teubner, 1940 and 1956.

The combined volumes bring the total number of fables
up to 289 and print all three recensions: the Augustana,
the Vindobonensis, and the Accursiana, wherever possible. Hausrath maintains that Augustana was the product of the schools of rhetoric. The second volume
contains an index of the fables and of proper names and
a concordance. The fables are also keyed to Perry's
edition.

522. ———. "Zeuskai ta theria: Die unbekannte Äsopfabel
      im Iambenbuch des Kallimachos." *Gymnasium*, 56 (1949),
      48-58.

A new collation of the pap. Oxyrh. 1011 offers the
opportunity to reevaluate Callimachus's fragments which
form P431 "Man's Loquacity," probably from the earliest
layer of Aesopic materials and further evidence for the

special nature of what Hausrath calls the Aesopic "Märchenfabel." Hausrath presents the fragments and suggests characterization for the fox and his motivation as well as a possibility of the etiological ending explaining why animals spoke at the time of Kronos but no longer do so.
See: Perry, "Demetrius of Phalerum."

523. Havet, Louis. *Phaedri Augusti liberti fabulae Aesopiae.* Paris: Hachette, 1895. xvi, 296 pp.

This edition of Phaedrus, based upon the *codex Pithoeanus*, includes a list of critics who have emended the text and a lengthy essay on Phaedrus as well as tables of concordances of the fables throughout the manuscript tradition, keyed to Hervieux.

524. ————. "Phaedrus." *Revue de philologie*, 20 (1896), 66; 146-148; 178-184; 188-190; and 22 (1898), 58-61.

Additions and corrections to his edition of Phaedrus. Numerous conjectural emendations.

525. ————. "Phaeder Appendix Perrotti 8." *Revue de Philologie*, 22 (1898), 176-177.

The text P536 "On Apollo's Oracle" is compared to similar material in Varro, Pliny, and others.

526. ————. "Sur le nom d'un protecteur de Phèdre et sur le nom de Phèdre lui-même." *Revue de philologie*, 24 (1900), 143.

The patron and protector mentioned in the fables is Eutyches; the name of the poet ought to be Phaeder, not Phaedrus.

527. ————. "Ad Phaedrum." *Revue de philologie*, 28 (1904), 44-48.

Notes containing six emendations to his editions of Phaedrus.

528. ————. "Phèdre 3, 4, 6-7." *Revue de philologie*, 30 (1906), 172.

Textual emendations to his edition of Phaedrus.

529. ————. "La Fable du loup et du chien." *Revue des Études anciennes*, 23 (1921), 95-102.

Havet considers Phaedrus III, 7, Babrius 100: P346
"Wolf and the Well-Fed Dog" (TMI L452.3) to be a thinly
disguised allegory. The two characters are Arminius,
the Cherusci chieftain and victor over Varrus, and his
brother Flavius who received a stipend from the Romans.
The essence of the dialogue is to be found in Tacitus.

530. ———. "Phèdre IV, 19. 19." *Revue de Philologie, de
      littérature, et d'histoire anciennes*, 48 (1924), 43.

      Suggests emendations in the text of P517 "Dogs send
      an Embassy to Jupiter" (TMI A2232.8, Q433.2).

531. Headlam, W.G. "Phaedrus App. ix." *Classical Review*,
      13 (1899), 135.

      A note on the similarity of motif to an Arabic proverb,
      with further notes on Pliny and Clemens Alexander.

532. Hedges, Ned Samuel. "The Fables and the Fabulous: The
      Use of Traditional Forms in Children's Literature."
      Dissertation, University of Nebraska, 1969.

      The narrative patterns and structures of most lasting
      works of children's literature are derived from the
      "ancient and traditional" literary forms: fables, myths,
      epic, and romance. Writers of new literature for children
      do not create new genres but rework the old. Hedges
      studies the uses of fabular motifs and structure in
      Kipling's *Just So Stories* and in other classics of
      children's literature.

533. Heeroma, Klaas. "Reinaert en Esopet." *Tijdschrift
      voor Nederlandse Taal- en Letterkunde*, 88 (1972),
      236-251.

      Heeroma discusses the fox fables to be found in the
      Reynard tradition with regard to the problem of whether
      or not the fables are interpolations inserted into the
      fabrics of the epic. The fables discussed do not
      always seem to fit into the narrative situation. *Esopet*
      and *Reinaert* are to be studied together.

534. Heidenhain, Frederich Jacob. *Zu den Apologi Aviani*.
      Program, Strassburg, 1894. 15 pp.

      The *apologi Aviani* are prose reworkings of the fables
      of Avianus, found in two manuscripts of the Bibliothèque
      Nationale (Cod. Lat. 347 A and B) without nos. 19, 25,
      26 and 38. Often the paraphrases are somewhat better

motivated than the originals. Heidenhain feels he has found an older tradition than the verse fables in the received tradition. Avianus 9, P65 "Travelers and the Bear" (A-T 179; TMI J1488), for example, has a lion in the paraphrase, which is taken as evidence of an earlier tradition.
See: Küppers, *Die Fabeln Avians*.

535. ————. "Rettung des Avianus." *Jahrbücher für classische Philologie*, 41 (1895), 837-855.

Assumes that Avianus used a text as his source that was fundamentally the same as that we have today and deduces from that that a more "complete" text of Avianus lies at the basis of the text we have received. The author uses Greek loan words and seemed to know the "Romulus" tradition, having used the latter at the end of P230 "Turtle and the Eagle" (A-T 225A; TMI J512, J657.2).

536. Heijbrock, Jan Frederik. *De fabel. Ontwikkeling van een literatuursoort in Noord-nederland en in Vlandern*. Dissertation, Utrecht. Published Amsterdam: H.J. Paris, 1941. 242 pp.

This dissertation begins with a survey of the history of the fable theory in general and in the the Netherlands. The bulk of the work is a history of fable literature in the Netherlands from the Middle Ages through the twentieth century, with sections on the fable as a political weapon, the fable as children's literature, and the new directions taken by the fable in modern times.

537. Heim, M. "Lomonosov's La Fontaine." *Slavic and East European Journal*, 20 (1976), 224-230.

Lomonosov used La Fontaine as a model in his *Brief Guide to Eloquence* (1747), the only neoclassical author included in an otherwise Graeco-Roman assembly. With translations of three La Fontaine fables (the basis for the article): "Le Loup devenu Berger," "La Femme noyée," and "Le Meunier, son Fils, et l'Ane."

538. Heineman, Max. "Merkwurdige Übereinstimmung zweier Fabeln." *Blätter für die Freunde der Antike*, 8 (1932), 67-68.

A Latin fable and an African one are surprisingly similar in content, as both are concerned with P60 "Old

Man and Death" (TMI C11), which Heineman was unable to
find among the classical fables.

539. Helber, Fritz. *Der Stil Gellerts in den Fabeln und
      Gedichten*. Dissertation, Tübingen, 1937. 127 pp.

      Discusses Gellert's style in light of his theoretical
      writings and comes to the conclusion that Gellert was
      considerably more advanced in theory than in his prac-
      tical applications. Helber demonstrates that Gellert
      stands on the borderline of Rationalism and Irrational-
      ism, showing characteristics of style and attitude that
      were prevalent both before and after Gellert's own work.

540. Held, Wolfgang. "Die Wünsche des Esels: 'Wahrheit' und
      'Moral' in G.C. Pfeffels Fabeln." *Acta Neophilologica*,
      7 (1974), 25-39.

      On the contrast between varying forms of truth (and
      reality) and the expressed morals in the fables of Gott-
      lieb Conrad Pfeffel.

541. Heller, Bernard. "Mikszath, Babrios: a mese es a
      legenda." *Ethnographia*, 29 (1930), 153-157.

      An examination of Babrian influence in the works of
      the Hungarian writer Mikszath.

542. Henderson, Arnold Clayton. "Moralized Beasts: The De-
      velopment of Medieval Fable and Beastiary, Particu-
      larly from the Twelfth through the Fifteenth Centuries
      in England and France." Dissertation, University of
      California, Berkeley, 1973.

      The morals and their use are seen as changing after
      the twelfth century. The morals after Marie de France
      become tools for social criticism. Extensive investiga-
      tion of various fable collections, especially Marie de
      France, Odo of Cheriton, and the Romulus traditions.
      Excellent bibliography.

543. ————. "'Of Heigh or Lough Estat': Medieval Fabulists
      as Social Critics." *Viator: Medieval and Renaissance
      Studies*, 9 (1978), 265-290.

      Well-presented, illuminating essay describing Marie
      de France, Odo of Cheriton and Berechiah ha-Nakdan as
      beginning something new in their fable collections:
      introducing social terms to replace the traditional
      moral terms. Also deals with the *Romulus* of Trier,
      Robert's *Romulus* in the context of Marie de France, and

and Nicole Bozon and John of Sheppey whose fables derive
from Odo. Describes the *Fabulae rhythmicae* as close to
the *Romulus Nilantus*.

544. ————. "Animal Fables as Vehicles of Social Protest
and Satire: Twelfth Century to Henryson." *Proceedings
of the Third International Beast Epic, Fable and Fabliau Colloquium.* Ed. Jan Goossens and Timothy Sodmann. Köln: Böhlau, 1981. 538 pp. (= Niederdeutsche
Studien, no. 30), pp. 160-173.

Deals with morals as social criticism in the fables
of Marie de France, Berechiah ha-Nakdan, Odo of Cheriton,
and Robert Henryson seen as relatively a new purpose.
Previously the moral was of a more general nature.

545. ————. "Medieval Beasts and Modern Cages: The Making
of Meaning in Fables and Bestiaries." *PMLA*, 97 (1982),
40-49.

Suggests that fables might be considered templates
for "unobstructed views of authentically medieval
moralizing." Emphasis upon Marie de France, Odo of
Cheriton, Berechiah ha-Nakdan, and especially Robert
Henryson as "social" fabulists and upon their new types
of moralization. Investigates stylistic shifts which
are illustrative of medieval meanings. Henderson concludes that fables are not as predictable as might have
been thought, given their recycled plots.

546. Henderson, J. "A Folklore Theme in Phaedrus, App.
Perotti 16 Perry, 14 postgate." *Proceedings of the
Cambridge Philological Society*, 23 (1977), 17-31.

The idea that the transmission of the Appendix Perot-
tina to Western Europe is traceable by noting its
presence in a series of subliterary versions is methodo-
logically unsound. This can be demonstrated to be at
least unlikely by means of a very close examination of
the nature and history of the Phaedrus corpus, with
particular reference to P544 "Two Suitors" (TMI K2213.1).

547. Heraeus, W. "Aus einer lateinischen Babriosübersetzung."
Archiv für Lateinische Lexikographie und Grammatik, 13
(1910), 129-130.

Notes on the Amherst Pap. II, 1901, no. 26.

548. Herbrand, Elizabeth. *Die Entwicklung der Fabel im 18.
Jahrhundert. Versuch einer historisch-materialisticher*

*Analyse der Gattung im bergerlichen Emanzipations-
prozess.* Studienreihe Humanismus. Wiesbaden: Athenaion,
1975.

This monograph begins with an introductory note by
way of literary justification of literary historical research on the fable in the eighteenth century, in which
Herbrand curiously suggests that the history of the
fable is closely connected with the struggle for emanci-
pation from feudalism. The main body of the work is
concerned with a discussion of the fable in the eighteenth
century, seen essentially as a reflection of the socio-
economical and political process of the day. The best
fabulists are discussed: Triller, Stoppe, Gellert, with
special attention given to the theoretical writings of
Lessing and the political fables of Pfeffel.

549. Herescu, N.T. "Glanures d'Histoire Littéraire I: Mar-
      tial III, 20, 5." *Rivista Classica Orpheus Favonius*,
      6-7 (1934-1935), 23-26.

      Remains unconvinced that Martial is speaking of
      Phaedrus in the line: "An aemulatur improbi iocos
      Phaedri." Argues against Friedländer, Plessis, and
      others.

550. Herlet, Bruno. "Studien über die sogenannte Ysopets
      (Lyoner Yzopet, Yzopet I und II)." *Romanische
      Forschungen*, 4 (1891), 219-309.

      The so-called Yzopets have had very different tradi-
      tions and histories. Herlet deals with the three Yzo-
      pets, the *Lyon Ysopet* I and II by describing each
      tradition and collating the works. Of the old French
      translations of the *Anonymous Neveleti*: the older is
      the *Lyon Yzopet*, the other is found in the I and II
      traditions. Textual criticism and history as well as
      individual fables are discussed.

551. ————. *Beiträge zur Geschichte der äsopischen Fabel
      im Mittelalter.* Program, Bamberg, 1892. 113 pp.

      Concerned first of all with the fables of Odo of
      Cheriton, especially with the original form of the col-
      lection. Herlet demonstrates Odo's familiarity with
      the Romulus collection in one or more versions but
      indicates some sort of knowledge of the Greek fable
      and does not know Avianus. Odo's work is well-known,
      with translations into Spanish and French used by
      Boner, Nicole Bozon, and John of Sheppey. Latter part

devoted to the *Romulus Monacensis*, which is compared
to the Breslau Cod. chart. 1376, to the Bern Ms. 674
and to Steinhöwel's *Esopus*, with the Breslau considered closest to the Rom. Monacensis; the relationship to Steinhöwel is second or third hand.

552. Hermes, Eberhard. *Petrus Alfonsi: Die Kunst, vernüftig
zu leben*. Zürich: Artemis, 1970. Now also: *The
Disciplina Clericalis of Petrus Alfonsi*. Trans.
P.R. Quarrie. Berkeley, Los Angeles: University of
California Press, 1977.

An edition and translation of the tales and fables
found in the *Disciplina Clericalis* of Petrus Alfonsi
with an extensive introduction discussing Alfonsi and
his position in literature as well as the relationships
to be found among the proverb, the exempla, and the
fable. Some modern analogues to the tales, a discussion
of the structure of the work as well as a bibliography
are included.

553. Hermes, Liesel. "Thurbers Fabeln im Englischunterricht."
Die neueren Sprachen, 24 (1975), 61-69.

The fable in its modern transformations and function
is the opening of this interesting article. The fable
has been a traditional source of material for language
instruction. Hermes demonstrates the use of the Thurber
fable in English instruction, showing that the goal of
such instruction lies in the promotion of a reflective
and critical attitude in the pupil.

554. Herrmann, Léon. "La Matrone d'Ephèse dans Petrone et
dans Phèdre." *Bulletin de l'Association Guillaume
Budé* (1927), 20-57.

Attempts to prove that Phaedrus, App. per. 15 "Vida
et miles," P543 "Widow and the Soldier" (A-T 1510;
TMI K2213.1) and Petronius did not work from a common
source but that Petronius would have been far more
likely to have been Phaedrus' source although Phaedrus
is apparently writing from an actual experience not
from a literary text. Most research is convinced that
Phaedrus' version is much the older. Thus the fourth
book of fables could not have appeared before 64 A.D.,
and similar arguments result in a date of 63 A.D. for
the third book.

555. ————. "Note sur le prologue du 1er livre des Fables

de Phèdre." *Revue Belge de philologie et d'histoire*,
6 (1927), 749-753.

Suggests the "speaking trees" which are mentioned in
Phaedrus' prologue but which do not appear in the
Phaedrine fables are an interpolation.

556. ————. "Princeps Tibicen (v, 7)." *Revue Belge de
Philologie et d'Histoire*, 12 (1933), 873-874.

Critical notes to Phaedrus V, 7, P529 "Prince and the
Fluteplayer" (TMI J953.3) suggesting "Notior paulo fuit"
to "notior poplo fuit," and other changes.

557. ————. "Apologues et anecdotes dans la tapisserie de
Bayeux." *Romania*, 65 (1939), 376-82.

Believes that the number of apologues represented on
the Bayeux tapestry ought to be twenty-nine, which he
lists.

558. ————. "Notes sur deux manuscrits anversois des
fables d'Avianus." *Latomus*, 8 (1939), 119-125.

Collation of MSS 340 and 140 of the Musée Plantin-
Movetus.

559. ————. "Esquisse d'une histoire des fables à Rome."
*Bulletin du Cercle de Philologie classique et orien-
tale. Phoibos*, 2 (1947-1948), 63-75.

The plan for the history of the fable at Rome seems
to incorporate not only the fabulists themselves but
also all those who used fables or fabular motifs in
their works from Hellenistic times to the invasion of
the barbarians.

560. ————. "Autour des fables de Phèdre." *Latomus*, 18
(1948), 197-207.

Connection among fabular material from Seneca, Horace,
Juvenal, and Gregory of Tours; however, these are not
directly connected to Phaedrus but more likely to
Conius Rufus. Influence of Phaedrus in other quarters
is shown.

561. ————. "L'Auteur du Querolus." *Revue Belge de philologie et d'histoire*, 26 (1948), 538-540.

The comedy of Querolus is supposed to be the last
work by the fabulist Avianus.

562. ————. "Une Caricature de Phèdre." *Mélanges d'Archéo-logie et de histoire offerts à Chr. Picard.* Paris: Revue Archéologique 29-32. Paris: Presses Univ., 1949, 435-437.

Herrmann feels he sees a representation of Phaedrus on a cup in the Gregorian Museum.

563. ————. "Recheiches sur Babrius." *L'Antiquité Classique*, 18 (1949), 353-367.

Highly speculative notes on Babrius, including an analysis of the Babrian prologue in which Herrmann reads an affirmation of a rivalry between Babrius and Phaedrus. Babrius is also the putative author of the *Batrachimyomachia* and of the *Roman d'Alexander*. Herrmann also sees points of contact between the works of Lucian and the Babrian fables.
See: Vaio, "A new Manuscript."

564. ————. "Quelques fables de Demetrios de Phalere." *L'Antiquité Classique*, 19 (1950), 5-11.

Discusses eight fables including P463 "Dancing Apes" (TMI J1908) found in Lucian (Piscat. 36), which Herrmann believes to have been invented or told by Demetrius of Phalerum in his putative collection of Acsopic fables. Part of the evidence seems to be the localization of fables in Ptolemaic Philadelphia where Demetrius lived as an exile in 280 B.C.
See: Perry, "Demerius of Phalerum."

565. ————. *Phèdre et ses fables.* Leiden: Brill, 1950. 371 pp.

An edition of Phaedrus' fables together with the "culex" and introduced by a highly speculative essay containing a short essay upon the "original" verse forms of the fables, the order of the books, the dates of certain sections and a reconstruction of the original work, and a biography of Phaedrus the man. The second part is an edition of the fables together with a translation and a reclassification of the fables into books and a new book of "sententiae," ascribed to Phaedrus together with the "culex." Herrmann concludes that there were originally four books, most with satirical intent. The "sententiae" are listed as the last work of the fabulist--on no evidence whatsoever. Published around the year 90 or 91, one or two years before he died. Very extensive bibliography.

566.   ————. *Les fables antiques de la broderie de Bayeux.*
       Brussels: Latomus, 1964.

       Well-illustrated study of the fables found on the
       Bayeux tapestry. Herrmann sees forty-two fables on the
       tapestry, all with Phaedrine analogues save one, "Les
       deux Pigeons," for which he lists a line from Horace
       and a reference to La Fontaine. Each fable is illus-
       trated and commented upon and described in the introduc-
       tion as well.

567.   ————. "Nouvelles recherches sur Babrius." *L'Antiquité
       Classique*, 35 (1966), 433-458.

       Corrects previous research on Babrius and adds some
       new materials attributed to Babrius.

568.   ————. *Avianus: Oeuvres.* Bruxelles: Latomus, 1968.

       The "Oeuvres" of Avianus consist not only of the
       fables but also of the comedy *Querolus* and some poems.
       The fables are discussed in detail in the introduction
       in which the authenticity of the morals is also dealt
       with.
       See: Küppers, *Die Fabeln Avians*, and Gaide, *Avianus*.

569.   ————. "Notes sur le texte d'Avianus." *Latomus*, 28
       (1969), 669-680.

       A series of notes to his edition of Avianus. The
       first section comprises various textual notes to the
       fables; the second on the putative authorship of
       Querolus; and the third on the "poems" of Avianus.
       See: Küppers, *Die Fabeln Avians*, and Gaide, *Avianus*.

570.   ————. "Hercule selon Seneque et selon Phèdre."
       Hommages à Marcel Renard. Ed. J. Bibaun. Bruxelles:
       Coll. Latomus, nos. 101, 102 and 103 (1969), 431-
       442.

       Sees a connection between the conception of Hercules
       in Seneca and in works attributed by Herrmann to
       Phaedrus.

571.   ————. "Les fables phèdriennes de Iulius Titianus."
       Latomus, 30 (1971), 678-686.

       Herrmann confirms his hypothesis concerning the con-
       jectured fables of Titianus as a collection of para-
       phrases of the fables of Phaedrus.

572. ————. *Babrius et ses poèmes*. Bruxelles: Coll. Lato-
     mus, no. 135, 1973. 250 pp.

     An edition of Babrius' fables based generally upon
     Perry without some six fables and epimythia for many
     others, with an alphabetical ordering restored. Also
     numerous other works including the *Batrachomyomachia*,
     attributed to Babrius on flimsy or no evidence. Ex-
     tensive bibliography.

573. ————. "Babrius et Titus." *Revue des Études Grecques*,
     92 (1979), 113-119.

     Babrius seems interested in the relationship between
     Titus and his father Vespasian, which seems disturbed
     by his projected marriage to Berenice. P369 "Rose and
     the Amaranth" (TMI J242.1), which does not survive in
     its original form, if indeed truly Babrian, is assumed
     by Herrmann to be not only genuine but to show Domitian
     with Titus.

574. Hertel, Johannes. *Das südliche Panchatantra: Übersicht
     über den Inhalt der älteren 'Panchatantra.'* Leipzig:
     Brockhaus, 1904. 68 pp.

     Comprehensive discussion of the processes involved
     in and results of the recensions of the southern branch
     of the *Panchatantra*--the Nepalese version and the
     Hitopadesa, both derived from the same source which was
     in many ways closer to the original received text.
     The frame and the secondary stories receive considerable
     attention, and parallel and comparative structures are
     thoroughly researched.

575. ————. *Über das Tantrakhayika: Die kasmirische Rezen-
     sion des Pancatantra*. Leipzig: Teubner, 1904. 154
     pp.

     The text of the Decc. coll. VIII. 145 manuscript dis-
     covered by Gertel and edited in 1909, considered the
     oldest known version of the *Panchatantra* containing the
     original order and phrasing of the author.

576. ————. "Von Panini zu Phaedrus." *Zeitschrift der
     deutschen Morgenländischen Gesellschaft* (1908), 113-
     118.

     P294 "Crane and Peacock" (TMI J242.5) and P101 "Jack-
     daw in Borrowed Feathers" (A-T 244; TMI J951.2), as
     Babrius 65 and 72; and P509 "Peacock Complains to Juno

about His Voice" (TMI W128.4) in Phaedrus III, 18 all
are discussed with Indian parallels.

577. ────. "Altindische Parallelen zu Babrius 32."
Zeitschrift des Vereins für Volkskunde (1912), 244-
252.

P50 "Weasel and Aphrodite" (TMI J1908.2), Babrius 32
is discussed together with various Indian parallels,
probable sources.

578. ────. *Das Pancatantra: Seine Geschichte und seine
Verbreitung.* Leipzig: Teubner, 1914. 460 pp.

Identifies two main streams of the *Panchatantra*
tradition: the Kashmiri *Tantrakhyayika* and "K," the
archetype of all known versions. There are various
intermediate steps, most notably the archetype "N-W"
responsible ultimately for the versions known as the
Hitopadesa, the Pahlavi, and those dependent upon
those versions. Great detail and well-illustrated
with literary stemmata. Little attention is paid to
oral transmission or mechanism but well-argued literary
relationships.

579. Hervieux, Léopold. *Les Fabulistes latins depuis le
siècle d'Auguste jusqu'à la fin du moyen âge.* 5 vols.
Paris: Firmin Didot, 1883-1889. 2nd ed. 1893-1899.
Reprint 1965.

Much criticized but indispensible collection of all
fable manuscripts (to the Renaissance) known to Hervieux in all the libraries of Europe. Description
and semi-diplomatic reproductions of all manuscripts.
Some errors but of great value. The first volume contains a lengthy discussion of the life and fables of
Phaedrus and begins the long collection of texts.
This is followed by an extensive investigation of the
manuscript tradition, beginning with François Pithou
(1598). Volume two contains texts of Phaedrus and
Romulus; volume three the Avianus tradition; volumes
four and five deal with Odo of Cheriton and John of
Capua and their derivatives.
See: Gaston Paris, *Les Fabulistes latins.*

580. ────. *Notice historique et critique sur les fables
latins de Phèdre et ses anciens imitateurs directs
et indirects, lue à l'academie des inscriptions et
belles-lettres.* Paris: Didot, 1884. 68 pp.

After a cursory discussion of the position of Phaedrus and the status of Phaedrus research at his time, Hervieux begins an attack on those who had criticized his first volume of *Les fabulists latines*. Asserts the genuineness of the Perotti Appendix; the *Anonymus Nilanti* is supposed to be the only direct imitator of Phaedrus. The first of two books of fables were published under the reign of Tiberius, the third perhaps also but with the dedication added later. Book four was written in the reign of Claudius. The relationship of various Phaedrus paraphrases follows.

581. ———. *Notice sur les Fables Latins d'origine Indienne*. Paris: Didot, 1898. 78 pp.

A lengthy demonstration of the thesis that India is the cradle of the fable. The first section is on John of Capua's *Directorium humanae vitae*, as a "modification" of the *Panchatantra*, followed by a biography of John of Capua and an analysis of the *Directorium*. The fables are discussed in detail, followed by the manuscript tradition and editions of the *Directorium*. The second chapter is concerned with Baldo and the manuscript tradition of his twenty-six fables. Chapter three deals with the fables of Raymond de Bezier with an analysis of the relationship between these fables and those of John of Capua. The essay ends with a table of correspondences.

582. Herwerden, H. van. "Babriana." *Mnemosyne*, 28 (1900), 157-175.

Extensive list of textual emendations and, in connection with a rigorous study of metrics, further interpolations and suggestions.

583. Hesseling, D.C. "On Waxen Tablets with Fables of Babrius (Tabulae cerate Assendelftianae)." *Journal of Hellenic Studies*, 13 (1893), 293-314.

Surveys texts found by the Dutch Naval officer H. van Assendelft in 1881 in the ruins of Palmyra. These seven tablets contain fourteen fables, a number of choliambs, unmistakably in the Babrian tradition. Tablets seem to be a schoolboy's exercise, which implies that Babrius was used as a school-text. The beginnings of the texts are relatively better preserved.

584. Heydenreich, Eduard. "Berich über die Litteratur zu

Phaedrus aus den Jahren 1873 bis 1882." *Jahres-
bericht für Alterthumswissenschaft*, 39 (1884), 1033;
39 (1884), 205-249 (On Phaedrus, 1883-1884); 43
(1885), 100-124 (On Phaedrus, 1885); 55 (1886-1887),
170-174 (Phaedrus, 1886-1887).

Various reports on critical literature concerning
Phaedrus. Heydenreich reports generally on German and
French materials; most other literature is not mentioned. Fairly complete listings of editions, including school editions but only partial bibliographies
of secondary materials. Continued by Hans Draheim (q.v.)
and Wilhelm Port (q.v.).

585. Hieatt, Constance B. "The Moral of the Nun's Priest's
      Tale." *Studia Neophilologia*, 42 (1970), 3-8.

The final three "morals" are stated at the end of
the tale in the structural equivalent of epimythia.
The problem: which of the morals is to be followed?
Hieatt demonstrates the essence of the moral content
is the common Chaucerian theme that man is by nature
unable to see the consequences of his own choices.

586. Hildebrand, J. *Robert Henrysons 'Moral Fabillis' im
      Rahmen der mittelalterlichen und spätmittelalter-
      lichen Tierdichtung.* Dissertation, Hamburg, 1973.

The structural and narrative techniques used by
Henryson in his *Fables* are detailed and discussed in
terms of their religious, and to a lesser extent, their
psychological considerations. The concept of the fable
is analyzed and compared to the parable and the allegory, which are then analyzed in their turn for their
religious content.

587. Hilka, Alfons. "Beiträge zur mittelalterlichen Fabel-
      literatur." *Jahresbericht der Schlesischen Gesell-
      schaft für vaterländische Cultur. 4. Abteilung,
      Sektion für neuere Philologie*, 91 (1913), 1-21.

On the Tours manuscript 468 and comparison to a
sister manuscript from Berne (no. 679) Hilka discovered.
The contents are described and twenty fables are printed
with sources and parallels. The manuscript is dated
to the fifteenth century although the collection is
clearly older.

588. ————. *Beiträge zur lateinischen Erzählungsliteratur
      des Mittelalters. I. Der novus Aesopus des Baldo.*

II. Eine lateinische Übersetzung der griechischen Version des Kalila-Buchs. Berlin: Weidmann, 1928.

Two essays on the Latin re-workings of the *Pancha-tantra*. I effects a new edition by bringing readings from new manuscript material Hilka discovered in the Stadtsbibliothek Heiligenkreuz from the fourteenth century. Contains seven new fables and tables of concordances of both manuscripts. II is concerned with an edition of *Stephanites kai Ichnelates*.

589. Hilligen, Wolfgang. "Didaktische Überlegungen zu Fabeln (und Märchen) in der Grundschule." *Gesellschaft, Staat, Erziehung: Blätter für politische Bildung und Erziehung*, 17: 2 (1972), 102-104.

Notes on the use of the fable and other narrative forms in the elementary grades in Germany.

590. Hillmann, Heinz. "Fabel und Parabel im 20. Jahrhundert-- Kafka und Brecht." *Die Fabel: Theorie, Geschichte und Rezeption einer Gattung.* Ed. Peter Hasubek. Berlin: Schmidt, 1982, 215-235.

This essay concentrates upon the parable as the fable is considered, following Brettschneider, a "special case in the general structure of the parable." Hillmann nevertheless apparently keeps the categories separate in his discussion of Brecht and Kafka, claiming parable status for some of the works discussed. The fable designation is not given to any.

591. Hirsch, L. *Die Fabel.* Cöthen: Herzoglich-Anhaltische Landesseminar zu Cöthen, 1894. 42 pp.

Treats the fable in broad scope but with precision. The history of the fable and fabulists (pp. 13-37) covers all major writers, editors, and collectors in classical times with specific characteristics of each fabulist.

592. Hoban, Thomas More. "The Contents and Structure of Dryden's *Fables Ancient and Modern*." Dissertation, University of Nebraska, 1971.

Hoban concludes that the term "fable" as used by Dryden and his contemporaries refers to a form of litera-ture which may or may not have a continuous narrative but which invariably has a moral. Thus the two genres found in his *Fables* were even more didactic in intent

than the classical forms. Hoban sees an inherent unity
in the work based upon explicit or implicit didacticism.

593. Hobbs, J. *Illustrated Fables: A Catalogue of the
      Library's Holdings.* 2 vols. London: Victoria and
      Albert Museum, 1972.

      A listing of the materials available in the Victoria
      and Albert Museum containing illustrated fables. The
      extensive holdings include numerous editions of Caxton
      and Ogilby.

594. Hodnett, Edward. "Elisha Kirkall c. 1682-1742: Master
      of Whiteline Engraving in Relief and Illustrator of
      Croxall's Aesop." *The Book Collector*, 25 (1976),
      195-209.

      Croxall's *Fables of Aesop and Others* (1722) was a
      landmark in Aesop collections and illustrations. It
      contained 196 oval illustrations and was one of the
      most substantial collections of the eighteenth century.
      The work was written to compete with the L'Estrange
      collection of 1692 and its illustrator has tentatively
      been identified as Elisha Kirkall. Hodnett here con-
      firms him in that honor and surveys what is known of
      Kirkall and analyzes his innovative technique.

595. ————. *Francis Barlow, First Master of English Book
      Illustration.* London: Scolar Press and Berkeley:
      University of California Press, 1978.

      An excellent introduction to the history of fable
      illustration through Marcus Gheeraerts to 1700. Con-
      tains a survey of Francis Barlow's career and his in-
      terpretative illustrations of Wenceslaus Hollar-Ogilby's
      Aesop Paraphrased (1665), *Aesop's Fables* (1666), and
      other works including his *Life of Aesop* series (1687).
      Good bibliography and numerous illustrations.

596. ————. *Aesop in England: The Transmission of Motifs
      in Seventeenth-Century Illustrations of Aesop's
      Fables.* Charlottesville: The Bibliographical Society
      of the University of Virginia, the Virginia University
      Press, 1979.

      Charts the transmission of motifs from, e.g., Pfister
      of Bamberg (1461) through Zainer of Ulm (1476) to
      Gheeraerts (1567) in Antwerp to Barlow in London, among
      many others. Discusses the illustrations of Caxton,
      Marcus Gheeraerts, and numerous seventeenth-century

book illustrations. Defines motif and the methods of transmission. The main body of the work is given over to a concordance of sources of motifs used in seventeenth-century English Aesop illustration. Bibliography and index and numerous plates.

597. Hofer, Phillip. "Francis Barlow's Aesop 1666, 1667." *Harvaid Library Bulletin*, 2 (1948), 279-295 + 16 plates.

Traces Francis Barlow's activity as a fable illustrator, as contributor to the second Ogilby edition (1665-68), and in his own *Aesop* (1666, 2nd edition), which is described as an unprofitable venture. Describes later "editions" (actually rebound and reduced reprintings from Barlow's plates) in relationship to the originals. Evaluates Barlow as artist. Includes a very complete bibliographical appendix.
See: Hodnett, *Francis Barlow*.

598. Hohmann, Ernest. *De indole atque auctoriatate Epimythiorum Babrianorum*. Dissertation, Königsberg, 1907.

Among the Babrian fables as transmitted in the A (Athous) Manuscript, some fifty-one have survived with epimythia. Hohmann discusses the genuineness of these epimythia and concludes that they were almost certainly added later. Now completely superseded by Perry.
See: Perry, "The Origin of the Epimythium."

599. Holbek, Bengt. "Hjorten, fåret og ulven: En fabelhistorie." *Arv: Journal of Scandinavian Folklore*, 15 (1959), 27-46.

An examination of P477 "Sheep, Stag and Wolf" (TMI J1383) and other versions of "De cervo, ove et lupo," including P478 "Sheep, Dog and Wolf" (TMI Q263) with relationships detailed so as to allow reconstruction of its development. At the base of Romulus 5 and Romulus 40 lies a lost version in Latin prose anterior to that of Phaedrus (I, 16 = P477) which was combined with the prose tradition of the fourth to fifth centuries.

600. ————. *Aesops levned og fabler: Christian Pedersens oversaettelse af Steinhöwels Aesop*. 2 vols. Copenhagen: J.H. Schultz Forlag, 1961-1962.

A facsimile edition of Christian Pedersen's translation of Heinrich Steinhöwel's *Esopus* with a second

volume of notes and introductory material. Extensive
source and parallel listings together with a history
of Aesop, the Aesop romance, and the fable. Good bibliography and extensive textual commentary with indices.
Fables are keyed to Perry, A-T Types, and Motif Index
numbers. Summary in English.

601. ————. "Äsop." *Enzyklopädie des Märchens: Handwörterbuch zur historischen und vergleichenden
Erzählforschung*. Ed. Kurt Ranke. Berlin: de Gruyter,
1977. 1, 881-889.

Reviews the historical basis for Aesop and discusses
this in relationship to the *Vita Aesopi*, which is analyzed
in various versions. The infusion of characteristics
from other folk characters, especially Diogenes, into
the figure of Aesop is outlined. Describes the Vita
as a product of the Hellenistic era and the figure
of Aesop as the exponent of a people oppressed by a
ruling Greek culture.

602. Holder, Alfred. "Zu Avianus." *Philologus*, 65 (1906),
91-96.

Avianus' Preface and some twenty-nine fables are
found in Karlsruh Codex LXXIII from the tenth century.
The manuscript appears to have no new variant readings,
but the collation has value for determining the family
tree of a group of manuscripts.

603. Holfelder, Hans Hermann. "Zu Horaz, *Ep.* I, 7, 29-33
and Cyrill, *Speculum sapientiae*, 111, 11." *Hermes*,
96 (1968-1969), 638-640.

The fables which traveled under the name of Cyrill
did not achieve their present form before the fourteenth
century and were widely known and appreciated during
the sixteenth century. They are therefore too young
to be of value in support of the manuscript tradition
of Horace. Ends with various notes on the influence
of the Cyrillian fables.

604. Homér, Gustaf. "L'Enxienplo del asno e del blanchete:
Quelques reflexions sur le génie poétique de l'Archi-
prêtre de Hita." *Moderna Språk*, 64 (1970), 59-71.

P91 "Ass and Master" (A-T 214; TMI J2413.1), as found
in Juan Ruiz's *Libro de Buen Amor*, is treated within its
context; Ruiz infuses color, vitality, as well as humor
into his *exempla*. The source is Walter of England,

perhaps through the medium of a French version, most
likely the *Isopet de Lyon*, although there are significant, fundamental differences between Ruiz's version
and the Aesopic tradition.

605. ————. "Une fable de André Chénier." *Moderna Språk*,
65 (1971), 341-354.

A discussion of André Chénier's version of P352
"Country Mouse and City Mouse" (A-T 112; TMI J211-1)
with comparisons to Horace and the Romulus and Isopet
traditions.

606. Holten, Ragmar von. "Gustave Moreau, Illustrateur de
La Fontaine." *L'Oeil*, 115-116 (1964), 20-27.

Twenty-three illustrations by Moreau from between
1880 and 1885 form a significant place in the work of
the artist. This article describes the accompanying
illustrations with a contextual commentary.

607. Hostetter, Winifred H. "A Linguistic Study of the
Vulgar Greek Life of Aesop." Dissertation, University
of Illinois, Urbana, 1955. 150 pp.

A study of the G version of the *Vita* in manuscript 397
of the Pierpont Morgan Library, published in Ben Edwin
Perry's *Aesopica* (q.v.) to determine if the unclassical
forms might represent the original version. G is compared to W in terms of orthography, syntax, and vocabulary with the conclusion that nearly all the unclassical
forms could be original readings. W appears to have
been revised to eliminate displeasing forms, but the
revision was careless and incomplete.

608. Hotson, J. Leslie. "Colfax vs. Chauntecleer." *PMLA*,
39 (1924), 762-781. Reprinted in Chaucer: *Modern
Essays in Criticism* (New York: Galaxy, 1959), 98-116.

Investigates Chaucer's "Nun's Priest's Tale" containing P562 "Partridge and Fox" (A-T 61; TMI K561.1, K721)
as a political satire, with Colfax and Chauntecleer
identified as Nicolas Colfax and Henry of Bolingbroke.

609. Houghton, Herbert Pierrepont. "Moral Significance of
Animals as Indicated in Greek Proverbs." Dissertation, Johns Hopkins University, 1907.

Discusses animals in Greek proverbs with an introduction to Greek paremiology and a comparison of the

moral content of animal proverbs compared to that of
animal fables, especially the Aesopic type. Other relationships between the proverb and the fable are discussed. No indices.

610. Housman, A.E. "Notes on Phaedrus." *Classical Review*,
      20 (1906), 257-259.

      On a number of emendations and other suggestions to
      six fables of Phaedrus generally in opposition to
      Müller.

611. Howarth, W.D. "La Fontaine." *Life and Letters in
      Seventeenth Century France: The Seventeenth Century*.
      London: Thomas Nelson, 1965, pp. 134-135.

      Uses La Fontaine's "Les Deux Rats, le renard et
      l'oeuf," Book 9, the last fable, attached to the philo-
      sophical discussion entitled "Discours à Mne. de la
      Sablière," to introduce an investigation of the Car-
      tesian animal-machine debate of the seventeenth century.
      La Fontaine is shown to be very much in step with the
      intellectual life of his time.

612. Hower, Charles Clare. "Studies on the So-Called
      Accursiana Recension of the Life and Fables of
      Aesop." Dissertation, University of Illinois, 1936.
      137 pp.

      The Accursiana recension of the fables, together with
      the *Vita Aesopi*, was printed by Bonus Accursius at
      Milan in 1480. Hower concludes that the printed re-
      cension represents the work of Maximus Planudes on the
      basis of a comparative study of style, syntax, and
      vocabulary from the letters of Planudes.

613. Hubert, Renée Riese. "Interprétation figurée des
      Fables de La Fontaine." *Kentucky Romance Quarterly*,
      14 (1967), 177-190.

      An approach to the illustrations of the fables by
      interpreting the illustrations as a work of literature.
      They are perforce selective, illustrating certain as-
      pects of the fables, passing over other features in
      silence. Thus the illustrator is interpreting the
      fables. Discussion ranges through the illustrators
      of La Fontaine, from François Chauveau, the illustrator
      of the original edition, through Chagall.

614. Hübschmann-Behrens, Gerda. "Die Ulmer Aesop-Holz-schnitte." Dissertation, Berlin (Humboldt), 1951.

    A discussion of the illustrations accompanying the Heinrich Steinhöwel *Esopus*. The woodcuts are identi-fied as belonging in part to the *Edelstein* tradition dating from 1461, the earliest printed illus-trated book. The woodcuts are closely connected to the editions and translations that followed.

615. Hudde, Hinrich. "La Mottes und Imberts literarische Repliken auf die Fabel von den Gliedern und vom Magen." *Romanistisches Jahrbuch*, 25 (1974), 94-122.

    Discusses the versions of P130 "Stomach and Feet" (A-T 293; TMI J461.1) by La Motte and Barthélemy Imbert as "repliques," as suggested by Von Stackelberg and defined as free imitations of a literary work with the intention of surpassing and perhaps refuting or re-butting the original. Hudde presents a diachronic study discussing the problems of composing fables in the shadow of La Fontaine; La Motte's "L'Estomac" and Imbert's "La Tête et les Pieds" are compared to numerous other forms in great detail. These two are concerned with political justice; the goal appears to be a har-monious relationship between those who govern and the governed. The message of the fable from Titus Livius through Marie de France and La Fontaine to the two fabulists studied here is a warning not to disturb the social symmetry.

616. ———. "Florians Fabeln: Regression angesichts der Revolution." *Zeitschrift für französische Sprache und Literatur*, 87 (1977), 99-141.

    Jean-Pierre Claris de Florian (1755-1794) published his fables during the French Revolution in contrast to the generally accepted idea that no significant work appeared during those years. Hudde explains Florian's much-disputed and complex relationship to the Revolution in essentially a sociological-historical textual analysis, but he sees the key in the Freudian psychoanalytical term: regression. Regression is seen as driving his art, as Florian, who lost his mother at the age of one, produces fables such as "La Mère, l'Enfant et les Sarigues," a "literarischen Ersatz." Regression is also a central problem with regard to Florian's political position. Hudde sees reflections of Florian's monarchism and his leanings toward the

Republic in "Le Poisson volant" (V,22) with the
poet's regressive wishes expressed in the character
of the fish. Ends with an interpretation of "Le Gril-
lon."

617. ————. "Das Schätchen und der Dornstrauch: Wand-
lungen einer Fabel von La Motte bis Wilhelm Busch."
Germanisch-Romanische Monatsschrift, 28 (1978), 399-
416.

An historical-sociological study of a fable invented
in the early eighteenth century, most likely by La
Motte. Seven versions in French, two in German and one
Latin, all from not very well-known authors, are investigated in the light of historical and social
changes. The fables range from the critical, emanci-
patory tendencies found in Hagedorn and to a lesser
extent in the Desbillions Latin version and the "anti-
Enlightenment" French pair to the sarcastic version
found with Busch.

618. Hueck, Monika. *Textstruktur und Gattungssystem: Studien
zum Verhältnis von Emblem und Fabel im 16. und 17.
Jahrhundert.* Kronberg/Ts.: Scriptor, 1975. 200 pp.

On the correlation of fable and emblem as distinct
genre systems found in the literary scheme of the
sixteenth and the seventeenth centuries. Begins with
a survey of research of the two together; then an outline of methodology to be followed and an analysis of
structural poetics, specifically Russian Formalism.
Contains a structural analysis of Taurellus' *Emblemata
Physico-Ethica* and Heinrich Steinhöwel's *Esopus*, followed by a careful description of the "evolutionary
process" involved. Appends illustrations, source bibliography, a limited general bibliography, and an index.

619. Huemer, Johannes. "Zu Avianus." *Wiener Studien*, 2
(1880), 158-160.

Presents variant readings of distiches from Avianus
22, 10-16; 21, 22; 31 and 32.

620. Huete, Sylvia B. "John Gay's *Fables I* and *II*: A Study
in the Eighteenth-Century Fable." Dissertation,
University of Southern Mississippi, 1973.

Attempts to account for sixty editions of John Gay's
Fables I and *II* before 1880 in the popularity of the
form as a literary genre. Examines Gay's unity of

structure and theme as well as poetic style. Gay's
fables show the influence of emblem literature as well
as the "courtesy books." The structural unity of
Fables I has no counterpart in *Fables II*; here Gay is
closer to Mandeville.

621. Hughes, Arthur Howard. "Notes on Steinhöwel's Aesop
and the Fables of Hans Sachs." *Modern Language Notes*,
47 (1932), 522-525.

Short notes demonstrating Hans Sachs to be dependent
upon Steinhöwel for a number of his fables (which are
not listed) and suggests that Steinhöwel's moral tags
were also used.
See: Carnes, "Heinrich Steinhöwel."

622. Hunger, Herbert. "Die Schildkröte im Himmel (Stephanites und Ichnelates I, 40)." *Wiener Studien*, 79
(1966), 260-263.

On a fable of a turtle carried up on a stick in
Stephanites und Ichnelates (cf. P230), used rhetorically
to describe the consequences of disregarding the helpful
suggestions of one's friends.

623. Huntley, Frank L. "A Background in Folklore for the
'Blind Mouths' Passage in Lycidas." *Milton News-
letter* (Athens, Ohio), 1: 4 (1967), 52-55.

Sees a tenuous secondary connection between the
phrase "blind mouths" in Milton's *Lycidas* and P688
"Wolf learns his letters" and other related fables.

624. Husselmann, Elinor Mulliet. "A Lost Manuscript of
Babrius." *Transactions of the American Philological
Association*, 66 (1935), 104-126.

A description of codex 397 of the Pierpont Morgan
Library from the tenth century containing four Babrian
fables not preserved in metrical form anywhere else.
Provides a critical survey of all the significant
variants of the Babrian text. The manuscript is the
oldest Aesopic text known.
See: Perry, *Studies in the Text History*.

625. ————. *A Fragment of Kalilah and Dimna from Ms 397
in the Pierpont Morgan Library*. London: Christophers,
1939. 35 pp. + 6 plates.

Three fragments from the Kalila and Dimna are here

identified as stemming from an incomplete model that
had been enlarged upon by its translator. The manuscript, which Husselmann identifies as the Cryptoferra-
tensis A33 from the tenth century which had disappeared
from a monastery in the Grottaferrata in the early
nineteenth century, varies so much from the tradition
of *Stephanites and Ichnelates* that reconstruction is
doubtful. Samples of the miniatures are appended.

626. Huygens, R.B.C. "Accessus ad auctores." *Latomus*, 12
      (1953), 296-311.

      Textual corrections and emendations on Avianus with
      various comments on each fable.

627. Ikeda, Hiroko. *A Type and Motif Index of Japanese
      Folk-Literature*. Folklore Fellows Communications,
      no. 209. Helsinki: Finnish Academy of Science and
      Letters, 1971.

      This comprehensive survey of Japanese Folktale
      materials includes extensive treatment of a number of
      fables, including the Aesopic type. P53 "Farmer's Sons:
      Strength in Unity" (A-T 910F; TMI J80, J1021), for ex-
      ample, is potentially attributed to the late sixteenth-
      century translation into Japanese of the Aesopic collec-
      tion.

628. Imendörffer, Helene. "Der Beitrag des Formalisten zur
      Gattungsgeschichtlichen Untersuchung der Fabel."
      *Poetica: Zeitschrift für Sprach- und Literaturwissen-
      schaft*, 9 (1977), 116-122.

      A useful and insightful presentation of Lindja Vindt's
      essay: "The Fable as Literary Genre" in the context of
      Russian Formalism. Imendörffer paraphrases the essen-
      tials of Vindt's essay and provides a commentary to
      this and other theoretical works, some antecedent to
      Vindt as well as more modern ones. Provides a concise
      history of the reception of fable studies in the Soviet
      Union in general and Vindt's work in particular.

629. Immisch, Otto. "Über eine Pflanzenfabel." *Philologus*,
      51 (1892), 560.

      Discusses Callimachus fragment 194 together with an
      old Lydian version of the fable, P439 "Laurel and Olive
      Tree" (TMI J411.7), suggesting that the fable was known
      in Assyria and attempting to connect this motif to

Phaedrus 3, 17: P508 "Trees under Patronage of the Gods" (TMI J241.1).

630. ———. "Babriana." *Rheinisches Museum für Philologie*, 79 (1930), 153-169.

Refers to the tablets found at Palmyra dating from the fourth century and containing fragmentary versions of the Babrian fables. Immisch surveys the research on the texts and concludes that either the text of the fragments or the "received tradition" of Babrius is not authentic, putting the authority of the Athous manuscript into question.

631. ———. "Ein Epodos des Archilochos." *Sitzungsbericht der Heidelberger Akademie des Wissenschaften, phil.-hist. Klasse* (1930-1931), no. 3.

Takes issue with Luria's reconstruction of P81 "Ape and Fox" (TMI K730.1). The entire question of reconstructing the fable from a few words, particularly the complex of motifs suggested by Luria, is labeled impossible.

632. Ingersoll, Ernest. *Birds in Legend, Fable and Folklore.* London: Longmans, Green and Co., 1923. Rpt. Detroit: Singing Trees, 1968.

Passing reference made to a few fables in this general survey of animals, especially birds, found in various folklore contexts and in iconographic traditions and literature.

633. Irmscher, Johannes. "Das mittelgriechische Tierepos: Bestand und Forschungssituation." *Aspects of the Medieval Animal Epic.* Ed. E. Rombauts and A. Wilkenhuysen. Louvain: Louvain University Press, 1955, pp. 207-227.

Deals with the fable incidentally in a discussion on the Middle Greek Beast Epic. Suggests the fable is only really available to us today in its Byzantine form. The oldest collection dates back to the third century A.D., but even this collection is considered a product of the Byzantine rhetorical schools. The popularity of the fable in Byzantine medieval society is analyzed as is the coming of the Indian fable (in Arabic form) to Byzantium during the tenth and the eleventh centuries.

634. ————. "Luthers Fabelbearbeitung." *Canadian Review
      of Comparative Literature*, 8 (1981), 324-333.

      Irmscher considers Luther collection to be essentially
      a reworking rather than a translation and, thus, a
      product of the Middle Ages. Describes Luther's manu-
      script and reviews the research on the fables. Para-
      phrases each fable.

635. Isaacs, Ann F. "Aesop, Common Sense and Giftedness."
      The Gifted Child Quarterly (Spring, 1974), 56-59.

      Apparently an attempt to make the point that a lack
      of common sense might cause the superior-gifted to
      appear to be stupid by means of a telling of P226
      "Tortoise and Hare" (A-T 275A; TMI K11.3).

636. Isenberg, M. "The Sale of Sacrificial Meat." *Classi-
      cal Philology*, 70 (1975), 271-273.

      A passage in the *Vita Aesopi* (Sec. 51 in Perry's
      Aesopica, p. 52) is discussed with emphasis upon the
      sacrificial nature of the pig meat involved, keying
      upon the word *tephymenon*. Sacrificial meats were ap-
      parently valued higher than non-sacrificial flesh.

637. Jack, R.D.S. "Caxton's *Mirrour of the World* and Henry-
      son's 'Taill of the Cock and the Jasp.'" *Chaucer
      Review*, 13 (1978), 157-165.

      Sees Caxton's work, chapter five, as the major source
      for Henryson's fable (on the basis of vocabulary, use
      of rhetoric, and, especially, parallels in the *morali-
      tas*) rather than the versions in the Romulus tradition
      and the *Isopet de Lyon*.

638. Jackson, George B. "Fabled Fireplaces." *Antiques*, 112
      (1977), 1148-1155.

      Well-illustrated article demonstrating the use of
      fables as themes for domestic interior architectural
      details, particularly fireplaces, a vogue in England
      during the eighteenth century, the model for which
      appears to have Barlow's Aesop (1666-1687). Most popu-
      lar fables are P426 "Fox and the Crane" and P133 "Dog
      and Piece of Meat." A few American fireplaces are
      known. Furniture, tile facing, and cast iron firebacks
      are also known.

639. Jacob, O. "Le rat de ville et le rat des champs."
      Les Études classiques, 4 (1935), 130-154.

Surveys fables throughout Roman literature focusing upon P352 "Country Mouse and City Mouse" (A-T 112; TMI J211.1) up to Horace's version and his specific use of the fable as satire. The characterization of the two mice is masterful; the country mouse personifying the Sabine peasant, the city mouse a metropolitan epicure gourmet. Action and stylistics are discussed and are compared to La Fontaine and a number of other fabulists especially from the seventeenth and eighteenth centuries.

640. Jacobs, Joseph. *The Fables of Aesop as First Printed by William Caxton in 1484 with Those of Avian, Alfonso and Poggio, Now Again Edited and Induced. Volume 1: History of the Aesopic Fable.* London: D. Nutt, 1889. Reprint, New York: Burt Franklin, 1970.

The second volume of this two volume set is a reprint of the Caxton edition of 1484 (for which now see: Lengahan, *Caxton's Aesop*). The first volume is a generally valueless study, often fanciful, of Aesop from the fables' earliest beginning. Now completely outdated.

641. ———. "Fable." *Encyclopedia of Religion and Ethics.* Ed. James Hastings. New York: Charles Scribner, 1920. 5, 677-678.

An eclectic and curious survey of the history of the fable and an investigation into its nature. Considers fables appealing to children because of the "primitive mind of a child" and because of the absence of "the sex motive." Essentially a summary of his earlier work and of little value.

642. Jacobsen, E. "The Fable Is Inverted or Donne's Aesop." *Classica et Mediaevalia*, 13 (1952), 1-37.

Deals with the problem of the snake in the classical tradition of P44 "Frogs Ask for a King" (A-T 277; TMI J643.1) that appears as a crane in John Donne's poem. The snake in Phaedrus and presumably in Babrius (see Halm 76) is preserved in the wide majority of medieval paraphrases of Phaedrus and in Marie de France. One thirteenth-century manuscript of the *Anonymous Neveleti* shows a radical departure, which is also found in some of the French series of "Ysopets." The stork appears also in the *Edelstein* of Ulrich Boner and finally in Heinrich Steinhöwel's late fifteenth-century edition, and from there to Julien Macho and Caxton. The version

in Donne may owe its existence to the stork or heron in
the Latin of William of Gouda much paraphrased in
England during his day. Ends with a note to Reynard
and a well-selected series of illustrations.

643. Jacquiot, Josèphe. "Les fables de La Fontaine dans
      les arts de la gravure et de la sculpture: Le perçu,
      le réel, l'imaginaire." *Cahiers de l'Association
      Internationale des Études Français*, 26 (1974), 159-
      172.

      Illustrated discussion of La Fontaine's fables in the
      plastic arts. The engravings are analyzed with the
      socio-historical implications brought about by differing
      attitudes across nearly three centuries. Bas-relief
      sculpture together with a wide variety of engraved
      illustrations.

644. Jambeck, Karen K. "Les fables de Marie de France:
      Edition critique de fables choisies." Dissertation,
      Univ. of Connecticut, 1980. 248 pp.

      A partial critical and virtually diplomatic edition
      of ten selected fables preparatory to a complete edi-
      tion, contrasting with Warnke's edition by faithful
      adherence to the manuscript. The apparatus provides
      variants and notes. The lengthy introduction is a com-
      prehensive survey of the fable, of Marie de France, and
      language problems found in the fables.

645. Jamieson, Ian W.A. "The Poetry of Robert Henryson: A
      Study of the Use of Source Material." Dissertation,
      University of Edinburgh, 1964.

      A wide-ranging investigation of the sources used by
      Henryson in all his work. The material on the fables
      surveys previous research on the sources, especially
      Diebler, and offers a number of specific details on
      the manner in which Henryson used his source materials.

646. ————. "Henryson's 'Fabillis': An Essay Towards a
      Revaluation." *Words: Wai-Te Atu Studies in Litera-
      ture* (Wellington, New Zealand), 2 (1966), 20-31.

      The sources of Henryson's fables ought to provide
      the material basis for a revaluation of his fables.
      Discusses various source possibilities, especially the
      French Ysopets. The *Isopet de Lyon* is a possible
      source for Henryson's "Sheep and the Dog" P478 "Sheep,
      Dog and Wolf" (TMI B270, Q263).

647. ————. "A Further Source for Henryson's *Fabillis*." *Notes and Queries*, 14: 1 [212] (1967), 403-405.

Henryson's debt to Odo of Cheriton's *Fabulae* in two fables is noted. Henryson apparently used materials from Odo in "Twa Myis" P352 "Country Mouse and City Mouse" (A-T 112; TMI J211.1) and the "Fox Trapped before the Lyone," cf. P187 and P638 (A-T 4/B; TMI 1608, K551.18).

648. ————. "Henryson's 'Taill of the Wolf and the Wedder.'" *Studies in Scottish Literature*, 6 (1969), 248-257.

An attempt to prove the idea that the *moralitas* are structured as a rhetorical device with the intention of shocking the reader/listener by involving him in the tale itself. Reiterates Henryson's dependence upon Steinhöwel/Caxton for his version of P705 "Dog, Wolf and Ram" (A-T 126; TMI K1715, K1839.3.1; cf. also P358).

649. ————. "The Beast Tale in Middle Scots: Some Thoughts on the History of a Genre." *Parergon*, 2 (1972), 26-36.

The apparent discrepancy between fable and *moralitas* is to be found in the shock of the unexpected interpretation, especially as found in Henryson's first fable "The Cock and the Jasp," P503 "Cock and Pearl" (TMI J1/61.1); his third, P562/P562A "Partridge and Fox" (A-T 6, cf. 61A; TMI K561.1, K721), and part of the fourth, P628 "Wolf Hearing Confession from a Fox/Ass" (TMI U11.1.1), as well as other poems.

650. ————. "'To preve thare preching be a poesye': Some Thoughts on Henryson's Poetics." *Parergon*, 8 (1974), 24-36.

Argues from Henryson's fifth fable: "The Trial of the Fox," P638 "Ass with the Privilege, the Fox and the Wolf" (A-T 47E; TMI K5551.18, J1608) and from his ninth: "Fox, Wolf and the Cadger," P625 "The Wolf and the Fox" (A-T 2; TMI K1021) as well as with evidence from other Henryson pieces, that there is a certain incompleteness in Henryson's fables, similar to that occasionally found in Chaucer, in which Henryson fails to "prove the preaching."

651. Janicke, Karl. "Die Fabeln und Erzählungen im 'Renner' des Hugo von Trimberg." *Archiv für das Studium der*

neueren Sprachen und Litteraturen, 32 (1862), 161-
176.

A source study for Hugo von Trimberg's fables, listing
essentially Latin sources, especially the Romulus tradition.
See: Seemann, *Hugo von Trimberg.*

652.   Janson, H.W. *Apes and Ape Lore in the Middle Ages.*
       London: The Warburg Institute, 1952.

       Following in general McDermott (q.v.), Janson traces
       the history of the perception and treatment of the ape
       in literature and iconography. The classical tradition
       is treated in detail during which the ape never achieved
       a clear-cut definition of character in relationship to
       the rest of the animal kingdom. Medieval fabulists in-
       herited this attitude and found themselves in something
       of a quandary about the stories of the apes. Treats
       ape fables from Bidpai and classical sources, especially
       P203 "Ape and Fisherman," P533 "Ape and Fox" (TMI J341.1,
       W152.1), and P643 "Ape and Merchant."

653.   Janssens, Jacques. *Le Fable et les fabulistes.* Brux-
       elles: Office de publicité, 1955.

       Traces the evolution of the fable from its beginnings
       through its "decline as a literary form." Sources and
       origins are now lost, but Janssens begins with the
       Indian fable although he does allow for the possibility
       of primacy to be given to the Greeks. Discusses the
       Panchatantra and "Aesop" and his possible precursors;
       the classical and medieval fable through to La Fon-
       taine, and then imitators of those forms, and finally,
       the "fable overseas." Concludes with a bibliography
       but no index of fables discussed.

654.   Jasinski, René. *La Fontaine et le premier recueil des
       fables.* 2 vols. Paris: A.G. Nizet, 1965 and 1966.

       Two volumes of tremendous erudition demonstrating
       Jasinski's main thesis that almost every single fable
       of the first edition (1668) is to be interpreted as a
       political allegory with the political affair connected
       with Foquet (1658-1678) as the primary focus.

655.   ———. "De quelques contresons sur les Fables."
       Europe, 515 (1972), 26-38.

       Insightful, commonsense essay on errors of reception

among readers and critics of La Fontaine. These errors involve misapprehensions of language, of misuse, or of prejudgment because of the sources and overall content of the fables.

656. Jason, Heda, and Aharon Kempinski. "How Old Are Folktales?" *Fabula*, 22 (1981), 1-27.

Interesting beginning to the extremely complex problem of the age of some of the most easily identified folktale types including a number of fables (although these are curiously never labeled as such): (5) "Tamarisk and Palm," closely related to P439 "Laurel and Olive" (TMI J411.7), (4) "Eagle and Serpent," related to P1 "Eagle and Fox" (A-T 69; TMI K2295).

657. Jauss, Hans Robert. *Untersuchungen zur mittelalterlichen Tierdichtung*. Beiheft zur Zeitschrift für romanische Philologie, no. 100. Tübingen, 1959. 314 pp.

Deals with all forms of medieval animal tales including the Aesopic fable, which is here characterized as exemplary in that, taken together, the fables display the "humanum morem." The animal figures are detailed in their Latin and French forms (especially in the beast epic) with regard to a sociological function that is considered far more important than any origin theory. Jauss makes a clear distinction between the fable and the beast epic (no common origin), breaking with nineteenth-century beast epic theory that alternatively derives the one from the other or suggests strong influence for one form to be found in the other.

658. Jech, Jaromír. "A Bohemian Medieval Fable on the Fox and the Pot." *Medieval Literature and Folklore Studies: Essays in Honor of Francis Lee Utley*. Ed. Jerome Mandel and Bruce A. Rosenberg. New Brunswick: Rutgers University Press, 1970, 275-289.

A satirical verse poem in the Bohemian Hradecký rukopis known also from a manuscript in Breslau, iv.Q.126, contains the fable of the fox that tries to drown a pot and causes his own death in the process (A-T 698; TMI J2131.5). Bohemian characteristics are highlighted to demonstrate the distinctly Czech flavor of the fable. With appendices containing four versions.

659. Jeffreys, M.D.W. "Some Ibibio Folk-Tales." *Folklore*, 78 (1967), 19-27.

Introductions to fifteen tales, mostly animal fables
and exampla from East Nigeria.

660. Jenkins, Anthony W. "Henryson's 'The Fox, the Wolf and
      the Cadger' Again." *Studies in Scottish Literature*,
      4 (1966), 107-112.

      An examination of the relationship between Henryson's
      fable and the Roman de Renart, particularly the Meόn text,
      where it is found as the tenth episode. Most of the
      confusion apparently is due to variations in the texts
      of the *Roman de Renart*, which seem to be fairly well
      worked out with the Meόn version. Jenkins demonstrates
      Henryson's dependence upon the French text even if
      slightly overstressed.
      See: Denton Fox, *The Poems of Robert Henryson*.

661. Jensen, Richard C., and Marie Bahr-Volk. "The Fox and
      the Crab: Coluccio Saluti's Unpublished Fable."
      Studies in Philology, 73 (1976), 162-168.

      The Crab fable dates from the 1370's or 80's and is
      probably a product of Saluti's youth, written after he
      began his study of the classics. The fable survives
      in five manuscripts and seems to be dependent upon
      Isidor and his description of the clam and the crab.

662. Jochum, Klaus Peter. "Die Fabeln James Thurbers." *Die
      Fabel: Theorie, Geschichte und Rezeption einer Gattung*.
      Ed. Peter Hasubek. Berlin: Schmidt, 1982, 236-252.

      A comprehensive discussion of Thurber's fable activity
      with particular attention paid to his sources, his
      themes, and stylistic considerations. Notes Thurber's
      internal transformations within his fables and links
      Thurber's fabular themes to common elements throughout
      his works. Details Thurber's play upon the traditional
      expectations of the classical fable. Properly details
      the "humorist" in the fables in comparison to Ambrose
      Bierce and George Ade.

663. Johnston, O.M. "The Episode of Yvain, the Lion and
      the Serpent in Chretien de Trois." *Zeitschrift für
      französische Sprache*, 31 (1907), 157-166.

      Sees strong similarities between P563 "Lion and the
      Shephard" (A-T 156; TMI B381, B431.2) and P563A "Andro-
      cles and the Lion" and the episode in Yvain in which
      the hero saves the lion from the serpent. Surveys the

research and concludes that the episode is ultimately dependent upon a complex of stories which included both versions of the fable.

664. Jones, William Robert. "The Text Tradition of Avianus." Dissertation, University of Illinois at Urbana, 1940.

Works out a complex classification scheme to categorize and evaluate the known manuscripts of Avianus. See: Küppers, *Die Fabeln Avians*, and Gaide, *Avianus*.

665. ―――. "Avianus, Flavianus, Theodosius and Macrobius." *Classical Studies Presented to B.E. Perry by His Students and Colleagues at the University of Illinois, 1924-1960*. Illinois Studies in Language and Literature, no. 58. Urbana, Ill.: University of Illinois Press, 1969, 203-209.

Suggests the possible identification of Avianus with Flavianus, who was supposedly in favor with the Emperor Theodosius, to whom the fables of Avianus appear to have been dedicated.

666. Josifovic, Stevan. "Beiträge zur Geschichte der äsopischen Fabel." *Godisnjak: Jahrbuch der philosophischen Fakultät in Novi Sud*, 6 (1961), 92-117.

Surveys the literature on the history of the Aesopic fable, essentially from the beginning through the twentieth century. Deals with the problems of origin and relationships with other forms, especially the riddle. The term "fable" is determined to be a catch-all category, with the origin not easily decided although some theories are easily disposed of.

667. ―――. "Zum Artikel *Aisopos*." *Supplement*. *Paulys Realencyclopädie*, 14 (1974), cols. 15-40.

Wide-ranging and concise review of the research on the fable in the past half-century. Manuscripts and editions of the Greek fable and of some of the Latin materials. Discusses opinions on the various terms used for the fable and allied forms. The life and figure of Aesop as well as the fable associated with his name is reviewed. The last part of the article is a particularly valuable discussion of the types of fables, of character in the fable, of the uses and functions of the genre as well as the political, comic, satirical, and philosophical implications of the Aesopic fable and allied forms. Each section is provided with a bibliography of the most pertinent research.

668. Kaczynski, Bernice, and Haijo Jan Westra. "Aesop in
      the Middle Ages: The Transmission of the Sick Lion
      Fable and the Authorship of the St. Gall Version."
      Mittellateinisches Jahrbuch, 17 (1982), 31-38.

      Useful and well-researched study of the transmission
      of the complex formed by P258 "Sick Lion, Wolf and Fox"
      (A-T 50; TMI B240.6, K961), known in Byzantium in the
      ninth century and by P585 "Sick Lion, Fox and Bear"
      (A-T 50; TMI B240.4), known from the St. Gall MS 899
      from the end of the ninth or early tenth century. A
      connection between the Greek and the Latin versions is
      suggested as found in the process of fable production
      and use in teaching materials. The St. Gall fable is
      considered a new formation, demonstrating a conflict
      from the point of view of the abbey. Notker is put
      forth as a possible author.

669. Kahlo, G. "Planudes und Aesop." *Helikon*, 1 (1961),
      686-688.

      Stresses the importance of the fables of Aesop and
      the specific edition of both the fables and the *Vita
      Aesopi* by Planudes for the study and the status of
      folklore.

670. Kaiser, Herbert. "Die Pädagogisierung der Fabel am
      Ende des 18. und zu Begin des 19. Jahrhunderts." *Die
      Fabel: Theorie, Geschichte und Rezeption einer Gattung*.
      Ed. Peter Hasubek. Berlin: Schmidt, 1982, 163-179.

      Describes the forty or so years after Lessing's work
      with the fable as a period of the "trivialization" of
      the fable and a period in which the fable was turned
      to essentially pedagogical uses. This process was de-
      termined by the reception of the fable and the charac-
      teristics of eighteenth-century pedagogy. Examples of
      wide variety of uses of the fables during the period
      are given.

671. Kalischer, Elias. *Parabel und Fabel bei den alten
      Hebräern*. Dissertation, Erlangen, 1899.

      Lists and discusses a number of parables, extended
      proverbs, and contest tales, among which are found a
      few non-Aesopic fables.

672. Käuffer, J. "Die Fabel im Bauermunde." *Rheinische
      Geschichtsblätter*, 7 (1903-1904), 151-153.

Publishes a short Rheinish version of P15 "Fox and
Grapes" (A-T 59; TMI J871) in dialect with notes.

673. Kay, Helen. "In Quest of Ms. Mouse." *Children's
      Literature*, 3 (1974), 165-168.

Elementary, naive, and inaccurate account of P619
"Mouse in Search of a Mate" (TMI L392, Z42), which suggests that the Aesopic tale "spread to India," and that
the original of the *Panchatantra* still survives, inter
alia. All toward "tracing the varying social attitudes"
toward marriagable women.

674. Kayser, Wolfgang. "Die Grundlagen der deutschen Fabel-
      dichtung des 16. und 18. Jahrhunderts." *Archiv für
      das Studium der neueren Sprachen und Literaturen*, 160
      (1931), 19-33.

A seminal essay on popular attitudes toward literature
in general and the fable in particular as well as the
position of the fabulist toward his readership. Kayser
contrasts the sociological basis for the popularity of
the fable in the sixteenth century with that of the
eighteenth century on all levels: the popularity in
the first case is due to its appeal to religious
morality, the second because of its appeal to reason.
In both, the fable is a medium for education and enlightenment.

675. Keidel, George C. "Die Eselherz- (Hirschherz-, Eberherz-)
      fabel." *Zeitschrift für vergleichende Literatur*, NS 7
      (1893), 264-267.

Notes on the tradition of P583 "Pig without a Heart"
(TMI K402) and P336 "Sick Lion, Fox and Stag" (TMI
K402.3, K813).

676. ————. "An Early German Edition of Aesop's Fables."
      Modern Language Notes, 11 (1896), 46-48.

Describes an early edition of Heinrich Steinhöwel's
Esopus bequeathed to the Johns Hopkins Library. The
copy is an example of the German language version printed
after the deluxe bilingual *editio princeps*; the volume
is not complete.

677. ————. *A Manual of Aesopic Fable Literature*. Romance
      and Other Studies, no. 2. Baltimore: Johns Hopkins
      University Press, 1896.

A bibliography of 178 incunabula as well as numerous
other works and a few manuscripts partially described.
The prologue points out some of the problems to be
found in the history and evaluation of the Aesopic
fable at the turn of the century. Cross listings of
the chronological entries are provided by extant copies
(together with location), by author, cities and printers,
size, language, cities where preserved, and lists of
sale catalogues. With bibliography of secondary
materials, and various plates.

678. ————. "Notes on Aesopic Fable Literature in Spain
       and Portugal During the Middle Ages." *Zeitschrift
       für romanische Philologie*, 25 (1901), 721-730.

       Lists Iberian manuscript fable sources building upon
       the three manuscripts mentioned by Hervieux. Keidel
       gives sixteen, including three Walter of England and
       five Vincent of Beauvais manuscripts together with two
       old French collections, a Catalan work supposedly con-
       taining fables and a Greek collection, dated roughly
       1350 to 1500.

679. ————. "An Aesopic Fable in Old French Prose." *Ameri-
       can Journal of Philology*, 22 (1901), 78-79.

       Finds a prose version of an ape fable in a Biblio-
       thèque Nationale (fonds français 435) manuscript.

680. ————. "Notes on Fable Incunabula Containing the
       Planudean Life of Aesop." *Byzantinische Zeitschrift*,
       11 (1902), 461-467.

       An account of the oldest fable editions in Western
       European vernaculars which contain the Westermann ver-
       sion of the *Vita Aesopi* from the Bonus Accursius edi-
       tion (Milan, 1479) and various editions of the Rinuccio
       D'Arezzo (here called Rimicius) collection.

681. ————. "The Edition Princeps of the Greek Aesop."
       American Journal of Philology, 24 (1903), 304-317.

       Description of the ten known copies of the first
       printed edition of Aesop's fables in Greek by Bonus
       Accursius in 1480: one in Florence, three in London,
       one in the John Rylands Library in Manchester, one in
       Munich, two in Oxford (Bodleian), one in Paris (BN),
       and one in the Library of Congress in Washington.

682. ———. "The History of French Fable Manuscripts."
    Publications of the Modern Language Association, 24
    (1909), 207–219.

    General bibliographical survey of Old French Fable
    manuscripts containing Aesopica together with a his-
    torical account of known collections. Lists 24 Marie
    de France manuscripts; one of the *Avionnet de York*;
    6 manuscripts of the *Avionnet de Paris*; one each of the
    Ysopet de Chartes, the *Ysopet de Lyon*, the *Ysopet de
    Chettenham*, *Avionnet de Milan*, *Ysopet de Milan*, 6 of
    the *Ysopet I de Paris*; 10 of Jehan de Vignay's *Ysopet
    de la Mireoir Histrial*; 2 of the *Ysopet II de Paris*,
    one of the Julien Macho version of Steinhöwel, 2 manu-
    scripts of the *Dialogue des Creatures* and one of the
    Ysopet III de Paris. A few general conclusions.
    See: Bastin, *Recueil général des Isopets*.

683. ———. "Problems in Medieval Fable Literature."
    Studies in Honor of A. Marshall Elliott. Vol. 1.
    Baltimore: The Johns Hopkins Press (1911), 281–303.

    Outlines a number of problems that had not yet been
    adequately investigated: the lines of transmission be-
    tween the classical fable and the Latin fable which
    emerged after the "Dark Ages"; Greek influence during
    the Middle Ages, lines of communication involving
    crusaders and pilgrims, and the role of the Byzantine
    fable during the Middle Ages. The lack of a comprehen-
    sive bibliography highlights the serious difficulties
    concerning the interrelationships of texts. Ends with
    an excellent bibliography to the end of the nineteenth
    century.

684. Keith-Falconer, I.G.N. *Kalilah and Dimnah, or the
    Fables of Bidpai*. Cambridge: Cambridge University
    Press, 1885. 320 pp.

    Contains a translation of the Syriac versions with
    synopses of longer pieces and an extensive introduction.
    Notes to the stories include a detailed accounting of
    the various origins of the elements of the collection.
    The texts are identified by language.

685. Keller, J.E., and J.H. Johnson. "Motif-Index Classifi-
    cation of Fable and Tales of *Ysopete Ystoriado*."
    Southern Folklore Quarterly, 18 (1954), 85–117.

    Presents a motif index following the general scheme
    of TMI numbers for the *Ysopete Ystoriado*, first printed

in Saragossa in 1489 and containing 173 fables and other
short forms.

686. Keller, Otto. *Die Schildkröte im Altertum.* Prag: Ver-
     lag des wissenschaftlichen Vereins für Volkskunde
     und Linguistik, 1897. 14 pp.

     Presents a comprehensive treatment of the turtle
     in classical times, its use as medicine, as musical
     instruments, and in tradition and literature, including
     its mention in fables.

687. Kennerly, Karen. *Hesitant Wolf and Scrupulous Fox.*
     New York: Random House, 1973.

     The introduction to this eclectic collection, brought
     together "to free the fable from constrictions of genre
     and of external form," contains much insightful thought
     but no clear statements about the fables in an ordered
     form. In comparing the fable to other forms, the author
     denies the fable the possibilities of satire or of
     allegory, and makes a curious distinction between the
     fable and the folktale, apparently equating this with
     the *Märchen.* Some interesting thoughts on characteriza-
     tion. Biographical sketches of some of the fabulists
     and an index of fables are included.

688. Ketelsen, Uwe-K. "Vom Siege der natürlichen Venunft:
     Einige Bemerkungen zu einer sozial-geschichtlichen
     Interpretation der Geschichte der Fabel in der
     deutschen Aufklärung." *Seminar,* 16 (1980), 208-23.

     An initial foray into the far-reaching questions of
     the development of literature and the justification of
     creating literary categories in the Formalist sense.
     The fable is examined in the social-historical context
     of the Enlightenment. The fable in pre-eighteenth-
     century Germany is not given autonomous genre-status.
     In the early Enlightenment it is connected with all
     other forms of Literature and was raised into a genre
     of Rationalization by Gottscheid and Christian Wolff.
     It was already outdated by the time of Lessing.

689. Khinoy, Stephan. "Tale-Moral Relationships in Henry-
     son's *Moral Fables.*" *Studies in Scottish Literature,*
     17 (1982), 99-115.

     Investigates the relationship of the moral to the nar-
     ration of the fables of Robert Henryson. The morals
     are not arbitrary and are central to Henryson's view of

art. The morals are used to teach his readership interpretation of figurative texts and proper perspective
on life. Narrative structures are closely examined.

690. Kindrick, Robert L. "Lion or Cat? Henryson's Characterization of James III." *Studies in Scottish Literature*, 14 (1979), 123-136.

This article is an attempt to delineate Henryson's
political viewpoints by examination of the political
satire in his *Moral Fables*. Henryson is a monarchist
although his attitude toward James III is complex.
James is identified here with the cat in Henryson's
"The Two Mice" P352, "The Country Mouse and the City
Mouse" (A-T 112; TMI J211.2) and as a Lion in "The
Trial of the Fox" P638, "Ass with Privilege, Fox and
Wolf" (TMI J1608) perhaps also as the Shepherd in the
"Taill of the Wolf and the Wether," P705 "Dog, Wolf and
Ram" (A-T 126; TMI J950, K1839.3.1) with the wolf most
likely referring to the rebellious barons.

691. ———. *Robert Henryson*. Boston: Twayne, 1979.

Well-rounded study of Robert Henryson and his works.
Chapter three deals with the fables, which he compares
to Chaucer in scope and which "illustrate the finest
literary techniques of both the allegorist and the
realist." The dates, witnesses, and sources are discussed. The prologue of each of the fables considered
to be a fundamental key for the understanding of the
text; extensive commentary on each of the fables including
an analysis of the social and political commentary that
is seen there. Excellent short bibliography.
See: Denton Fox, *The Poems of Robert Henryson*.

692. Kindstrand, Jan Fredrik. "The Greek Concept of Proverbs."
Eranos, 76 (1978), 71-85.

Deals in detail with the interest in the proverb found
among ancient Greek writers and in passing with that of
the Aesopic fable as being very close to the proverb
from a stylistic point of view. Both forms stress conciseness. Any attempt to find a clear distinction would
be mere speculation.

693. Kinzel, Karl. "Gottschick: Über Boners Fabeln." *Zeitschrift für deutsche Philologie*, 19 (1897), 255-256.

A review of Gottschick's work on Boner, generally
favorable, with a few suggestions on sources and influences.

694. Klinger, Witold. *Ze stujow nad liryka grecka*. Philo-
      logical Series, 62. Warsaw: Polish Academy, 1930.

      The first essay deals with the fragments of Archi-
      lochus' version of Pl "Eagle and Fox" (TMI K2295,
      L315.3) and its connection to Lycambes.

695. ————. "Dzisiejszy baśń o rybaky i złotej rebcei
      jej strogreckie korzenie." *Eos: Commentarii Societatis
      Philologae Polonorum*, 51 (1961), 217-227.

      On the origin of a complex of tales and fables with
      talking fish and fish with gold. Connects P18 "Fisher-
      man with Little Fish" (TMI J321.12) with P173 "Hermes
      and Woodcutter" (A-T 729; TMI F420.5.1.7, Q3.1), and
      investigates the transmission of tales from India.

696. Knab, Bernard M. *Otto Knab's Fox-Fables*. Pullman,
      Washington: Washington State University Press, 1966.

      Historical account of the *Fuchsenfabeln* by Otto
      Michael Knab, a series of anti-Nazi satirical fables,
      which began to appear in the *Deutsche Briefe* in Switzer-
      land in 1936. There are twenty-one fables. Generally
      mirroring Nazi totalitarianism and forming a loosely
      connected beast epic. Extensive commentary, texts, and
      notes.

697. Knapp, Fritz Peter. *Das lateinische Tierepos*. Darm-
      stadt: Wissenschaftliche Buchgesellschaft, 1979.
      x + 178 pp.

      Comprehensive treatment of the Latin Beast epic of
      the Middle Ages. Begins with *Ysengrimus* and the *Ecbasis
      Captivi*, discussing the transmission and origin of the
      form and material as well as stylistic considerations.
      The concept of the Beast Epic as literary genre leads
      to an attempt to define certain narrative genres, in-
      cluding the fable. Knapp sees a progressive evolution
      from the fable to the "Tierschwank" to the Beast Epic.

698. ————. "Das mittelalterliche Tierepos: Zur Genese
      und Definition eines grossepischen Literaturgattung."
      Sprachkunst: Beiträge zur Literaturwissenschaft, 10
      (1979), 53-68.

      Essentially a condensed reworking of Knapp's *Das
      lateinische Tierepos* (q.v.) although the historical
      presentation and the progression from *Tierfabel* to
      Tierschwank to *Tierepos* is perhaps more easily appreciated

in the shortened form. Suggests that those working
in the Middle Ages within the genre of "Tierschwank"
to Beast Epic would have agreed with the medieval designation of *fabula* for what they were composing.

699. Knöll, Pius. *Die Babrianischen Fabeln des Cod. bod-
      leinus 2906*. Program, Vienna, 1876. 32 pp.

      Discusses in detail the prose paraphrases of Babrius
      found in the 148-fable collection in folios 163^V-192^V
      of the Codex Bodleianus, Auct. F.4.7 once no. 2906.
      The readings are of little importance for the text of
      Babrius.

700. ———. *Fabularum Babrianarum Paraphrasis Bodleinana*.
      Vienna: Hölder, 1877.

      Edition with extensive apparatus from two other manu-
      scripts in the same tradition of the 148 prose paraphrase
      of Babrian fables in the Codex Bodleianus (Auct. F.4.7),
      dating from the thirteenth century. Introduction and
      index.

701. ———. "Neue Fabeln des Babrius." *Sitzungsbericht
      der philosophisch-historische Klasse der Akademie der
      Wissenschaften in Wien*, 91 (1878), 659-690.

      Describes the Codex Vaticanus Gr. 777 dating from
      the fifteenth century and containing thirty fables of
      Babrius in choliambic verse scattered throughout numerous
      other fables in prose from various other sources.
      Twelve fables here are not in the Codex Athous; six
      of which are published as an appendix.

702. ———. "Zum Codex Athous und zum ersten Prooemium
      des Babrios." *Wiener Studien*, 3 (1881), 184-195.

      Investigates the manuscript tradition of Babrius
      preparatory to an edition of the Babrian fables, which
      did not appear. Describes the Codex Athous in the
      British Museum, especially the paleographic features.

703. ———. *Die Athoshandschrift des Babrios*. *Wiener
      Studien*, 31 (1909), 200-210.

      On those points in the Codex Athous rendered illegible
      by the second hand in the manuscript. The second hand
      appears to be not much younger than the first (tenth
      century); the third considerably later. Numerous textual
      notes, readings, and suggested emendations to Crusius'
      edition.

704. Knust, Hermann. "Steinhöwel's Äsop." *Zeitschrift für deutsche Philologie*, 19 (1887), 197-218; 20 (1888), and 237.

Consists of a listing of all editions and reprints of Steinhöwel's "Esopus" (ca. 1476) as well as most translations. The contents of most editions are listed insofar as they vary from the original. The additions to the Caxton version are reprinted as well as very extensive sections from the Spanish edition of 1484.
See: Carnes, "Heinrich Steinhöwel."

705. Koch, Ruth. "Die Fabel als didaktisches Problem des Literaturunterrichts." Dissertation, Marburg, 1973. Published as *Theoriebildung und Lernzielentwicklung in der Literaturdidaktik--ein Entwurf gegenstands-orientierter Lernzielentwicklung am Beispiel der Fabel*. Weinheim: Beltz, 1973. 298 pp. (= Marburger Pädagogische Studien, Neue Folge, no. 13).

This thoroughgoing treatment of the fable as a didactic unit in German elementary instruction is in fact a comprehensive work on the history of fable theory, of the sociological aspects of the fable, and on the fable in pedagogy in general. Extensive study of the form and structure of the fable. The fable is also used as a medium for insights into sociological and historical changes in literary forms. With notes and bibliography.

706. ————. "Erneuerung der Fabel in der zweiten Hälfte des 20. Jahrhunderts?" *Die Fabel: Theorie, Geschichte und Rezeption einer Gattung*. Berlin: Schmidt, 1982, 253-271.

Suggests a renaissance of sorts in the modern fable, in which there is a release from the traditional themes. The modern fable sees the animal in man, rather than the man in the animal. Social criticism is a primary subject and function of the modern fable in its early stages, the postwar stage; Thurber, Helmut Arntzen, and Wolfdietrich Schnurre are all social critics but deal with the problems of human existence. Form, structure (the loss of the epimythium), and the humor in the irony of traditional materials are all characteristic of the modern fable.
See: Carnes, "The Fable Joke."

707. Koep, L. "Fabel." *Realexikon für Antik und Christentum*.

Vol. 7. Ed. Theodor Klauser. Stuttgart: Hiersemann, 1966, 128-154.

An exhaustive history of the fable beginning with the concept and definition of the form, surveying its tradition in Egypt and the Near East with special attention paid to the Old Testament. The classical forms of Aesop, Phaedrus, and Babrius are covered in context followed by an investigation of the origins of the genre and its use in various art forms. A discussion of the fable (actually as parable) in the New Testament and in Patristic writings and its use in sermons and in iconography ends this informative article.

708. Kohler, L. *Die Fabel von der Stadt- und Feldmaus in der deutschen Literatur.* Program, Mährish-Osorau, 1909.

A chronological survey of P352 "Country Mouse and City Mouse" (A-T 112; TMI J211.2), with mention of classical forms (Horace, Phaedrus), and German versions (Boner, Gerhard von Minden, as well as Steinhöwel, Luther and Waldis).
See: Jacob, "Le rat de ville et le rat de champs."

709. Kohn, Renée. *Le Goût de La Fontaine.* Paris: Presses Universitaires de France, 1962. 457 pp.

Begins with the idea of "le goût" that was so very important for La Fontaine and his contemporaries. Three chapters are devoted to the fables; three themes are distinguished in the first edition: the man and his natural environs, his future, and his liberty. The second edition of the fables is discussed in terms of the political and philosophical character of the fables, with special attention to the narrative techniques in various aspects of the lyrical form. Includes illustrations from La Fontaine's fables and from other earlier editions.

710. ──────. "La Fontaine et le merveilleux." *Cahiers de l'Association Internationale des Études Français,* 26 (1974), 117-129.

La Fontaine's concern with the marvelous is difficult to define, as much is found within satire and parody. The metamorphosis of Ulysses' men in 12, 5 "Les Compagnons d'Ulysse" demonstrates a rare concern with the marvelous. La Fontaine's long and intimate involvement with the sources of his fables brought him into close touch with numerous fabulous tales and mythic elements.

711. König, Karl. "Der elsässische Fabeldichter Gottlieb
     Conrad Pfeffel. Ein Charakterbild aus der Zeit der
     elsässischen Schicksalswende um 1800." *Elsass-
     Lothringen*, 12 (1934), 113-116; 156-161; 215-224.

     A sociological presentation of the external factors
     and the poet's mental condition that helped to shape
     various sides of Gottlieb Conrad Pfeffel's character
     and work. Pfeffel's fabular output, consisting of
     over three hundred pieces, is shown to be very much
     representative of his time.

712. Könneker, Barbara. "Die Rezeption der aesopischen Fabel
     in der deutschen Literatur des Mittelalters und der
     frühen Neuzeit." *Die Rezeption der Antike: Zum
     Problem der Kontinuität zwischen Mittelalter und
     Renaissance*. Wolfenbütteler Abhandlungen zur
     Renaissanceforschung, I. Ed. August Buck. Hamburg:
     Hauswedell, 1981, 209-224.

     A highly interesting, if highly speculative, essay on
     the reception of the German language fable from the
     thirteenth century to the beginning of the sixteenth.
     Könneker sees two types of fables, the "Moral Type,"
     typified by P133 "Dog and Meat" (A-T 34; TMI J1791.4);
     and the "Social Type," as exemplified by P149 "Lion's
     Share" (A-T 51; TMI J811.1). The latter type is the
     more common, and this is partly the key to understanding
     the reception of the vernacular fable. The fact that
     the fable is aimed more at worldly conditions, to the
     ideas of injury and usefulness and the like in contrast
     to addressing such questions as good and evil, leads
     Könneker to the idea that the fable had to wait for
     social progress that would demonstrate this difference
     in actual social organization on the one hand and a
     relaxation of the hold on literature the clergy had on
     the other. The progress from Stricker through Boner
     to Steinhöwel along these lines is investigated, which
     also suggests an answer to the very negative response
     by Martin Luther to the Steinhöwel collection.

713. Körner, Renate. "Die russische Rezeption von Ewald
     Christian von Kleists Fabel "Der gelähmte Kranich.'"
     Festschrift für Alfred Rammelmeyer. Ed. Hans-Bernd
     Harder. Munich: Fink, 1975, 111-122.

     An investigation of the Russian response to Ewald von
     Kleist's fable from the pre-1802 translation by Radiščev
     and other early nineteenth-century translations with

particular reference to the reason for the Russian
interest in the motif, which is most likely the elegaic-
sentimental character of the work.

714. Korsch, Th. "Ad Babrium." *Filologiczesskoje obozrjen-
ije*, 7: 1 (1895), 125-130.

Treats Babrius 97, P143 "Lion and Bull" (TMI J644.1.2)
in context, and presumes that a proverb underlies the
epimythic last verse concerning the sacrificial victim.

715. Kosack, Wolfgang. "Der Gattungsbegriff 'Volkserzählung.'"
Fabula, 12 (1971), 18-47.

An attempt to come to grips with the lack of a precise definition for "folk narrative" terms of all sorts,
including the fable. Concentrates upon the *Märchen*
with passing reference made to other forms, including
the fable, which is classed as within the prose narrative
group as opposed to the rhythmic narrative forms. Examples are given from Arabic and Coptic folk narratives.

716. Kötz, Otto. "Der Sprachgebrauch La Fontaines in seinen
Fabeln." *Die neueren Sprachen*, 17 (1906), 257-278;
321-401; 402-420.

Wide-ranging and only loosely connected thoughts on
La Fontaine's language and style, interesting for the
demonstration that modern colloquial French is very
close to some La Fontaine usage. Kötz lists a number
of specific instances of "folk speech" that certainly
proceeded from the *Fables*.

717. Kovacs, Ruth Stafford. "The Aesopic Fable in Ancient
Rhetorical Theory and Practice." Dissertation,
Illinois (Urbana), 1950. Abstract: Urbana: Univer-
sity of Illinois Press, 1950. 6 pp.

Identifies and discusses various uses of the Aesopic
fable in classical and Hellenistic Roman texts as well
as in theoretical treatments of the form. Works from
the views of Hausrath who had asserted that the texts
in the most ancient collections represent schoolboys'
exercises. Hausrath and others had then maintained
that the use of the fables as described by the ancient
rhetoricians represented something later and unclassical.
The problem is one of collections. Kovacs argues
against the theories established on the basis of fables
in the Halm collection, as the fables were not, on all
available evidence, commonly in collections but conformed

to the earliest rhetorical theory, that of Aristotle,
who defined the fables as essentially a rhetorical
device. The first known collection, that of Demetrius
of Phalerum, was almost certainly a rhetor's handbook
of sorts. If the Rylands papyrus 493 is in fact a survival of that collection, then the promythic elements
confirm this function.

718. Kožešnik, Karl. "Kunstproblem und Moral in La Fontaines
      Fabeln." *Zeitschrift für französische Sprache und
      Literatur*, 56 (1932), 479-490.

      Review article prompted by the appearance of F. Gohin's
      L'art de La Fontaine dans ses fables, 1929. Kožešnik's
      conception of the relationship of art and didactic
      content in La Fontaine is compared to see-sawing back
      and forth with the moral and the wisdom materials of
      society.

719. Kragelund, P., and J. Krogh, M. Skafte Jensen, and
      K. Friis-Jensen. "Fabel og samfund." *Museum Tuscu-
      lanum* (Copenhagen), 32-33 (1978), 55-75.

      Discusses the role of the narrator in the Phaedrine
      tales and the social classes displayed within the fables.
      Discusses P339 "Lion and Ass, Partners in the Hunt"
      (A-T 51; TMI J811.1.1) in detail; and the order of
      nature in this and other fables.

720. Kramer, Samuel N. *From the Tablets of Sumer: Twenty-
      Five Firsts in Man's Recorded History*. Indian Hills,
      Col.: Falcon's Press, 1956. (Reprinted as *History
      Begins as Sumer*.)

      Chapter seventeen "Aesopica: The First Animal Tales,"
      describes the recording of Aesopic type fables a full
      thousand years before Aesop and suggests that they
      might be considerably older. Most have no modern
      equivalents, but some are similar im motif and a few
      are identical to Aesopica. Most of the examples are
      in the form of proverbs.
      See: Lambert, "Babylonian Wisdom Literature."

721. Kranz, Dieter. "Ambivalente Formen des 'style indirect
      libre' in der Fabeln La Fontaines." *Archiv für
      Studium der neueren Sprachen*, 207 (1970), 36-42.

      The lines drawn among direct, indirect and "erlebte"
      speech are directed toward discussion of seven of La
      Fontaine's *Fables*. This stylistic mechanism is used

effectively by La Fontaine, especially as "ambivalent
forms" which Kranz prefers. These forms are also used
to repeat actual dialogue.

722. Krappe, Alexander Haggerly. "The Source of Detlev von
Liliencron's *Abschied.*" *Journal of English and Germanic
Philology*, 25 (1926), 79-83.

Finds a strong parallel between Liliencron's poem and
P299 "Farmer and the Tree" (TMI J241.2) and notes the
usage of the motif by Florian and by Pfeffel (1793).

723. Kratz, Bernd. "Maulesel und Maus auf der Suche nach
einer Braut." *Niederdeutsches Jahrbuch*, 91 (1968),
87-92.

Deals essentially with the use of "nul" as the main
character in the Wolfenbütteler Äsop's version of P619
"Mouse in Quest of a Mate" (TMI L392, Z42), perhaps
evidence of the author using a particular Latin model
with "mulus".

724. Kreis, Rudolf. "Fabel und Tiergleichnis." *Project
Deutschunterricht*, 1 (1971), 57-103.

This comprehensive essay on the pedagogical potential
of the fable begins with an attempt to define both the
form and a methodology that might be valid in understanding it, concluding that the fable must be seen
in its historical context. Deals with the "dialectical"
structure of the form, and this is followed by interesting
text interpretations of a long list of fables from
various authors for various levels in school. Fables
from Pestalozzi, Lessing, La Fontaine, Krylov, Busch,
Kirsten, Kreis, Schnurre, and Thurber as well as classical versions are interpreted. Theoretical material
from Lessing is introduced and the essay ends with
Kafka's parables.

725. Kreisler, Nicolai von. "Satire in *The Fox and the Wolf.*"
Journal of English and Germanic Philology, 69 (1970),
650-658.

Discovers a rich pattern of allusion in the Middle
English poem with priests as its target. The satire
beneath the surface humor is best seen by considering
the tale in relationship to the French sources or
parallels. The Wolf thus also emerges as a target.

726. ———. "An Aesopic Allusion in the Merchant's Tale."
      Chaucer Review, 6 (1971), 30-37.

      Sees an allusion to P119 "Gardener Watering his Vege-
      tables" (TMI J1033) from the *Vita Aesopi* in the phrases
      "panger ful of herbes/ of scole-termes" in "The Mer-
      chant's Tale"; supposing oral transmission from the
      Byzantine tradition.

727. ———. "Henryson's Visionary Fable: Tradition and
      Craftsmanship in the 'Lyoun and the Mous.'" *Texas
      Studies in Literature and Language*, 15 (1973), 391-
      403.

      Henryson's version of P563/P563A "Lion and Shepherd/
      Androcles" (A-T 156; TMI B381) is considered the most
      innovative of all the *Moral Fables*, particularly because
      of the frame in which Aesop appears in a dream, thus
      fusing dream-vision literature to fable literature. A
      discussion of the political cast of the fable leads
      Von Kreisler to suggest that Henryson meant to deliver
      an admonishment to king and country. The dream-vision
      frame softens the imperative.

728. Krohn, Kaarle. *Bär (Wolf) und Fuchs*. Helsinki, 1886.

      A classic using the historical-geographical method
      to investigate P625 "Wolf as Fisherman and the Fox"
      (A-T 2 "Tail Fisher"; TMI K1021), P693 "Unlucky Wolf,
      Fox and Mule" (A-T 47; TMI K551.18) and other fox and
      wolf tales and fables. Krohn deals with literary and
      orally circulated versions.

729. ———. *Mann und Fuchs*. Helsingfors, 1891.

      Deals with numerous versions of P176 "The Man who
      warmed a Snake" (A-T 155; TMI J1172.3), generally with
      a bear or fox. Treats the tales (also type 154, and
      others) in eleven literary and twenty-six oral forms.
      Krohn confirms the very small influence of the animal
      epic upon the tale and suggests the original form must
      have been an Egyptian one with a crocodile.
              See: McKenzie, "An Italian Fable," and Draak, "Is
      Ondank."

730. Kruyskamp, C. "Van de os op de ezel." *Tijdschrift voor
      Nederlandse Taal- en Letterkunde*, 81 (1965), 85-93.

      This article deals with the titular Dutch proverbial
      phrase and working out from that phrase discusses a

number of related texts including fables with asses and oxen.

731. Krzyzanowski, Julian. "Sprichwort und Märchen in der polnischer Volkserzählung." *Volksüberlieferung: Festschrift für Kurt Ranke zur Vollendung des 60. Lebenjahres.* Ed. Fritz Harkort et al. Göttingen: Schwartz, 1968, 151-158.

This essay discusses the possibility of the generation of proverbs from various forms of folktales, including fables. The relationship of proverbs to other forms of folk literature is complex, but many Polish proverbs seem to come from reduced forms of longer narratives.

732. Kumaniecki, Casimir Felix. "De Aesopi Vita supplenda." *Aegyptus*, 13 (1933), 51-52.

Fills in a number of gaps in the papyrus tradition of the *Vita Aesopi* as published in the Westermann text.

733. Küppers, Jochen. *Die Fabeln Avians: Studien zu Darstellung und Erzählweise spätantiker Fabeldichtung.* Bonn: Habelt, 1977. 252 pp.

Küppers spends much energy in reordering Avianus research by setting aside the previous work of Ellis and Herrmann especially, and to a lesser extent, Crusius and Cameron, as well as Jones and Thraede. Küppers deals with all the major issues: the name of the poet, the *Theodosio* problem, and the origin of the fables themselves. Küppers deals with the divergences from the Babrian original as Avianus' own artistic contribution and argues for Avianus' translation as coming directly out of the Greek, rather than through a Latin intermediary. Full and useful bibliographies and indices.

734. Küster, Christian Ludwig. *Illustrierte Aesop-Ausgaben des 15. und 16. Jahrhunderts.* Dissertation, Hamburg, 1970. 324 pp. + 253 illustrations.

This dissertation is a particularly useful detailed listing and comprehensive description with examples of the illustrated editions of Aesopica during the fifteenth and sixteenth centuries beginning with Steinhöwel and carrying through Italian, French, and other editions. The study contains extensive listings of iconographic motifs, a summary of fable illustration history, and a bibliography.

735. Labriolle, F. de. "Krylov et La Fontaine." *Revue de
      la littérature Comparée*, 40 (1966), 91-109.

      Informative discussion of the borrowings from La Fon-
      taine by Krylov. Deals also with the years various
      fables were adapted and the type of adaptation prac-
      ticed by Krylov. Krylov's work is hardly to be con-
      sidered translation from La Fontaine, but rather a
      specialized type of adaptation. Labriolle compares
      the forms of satire common to both fabulists as well
      as characterizations within the fables themselves.

736. Lafay, Henri. "*L'Homme et la Couleuvre* ou la parole
      de La Fontaine: Analyse de fonctionnement textuel,"
      Mélanges offerts à Georges Couton. Lyon: Presses
      Universitaires de Lyon, 1981, 373-382.

      An interesting stylistic, specifically an inter-
      textual, analysis of the language and information
      transferal technique of La Fontaine's version of P640
      "Soldier and Serpent" with the often noted inversion
      of action. The material is analyzed under the rubrics
      "Parole fable," "Fable parole," "Texte anaphore," and
      "Texte figure."

737. La Fontaine, Gilles Emilio de. "Les interventions per-
      sonnelles de La Fontaine dans ses fables." Disserta-
      tion, The Ohio State University, 1965. 268 pp.

      An extended discussion of the nearly 250 personal
      interventions of La Fontaine into his fables, divided
      into various categories, all examined with regard to
      content and technique with a view toward establishing
      the direct contribution of personal intrusion to the
      aesthetics of the poetry. Each author intrusion is
      examined within the context of the fable in question.
      One of the most interesting aspects is the extreme
      variety of intrusions, ranging from the satirical to
      the comic, from the objective to the very subjective.
      La Fontaine's shifting viewpoints are expounded, il-
      luminating a number of aspects of the poet's literary
      techniques.

738. ―――. *La Fontaine dans ses fables: Comment l'homme
      perce à travers l'oeuvre*. Ottawa: Le Cercle du Livre
      de France, 1966. 252 pp.

      Essentially an expanded rewrite of the author's dis-
      sertation (see above) with an introduction identifying
      La Fontaine and his place in the history of fable writing

and narrowing down the subject to the subject in the
main portion of the text: the idea of the personal interventions, remarks, and digressions found in the
Fables.

739. Lall, Rama Rani. *Satirical Fables in English: A Critical Study of the Animal Tales of Chaucer, Spenser,
Dryden and Orwell*. New Delhi: New Statesman Publishing, 1979.

An investigation of the animal tales and allusions
to animal tales in the authors mentioned in the title,
including superficial mention of a few titles. Generally
concerned with the allegorical use of animals in satirical pieces.

740. Lambel, Hans. *Lessing, Abhandlungen über die Fabel für
den Schulgebrauch herausgegeben*. Leipzig: Witzel,
1920. 25 pp.

An introduction to Lessing's fable theory and a
general survey of the literature in an edition meant
for school use. Lambel emphasizes Lessing's freeing of
the fable from its literary genre and his views on the
action and the narrative of the form.

741. Lambert, W.G. *Babylonian Wisdom Literature*. Oxford:
Clarendon Press, 1960. Especially pages 150-212.

This very well-presented volume contains a general
introduction to the fable and its position in Sumerian
and Akkadian. In addition to the Aesopic type of fable
and the proverbial fable fragment, Lambert also describes
and provides texts for the verbal contest sort of fable
which had a wide distribution throughout the Middle
East. Provides numerous fabular motifs in the text,
especially "Eagle and Snake" and "Tamarisk and Palm"
both of which have Aesopic reflexes: P1 "Eagle and Fox"
(TMI K2295; L315.3) and P439 "Laurel and Olive" (TMI
J411.7).

742. Lämke, Dora. *Mittelalterliche Tierfabeln und ihre
Beziehungen zur bildenden Kunst in Deutschland*.
Dissertation, Greifswald, 1937. 112 pp. Printed
Greifswald: Universitätsverlag L. Bamberg, 1937.

Excellent presentation of the use of fabular motifs
in the iconography of the Middle Ages, especially in
churches and cloisters. Begins with an analysis of
the use of the fable in the medieval sermon, in the

school and in literature compared to its use in illustrations. The use of illustrations, especially in the
church, is then detailed, and the author ends with a
detailed study of the four most popular motifs found
in the plastic arts during the Middle Ages: P426 "Fox
and Stork" (A-T 60; TMI J1565.1), P156 "Wolf and Heron"
(A-T 76; TMI W154.3), P688 "Wolf learning his Letters,"
and various forms of P671 "Fox and Dove" (A-T 62;
TMI J1421). With illustrations and bibliography.

743. Lancaster, H. Carrington. "The Sources and Medieval
     Versions of the Peace-Fable." *Publications of the
     Modern Language Association*, 22 (1907), 33-53.

     Lengthy, detailed investigation of P671 "Fox and Dove"
     (A-T 62; TMI J1421) in over thirty versions from
     Ysengrimus to Guillaume Tardif (ca. 1490) together with
     dozens of versions in the modern era indicated. Lan-
     caster sees a tripartite stemmata, with the original
     form the ancestor of the Ysengrimus, Romulus, and
     Renart versions. All other forms listed can be derived
     from these three. The original form apparently had a
     fox with either a cock or a dove. With an appended
     "version tree" and bibliography.
     See: Lumpkin, "Fox and Goose."

744. Lanckorońska, Maria. "Der Zeichner der Illustrationen
     des Ulmer Aesop." *Gutenberg-Jahrbuch* (1966), 278-
     283.

     Cursory investigation, without definitive results,
     into the questions of the identity and the tradition
     of the illustrator of the Heinrich Steinhöwel *Esopus*
     of 1476/77.
     See: Küster, *Illustrierte Aesop-Ausgaben*.

745. Landwehr, John. *Fable-Books Printed in the Low Coun-
     tries*. Nieuwkoop: De Graaf, 1963. xvii + 43 pp.

     Bibliography of editions of Aesopica from various
     sources: most general European fable collections,
     especially in Latin, and translations from these into
     Dutch and Flemish, as well as original collections in
     these languages. Begins with the introduction of
     printing (Lorenzo Valla's collection, printed in Utrecht
     in 1472) with over 300 entries through the seventeenth
     century. Well-detailed materials with an index.

746. Langemeyer, Gerhard. "Aesopus in Europa: Bemerkungen

zur politisch-satirisch Graphik des Romeyn de Hooghe."
Dissertation, Münster, 1973. 238 pp.

Describes Romeyn de Hooghe (1645-1706) as Aesop first
for his graphically realistic and satirical style and
for the *physiologus* interpretation of animal subjects.

747. La Penna, Antonio. "La morale della favola esopica
come morale delle classc subalterne nell'antichita."
Societa, 17 (1961), 459-537.

A detailed and comprehensive, if not entirely con-
vincing, investigation of the congruence of the morals
of the traditional Aesopic corpus with society. La
Penna deals with an impressive list of examples and
concludes that the Aesopic fable expresses in simple
form the observations and the opinions, to a limited
extent and in simple form, of simple, ordinary folk.

748. ————. "Il Romanzo di Esopo." *Athenaeum*, 40 (1962),
264-314.

In an extensive investigation of the *Vita Aesopi*, La
Penna examines the relationship of the G redaction to
the W with particular emphasis upon those points in
which the W might conserve original readings. The G
redaction appears to have originated in Syria or in
Palestine, the W in Sicily. The relationship of the
Vita to the Babylonian *Ahiqar* and to oral tradition is
stressed as are the strong differences between the
Vita and other types of Aesopic material.

749. ————. "Marginalis Aesopica." *Miscellanea Terzaghi*.
Genoa: University of Genoa Institute of Classical
and Medieval Philology, 1963, 227-236.

Critical notes to passages in Phaedrus and medieval
fables and textual notes to Aesopica in Greek. Variant
readings, emendation suggestions, and ideas for interpretations.

750. ————. "Letteratura esopica e letteratura assiro-
babilonese." *Rivista di filologia e di istruzione
classica*, 92 (1964), 24-39.

Very interesting, well-detailed analysis of some of
the connections between Assyrian-Babylonian literary
materials and the Aesopic fable tradition. Treats a
number of motifs shared by both traditions, especially
the connection found between Archilochus' P1 "Eagle

and Fox" (TMI K2295, L315.3) and the myth cycle of
Etana. The *Vita Aesopi* is also related to Babylonian
material.
See: Williams, "The Literary History of a Mesopotamian
Fable."

751. ———. "Il ritratto paradossale da Stil a Petronio."
      Rivista di filologia e di istruzione classica, 104
      (1976), 270-293.

      This lengthy article contains a short section on
      Phaedrus comparing the stylistic features of Phaedrus
      and Petronius.

752. Larkin, Neil M. "Another Look at Dante's Frog and
      Mouse." *Modern Language Notes*, 77 (1962), 94-99.

      Discusses Dante's allusion to P384 "Mouse and Frog"
      (A-T 278; TMI J681.1) in the twenty-third Canto of the
      Inferno. In contrast to most commentators, Larkin
      suggests that the demons be equated to the role of the
      frog and that of Dante and Virgil are represented by
      the mouse.

753. ———. "Inferno XXIII, 4-9 Again." *Modern Language
      Notes*, 81 (1966), 85-88.

      Deals with Pudoan's essay on Dante's allusion to P384
      "Mouse and Frog" (A-T 278; TMI J681.1). Larkin re-
      affirms his original identification of Dante and Virgil
      as the mouse and the demons as the frog.

754. Laubscher, G.C. "Notes on the Spanish *Ysopo* of 1496."
      Modern Language Notes, 24 (1909), 70-71.

      The edition is identified as a Spanish version of
      the Steinhöwel collection with fables added from an
      unknown source.

755. Laufer, Roger. "Genre et idéologie: La fable de La
      Fontaine à Florian." *Les Lumières en Hongrie, en
      Europe centrale et en Europe orientale: Actes du
      Troisième Colloque de Mátrafüred, 28 Sept.-2 Oct.
      1975.* Budapest: Akad. Kiadó, 1977, 291-298.

      Investigates the French fable of the Enlightenment,
      beginning with a structural and ideological analysis
      of La Fontaine then numerous other fabulists through
      the eighteenth century: La Motte-Houdart, Imbert,
      Grécourt, Le Bailly, Florian, and others. Identifies
      types of fables specific to the eighteenth century.

756. Lazzatto, M.J. "Due note al test di Babrio." *Maia: Rivista di letterature classische*, 27 (1975), 49-51.

Suggests readings for Babrius 95 and Babrius 115.

757. Lebois, André. *Sources négligées des Fables de La Fontaine.* Paris: Minard, 1960. First in *Archiv des lettres modernes*, no. 27 (1959). 36 pp.

Tracks down a number of overlooked sources for the *Fables* of La Fontaine. Discusses the Roman de Renard, a number of authors, including Rabelais; the *Aventures du Baron de Faeneste*, and many others. Some are possible, others less likely.

758. Le Comte, Edward. "Samson's Bosom Snake Again." *Milton Quarterly*, 9: 4 (1975), 114-115.

Jackson Boswell's "Samson's Bosom Snake" (q.v.) tries to resolve the motif underlying the reference in *Samson Agonistes* by referring to Aesop, Virgil, and others. Le Comte supplies an analogy in Aeschuylus' *The Choephoeri*.

759. Lecoy, Felix. *Recherches sur le libro de buen amor.* Paris: Belin Frères, 1938.

Wide-ranging series of materials on Juan Ruiz's *Libro de Buen Amor* containing a number of references to the fables. Builds upon Tacke's source study by agreeing that most of the fables are ultimately to be derived from the Latin "Walther of England" versions but does not agree with Tacke's conclusion that Ruiz was also strongly influenced by a specific translation of Walther into French, the *Lyoner Ysopet*.

760. Lee, A.G. "Avianus, fabula xxi, 12." *Proceedings of the Cambridge Philological Society*, 181 (1950-1951), 3-4.

Textual notes to P325 "Lark and Farmer" (A-T 93; TMI J1031).

761. ————. "Two Linguistic Parallels from Babrius." *Novem Testamentum. An International Quarterly for New Testament and Related Studies*, 9 (1967), 41-42.

Uses a phrase from Babrius 45 to explain Acts XXIV, and another from Babrius 143 for Acts XVI, 6.

762. Leemann-Van Elch, Paul. "Der züricherische Äsop."
      Stultifera navis, 1 (1944), 80–83.

      A note on Hans Ludwig Meyer von Knonau's fables,
      with a table of concordances and two illustrations.

763. Leeuwen, J. van. "De codicillis nuper bibliothecae
      Lugduno-Batavae donatis." Mnemosyne, 22 (1894), 222–
      230.

      A report on the tablets donated to the Batavian
      Academy by the brother of A.D. van Assendelft, found
      in Palmyra in 1881 and discussed by Hesseling in the
      Journal of Hellenic Studies. Leeuwen describes the
      tablets and offers a transliteration which is compared
      to the Greek of Babrius. Line drawings accompany the
      text.

764. Lefeve, B. Une version syriaque des fables d'Esope.
      Paris: Firmin-Didot, 1941.

      An edition and translation of a Syrian collection of
      fables. No introduction, no notes. The collection is
      not identified save by language.

765. Le Hir, Yves. "Visages de La Fontaine." Missions et
      démarches de la critique: Mélanges offerts au Pro-
      fesseur J.A. Vier. Université de Haut-Bretagne,
      1973, 755–761.

      This essay consists essentially of a statistical
      analysis of the lexicon of the two editions of La Fon-
      taine's Fables. Le Hir concludes there is a significant
      difference in attitudes, in truths, in the "faces of
      the poets," as La Fontaine himself had maintained.

766. Lehmann, W.R. "Fabel und Parabel als literarisches
      Bildungsgut." Pädagogische Rundschau, 15 (1961),
      696–707.

      An historical survey of the treatment of the fable
      as an element in education, especially teaching litera-
      ture and the humanities. Particular attention is paid
      to Gellert and Lessing.

767. Leibfried, Erwin. "Philosophisches Lehrgedicht und
      Fabel." Neues Handbuch der Literaturwissenschaft.
      II: Europäische Aufklärung (I. Teil). Ed. Walter
      Hinck. Frankfurt: Athenaion, 1974, 75–90.

      A short historical survey of the fable in the eighteenth

century with reference to other fabulists in Europe.
The popularity of the form proceeds from the affinity
of the era for didactic poetry. This led to a preference for the fable as a vehicle for literary expression.
The traditional motifs were recycled and La Fontaine
was taken as model. Lessing's reaction to this and the
fable theories of the century conclude the essay.

768. ─ ──. *Fabel.* Stuttgart: Metzler, 1967. 3rd ed.,
1976. 114 pp.

This monograph presents an historic and systematic
presentation of the fable, especially in Germany. The
opening sections attempt to define the fable by surveying
the various theories and the related forms. Leibfried
then discusses variations, stylistic characterizations,
structural types of oral and literary fables. The history of the fable in Germany is covered in the last two
thirds of the work. Each section ends with a complete
bibliography, and the study concludes with notes on the
fable in education and final words on problems for research.

769. ──── . "Autorposition, Leserbild: Zerstreute Bemer-
kungen zu unterschiedlichen Problemen." *Die Fabel:
Theorie, Geschichte und Rezeption einer Gattung.*
Berlin: Schmidt, 1982, 13-26.

Highly interesting and well-argued thoughts on the
position the author takes in writing fables and the
implied reader as well as the options open to the actual reader. The author lays claim to the truth and
to authority. He takes part in political and ethical
as well as moral problems, and he is either authorita-
tive or trivial. The author also is likely to run
into contradictions, which are to him either minor or
non-existent. The reader on the other hand, is pro-
grammed into a certain role by the author. It is important that the text be received in a certain way.
The reader, however, has the chance to take issue with
the author.

770. ────, and Josef Werle. *Textc zur Theorie der Fabel.*
Stuttgart: Metzler, 1978.

This useful work provides a selection of materials
for the historical study of the theory of the fable in
Germany, ranging from the introduction to Boner's
Edelstein (ca. 1350) to Emmerich's 1960 essay "Der

Wolf und das Pferd." Werle's commentary provides brief
historical background sketches to each section and a
bibliographical note as well as annotations to various
points in the text.

771. Leite de Vasconcelles, J. *O Livro de Esopo: Fabulario
      Português Medieval*. Lisbon: Imprensa Nacional, 1906.
      iv + 168 pp.

      Reports on a Viennese manuscript: *Fabulae Aesopi in
      lingua lusitana*, a collection of fables written in
      prose with an admixture of native Portuguese materials,
      especially proverbs. The manuscript is descended from
      the Walther of England tradition, contains 62 fables
      and is dated within the fifteenth century.

772. Leitzmann, Albert. *Die Fabeln Gerhards von Minden in
      mittelniederdeutscher Sprache zum ersten Mal herausge-
      geben*. Halle/Salle: Niemeyer, 1898. 304 pp.

      A complete edition of the Wolfenbütteler manuscript
      of the Low German fables of Gerhard von Minden in re-
      sponse to the uncritical partial edition of the same
      by von Fallersleben in 1870 and to the 1878 edition of
      Gerhard's fables based upon a Magdeburg manuscript.

773. ————. "Zu Burkhard Waldis." *Beiträge zur Geschichte
      der deutschen Sprache und Literatur*, 52 (1928), 291-
      304.

      Various notes to Burkhard Waldis, including sources
      for his fables.

774. ————. "Studien zum Magdeburger Äsop." *Jahrbuch
      des Vereins für niederdeutsche Sprachforschung*, 59-60
      (1943-1947) [1948], 56-66.

      Deals with the Magdeburger Aesop dependent upon, but
      not identical with, the Wolfenbütteler Aesop almost
      certainly by Gerhard von Minden. The two traditions
      are compared, and the components of the Magdeburger
      Aesop are listed: essentially the same motifs, but also
      the proverbs found in the fables, as well as citations
      from Cato, perhaps from Horace, and the Bible, and the
      numerous Middle High German parallel phrases. Ends
      with extensive textual emendations.

775. Lejard, J. *Phaedri fabulae*. Paris: Libraire Poussielque
      frères, 1878. 160 pp.

Reports on the research concerning the life of Phaedrus and upon the fables of François Desbillons (1711-
1789). Twenty of Desbillons' fables are published and
annotated here.

776. Lenaghan, Robert T. "The Nun's Priest's Tale." *PMLA*,
      78 (1963), 250-257.

      Attempts a definition of the tale by identification
      of reference points which define the social or dramatic
      context of the poem, beginning with the relationship
      of the tale to a well-established literary type: the
      fable. The term fable is used to illustrate both tale
      and methods, the rhetorical features and the construc-
      tion of the material. The specific type of *narratio*
      that is roughly the Aesopic fable is a third point,
      offering the opportunity of irony.

777. ————. "William Caxton's Translation of the 'Subtyl
      Histories and Fables of Esope': An Annotated Edition."
      Dissertation, Harvard, 1957. Revised and Published,
      Caxton's Aesop. Cambridge, Mass.: Harvard University
      Press, 1967. 264 pp.

      Very well-presented edition of Caxton's *Aesop* with
      a comprehensive introduction dealing with the history
      of the text, of the woodcuts, and the text's position
      in the history of the Heinrich Steinhöwel *Esopus* tradi-
      tion. Extensive notes, a glossary, together with an
      index of fables, and a comparative table of Perry
      Aesopica numbers make the work very useful.

778. ————. "Steinhöwel's 'Esopus' and Early Humanism."
      *Monatshefte für deutschen Unterricht, deutsche
      Sprache und Literatur*, 60 (1968), 1-8.

      Excellent, concise description of Heinrich Stein-
      höwel's *Esopus* (1476/77) in the light of his Humanistic
      tendencies demonstrated by his editorial decisions.
      This collection is the first to add the Italian Humanist
      fable translation tradition in the form of the fables
      of Rinuccio D'Arezzo.
      See: Carnes, "Heinrich Steinhöwel."

779. Lengyel, Dénes. "La Fontaine en Hongrie." *Europe*, 515
      (1972), 148-155.

      Concise historical presentation of La Fontaine's
      fables in Hungary to the present day. Political as
      well as literary influence is claimed for the fables

which were first translated into Hungarian by Jozsef
Peczel who outfitted the fables with Hungarian oikotypes.
Later translators and imitators discussed with limited
bibliographical details.

780. Lentzen, Manfred. "Tomás de Iriartes Fabeln und der
    Neoklassizismus in Spanien: Ein Beitrag zur Er-
    forschung des spanischen 18. Jahrhunderts." *Roman-
    ische Forschungen*, 79 (1967), 602-620.

    An historical, contextual presentation of the fables
    of Tomás de Iriarte. Iriarte's fables are seen to fol-
    low the structure and form of the fable as established
    during the Middle Ages; they follow La Fontaine es-
    pecially. The form of narration (*corps*) and moral
    (*âme*) is the general structure Iriarte uses although
    other special structural characteristics are noted.
    Iriarte's fables are seen as illustrations of the essen-
    tial principles of classical literary theory after a
    survey of the introduction of classical theory into
    Spain.

781. Lévêque, Eugène. *Les Fables ésopiques de Babrios tra-
    duite en totalité pour la première fois comparées
    aux fables d'Horace et de Phèdre, de Corrozet et de
    La Fontaine avec une étude sur leurs origines et
    leur iconographie.* Paris: Belin-Frères, 1890.
    lxxxviii + 468 pp.

    Lengthy, comprehensive historical survey of the
    origin of the fable. The Assyrian, Hebrew, Egyptian,
    Indian, Greek, and Roman contributions are studied
    apparently with an eye toward explicating the Babrian
    fables, but with a long discourse on the French fables
    of the Middle Ages. The history of the Babrian fables
    begins with a comparison of Babrius to Horace, Phaedrus,
    Avianus, Faerne, Corrozet, and La Fontaine. The work
    ends with an extensive list of sources.

782. ————. *Iconographie des fables de La Fontaine, La
    Motte, Dorat, Florian avec une étude sur l'iconographie
    antique.* Paris: E. Flammarion, 1893. 228 pp.

    This monograph deals with the iconography of the
    fable from the earliest times (Assyrian, Egyptian,
    Phoenician, and Greek and Roman) through the Middle
    Ages and the Renaissance to the fables of Florian.
    Numerous examples of sixteenth- and seventeenth-century
    fable illustration are given together with a running
    commentary. Over one hundred illustrations.

783. Levrault, Léon. *La Fable: Évolution du genre.* Paris:
      Paul Delaplane, 1905. 151 pp.

      This interesting monograph begins with a survey of
      the fable from its earliest stirrings, explained by
      means of an anthropological approach, through a rehear-
      sal of the Indian and classical forms. The history of
      the fable in France from the Romulus Latin versions
      through the fable at the end of the nineteenth century
      makes up the latter part. The popular forms are em-
      phasized in the medieval fable up to the wave of
      Humanists and through the sixteenth century. The most
      productive era is seen as the seventeenth and eighteenth
      centuries with La Fontaine standing at the apogee. The
      decline of the genre had already begun with the con-
      temporaries of La Fontaine.

784. von der Leyen, Friedrich. "Tierepos und Tierfabel."
      *Volkstum und Dichtung: Studien zum Ursprung und zum
      Leben der Dichtung.* Jena: Eugen Diederich, 1933,
      74-77.

      Von der Leyen distinguishes clearly the Animal Tale,
      in part indigenous to Northern Europe, the Indian and
      the Greek Animal Fable traditions and the "Tierepos,"
      which is in no sense an epic but a loosely connected
      collection of motifs.

785. Ligacz, Richard. *Aesops Einfluss auf die deutsche
      Literatur des 16. Jahrhunderts.* Dissertation, Krakau,
      1945. 82 pp.

      After an introductory survey of the fable, Ligacz
      deals with the specific uses of "Aesop," which is no-
      where defined but which apparently means the entire
      corpus of fables through the Middle Ages. Aesopic
      collections, including Dorp, Camerarius, Alberus,
      Waldis are discussed by stressing the extent of the
      Aesopic contribution within the collections. Other
      literature using Aesopic motifs through the Baroque is
      outlined. The second section deals with the fable
      in structure and characterization, with the fable in
      the eighteenth century, with evaluation of materials
      in the fable, and the "new" fable of the twentieth
      century.

786. ————. "Aesops Einfluss auf die deutsche Literatur
      des 16. Jahrhunderts." *Zeitschrift für deutsche
      Philologie*, 75 (1956), 356-362.

A general survey of Aesopic literature in Europe in
the sixteenth century, considered in terms of reflexes
of the three branches of the Greek Prose tradition, the
existence of which is attributed to the *Rhetorenschulen*
of the Greek Middle Ages. Lists paraphrases and manuscripts and outlines the fable collections of the
sixteenth century in Germany: Dorp, Alberus, Osius,
Pothius, Schopper, and a few Baroque writers.

787. Lindner, Hermann. *Didaktisches Gattungsstruktur und*
      narratives Spiel: Studien zur Erzähltechnik in La
      Fontaines Fabeln. First dissertation, Munich, 1973;
      later Romanica Monacensia, 10. Munich: Fink, 1975.
      223 pp.

A thoroughgoing and well-argued presentation of La
Fontaine's fables and his putative fable theories as
exhibited by the collection, the presentation, the
organization, and the writing of the fables themselves
seen against the background of the fable theories of
his time. Discusses La Fontaine's writing of fables
in verse, the implications of which are of great importance for the history of the fable. La Fontaine
insured a certain amount of variety by alternating
well-known with little-known stories. Good bibliography and indices are provided.

788. ———. "Bibliographie zur Gattungspoetik (5): Theorie
      und Geschichte der Fabel (1900-1974)." *Zeitschrift*
      für französische Sprache und Literatur, 85 (1975),
      246-259.

A bibliographical list without annotations or commentary with 56 items on the theory of the genre and
another 136 on the history of the form.

789. ———. "Vers le Vrai La Fontaine? Anmerkungen zu
      einigen neueren Tendenzen der La Fontaine-Kritik aus
      Anlass des jüngsten Forschungsberichts zu La Fon-
      taines Fabeln." *Zeitschrift für französische Sprache*
      und Literatur, 87 (1977), 142-164.

Jürgen Grimm's *La Fontaines Fabeln* is the specific
motivation for this essay on new tendencies in La Fontaine research. Takes issue with Grimm's assertion
that there is a dichotomy "aesthetically oriented" vs.
"content specific" to be seen in the La Fontaine
studies he deals with. Disputes the categories and
the interpretations of the works cited. Adds a number

of bibliographical entries not mentioned in Grimm's work. Lindner uses the work of Jasinski to analyze Grimm's "content oriented" approach to La Fontaine and concludes that Grimm's methodology is questionable at best.

790. ———. "Historisch-strukturalistische Literaturwissenschaft versus historisch soziologische Essayistik: Klarstellung zu J. Grimms 'La Fontaine--Être de Papier?'" *Zeitschrift für französische Sprache und Literatur*, 88 (1978), 122-138.

Presents a commentary in the form of a rebuttal to Grimm's work on La Fontaine's fables, in particular to Grimm's response to Lindner's series. Lindner discusses the genre tradition of the fable, the particular political structure of the fables, the reception of the fables, both in La Fontaine's time and by the modern reader, as well as various aspects of the stylistic problems of La Fontaine's verse. Answers to a number of the attacks by Grimm are attempted, and an outline of the main points considered essential by Lindner in opposition to Grimm's views is carefully presented. See: J. Grimm, "La Fontaine--Être de Papier?"

791. ———. *Fabeln der Neuzeit: England, Frankreich, Deutschland*. Munich: Fink, 1978.

Presents an extraordinarily rich assortment of modern (i.e., after ca. 1500) fabulists and an equally varied selection of materials from fable theorists, including translations into German for the English and French sections and lengthy annotations. The introductory materials describe the work as a philological reader, but the work is far more than that with a comprehensive set of mini-essays on various aspects of the fable, especially structure and problems of definition.

792. Lindstrom, James David. "Metaphoric Structure in the Verse Fables and Horatian Imitations of Jonathan Swift; An Introduction to His Poetic Style." Dissertation, UCLA, 1969. 257 pp.

Suggests a metaphoric analysis in which the original and the imitation are related as the two terms of a metaphor. The fables are best exhibited when they are explicated within this sort of a framework, which shows the fable to be composed of four separate, co-existing parts: fable and moral, and also the applied fable and

the applied moral. Two distinct metaphors govern these
parts and the interactions that occur among them. Lindstrom suggests that this relationship is conventional
and exists in all fables, and which in this case, related Swift's poetry to his moral-instructive style.

793. Llinarès, Armand. "Deux versions médiévales espagnoles
de 'La Laitière et le pot au lait.'" *Revue de Littérature Comparée*, 33 (1959), 230-234.

A note on La Fontaine's version of the Milkmaid and
the Pot of Milk with the Bidpai version and that of
Juan Manuel (1282-1348). Mention is made of the motif
in Rabelais as well.

794. Lockwood, Dean Putnam. "De Rinucio Aretino Graecarum
Litterarum Interprete." *Harvard Studies in Classical
Philology*, 24 (1913), 51-109.

A complete listing and detailed examination of the
works of Rinuccio d'Arezzo's translations from the
Greek, including the one hundred fable collection and
the *Vita Aesopi*. Informative presentation of the
manuscript tradition and the early printed versions.

795. Lohof, Bruce A. "A Morphology of the Modern Fable."
Journal of Popular Culture, 8 (1974), 15-27.

The short stories in *Good Housekeeping* magazine are
compared to fables: they are brief, entertaining,
familiar, and didactic. They are meant to convey
some moral or useful lesson, and this essay investigates the nature of the systems of morality, using the
structural approach of Claude Lévi-Strauss. The moral
system found in these stories is compared to the picture of the American middle class by the anthropologist
Cora Dubois.

796. Lorenzo, Attilo de. *Fedro*. Florence: La Nuova Italia,
1955. 215 pp.

The most complete presentation of the life, fables,
the Perotti Appendix, and the paraphrases. De Lorenzo
makes a number of well-argued but still somewhat speculative suggestions concerning the life of Phaedrus:
that Phaedrus was a personal servant of the emperor
Augustus teaching his grandson Greek and therefore at-
tended the Verrius Flaccus school on the Palatine and
many others. Deals with the problem of Phaedrus'
birthplace, the chronology of his life, his life as a

Freeman, the political allusions in the fables, the
three dedications, and the probable course of the fables
after Phaedrus' lifetime. The special literary problems
of the silence of Quintilian and the Martial quote are
given separate chapters. The monograph ends with an
extensive list and index of fables, all keyed to standard
editions, and an index of names mentioned in the text
which somewhat makes up for the lack of a bibliography.

797. Loukatos, Démetrios. "Le proverbe dans le conte." *IV*
      International Congress for Folk-Narrative Research
      in Athens 1964: Lectures and Reports. Ed. Georgios
      A. Megas. Athens, Laographia, 1965, 229-233.

      Notes on various types of short narrative forms and
      their relationship to the proverb. The fable and the
      origin of the fable are discussed as is the function
      of the proverb within the fable.

798. ———. "La Classification des Fables." *Lares*, 35
      (1969), 17-21.

      Discusses four systems of classification for fables:
      (1) an alphabetical system, according to the first word
      in the fable, not very useful in modern collections,
      (2) a nominative system, in which key names of charac-
      ters or of a title are used, not easily transferred to
      modern collections with changes of character or with
      titles that are not everywhere recognized, (3) a thematic
      system, in which the tale is typed according to the
      acts or the environment of the characters, as in the
      Halm collection, and which has the advantage of in-
      corporating the previous two systems, and (4) an ideo-
      logical system in which the fables are classified
      according to the abstract subjects, often correspond-
      ing to a perceived moral and thus always necessary for
      fable collections.

799. ———. *Neoellenikoi Paroimiomythoi.* Athens: Ekodotike
      Ermes, 1972.

      Discusses the close relationship of proverbs to
      fables as part of an extensive descriptive history of
      modern Greek proverbs. Good bibliography.

800. Lowe, Gladys, and Myra E. Shimberg. "A Critique of the
      Fables as a Moral Judgement Test." *Journal of Applied*
      Psychology, 9 (1925), 52-59.

      Apparently a report on testing for delinquency by

means of successful recognition of the intent of certain morals. The essay details reasons for the failure
of such a testing system and demonstrates a possible
correlation between the subject's intelligence and
recognition of the moral, rather than a correspondence
between ability to perceive the intended moral in a
given fable and moral action.

801. Lukas, Ruta Ona. "French Opinion of La Fontaine (1654–
      1800)." Dissertation, Columbia, 1980. 397 pp.

      Discusses the reception of La Fontaine by his con-
      temporaries, even though he used genres considered so
      minor that they were not even treated in their *Poetics*.
      His image in the eighteenth century is an idealized one,
      as he assumes the position of the preeminent fabulist.
      Fable theory everywhere bears the stamp of his prece-
      dent. The final chapter is an investigation of the
      fable as a pedagogical tool and as children's litera-
      ture. This appears to have brought about a somewhat
      more discriminating use of the *Fables*. With bibliog-
      raphy.

802. Lumpkin, Ben G. "'The Fox and the Goose': Tale Type 62
      from South Carolina." *North Carolina Folklore*, 18
      (1970), 90–94.

      P671 "Fox and Dove" (A-T 62; TMI 1421) is compared
      in numerous versions; mention is made of the fabular
      origin of the tale and its inclusion in the collections
      of Marie de France and others. American versions include
      that of J. Frank Dobie.

803. Luria, S. "Der Affe des Archilochis und die Brautwer-
      bung des Hippokleider." *Philologus*, 85 (1929), 1–22.

      Reconstructs P81 "Ape and Fox" (TMI K730.1) from
      fragments of Archilochus. Luria sees an echo of this
      fable in Herodotus VI, 129–130 (the marriage of Hippo-
      klides) from a time just before the triumph of the
      democracy.
      See: Immisch, "Ein Epodos des Archilochus."

804. ———. "L'asino nella pella del leone (un parallelo
      fra le favole dell'India e quelle dell'antica Grecia."
      Rivista di Filologia e di Istruzione Classica, 12
      (1934), 447–473.

      Discusses the relationships of a specific group of
      fables concerned with the theme of an upstart who earns

the mockery of his society with his empty boasting. In
the Greek fable, the Ass plays the role, specifically
P188 and P358 "Ass in Lion's Skin" (A-T 214B; TMI
J951.1), P151 "Lion and Ass Hunting" (TMI J952.2),
and P82 "Ass, Cock and Lion" (TMI 952.2). Similar
characteristics are often attributed to the ape. Luria
adds a number of Indian motifs and suggests Indian origin for all, adding that the motif of the upstart is a
reflection of the caste system.

805. Lüttecken, L. *Lessing, Abhandlungen über die Fabel,*
Literaturbriefe mit ausführlichen Erläuterungen für
den Schulgebrauch und das Privatstudium herausgegeben.
Paderborn: Schmidt, 1904. 199 pp.

Presents a general introduction to Lessing's *Abhand-*
lungen zur Fabel in connection with an historical outline of the genre. Lessing's fable theory is to be
reconciled to his other theoretical writings. Reference
is made to the ideas of Herder and Grimm and these are
contrasted to those of Lessing.

806. Lutz, C.E. "A Medieval Textbook." *Yale University*
Library Gazette, 49 (1974), 212-216.

Describes Ms 513 of the Beinecke Library at Yale,
written in Latin in England roughly 1300, and including
an evaluation of works read in medieval curricula in
the twelfth and thirteenth centuries. Contains the
fables of Avianus and others.

807. Luzzatto, Maria Joada. "La cultura letteraria di Babrio." *Annali della scuola normale superiore di*
Pisa, Classe di Lett., Series III, 5 (1975), 17-97.

Lengthy and lucid study of Babrius, including an extensive discussion of his style, demonstrating the
impressive vocabulary of the fabulist and his skills
in the writing of the prose and the rhetoric of his day.
The large number of correspondences seen to the Greek
New Testament and the Greek Septuagint leads the author
to suspect that Babrius knew the Near East at end of
the second century A.D.

808. ———. *Fedro, un poeta fra favola e realtà.* Torino:
Paravia, 1976. xiv + 254 pp.

Discusses Phaedrus' life and works as essentially
of one piece. Sees the fables as revelatory to Phaedrus'
life at every turn, with a complete evaluation of pre-

vious research regarding Phaedrus' metaphorical allusions to the political events surrounding him.

809.   Lyall, Roderick J. "William Dunbar's Beast Fable."
       Scottish Literary Journal, 1: 1 (1974), 17-28.

       Dunbar's "This hindir nicht in Dumfermeling" belongs
       primarily to the genre of the fable, and the mention
       of Dunfermline and fable together in the same poem
       might be an allusion to Robert Henryson.

810.   ————. "Henryson and Boccaccio: A Problem in the
       Study of Sources." *Anglia*, 99 (1981), 38-59.

       Considers Boccaccian influence upon the *Moral Fables*
       to be unlikely; those places are explicable by refer-
       ence to other, more obviously traditional sources.

811.   Lyons, John D. "The Author and the Reader in the
       Fables." *French Review*, 49 (1975), 59-67.

       Discusses the special *rapport* between author and
       audience. In many fables a specific literary exis-
       tence as language and as text is consciously promoted,
       and this requires an awareness of the text as a text.
       La Fontaine's language does not appear to interfere
       with communication, but La Fontaine also promotes the
       consciousness of the text as a literary artifact by re-
       ferring to other fabulists and contemporary writers.
       The reader is called upon to help recreate the scene,
       thus becoming an explicit part of the fable.

812.   McDermott, William Coffmann. "The Ape in Greek Litera-
       ture." *Transactions of the American Philological
       Association*, 66 (1935), 165-176.

       A general discussion of the Ape in Greek literature,
       including fables in various authors, pointing out the
       Eastern and Egyptian origins of the ape and ape lore.
       Mentions briefly P14 "Ape Boasting to Fox" (TMI J954.2),
       P73 "Ape and Dolphin" (TMI M205.1.1), P81 "Ape and
       Fox" (TMI J952.2) and P203 "Ape and Fisherman."
       See: Janson, *Apes and Ape Lore*.

813.   ————. "The Ape in Roman Literature." *Transactions
       of the American Philological Association*, 67 (1936),
       148-164.

       Discusses the influence of Greek literature and the
       proximity of Africa to explain the presence of apes in

Latin literature from Ennius to Avianus, with the
later as imitator of Greek models. Treats P364 "Ape
Mother and Zeus" (TMI T681), P474 "Wolf and Fox before
Judge Ape" (TMI B270, B274), P533 "Ape and Fox" (TMI
J341.1, W152.1), P569 "King of the Apes" (TMI B221.1,
J815.1) in detail.
See: Janson, *Apes and Ape Lore*.

814. McDonald, Craig. "The Fox, the Wolf and the Husband-
      man." *Medium Aevum*, 49 (1980), 244-253.

Discusses "the rash promise" in Henryson's "Fox,
Wolf and Husbandman" (A-T 154; TMI C25, K2061.4), a
variant of P158 "Wolf and Old Woman Nurse." The
promise forms the basis for legal action by the wolf.
The dispute is settled by arbitration, with Fox as
judge and accepting bribes, which McDonald suggests is
a response to a period of lawlessness.

815. McDonald, Donald. "Narrative Art in Henryson's Fables."
      Studies in Scottish Literature, 3 (1965), 101-113.

Discusses Henryson's sources and the expansion of
those sources, especially "Wolf and the Wether," P705
(A-T 126; TMI K1839.3.1, K1715) and "Cock and the Fox,"
P562 (A-T 61; TMI K561.1) in an attempt to reveal important characteristics of Henryson's narrative prac-
tices. The expansion of source material is a highly
selective process concentrating upon the comic as well
as the logical and plausible.

816. ————. "Henryson and Chaucer: The Cock and the Fox."
      Texas Studies in Literature and Language, 8 (1966),
      451-461.

Demonstrates borrowings, probable and possible, from
Chaucer's Nun's Priest's Tale by Henryson in the Cock
and the Fox, P562 and P562A "Partridge and Fox" (A-T 6,
cf. 61A; TMI K561.1, K721). A number of elements apparently original to Chaucer appear in Henryson's
version of the fable.

817. ————. "Chaucer's Influence on Henryson's Fables:
      The Use of Proverbs and Sententiae." *Medium Aevum*,
      39 (1970), 21-27.

Henryson's use of proverbs and in part the proverbs
themselves are specifically Chaucerian.

818. McGaughy, Lune C. "Pagan Hellenistic Literature: The
      Babrian Fables." *Society of Biblical Literature:*
      Seminar Papers, 11 (1977), 205-214.

      A cursory survey of the Babrian fables as representa-
      tive of the moral support system in Hellenistic litera-
      ture, here curiously characterized as "pagan."

819. McGowan, Margaret M. "Moral Intention in the Fables of
      La Fontaine." *Journal of the Warburg and Courtauld*
      Institutes, 29 (1966), 264-281.

      Decries the modern La Fontaine scholarship that under-
      plays his role as a moralist. Moral intent is seen in
      his relationship to emblems and in La Fontaine's com-
      ments to his fables indicating their didactic purposes.
      The fable is discussed as closely related to emblem
      literature and working in the same tradition, thus the
      illustrations that invariably accompany the fables.
      The result is not a clear set of morals, rather
      limits of behavior.

820. McGrady, Donald. "The *sospiros* of Sancho's Donkey."
      MLN, 88 (1973), 335-337.

      Accounts for the belief that the flatulence of Sancho's
      Donkey in *Don Quixote* is a good omen by means of P699
      (TMI J2066.4). Notes also Cervantes' mention of Aesop
      in I, chap. 25 and II, chap. 42.

821. McKendry, John L. *Aesop: Five Centuries of Illustrated*
      Fables. New York: The Metropolitan Museum of Art,
      1962. 95 pp.

      Occasioned by a Museum of Art exhibition, this volume
      presents a highly selective history of fable illustra-
      tion from Caxton through Franconi and Low with examples
      from many of the great fable illustrators. Illustra-
      tions are reproduced with the corresponding fables in
      modern translation on facing pages. A short introduc-
      tion covers the entire period of printed fable illus-
      trations with summary introductions to various illus-
      trators.

822. Mackensen, Lutz. "Fabel." *Handwörterbuch des deutschen*
      Märchens. Ed. Lutz Mackensen and Johannes Bolte.
      Berlin, 1934. 2, 1-3.

      Surveys the fable in popular literature, followed by
      a superficial history of the fable in Europe, especially
      in Germany. Short, now outdated bibliography.

823. McKenzie, Kenneth. "A Sonnet Ascribed to Chiaro Davanzati and Its Place in Fable Literature." *PMLA*, 13 (1898), 205-220.

Discusses the authorship of a sonnet containing versions of P101 and P472 "Jackdaw in Borrowed Feathers" (A-T 244; TMI J951.2), suggesting that the Greek versions circulated orally during the Middle Ages.

824. ————. "Dante References to Aesop." *17th Annual Report of the Dante Society* (1898), 1-14.

On Dante's references to fables: P503 "Cockerel and Pearl" (TMI J1061.1) in *Convito* (iv, 30) and the reference in *Inferno* (23, 4-9), P384 "Mouse and Frog" (A-T 278; TMI J681.1). Dante undoubtedly knew one of the Romulus versions.

825. ————. "An Italian Fable, Its Sources and History." *Modern Philology*, 1 (1904), 497-524.

Deals with the textual and source history of a fable found in a fifteenth-century Italian manuscript. Similar to P518 "Fox and Dragon" and P640 "Soldier and Serpent" (A-T 155; TMI J1172.3, W154.2.1).

826. ————. "Unpublished Manuscripts of Italian Bestiaries." *PMLA*, 2 (1905), 380-433.

Contains the text and complete bibliographical materials to the dozen or more manuscripts of the *il libro della natura degli animali* with some sixteen fables.

827. ————. "Italian Fables in Verse." *PMLA*, 21 (1906), 226-278.

Begins with a brief history of Italian verse fables: several translations of the Walter of England collection, followed by the Marie de France collection and its reflexes in Italy, the Bestiary tradition, and miscellaneous fables. Texts of verse fables, followed by an extensive "Sources and Parallels" section.

828. ————. "Italian Fables of the Eighteenth Century." *Italica*, 12 (1935), 39-44.

After a short history of the Italian fable, the eighteenth-century fabulists are discussed: seven in particular: Roberti, Passeroni, Bertola, Manzoni, Pignotti, De Rossi and Clasio, others mentioned in passing.

Lists of fabulists, both original and those who reworked the Aesopic corpus, are appended. The eighteenth-
century fabulists are rated as not great but typical of
their times.

829. ————. "Some Remarks on a Fable Collection." *Prince-
      ton University Library Chronicle*, 5: 4 (1944), 137-
      149.

Describes the collection in the Princeton Library
devoted to fables, apparently once McKenzie's own.
Generalizations on the fable and an attempt at a
definition begins the history of the fable, concentrating on McKenzie's specialty, the medieval period
but ranging from the beginnings to modern reflexes of
the fables. Primary collections represented by the
volumes in the collection are described and their relationships established. Numerous fabulists are mentioned and briefly discussed, notably the Italian fabulists of the sixteenth and eighteenth centuries as
well as dozens of others from all over Europe. Ends
with a bibliography of McKenzie's writings on the fable
and the bestiaries.

830. ————, and William A. Oldfather. *Ysopet-Avionnet: The
      Latin and French Texts*. Illinois Studies in Language
      and Literature, no. 5. Urbana, Ill.: University of
      Illinois Press, 1919. 262 pp.

The author and editors present here the text of the
Walter of England collection of sixty-five fables in
Latin verse accompanied by a French translation from
the fourteenth century, presented in three clearly related manuscripts called Isopet I. That portion which
stems from the Avianus tradition is treated separately
and called the Avionnet. The collection dates ultimately from the twelfth century. The lengthy introduction
contains an extensive discussion of the history of the
fables and their interrelationships as well as a description of the manuscripts and their illustrations. With
tables of correspondences, an index of proper names, a
Latin glossary, and a series of illustrations from the
manuscripts.

831. McKnight, G.H. "The Middle English *Vox and Wolf*."
      PMLA, 23 (1908), 497-509.

Treats the Middle English Beast Tale, *Vox and Wolf*,
a version of P593 "Fox and Wolf in the Well" (cf. A-T 31;

TMI K651, K652). Sources and parallels are examined, ranging from remote possibilities (a Zulu Tale) to various medieval exempla. Possible Hebrew origin of the tale is investigated, followed by a tracing of the modern history of the fable.

832. MacQueen, John. "The Text of Henryson's *Morall Fabilis*." *Innes Review*, 14 (1963), 3-9.

Uses the Bannatyne manuscript, compiled by George Bannatyne in the 1560's, for the establishment of the text of the fables.
See: Denton Fox, *The Poems of Robert Henryson*.

833. ————. *Robert Henryson: A Study of the Major Narrative Poems*. Oxford: Clarendon Press, 1967.

Presents an overall investigation of the narrative poems of Robert Henryson including the *Moral Fables*. Gives a general evaluation and a concise, thoroughgoing analysis of each fable. Appendices on text tradition and on sources, in which lines are drawn between Henryson and the Walter of England fables for techniques as well as material. The third appendix discusses the relationship of the beast epic to the fables with five fables counted as coming directly from that tradition.

834. Mader, Ludwig. *Antike Fabeln*. Zurich: Artemis, 1950. Reprint, Munich: DTU, 1973. 367 pp.

An edition of fables from Hesiod through classical forms to Romulus and other medieval Latin fables with illustrations from the Steinhöwel edition. Informative introduction, historical in approach, with criticism of individual fables, dealing with questions of pre-fabular models and countries of origin. Assumes a sociological function for the Aesopic version of the fable and its development through later stages.

835. Magill, C.P. "Im Dienste der Wahrheit: Observations on Some German Prose Fables." *Publications of the English Goethe Society*, 43 (1973), 57-71.

Examines various uses of the parable and fable by Hebel and Kafka, with Brecht mentioned. No clear distinction between genres is given; the only fable touched upon is Kafka's "Kleine Fabel."

836. Malandain, Pierre. *La Fable et l'intertexte*. Paris: Temps actuels, 1981. 128 pp.

Investigates the possibility of using the idea of
intertextualism with fabular literature, using La
Fontaine as text. Begins with a lexicon of terms used
in "intertextology," with applications generally to
fables and specifically to La Fontaine. An *ars poetica*
is constructed using specific examples from La Fontaine. A summary is followed by a list of fables discussed.

837. Mall, E. "Zur Geschichte der mittelalterlichen Fabelliteratur und insbesondere des Esope der Marie de
France." *Zeitschrift für romanische Philologie*, 9
(1885), 161-203.

Investigates the Latin and English antecedents to
the fables of Marie de France. Discusses a set of
manuscripts found in London, Brussels, and Göttingen
(thus the "LBG" designation), which is off the main
line of Romulus fable tradition but which contains
over half of Marie de France's fables. Mall concludes
that the LBG are more likely a translation from Marie
de France than the source, and that Marie did use an
English source but that it must have been a Middle
English one from the early to mid-thirteenth century.
See: Warnke, *Quellen*.

838. Mandowsky, Erna. "Pirro Ligorio's Illustrations to
Aesop's Fables." *Journal of the Warburg and Courtauld
Institutes*, 24 (1961), 327-331.

A discussion with illustrations of Pirro Ligorio's
engravings made to accompany Faërno's *Fables*, first
with an eye toward establishing the authenticity of
the engravings and then as an evaluation of the work.

839. Manitius, Maximillian. "Beiträge zur Geschichte
römischer Dichter im Mittelalter." *Philologus*, 51
(1890), 520-535.

Notes on various manuscripts of Avianus' fables.

840. ———. *Philologisches aus alten Bibliothekskatalogen.*
Rheinisches Museum, Ergänzungsheft 47. Frankfurt:
Sauerländer, 1892. viii + 152 pp.

Contains, among much else, an extensive listing of
the manuscripts of Avianus and evaluates their availa-
bility at various times and places during the Middle
Ages, especially the ninth century. Lists and describes
six manuscripts from the ninth century, five from the

tenth, seven from the eleventh, nine from the twelfth
and seven from the thirteenth.

841. ————. *Handschriften antiker Autoren in mittelalter-
      lichen Bibliothekskatalogen*. Leipzig: Teubner, 1935.

      This posthumously-appearing work lists those classi-
      cal authors mentioned in library catalogs from the
      Middle Ages to 1933. Lists Phaedrus and "Aesopus" (i.e.,
      the Romulus tradition), with special attention given
      to the very widespread Avianus tradition.

842. Mann, Jill. "'Luitur illusor': The Cartoon World of
      Ysengrimus." *Neophilologus*, 61 (1977), 495–509.

      Discusses difficulties in interpreting Isengrimus
      in specific terms. Fables are discussed in passing.

843. Manning, Stephen. "Nun's Priest's Morality and the
      Medieval Attitude toward Fables." *JEGP*, 59 (1966),
      403–416.

      Well-argued essay based upon the premise that fables
      were used in various narratives on the grounds that
      the stories attracted readers and entertained them.
      These readers then profited from the moral system in-
      herent in the fables.

844– Numbers omitted.
847.

848. Marc, Paul. "Die Überlieferung des Äsopromans."
      Byzantische Zeitschrift, 19 (1910), 382–421. Origin-
      ally dissertation, Munich, 1904.

      Extensive handling of the textual tradition of the
      Vita Aesopi. The Westermann *Vita* and its manuscript
      tradition is followed by the *Accursiana Vita* connected
      with the name of Maximus Planudes and a section re-
      lating the two. Follows Hausrath in postulating a
      "Volksbuch" supposedly containing the original form of
      the romance.
      See: Perry, *Studies in the Text History*.

849. Marchesi, Concetto. *Fedro e la favola latina*. Florence:
      Vallecchi, 1923. 118 pp.

      Deals with the relationships of Phaedrus to the Greek
      tradition and his position relative to the Latin fable
      in the Middle Ages.

850. Marchiano, Michele. *Babrios fortuna de suoi mitiambi,*
      et à e patria del poeta. Trani: Vecchi, 1899.

      Historical presentation of the life and fable collec-
      tion of Babrius, especially the manuscript and verse-
      form tradition.
      See: Perry, *Babrius and Phaedrus.*

851. ————. *L'Origine della favola greca e i suoi rap-*
      porti con le favole orientali. Trani: Vecchi, 1900.
      xii + 504 pp.

      Describes the theories of the Indian origin of the
      fable and attempts to draw lines of correspondence
      between Babrius and the *Panchatantra* and, from there,
      more general analogues between the body of Greek fables
      and Indian forms. Conclusions are generally against
      the idea of Indian origin. Fables of Arabian, Hebrew,
      and other Near-Eastern origins are discussed as are
      fables from all over the world with no firm conclusions.
      The idea of the fable as a literary genre seems to be
      specifically Greek. Fables are not keyed to any
      standard collection.

852. Marco, Maria de. "Una favola della volpe, dell'agnetto
      e de leone nel secolo xii." *Aevum,* 36 (1962), 532-
      533.

      A note on the probable allusion to an unknown fable
      in the *Responsio Catilinae.*

853. Marenghi, Gerardo. "I mitiambi di Babrio e la tradi-
      zione esopiana." *Giornale Italiano di Filologia,* 7
      (1954), 341-348.

      Reviews the textual history of the Babrian fables
      and summarizes previous research; discusses various
      passages that demonstrate Babrius' linkage with the
      Greek Aesopic tradition.

854. ————. "Babrio e la favola romana." *Athenaeum,* 33
      (1955), 233-246.

      Babrius represents a return of a sort to the Aesopic
      type within the Roman fable tradition, especially as
      regards the attitude toward the pedagogical aspect,
      when compared to Phaedrus and Horace.

855. ————. "Questioni di lingua stile e metrica per una
      collocazione romana di Babrio." *Giornale Italiano*
      di Filologia, 8 (1955), 116-130.

Survey of Babrian research followed by a phonetic and lexical analysis (particularly the vowel system) as well as Babrian metrics to demonstrate that Babrius was a Roman.

856. ————. "Ignazio Diacono e i tetrastici giambici." *Emerita*, 25 (1957), 487-497.

Discusses the iambic tetrasticha, the Byzantine paraphrases of Babrian written by Ignatius Diaconus and his imitators in the ninth century. Manuscripts listed and classified together with an analysis of Ignatius' techniques which are compared to Babrius.

857. Marin, Louis. "Le Récit originaire, l'origine du récit, le récit de l'origine." *Papers on French Seventeenth Century Literature*, 11 (1979), 13-28.

Deals with the anecdote of Aesop and the Figs in La Fontaine's Life of Aesop and with his "Le Corbeau et le Renard," P124 "Fox and Crow" (A-T 57; TMI K334.1). Complicated analysis of structure and meaning.

858. Markschies, Hans Lothar. "Lessing und die Äsopische Fabel." *Wissenschaftliche Zeitschrift der Karl-Marx-Universität, Gesellschafts- und Sprachwissenschaftliche Reihe*, 4 (1954-1955), 120-142.

Analyzes the methods in Lessing's *Abhandlungen zur Fabel*. Suggests that Lessing recognized the usefulness of fable theory operating within its historical genre, and thus Lessing's primary accomplishment consists of the "rediscovery" of the "Aesopic" genre. At the base of this idea is the "truth" from which the fable must ultimately gain its form. Here Lessing's fable theory and fable production come together. Markschies sees Lessing's attitude toward a number of fables as "socio-revolutionary."

859. ————. "Fabel." *Reallexikon der deutschen Literaturgeschichte*. 2nd ed. Ed. Werner Kohlschmidt and Wolfgang Mohr. Berlin: De Gruyter, 1958. I, 433-441.

Concise accounting for the fable in German literary tradition with bibliographical entries for each section. The fable is presented historically from the beginnings through the early nineteenth century, with emphasis upon the period of its highest popularity--the eighteenth century, which Markschies denotes as also the end of

the genre in a sense. Good summaries of research and
capsule presentations of each era.

860. Marquardsen, Mary Andrews. "Rhetoric in the Fables of
La Fontaine." Dissertation, Tulane, 1975. 204 pp.

La Fontaine's fables reflect the influence of elocu-
tion as a division of the study of rhetoric, and his
style within the fable collection is better understood in terms of an analysis of his rhetorical skills.
La Fontaine clearly saw the poetic potential in the
fables, and he used rhetorical features, often highly
stylized figures, to present his materials in an
agreeable manner.

861. Martens, Ernst. *Entstehungsgeschichte von Burkhard
Waldis' Esopus*. Dissertation, Göttingen, 1907.
110 pp.

Deals primarily with the language of the fables, especially stylistic problems, formulae, rhyme schemes,
but also outlines some of the sources. The massive
Latin collection of Martin Dorp, which in its later editions provided 281 of Waldis' 400 fables, is described
in detail. Other sources are mentioned although no
other systematic borrowing is seen. Short bibliography but no index of fables.

862. Martin, Ernst. "Zur Geschichte der Tiersage im Mittelalter." *Prager Deutsche Studien*, 8 (1908), 273-287.

Concerned primarily with the figure of Isengrim and
speaks to the relationship between the beast epic and
the Aesopic fable. Grimm's theory of the evolution of
the "Tiersage" from Old-Germanic animal epics is considered unlikely although not completely excluded as
is the Hausrath addition to the theory that assumes
Germanic material reached the Byzantine rhetorical
schools and reformation of these materials there re-
sulted in many of the fables common today. The fable
is to be found everywhere and this makes specific
origins improbable. Martin notes relationships between the medieval mimes and wandering poets, on the
one hand, and the fable and kindred forms on the other.
Stresses the secular nature of such writings and the
fact that they stand in opposition to clerical materials.

863. Martin, Mary Lou. "The Fables of Marie de France: A
Critical Commentary with English Translation."
Dissertation, University of Texas at Austin, 1979.

An edition of the 102 fables of Marie de France
with translation and commentary which is, in effect,
a listing of the problems encountered in the process
of translation. The introduction deals with the relationship of the fables to the *lais* and to the Aesopic
tradition and contains a text criticism bibliography.
See: Warnke, *Die Fabeln der Marie de France*.

864. Masoin, F. "La Morale dans les fables de Phèdre."
     Bulletin du Musée de Beyrouth, 28 (1924), 69-71.

     Social life as well as political and literary aspects
     of Roman civilization is reflected in the Phaedrine
     fables, the primary message of which is to be found
     in the acquisition of wisdom.

865. Maspero, G. "Fragment d'une version égyptienne de la
     fable des members et de l'estomac." *Études Egypt-
     iennes*, 1 (1886), 260-267.

     Notes on a partial reconstruction of a fragment of
     an Egyptian version of P130 "Stomach and Feet" (A-T 293;
     TMI J461.1).

866. Massaro, M. "Variatio e sinonimia in Fedro." *Invigilata
     lucernis Rivista dell'Istituto di latino, Università
     di Bari*, 1 (1979), 89-142.

     A comprehensive examination of the Phaedrine fables
     from the point of view of language analysis, especially
     as regards Phaedrus' vocabulary and specific rhetorical
     features. The aesthetic techniques employed by Phaedrus
     appear to have included not only intentional brevity
     balanced by variety but also a thoroughgoing command
     of the lexicon and commonplaces from the standard
     authors.

867. ———. "La redazione fedriana della Matrona di Efeso."
     *Materiali e contributi per la storia della narrativa
     greco-latina*, 3 (1981), 217-237.

     Exhaustive comparison of Phaedrus, Appendix 15 with
     Petronius, Sat. cxi-cxii, versions of P543 "Widow and
     Soldier" (A-T 1510; TMI K2213.1).

868. ———. "Una caratteristica dello stile di Fedro. La
     variatio sermonis." *Quaderni dell'Associazione italiana
     di cultura classica*, 1 (1981), 49-61.

     A listing of examples illustrative of the points
     made in Massaro's 1979 article (q.v.).

869. Mast, Hans. *Stilistische Untersuchungen an den kleinen*
      Dichtungen des Strickers mit besonderer Berücksichti-
      gung des volkstümlichen und formelhaften Elementes.
      Dissertation, Basel, 1929. 128 pp.

      Investigates the stylistic elements, generally lexical,
      in the works of Der Stricker, including the fables.
      The introduction deals with the transition from the
      Novelle to the bîspel, a term meant to include a number
      of short didactic forms including the fable with rela-
      tively indistinct genre boundaries. Numerous features
      of language and folk speech patterns such as commonplaces
      and formulae are noted.

870. Matl, Josef. "Antike Gestalten in der slawischen
      literarischen und Volksüberlieferung. Ein Beitrag
      zur europäischen Geistesgeschichte." *Saeculum:*
      Jahrbuch für Universalgeschichte, 6 (1955), 407-431.

      A far-reaching but somewhat superficial overview of
      the survival of classical materials in Slavic literary
      and folk tradition. Among the texts discussed are the
      Historia septem sapientum and various manifestations of
      Aesopic materials. Lists texts and translations in
      the Slavic countries and suggests that Aesop is known
      in Eastern tradition more as a literary figure than
      through his fables.

871. May, Kurt. "Fabel." *Lessings und Herders kunsttheore-*
      tische Gedanken in ihrem Zusammenhang. Germanische
      Studien, 25. Berlin: Matthiesen, 1923, 124-136.

      Compares and contrasts Herder's theoretical writings
      on the fable with Lessing's *Abhandlungen*. Deals with
      their concept of the moral system and its reasons for
      being, with the action in the narrative, and especially
      the use of animals in the fable. Stylistic problems
      concerned both, with Herder shown to be far more
      liberal than Lessing in questions of verse forms and
      poetic ideals in general. Lessing's ideas of classifi-
      cation are quite different from those of Herder although
      the latter was more concerned with his system than
      Lessing was.

872. Mayer, Anton. *Die Quellen zum Fabularius des Konrad*
      von Mure. Dissertation, Nürnberg, 1916. 45 pp.

      A philological investigation of the *Fabularius*, an
      eclectic collection of verses from around 1200, con-
      taining, among much else, some verses from Avianus.

873. ————. *Studien zum Aesoproman und zur aesopischen Fabel im lateinischen Mittelalter.* Program, Lohr, 1916-1917. 40 pp.

The *Vita Aesopi* in Latin through the Middle Ages is outlined together with the fable tradition with which it traveled. Discussion centers on the Westermann and the Accursiana traditions as seen in the Rinuccio version. The fables are traced from the Romulus forms through various exempla collections.

874. Mayer, Gerd-Rainer. *Die Funktion mythologischer Namen und Anspielungen in La Fontaines Fabeln.* Dissertation, Bonn, 1969. 220 pp.

Treats aspects of the mythological elements in La Fontaine's *Fables* from the points of view of an educational milieu and the use of these elements in classical literature. Most of the mythological elements seem to have been intentionally included by La Fontaine; Mayer then tries to determine the reason for their inclusion by close readings of the fables.

875. Mazzoli, G. "Due note anneane: I--Fedro e Sen. *cons. ad Pol.* 8, 3." *Athenaeum,* 46 (1968), 354-368.

Attempts to connect Phaedrus to Seneca's mention of fables.

876. Megas, Georgios A. "Some Oral Greek Parallels to Aesop's Fables." *Humaniora: Essays in Literature, Folklore and Bibliography Honoring Archer Taylor on His Seventieth Birthday.* Ed. Wayland Hand and Gustav O. Arlt. Locust Valley, New York: Augustin, 1960, pp. 195-207.

Beginning with the premise that the oral tradition better preserves the "original relationships" than does literary tradition, Megas suggests that this is especially true for the Aesopic fables (somewhat curiously because they were used for centuries for the purpose of teaching writing) and calls for collection of those relationships not found in the literary versions. Demonstrations follow, with a number of fables, especially P196 "Snake and Crab" (A-T 279; TMI J1053), P51 "Farmer and Snake" (A-T 285D; TMI J15), and a number of other motifs. Examines a number of modern tales for contrast.

877.   ————. *To elleniko paramythi*. *Analytikos katalogos*
        typon kai parallagon kata to systima Aarne-Thompson
        (FFC 184). *Teychos proton mythi zoon*. Athens:
        Akademia Athinon, 1978. xxxii + 112 pp.

    The first section of the Greek Tale catalog deals
    with a number of fabular motifs, especially P226
    "Tortoise and Hare" (A-T 275A; TMI K11.3) with 384
    variants; P176 "Man who Warmed a Snake" (A-T 155; TMI
    J1172.3, W154.2) with 132 variants; P150 "Lion and
    Mouse" (A-T 75; TMI B371.1, B363) with 116 variants
    and a number of others. A significant number of these
    tales do not have A-T numbers (nearly one fourth) and
    Megas has followed convention by issuing numbers for
    these. Thus P252 "Dog, Rooster and Fox" (TMI K579.8)
    is given the A-T number *62A. A number of fables are
    demonstrated to have taken on a distinctive Greek
    character, but, most importantly, Megas has shown that
    the Aesopic tradition is remarkably alive.

878.   Meisser, Ulrich M. "Tiersprichwörter und Verhaltens-
        forschung: Zur gegenseitigen Erhellung von didaktischer
        Literatur und Naturwissenschaft." *Studium Generale*,
        22 (1969), 861-889.

    This highly interesting study of animal proverbs,
    especially in the Sebastian Franck and Eberhard Tappe
    collections of the sixteenth century, also discusses
    the interrelationship of the fable to the proverb and
    the stereotypical characteristics of the animals
    common to both forms.

879.   Melella, O. "Esopo y la fábula esópica." *Annales del*
        Instituto de Literaturas Clásicas, 3 (1945-1946),
        291-329.

    Investigates a number of different designations for
    the fable and pursues some of the evidence for the
    historicity of the person Aesop and the production of
    fables.

880.   Mendell, Clarence. "Phaedrus." Latin Poetry: *The Age*
        of Rhetoric and Satire. NP: Archon Books, 1967, pp.
        20-33.

    Begins with the curious premise that the fable has
    never attained high standing in any literature, that
    the form stems from "primitive folklore" and that it
    is to be associated with "children's books." Dis-
    cusses the introductions to Phaedrus' fable books,

describing the fabulist as a second-rate satirist.
Some of the fables cursorily treated.

881. Mendoza, Vincente T. "El Apólogo Español en la pro-
ducción folklórica de México." *Universidad: Mensual
de Cultura Popular*, 27 (1938), 11-19.

On the use of fables and fabular motifs in various
folklore manifestations, especially the folksong.
Fables are partly native materials in the Aesopic
manner, partly from imported motifs.

882. Merendino, Anna. "La pecora zoppa. Analisi strutturale
di una fiaba di magia del Salento." *Lares*, 39 (1973),
163-172.

A Proppian analysis of P572 "Kid and Wolf" (A-T 123;
TMI J144) in a Salentine version. Individual elements
are divided among the Proppian functions with only
partial success.

883. Merone, E. "Suflo e sufflo (a proposito di Aviano 29,
18)." *Giornale Italiano di Filologia*, 11 (1958),
45-50.

Textual notes to a passage in Avianus; concludes
that no reading is clearly indicated but that some
are more difficult to support.

884. Metzker, Otto. "Die wertvolle und die minderwertige
Tiergeschichte." *Der Deutschunterricht*, 9: 4 (1957),
33-50.

Deals with the fable incidentally in the broader
scope of "animal story." The child does not like the
fable; it is too short, and he enjoys expanded forms.
Lists recommended animal stories.

885. Meuli, Karl. "Herkunft und Wesen der Fabel." *Schweizer-
isches Archiv für Volkskunde*, 50 (1954), 65-88.

Deals with two complex issues: the function of the
original fable and the problem of its origin. Sees
the fable as essentially the same in function as the
Homeric *ainos* and thus is the diplomatic representative of a very specific truth, and therefore a rhetorical device. From this, Meuli concludes the origin
of the fable is to be found among "gifted people,"
such as the Hellenes, the people of India, and the
people of the "Old Orient."

886. Michel, Alain. "Rhétorique et philosophie de l'emblème:
      Allegorie, realisme, fable." *Emblèmes et devises au
      temps de la Renaissance*. Ed. M.T. Jones-Davies.
      Paris: Touzot, 1981, 23-31.

      Deals with the interrelationships of the allegorical
      level of the emblem and the animal fable. Notes the
      similarity of the epigram with regard to brevity and
      allegorical content. Stresses the rapport between the
      image and the poetic theme, which does not depend en-
      tirely upon sensual reception but upon cultural aspects
      as well. The fabular motifs of La Fontaine, for ex-
      ample, are among the many to which a specific response
      is expected.

887. Number omitted.

888. Mickel, Emanuel J. "Fables." *Marie de France*. New
      York: Twayne, 1974, 34-40.

      Short introduction to the fables of Marie de France
      within the larger context of her life and works. The
      fable as form is discussed, essentially following M.
      Ellwood Smith (q.v.). The chapter ends with a con-
      sideration of the structure of the collection.

889. Mieder, Wolfgang. *Deutsche Sprichwörter und Redensarten*.
      Stuttgart: Reclam, 1979. 199 pp.

      Although essentially devoted to proverbs, this collec-
      tion of German materials by one of the leading paremio-
      logists of the day contains a number of references to
      fables, especially those of the German sixteenth
      century.

890. Millé y Gimenez, Juan. "La Fábula de la lechera a tra-
      vés de las diversas literaturas." *Nosotros*, 43 (1924),
      203-225.

      Traces the history of "Dairy Maid and Pot of Milk"
      (La Fontaine 7, 10) from the *Panchatantra*, the *Hito-
      padesa* from India to the *Thousand and One Nights*, the
      Kalila wa Dimna and the Latin versions in Europe, as
      well as various modern European forms.

891. Miner, Robert G. "Aesop as Litmus: The Acid Test of
      Children's Literature." *The Great Excluded: Critical
      Essays on Children's Literature*. Ed. Francelia
      Butler. Storrs: University of Connecticut Press,
      1972, pp. 9-15.

Declares, curiously, that the basic English children's edition of Aesop is the Roger L'Estrange translation (2 vols., 1692, 1699), followed by a somewhat naive overview of a few editions of Aesop both before and after L'Estrange.

892. Minor, Jacob. "Einleitung." *Fabeldichter, Satiriker und Popularphilosophen des 18. Jahrhunderts*. Berlin: Speman, 1899.

The fables of Lichtwer and Pfeffel are introduced with outlines of the fabulists' life and works. Lichtwer and the history of his 100-fable collection (1748) is the subject of a comparison with Lessing. Pfeffel's collection (Basel, 1783) established him as a true fabulist; his fables are characterized by their many-sidedness and their finely drawn morals.

893. Miquel, André. "La Fontaine et la version arabe des fables de Bidpai." *Revue de littérature comparée*, 38 (1964), 35-50.

On the influence of the *Kalila wa Dimna* upon La Fontaine, not only with source materials but also style and structure, some of which arises from the milieu of eighth-century Baghdad.

894. Mitchell, P.M. "Aspekte der Fabeltheorie im 18. Jahrhundert vor Lessing." *Die Fabel: Theorie, Geschichte und Rezeption einer Gattung*. Ed. Peter Hasubek. Berlin: Schmidt, 1982, 119-133.

Presents a detailed and highly interesting history of the German fable and especially fable theory from the sixteenth century through the eighteenth century up to Lessing. Mitchell sees no true German fable theory developing in Germany before Lessing, yet the fable becomes a viable recognized genre in this period. The fable is traced through its popularity from the seventeenth century on a level likened to that of the broadside to the early eighteenth century with the fable of La Fontaine highly visible and popular together with the theoretical writings of La Motte and Fontenelle. Mentions the moral weekly-fable publications: *Der Teutsche Lockman* (1739) and *Der deutsche Aesop* (Königsberg, 1743) as symptomatic of the increasing synthesis of German and French ideas. The fables and writings of Gellert, Daniel Triller, Friedrich Hagedorn, Daniel Stoppe, Breitinger, and Gottsched are all evaluated.

895. Mogilianskii, A.P. *I.A. Krylov: Basni.* Moscow: Academy
     of Sciences of the U.S.S.R., 1956. 634 pp.

     Sources, parallels, and historical background are
     provided for each of the fables in this definitive
     edition of Krylov's fables. Mogilianskii provides an
     extensive commentary on personal aspects of Krylov's
     life and their relationship to specific fables, together
     with a chronology of fable production and reproductions
     of illustrations from earlier editions.

896. Moldenhauer, Gerhard. "Zur Geschichte der Tiererzählung
     in der mittelalterlichen spanischen Literatur."
     Philologische Studien: Festschrift für Karl Voretzch.
     Halle/Salle: Niemeyer, 1927, 480-513.

     A general survey of animal literature, including some
     few fable collections and their manuscript tradition,
     found in medieval Spanish materials. Lists and descrip-
     tions of Spanish translations from Latin and other lan-
     guages.

897. Mombello, Gianni. "La Vie d'Esope tradotto da Antoine
     du Moulin." *Mélanges à la mémoire de Franco Simone.*
     Geneva: Slatkine, 1980, 157-179.

     The du Moulin translation of the *Vita Aesopi* is com-
     pared to its source with textual annotations. The text
     is reproduced together with variants.

898. ————. "Un problème de propriété littéraire: Jean
     Baudoin, Pierre III de Boissat et l'Anonyme de 1547."
     Studi Francesi, 70 (1980), 14-34.

     Concerns the problem of the connection between Jean
     Baudoin and an edition of Aesopic fables which appeared,
     without his name, in 1631. Mombello concludes that
     Baudoin is responsible for the edition and traces the
     transmission of the text from its anonymous beginnings
     in 1547 through 1649.

899. Monaci, E. *Apologhi verseggiati in antico volgare
     reatino.* Rome, 1894.

     Publishes the codex Vat. 4834, containing twenty-
     three fables from the Gualtherius Anglicus collection
     tradition as well as other writings.

900. Moral, W. "Some Emendations in Late Latin Texts:
     Avianus, *Fabulae*, 40." *Classical Quarterly*, 35

(1941), 136-138.

Suggests various readings, e.g., "ibat in astra."

901. Moravcevitch, June. "Reason and Rhetoric in the
Fables of La Fontaine." *Australian Journal of French
Studies*, 16 (1979), 347-360.

Deals with the dialogues among the characters in the
Fables who use logical fallacies and empty rhetoric.
This is part of La Fontaine's concept of the genre,
the function of which is to offer wisdom rather than
a moral system.

902. Moraveski, Gyula. "'Hund in der Krippe': Zur Geschichte
eines griechischen Sprichwortes." *Acta Antiqua Academiae Scientiarum Hungaricae*, 12 (1964), 77-86.

The metaphor found in the Thomas Gospel and in
Lucian's *Adversus indoctum*, c. 30, P702 "Dog in the
Manger" (TMI W156), is likely to be traced to a classi-
cal proverb.

903. Moreau, Pierre. *Thèmes et variations dans le premier
recueil des 'Fables' de La Fontaine*. Paris: Cours
de Sorbonne, 1960. 95 pp.

General introduction of the first edition of La Fontaine's *Fables*. Covers the person of La Fontaine and
his ideas on art in general and literature, especially
the fables in particular. The form, structure, and
poetic forms of the first edition are discussed in detail.

904. Morel-Fatio, A. "L'Isopo Castillan." *Romania*, 23
(1894), 561-575.

Reports on the 1496 folio edition of the Spanish
translation of the Steinhöwel collection, assumed by
some to have been done by the son of Ferdinand. Some
differences in the Spanish version are noted.

905. Moroncini, G. "Phaedrus." *Rivista di filologia*
(1895), 23-92.

Historical overview on the history and problems of
the Phaedrus text from Pithou (1596) through Hervieux.
Concludes: books one and two published under Tiberius,
last three under Caligula, with the division into
books original with Phaedrus. Political details abound;

date seems confirmed in the metrics and the language.
Nothing speaks against genuineness of the Perotti Appendix.

906. Morreale, Margherita. "'Fallo cafir golpado' 1387C:
Análisis e la adaptación de una fábula esópica en el
libro de buen amor." *Studia Hispanica in Honorem*
R. Lapesa. Madrid: Gredos, 1975, pp. 369-374.

Deals with the adaptation by Juan Ruiz of P503 "Cock-
eral and Pearl" (TMI J1061.1) in the *Libro de Buen Amor.*
Textual and language problems are discussed as is the
immediate source, most likely the Lyon copy of the
Walter of England collection.

907. Moser-Rath, Elfriede. "Erzähler auf der Kanzel."
Fabula, 2 (1958), 1-29.

A discussion of the modes and uses of various motifs
found in the Baroque sermon, including a number of
fables.

908. ———. "Das streitsüchtige Eheweib, Erzählformen des
17. Jahrhunderts zum Schwanktyp ATh 1365." *Rheinisches*
Jahrbuch für Volkskunde, 10 (1959), 40-52.

A discussion of P682 "Contrary Wife" (A-T 1365; TMI
T255.2) in various texts from the seventeenth century.

909. ———. *Predigtmärlein der Barockzeit.* Berlin: de
Gruyter, 1964. 545 pp.

Monumental investigation of 270 *exempla*, *Schwank*,
fabular as well as other short narrative motifs distributed over the sermons of a number of seventeenth-
century preachers. An extensive introduction is followed by the 270 texts, followed by a commentary with
copious notes, variants, sources, and bibliographical
notes. Fables are keyed to A-T numbers and provided
with TMI numbers.

910. ———. "Scherz und Ernst beysammen: Volkskundlicher
Erzählgut in geistlichen Schriften des 18. Jahrhunderts." *Zeitschrift für Volkskunde*, 61 (1965),
38-73.

Continues her search for traditional narrative materials (see her *Predigtmärlein*) in the eighteenth century.
In addition to a comprehensive overview of the subject,
a wide-ranging series of texts is included which contain a number of fabular motifs.

911. ————. "Die Fabel als rhetorisches Element in der
     katholischen Predigt der Barockseit." *Die Fabel:*
     Theorie, Geschichte und Rezeption einer Gattung. Ed.
     Peter Hasubek. Berlin: Schmidt, 1982, 59-75.

     This informative essay covers both the pros and cons
     of the seventeenth century debate concerning the use of
     fables and tales in sermons, a debate which might have
     itself been something of a literary topos. Lists
     priests who used fables and describes their technique,
     focusing upon Andreas Strobl for whom Moser-Rath lists
     32 sermons out of one hundred as having fables or fable-
     like tales. These are listed with A-T numbers where
     applicable. The fable wins back one of its original
     functions, that of rhetorical device, in this century.

912. Mosino, F. "Simonide, Esope e le mule." *Quaderni*
     Urbinati di cultura classica Roma, 28 (1978), 93-96.

     Connects P315 "Mule" (TMI L465), in which the mule
     exclaims that his mother was a horse, to a verse in
     Simonides, a witness to the triumph of the Tyrant
     Anaxilaos whose chariot was pulled by a vainglorious
     mule. Mosino thus urges "mother" rather than "father"
     in the line "my father was a horse."

913. Moss, Joy. "Fable and Critical Thinking." *Language*
     Arts, 58 (1980), 21-29.

     Literary fables are used as "focus units" to help
     children discover basic characteristics of the literary
     genre and to guide them toward understanding the idea
     of "oral tradition." Bibliography of modern children's
     fables and similar literature.

914. Mourgues, Odette de. *O Muse, fuyante proie: Essai sur*
     la poésie de La Fontaine. Paris: Corti, 1962.

     A sensitive and illuminating study concerned with
     highlighting La Fontaine the literary artist at the
     expense of La Fontaine the moralist. De Mourgues
     makes the point that La Fontaine is not writing a
     manual of conduct, and the fables are therefore to be
     considered on their literary merit. La Fontaine's es-
     thetic is seen to be unique and remarkably varied.

915. ————. "Two Speeches in La Fontaine's *Fables*. VII,
     1." *Modern Language Review*, 58 (1963), 70-73.

     A stylistic note to the lion's speech in VII, 1 and

to one by the fox. La Fontaine's vocabulary, imagery, and fluctuations in stylistic considerations are all investigated.

916. Mowry, Hua-yuan Li. "The Wolf of Chung-Shan." *Tamkang Review*, 11 (1980), 139-159.

Deals with the *Chung-shan lung chuan* "Story of the Wolf of Chung-shan" by Ma Chung-hsi (1446-1512), a Ming form of a wolf tale identical in motif to P640 "Man and Serpent" (A-T 155; TMI J1172.3) known from the *Panchatantra* to modern collections as well as in the Reynard the Fox cycle. Mowry sees the earliest Chung-shan Wolf variant in the *Disciplina clericalis* (twelfth century); the Chinese form is determined to be dependent upon the *Panchatantra*.

917. Müller, Carl Werner. "Ennius und Äsop." *Museum Helveticum*, 33 (1976), 193-218.

An exhaustive investigation of P325 "Lark and Farmer" (A-T 93; TMI J1031) from Quintus Ennius' *Satura* (21-58). Begins with a study of the fable in Gellius with emphasis upon the action. The fable is discussed as satire; the two concepts are said to have a natural affinity for each other. The Ennius fable is compared to Babrius, and Müller demonstrates that Babrius was not the source, postulating a Hellenistic model of some sort.

918. Muller, J.W. "De Twee Dichters van Reinaert I." *Tijdschrift voor Nederlandse Taal- en Letterkunde*, 31 (1912), 177-276.

A very extensive linguistic and stylistic analysis of the two assumed authors of *Reinaert I*, which includes in passing a series of fables used by Author B. These are analyzed to determine dialect, formulae, and lexicon so as to determine the poet's distinct status.

919. Müller, Lucian. *De Phaedri et Aviani fabulis libellis*. Leipzig: Teubner, 1875. iii + 34 pp.

Numerous notes preparatory to critical editions of the fabulists mentioned. The metrics of Phaedrus are discussed extensively, Avianus' mention of Phaedrus is discounted.

920. ————. "Phaedriana." *Rheinisches Museum für Philologie*, 30 (1875), 618-619.

Short note on the metrical forms found in Phaedrus
and the necessity to base textual criticism upon a
sound knowledge of these forms.

921. ———. "Über Naucks Phaedrusstudien." *Berliner
Philologischer Wochenschrift* (1890), 130-140. Also
Berlin: Calvary, 1890. 16 pp.

A rebuttal of Nauck's 1880 commentary on Müller's
Phaedrus edition, demonstrating that two of the proposed emendations are not necessary and that four
others lack evidence.

922. Müller, Max. "On the Migration of Fables." *Chips from
a German Workshop*. London: Longmans, 1875. 4, 145-
209. Also in *Selected Essays on Language, Mythology
and Religion*. 1, 500-576. Also reprinted in *World's
Best Literature*. Ed. Charles Warner. New York:
Hill, 1902, 10429-10441.

The fable of the Dairy Maid and the Milkpot (La Fontaine's "La laitière et le pot au lait") is traced from
the *Panchatantra* to the *Hitopadesa*, the *Kalila wa Dimna*
and through various versions during the Middle Ages in
Arabic, Persian, and Latin. La Fontaine's version is
traced back to the medieval *Dialogus creaturam moralisa-
tus* with a number of intermediate stages. All done in
support of Müller's theory of the migration of fable
motifs from one culture to another.

923. Müller, Rolf. "Die Cyrillische Fabel und ihre Verbreitung in der deutschen Literatur." Dissertation,
Mainz, 1955. 303 pp.

Traces the effects of the Cyrillian Fables upon German literature, both in Latin and in Ulrich von Pottenstein's translation: *Buch der natürlichen Weisheit*
(1410). The influence of the *Speculum sapientiae* is
traced through collections in German and Latin especially in the sixteenth century. The structure of
the Cyrillian fable and the types of narratives found
in the collection are investigated, with significant
differences between this form and the more common
Aesopic type noted.

924. Murtaugh, Daniel M. "Henryson's Animals." *Texas
Studies in Literature and Language*, 14 (1972), 405-
421.

This article uses three of Henryson's fables: "The

Preiching of the Swallow," P39 (A-T 233C; TMI J652.2);
"The Taill of the Uponlandis Mous and the Burges Mous,"
P352 "Country Mouse and City Mouse," (A-T 112; TMI
J211.1); and "The Taill of the Paddock and the Mous,"
P384 (A-T 278; TMI J651.1) to illustrate the irony inherent in the recognition of one's circumstances in an
identification with the animal characters in these
fables. Murtaugh demonstrates the three fables deal
essentially with the same problem: man at the mercy of
a random power.

925. Nancy, Jean-Luc. "Mundus est Fabula." [Translated by
      Daniel Brewer.] *Modern Language Notes*, 93 (1978),
      635-653.

      A discussion of Descartes' "fabulatory law," which
      ranges in and out of the literary fable, with various
      undefined forms of "fabulation" considered as being all
      the same. Nancy often uses "fable" to mean the Aesopic
      type of fable but also apparently as a synonym for fic-
      tion.

926. Nedden, Rudolf. *Quellenstudien zu Gellerts Fabeln und
      Erzählungen*. Dissertation, Leipzig, 1899. 81 pp.

      A short listing and discussion of the sources of
      Christian Fürchtegott Gellert's stories and fables,
      other than the most obvious sources pointed out by
      earlier works and by Gellert himself. Nedden suggests
      that Gellert used more traditional material for his
      fables than any of his contemporaries although many of
      his sources are literary and include the "moral" journals
      of his day. A short discussion of Stoppe's fables
      style is appended.
      See: H. Handwerk, *Studien über Gellerts Fabelstil*.

927. Needler, Howard. "Introduction." *Fables from Old
      French*. Translated by Norman R. Shapiro. Middle-
      town, Conn.: Wesleyan University Press, 1982, xi-lix.

      A historical and incisively critical survey of the
      fable from its beginnings up to Marie de France's
      translation/collection provided as an introduction to
      a series of translations from Old French. Various
      moral stances by various fabulists are discussed,
      followed by a rehearsal of what is known of Marie and
      the circumstances of her collection. Detailed dis-
      cussion of each of the thirty-seven fables in the
      book.

928. Neff, Karl. *Die Gedichte des Paulus Diaconus: Kritische und erklärende Ausgabe.* Munich: Beck, 1908. 220 pp.

The introduction to this edition of the poems of Paulus Diaconus provides an important catalogue and description of the manuscripts for the tradition of the three fables that are attributed to him. These three fables are the earliest known versions of the motifs: P585 "Sick Lion, Wolf and Fox" (cf. P258, A-T 50; TMI B246.4, K961); P586 "Calf and Stork" (TMI J2214.5); P587 "Flea and Gout" (TMI J6.2.1.1), and each is provided with an introduction and an *apparatus criticus*.

929. Nestle, Wilhelm. "Die Fabel des Menenius Agrippa." *Klio*, 21 (1927), 350-360. Reprinted in *Griechische Studien*. Stuttgart, 1944, 502-516.

The fable of Menenius Agrippa, P130 "Stomach and Feet" (A-T 293; TMI J461.1) is an isolated case in history. Its authenticity is not to be doubted. The traits discussed include affinities with Plato (the concept of the state as an organism) and with Judaic literature.

930. ————. "Ein pessimistischer Zug im Prometheusmythus." *Archiv für Religionswissenschaft*, 34 (1937), 378-381.

A note on P430 "Creation of Man" (from Themistius, *Orat.*) and P266 "Two Wallets" which have Prometheus as creator. Both are pessimistic in nature which seems to be a fabular adaptation to the Prometheus myth cycle.

931. Neuhaus-Koch, Ariane. "Die gesellschaftliche Funktion der Fabel in der Restaurationszeit." *Die Fabel: Theorie, Geschichte und Rezeption einer Gattung.* Ed. Peter Hasubek. Berlin: Schmidt, 1982, 180-197.

Informative essay on the fable activity of a number of turn of the century writers in Germany. The fables of August Friedrich Langbein (1757-1835), Friedrich Haug (1761-1829), Abraham Fröhlich (1796-1865) are discussed with an eye toward demonstrating the contrast of traditional materials with the contemporary social criticism of the form. Franz Grillparzer is shown using the fable as a crystallization point of liberal political thought. Heinrich Heine uses the form as a satirical vehicle to delineate his times. In general, the particular understanding of society articulated in

the fable in Germany from roughly 1815 to about 1855
helps to explain the social function of the genre as
seen and practiced by these authors.

932. Neumann, Siegfried. "Aspekte der Wellerismen-Forschung."
      Proverbium, 6 (1966), 131-137.

      Deals with various problems of Wellerism research
      and discusses the relationship of the form to the
      fable, among other things. Extensive bibliography.

933. Newbigging, Thomas. *Fables and Fabulists Ancient and
      Modern.* London: E. Stock, 1895 and New York: Fredrick
      Stokes, n.d. [1904?]. 152 pp.

      Defines the fable as a special branch of literature
      in which the imagination has full play, wherein the
      fabulist gives the power of speech to "humbler subjects"
      and in which the narration is true only in its applica-
      tion. This introduces a discussion of the characteris-
      tics and applications of fables, now generally outdated,
      followed by a historical survey of the form from
      Aesop through the nineteenth century. Appended is an
      index of fables and fabulists.

934. Newlyn, Evelyn S. "Robert Henryson and the Popular
      Fable Tradition in the Middle Ages." *Journal of
      Popular Culture*, 14 (1980), 108-118.

      An illuminating essay working out from the popularity
      of the fable in the Middle Ages to discuss Henryson's
      Moral Fables as used for education on political and
      social issues as well as for entertainment.
      See: Baumann, "The Folktale and Oral Tradition," and
      Fox, *Poems of Robert Henryson.*

935. Ničev, A. "Sophronios' Aisopus." *Jazik i Literatura,*
      18: 6 (1963), 61-74.

      Notes to the fable translations of Sophronios Branasky
      (1739-1813).

936. Nickisch, Reinhard M.G. "Über die Fabeltheorien des
      19. Jahrhunderts und ihr Verhältnis zur Tradition."
      *Die Fabel: Theorie, Geschichte und Rezeption einer
      Gattung.* Ed. Peter Hasubek. Berlin: Schmidt, 1982,
      198-214.

      Builds upon Briegel-Florig (q.v.) for an investiga-
      tion of critical materials on the fable of the nineteenth

century. Nickisch suggests this century was perhaps
more concerned with the fable's "volkspädagogisch"
function than any other and investigates the very wide-
spread interest in fable theory from Herder to modern
fable critics.

937. Niess, Robert Judson. "A Study of the Influence of
Jean de La Fontaine on the Works of Felix M. de
Samaniego." Dissertation, Minnesota, 1937. 162 pp.

A thoroughgoing study of the influences of La Fontaine upon Samaniego and other Iberian fabulists with
particular attention paid to the sources of the fables.

938. Nikitine, B. "Quelques fables kurdes d'animaux."
Folk-Lore, 40 (1929), 228-244.

Reviews, with commentary, Kurdish animal tales including a number of fables received by the author in 1917-
1918. The fables are related to Greek and Indian analogues.

939. Nikliborg, Anna. "La Fontaine en Pologne." *Europe*,
515 (1972), 155-162.

Begins with a summary of the history of the fable,
which begins in Poland long before La Fontaine. The
entry of La Fontaine's fables is traced to Christophe's
translation of forty fables in imitation of the La Fontaine form. 1731 saw Jablonowski's work and others
written in imitation of the collection, and La Fontaine's influence in Poland continues up to the 1971
edition of La Fontaine's *Bajki*.

940. Noel, Thomas Lawrence. "The Rise and Fall of a Genre:
Theories of the Fable in the 18th Century." Dissertation, Illinois (Urbana), 1971. Later: *Theories
of the Fable in the Eighteenth Century*. New York:
Columbia University Press, 1975. 177 pp.

This monograph, rewritten from the author's dissertation, presents a very thorough review of the major
theories of the fable which were expounded and espoused
in Western Europe during the eighteenth century. Beginning with La Fontaine and other seventeenth-century
forerunners, most major fabulists through Herder and
the Romantics are highlighted generally by country
although this is not strictly maintained. Most theories
are paraphrased and analyzed, compared and contrasted.
Fable theory in England from Locke, Roger L'Estrange,

and John Ogilby is delineated; in France from La Fontaine through Baudoin and La Motte and Richter. Germany is represented by Hagedorn and Gottsched, Daniel
Triller and Daniel Stoppe followed by Gellert, and
Lessing who dominates the middle section of the monograph. Herder and the theories of Lessing are contrasted, and the fable in Spain together with the dis-
solution of the fable as a viable literary genre end
the work, mentioning at the very end Grimm's view
which set the fable into the realm of folklore. Limited
bibliography.

941.   Noelle, August. *Beiträge zum Studium der Fabel mit
       besonderer Berücksichtigung Jean de La Fontaine,
       nebst vergleichenen Texten und metrischen Verdeutsch-
       ungen.* Program, Cuxhaven: Raschenplatz, 1893.   57 pp.

       Short introduction to the idea of the fable as a
       literary genre with an analysis of the La Fontaine
       fable. Paraphrases and metrical translations and a
       listing of the "unaesopic" rhetorical intrusions.

942.   Nøjgaard, Morten. "Le Cerf, le cheval, et l'homme."
       Classica et Mediaevalia, 24 (1963), 1-19.

       Deals with P269A "Stag, Horse and Man" (TMI K192)
       in a number of versions including Sumerian, Greek, and
       Latin. Two main versions, P269 "Wild Boar, Horse and
       Hunter," and the version with the Stag, are discussed
       in detail. The Romulus tradition seems to represent a
       mixture of the two.

943.   ————. *La fable antique.* Tome 1: *La Fable grecque
       avant Phèdre.* Copenhagen: Nordisk Forlag, 1964.
       Tome 2: *Les grands fabulisten.* Copenhagen: Nyt Nor-
       disk Forlag, 1967.   600 and 471 pp.

       This massive rewrite of the author's dissertation
       begins with the idea of a fable as a world self-suf-
       ficient but intruding into that of the reader. Ancient
       fable collections and fable theory are examined, but
       ancient theory does not deal with the fable in anything
       but the simplistic terms of a fiction displaying a
       truth. Nøjgaard deals with the form structurally as
       a literary genre with each element related to each
       other element in any given piece. The fables are thus
       examined without externally enforced standards for eval-
       uation. The fables of the *recensio Augustana*, most
       likely from the first century and likely to be before

Phaedrus (indeed possibly his source), are investigated
under a very complex series of criteria. This results
in the idea that the typical fable is a conflict between
two characters, with the overriding conclusion that the
weaker of the two was silly to have undertaken the conflict in the first place. The fable is most likely of
Near Eastern origin, ultimately Sumerian. The second
volume continues essentially the same type of criticism
with the fables of Phaedrus and Babrius. The morals
of the two fabulists are compared and contrasted, Phaedrus continuing in the Aesopic mold, Babrius being more
concerned with character and displaying a certain con-
tempt for the lower classes. With appendices, bibliography, and a list of fables treated.

944.   ————. "The Moralization of the Fable: From Aesop to
       Romulus." *Medieval Narrative: A Symposium. Proceed-
       ings of the Third International Symposium Organized
       by the Centre for the Study of Vernacular Literature
       in the Middle Ages.* Ed. Hans Bekker-Nielsen, et al.
       Odense: Odense University Press, 1979, 31-43.

       Nøjgaard sees a constant tension between the fable
       and its moral and demonstrates in this essay changes in
       the fables as differing moralistic tendencies shaped
       the attitudes of the fabulists. In the ancient fable
       values of justice and virtue are ignored, and the only
       positive qualities are strength and cunning. Nøjgaard
       sees three stages in a demonstrable change: first, in
       the Augustana recension, second, in Phaedrus, and,
       third, in the Romulus collection. Each of these is
       shown to be different in using P155 "Wolf and Lamb"
       (A-T 111A; TMI U31) as a constant. Phaedrus, for ex-
       ample, gives the moral a narrative function; in Romulus,
       however, it is characteristically independent from the
       narration.

945.   Nouaros, André M. *Une fable grecque moderne: Structure-
       éléments originaux qui dénotent la mentalité particu-
       lière du jeune Grec.* Athens: Athanassios Altintzi
       Salonique, 1979. 108 pp.

       Proceeds from the concept that folktales of various
       kinds are a symbolization of particular psychological
       experiences and, especially, experiences of a type that
       is somewhat recoverable from the natural world of the
       child. This is based upon the idea that *Märchen* and
       fables contain exactly that which is pleasing to children.

The proof for this is that children react negatively
to that which they do not like. One needs then only
analyze the tales to discover the secrets of the nature
of the child. Nouaros uses P562 "Partridge and Fox"
(A-T 61; TMI K561.1, K721) and other tales to determine
the attention span of the child and to determine set
"units of narration" out of which the material is constructed. Nouraos seems to feel that he can determine
certain national characteristics (here, among the Greeks)
through these and allied techniques.

946. Novotný, Miloslav. *Ezop Václava Hollara*. Prague:
      Sfinx, 1936. 34 pp.

      Introduction to the plates by Hollar used in the
      1665 edition of John Ogilby's *Aesop Paraphras'd*. With
      reproductions and listings of fables.

947. Olájubŭ, Oludáre. "The Use of Yoruba Folktales as a
      Means of Moral Education." *Fabula*, 19 (1978), 211-
      224.

      Deals with fables and other folktales used in the
      moral education of the Yoruba in the Federal Republic
      of Nigeria. The methodology is traditional as are the
      materials. The article contains examples of the tales
      and their moral content and a commentary on the decline
      of traditional moral education as a result of the intro-
      duction of Western culture and educational systems.

948. Oldaker, W.H. "Greek Fables and Babrius." *Greece and
      Rome*, 3 (1934), 85-93.

      Discusses the origin and development of the fables
      in Greece and traces the rediscovery of Babrius and
      his position within this tradition. A few Babrian
      fables and manuscripts are discussed.

949. Oldfather, William A. "New Manuscript Material for the
      Study of Avianus." *Transactions of the American
      Philological Society*, 42 (1911), 105-121.

      Traces the history of Avianus scholarship, with par-
      ticular regard to the establishment of the corpus.
      Lists numerous manuscripts and the Heinrich Steinhöwel's
      Esopus which contains twenty-seven fables from Avianus
      and which is the first known (partial) edition, as well
      as a number of *florilgeia* and other collections. Five
      newly noted medieval texts and introductions to Avianus
      are described as are six collections of imitations and
      paraphrases.
      See: Küppers, *Die Fabeln Avians*.

950. ———. "Bibliographical Notes on the Fables of Avianus." *Papers of the Bibliographical Society of America*, 15: 2 (1921), 61-77.

Lists materials not found in Hervieux or incompletely described there. Issues a call for a systematic bibliography of Avianus, including all incunabula and prose re-workings during the Middle Ages.

951. ———. "A Fleury Text of Avianus." *Philological Quarterly*, 5 (1926), 20-28.

Builds on Rand's assumption that the Codex Leidensis Vossianus Lat. Q 86 came from Fleury. Oldest known manuscript comes from St. Gallen from which emanate three branches in the manuscript tradition.

952. ———. "An Aesopic Fable in a Schoolboy's Exercise." *Aegyptus*, 10 (1929), 255-257.

Discusses a variant of P9 "Fox and Goat in the Well" (A-T 31; TMI K652), as a schoolboy's exercise working off an original cast in iambics. The moral of the fable is very close to a Babrian fable.

953. Omont, H. "Sur un ms de Phèdre." *CRPI* (1912), 11.

A note to variant reading of the Rheims manuscript.

954. O'Neill, E.W., Jr. "A Trend in Fable Literature after La Fontaine: The Fable Play." *French Review*, 27 (1953/54), 354-359.

Discusses the reception of La Fontaine's fables, particularly as they relate to oral recitation or dramatic reworking, and the popularity of the fable in France after La Fontaine (some 200 fabulists areknown before 1900). Twelve playwrights who used fables are touched upon, from Boursault (*Esope à la ville* 1690) to the Vicomte de Marignac (*Esope chez Xanthus* 1801, presented at the Théâtre du Vandeville.) A discussion of the nature of these plays with their common elements ends the article

955. Österley, Hermann. *Romulus: Die Paraphrasen des Phaedrus und die aesopische Fabel im Mittelalter*. Berlin: Weidmann, 1870. 124 pp.

The introduction to this edition of the Romulus contains an illuminating essay on the history of the fable during the Middle Ages, now outdated, but containing a

still convenient listing of the more important manuscripts and their features. These are reviewed in an
attempt to bring their relationships into alignment.
The Romulus collection is treated as essentially a
single prose version of Phaedrus. Österley deals with
the corpus in a literary-historical context.

956.   ———. *Steinhöwels Äsop*. Tübingen: Litterarischer
        Verein in Stuttgart, 1873. 372 pp.

Steinhöwel's 1476/1477 *Esopus* is edited and minimally
annotated in this edition. The introduction provides
a cursory historical background, including a partial
history of the collections from which it is formed, as
well as the printing history of the *Esopus* itself.
See: Carnes, "Heinrich Steinhöwel."

957.   Ott, Karl August. "Lessing und La Fontaine: Von dem
        Gebrauch der Tiere in der Fabel." *Germanisch-
        Romanische Monatschrift*, 40 (1959), 235-266.

Lessing's *Abhandlungen über die Fabel* are used as the
starting point for a compelling and wide-ranging essay
on the nature of the proverb and its relationship to
the fable (the common didacticism and the idea of
whether some fables are expanded forms of proverbs
or some proverbs reduced forms of fables), and on
another complex of ideas: the fable as imitation and
its unity within its literary replications, especially
with regard to its ability to maintain its didactic
element.

958.   ———. "La Fontaine als Vorbild: Einflüsse franzö-
        sischer Fabeldichtung auf die deutschen Fabeldichter
        des 18. Jahrhunderts." *Die Fabel: Theorie, Geschichte
        und Rezeption einer Gattung*. Ed. Peter Hasubek.
        Berlin: Schmidt, 1982, 76-105.

Building upon the dichotomy between the history of
the fable and the history of fable theory, this illuminating essay covers the period in German fable writings
from the point wherein the history of the two activities
reunited. This turning point was brought about by La
Fontaine and was especially manifest in Germany by
Lessing. La Fontaine's influence is discussed in detail
from form and stylistic considerations to characterizations.

959. Otto, Paul (Elais Erasmus). "Lichtwer und seine
     Fabeln." *Von Büchern und Menschen: Festschrift für
     Fedor von Zobeltietz.* Weimar: Gesellschaft der
     Bibliophilen, 1927, 165-187.

     A thoroughgoing discussion of Lichtwer's fables with
     an eye towards casting more light on his biography.
     Follows the poet's life by means of the editions and
     the various changes in the contents of his fables.

960. Pabst, Walter. "La Fontaines Narziss und Moses: Kleine
     Beiträge zur Prüfung des Begriffs *Fable.*" *Romanis-
     tisches Jahrbuch,* 22 (1971), 123-129.

     La Fontaine's "L'Homme et son image" (I, 11) is ex-
     pressly connected to a mythic image ("Que fait notre
     Narcisse?"), yet the hero of the poem is an Anti-
     Narcissis who fears rather than desires, his image.
     Pabst also connects "Le Berger et le Roi" (X, 9) with
     Moses generally on the basis of the similarity of the
     snake transformation, and the essay ends with a dis-
     cussion of La Fontaine's concept of the fable, which
     involves a conscious fusion of various ideas inherent
     in the word.

961. Padoan, Giorgio. "Il *Liber Esopi* e due episodi dell'
     Inferno." *Studi Danteschi,* 16 (1964), 75-102.

     Suggests that Dante's allusion to P384 "Mouse and
     Frog" (A-T 278; TMI J681.1) in Canto XXIII of the *In-
     ferno,* 4-8 is to be understood in those parts mentioned
     by Dante and not necessarily in a process that recalls
     the entire fable. The deceit of the frog corresponds
     to a similar trait in Ciampolo who is often called a
     frog; the idea that such false action leads to self-
     destruction corresponds to the demons' battle.
     See: Larkin, "*Inferno,* XXIII, 4-9 Again."

962. Paepre, F. "Die Fabel vom Eichbaum und vom Schilfrohr.
     Eine Deutung von La Fontaine: Le chêne et le roseau."
     Neophilologische Zeitschrift, 3 (1951), 89-101.

     Examines P70 "Oak and Reed" (A-T 298C; TMI J832) to-
     gether with various attempts to connect the fable to
     political events of La Fontaine's day.

963. Pallas, D.I. "Peri tēn eikonographian ton Aisopeion
     Mūthon." *Epeteris Hetaireias Buzantin Spoudon,* 34
     (1965), 332-335.

     Deals with a number of representations of Aesopic

fables in Byzantine art forms, sculpture, and mosaics.
A number of scenes are described as having been inspired
by various fables.

964.   Palm, E.W.   "Diego Velazquez: Aesop und Menipp."
       Lebende Antike: Symposium für R. Sühnel.   Ed. H.
       Meller und H.J. Zimmermann.   Berlin: Schmidt, 1967,
       207-217.

       Deals with Velazquez' "Two Philosophers," characterized
       here as working with an equation with two or more un-
       knowns.   Identification of the two has been the main
       topic of discussion.

965.   Pannwitz, Rudolf.   "Äsop."   *Antaios*, 8 (1967), 47-65.

       Aesop is compared to the Seven Wise Ones and to other
       givers of wisdom in this essay which suggests that the
       Sententiae and other collections of gnomic materials
       are very much like the fables.   The fable material is
       something original and can be described in terms of a
       cosmic and a moral fable form.   The first contains ele-
       ments of the divine and the demonic, with mythic ele-
       ments surviving in a number of fables.   The moral fable
       was perhaps not originally moralistic but became so
       inclined by the time fables were recorded.   A short
       historical survey of the Babylonian, Egyptian, and
       Assyrian fable, together with an argument for the proper
       designation of the fable ends the essay.   No bibliog-
       raphy and no listing of fables discussed.

966.   Papademetriou, John-Theophanes.   "Studies in the Manu-
       script Tradition of *Stephanites kai Ichnelates.*"
       Dissertation, University of Illinois at Urbana, 1960.
       207 pp.

       Presents the Greek text of the Fables of Bidpai in
       the eleventh century translation from the Arabic into
       Greek by Symeon Seth in thirty-five manuscripts.
       Traces its history and success.

967.   ————.   "The Sources and Character of Del Governo de'
       Regni."   *Transactions of the American Philological
       Association*, 92 (1961), 422-439.

       Describes the *Del governo de' regni*, a 1583 Italian
       translation of the *Fables of Bidpai*, printed at Ferrara.
       The history of the material and the nature of the
       translation follow.   The alterations do not seem to be
       systematic ones, rather haphazard; no stories were
       added or omitted.

968. ————. *Archaion Ellenikon mythographikon thema kai mythoi tou Vatikanou Kodikos 1139*. Athens: n.p., 1968. 30 pp. Also in *Epeteris Etaireias Byzantinon Spoudon*, 36 (1968), 241-259.

The motif of iron- or gold-eating mice is found in a number of Greek and Roman authors but appears to have had its origins in Oriental sources. The fable containing this motif is found in the *Panchatantra* and its derivatives and ultimately makes its way to La Fontaine (IX, 1 "Le Dépositaire infidèle"). The texts of the fables and others containing this motif are discussed as translations from the Greek.
See: Papademetriou, "The Mutations of an Ancient Greek Proverb."

969. ————. "Ta Schedê tou Myos: New Sources and Text." *Classical Studies Presented to Ben Edwin Perry by His Students and Colleagues at the University of Illinois, 1924-1960*. Illinois Studies in Language and Literature, no. 58. University of Illinois Press: Urbana, 1969, 210-222.

Treats three codices containing the *Schedê tou myos* toward the establishment of a better text of the work which contains a fable similar in motif to P592 "Cat as Monk" (TMI K1961 and K2010) known from Odo of Cheriton. The text was intended as an amusing dialogue with humor from the ironic positioning of scripture in an absurd context. Prints texts and offers a stemma of textual relationships.

970. ————. "Kritika, Glossika kai Ermeneutika eis ten Peri Aisopoi Mythistorian. Symbole A." *Platon*, 21 (1969), 251-269.

Presents a number of emendations to the G version of the *Vita Aesopi* as edited by Ben Edwin Perry in *Aesopica* and named here the *Perriana*. Lengthy discussion of lexical items building upon the work of earlier scholars.

971. ————. "The Mutation of an Ancient Greek Proverb." *Revue des Études Grecques*, 83 (1970), 94-105.

Although the belief in iron-eating mice seems to have died out, still the proverbial use of the image has survived in Greek oral tradition in the form of a widely used modern Greek proverb. The proverb is not likely to have come into being without the background

of story, and the motif is traced to the *Panchatantra*
and Greek forms derived from Indian and Near Eastern
sources. The motif travels with the Indian tales
reaching La Fontaine's collection (IX, 1 "Le Dépositaire
infidèle"; TMI J1531.2).

972.   ———. "Kritika, Glossika kai Ermeneutika eis ten
        Peri Aisopou Mythistorian: Symbole B." *Athena*, 73/74
        (1973), 231-44.

        Continues Papademetriou's earlier emendations and com-
        mentary on the *Vita Aesopi* as edited by Perry in his
        Aesopica. Introduction to the manuscript and history
        of the Romance together with bibliographical notes and
        lexical suggestions.

973.   ———. "Notes on the Aesop Romance New Series, I."
        Rheinisches Museum für Philologie, 123 (1980), 25-40.

        Extensive commentary on the *Vita Aesopi* with special
        attention to the *G Vita*, edited by Perry in his *Aesopica*,
        dating from the tenth century, in contrast to the Wester-
        mann version. Details much earlier research and makes
        a number of emendations and corrections.

974.   Papathomopoulos, Manolis. "Aesopica I." *Platon*, 26
        (1974), 51-52 and 289-302.

        Suggestions and emendations to various Aesopic
        materials including the *Vita Aesopi* in the Perry edi-
        tion of *Aesopica*.

975.   Parassoglou, George. "A Latin Text and a New Aesop
        Fable." *Studia Papyrologica*, 13 (1974), 31-37.

        A description of P. Yale inv. 1158V, noting that
        P. Mich 456 and 457 join allowing better reconstruction
        of the fable of the Swallow, P39 "Wise Swallow" (A-T
        233C; TMI J652.2), as first in C.H. Roberts (q.v.).
        New version has the bird urge the destruction of the
        flax. With texts and notes.
        See: Perry, "Demetrius of Phalerum."

976.   Paris, Gaston. "Les Fabulists latines." *Journal des
        Savants* (1884/1885). Published separately, Paris:
        Imprimerie nationale, 1885. 31 pp. Rpt. New York:
        Burt Franklin, 1972.

        Very extensive criticism of Leopold Hervieux's *Les
        Fabulistes latines*, generally helpful, but with numerous

examples of errors. Paris himself commits the same
sort of fault, as in his identification of Ademar with
the *Anonymous Nilanti* and in his version of the manuscript tradition of Romulus. There is also no evidence
that Phaedrus composed 200 fables. Nevertheless,
Paris' essay is now a necessary adjunct to Hervieux's
edition.

977. ———. "Une fable à retrouver." *Romania*, 31 (1902),
100-103.

Verse 3053 of *Aliscans* contains a reference to a fable
which has been variously identified as P553 "Crow and
Sheep" (TMI W121.2.3) and a number of others. The
fable is tentatively given the characters *tor* and *nuiton*
but is not identified.

978. ———. "Raimond de Béziers: Traducteur et compila-
teur." *Histoire littéraire de la France*, 33 (1906),
191-253.

The story of Raimond de Béziers translating a Cas-
tilian version of the *Kalila wa Dimna* into Latin for
Jeanne de Navarre-Champagne leads to a lengthy and
comprehensive introduction to the transmission of the
Bidpai fables and an exposition of the tradition in
Medieval Europe. The material is traced from Sanscrit
to Pahlavi to Syriac, Arabic, Hebrew, and Spanish.
Manuscript families are traced and some individual
fabular motifs are highlighted. Extensive bibliographical
references in the notes.

979. Parmée, Douglas. "'Cric? Crac!': Fables of La Fontaine
in Haitian Creole. A Literary Ethno-Socio-Linguistic
Curiosity." *Nottingham French Studies*, 15: 2 (1976),
12-26.

Presents a discussion of Georges Sylvain's *Cric? Crac!*,
a Haitian Creole version of 31 La Fontaine fables first
published in 1902. The title refers to a Haitian narration custom: a "cric?" from a story-teller receives
an answering "crac!" which hints toward the use to which
the fables are put. They are told for their entertainment value. All the fables are longer in the Haitian,
and Parmée gives examples of the added descriptive
materials and describes the proverbs used for epimythia.

980. Partridge, Emely, and George Partridge. "Fables and
Other Purposive Stories." *Storytelling in School and
Home*. New York: Sturgis, 1912.

All fables and other moral tales are designed to be told with a purpose. The purpose is to teach, and this is effected by an encoding device which at once conveys the teaching point but which also calls to mind other forms of traditional material. Examples of fabular motifs are given but not indexed.

981. Pascal, Carlo. *Letteratura Latina Medievale: Nuovi Saggi e Note Critiche.* Catania: Battiato, 1909. Esp. pp. 91-102.

Deals extensively with the history and spread of P130 "Stomach and Feet" (A-T 293; TMI J461.1) and its popularity in the Middle Ages. Pascal suggests the fable originated with Ovid.
See: David Hale, "Intestine Sedition," and *The Body Politic.*

982. Patterson, Anne Elizabeth. "Descartes' Animal-Machine and Neoclassical Satire: Animal Imagery in Selected Works of La Fontaine and Swift." Dissertation, Wisconsin, 1973. 329 pp.

La Fontaine's initial traditional use of the fable image for man and then his direct criticism of the Animal-Machine are the focuses of this dissertation, with Swift also discussed. La Fontaine's criticism takes three forms: comic exaggeration of the "happy beast" theme, emphasis upon the animal as animal, and reinterpretation of the Cartesian language criteria for separation of man from animal. La Fontaine's attack is direct in the second collection.

983. Pecere, Oronzo. *Petronio, La Novella della Matrona di Efeso.* Miscellanea Erudita, no. 27. Padua: Editrice Antenore, 1975. xv + 150 pp.

This monograph provides a lengthy commentary on the Phaedrus and Romulus version of this famous story, P543 "Widow and Soldier" (A-T 1510; TMI K2213.1), and suggests the Phaedrus form began the moralistic tendencies that are seen in Petronius. The common source of both is likely to have shown less of this tendency.

984. Périvier, Jacques-Henri. "'La Cigale et la fourmi' comme introduction aux fables." *The French Review,* 42 (1969), 419-429.

This informative and well-argued article discusses the position of "La Cigale et la fourmi," P373 "Ant and

Cicada" (A-T 280A; TMI 711.1) in the collection. Although little is known concerning the composition of the *Fables*, it seems clear that organization is the rule, not chance. By placing this fable at the beginning, La Fontaine is apparently sending a signal to his reader. The first fable is not only good (bonne) but also concise (brève). This is in effect the only rule of the genre.

985. ———. "Fondement et mode de l'éthique dans les *Fables* de La Fontaine." *Kentucky Romance Quarterly*, 18 (1971), 333-347.

Highly interesting essay dealing with the moral system and the amoralism of a determinist conception of human nature in La Fontaine. The essential division is not one of good and evil but of wise and foolish. Stylistic analysis of various passages, highlighting La Fontaine's irony.

986. Permiakov, G.L. *Ot pogovorki do skazki: Zametki po obschei teorii klishe.* Moscow: Nauka, 1970. Also *From Proverb to Folk-tale: Notes on the General Theory of Cliché.* Moscow: Nauka, 1979. Esp. pp. 205-227.

This monograph presents a wide-ranging discussion of proverbs and proverbial phrases, including "fablettes" (extended metaphors) and fables. On the theory of cliché (by Y.V. Rozhdestvensky, "Folkloristic in Material, Linguistic in Method") there is an attempt to produce reproducable units or to approach clichés from the standpoint of grammar with proverbs and fables as texts.

987. Perozo, V.M. Pérez. "Fables and Fable-Writers." *Books Abroad*, 20 (1946), 363-367.

A popular survey of the history of the fable is followed by a call to do something to save the fable, described as a literary fossil, in this uncritical essay. "The Grateful Lion" by Trilussa and a paragraph on Walt Disney end the argument.

988. Perrin-Naffakh, Anne-Marie. "Locutions et proverbs dans les Fables de La Fontaine." *L'Information Littéraire*, 31 (1979), 151-155.

Consists of a survey of the proverbs and proverbial phrases found in the *Fables* of La Fontaine, arranged

by type and source and even by dialect. The use of the
proverb within the fable, especially the integration
of the texts, is discussed as is the influence of oral
and literary traditions.

989. Perry, Ben Edwin. "The Origin and the Date of the
      Fables Ascribed to Syntipas." *Proceedings of the
      American Philological Association*, 63 (1933),
      xliv-xlv.

      The oldest version of this curious recension of
      fables is codex Monacensis 525 and Mosquensis 436,
      both from the fourteenth century. This group is dated
      by Perry to the eleventh century and is seen as having
      been very popular in the Near East.

990. ————. "The Text Tradition of the Greek Life of
      Aesop." *Transactions of the American Philological
      Association*, 64 (1933), 198-244.

      Traces three principal versions of the *Vita Aesopi*:
      the "G" (ms 397 in the J. Pierpont Morgan Library),
      the Westermann version, and the Planudean version which
      is ultimately dependent upon the Westermann. Manu-
      scripts are listed and relationships are established
      among these and another, a "mixed" class.
      See: Perry, *Studies in the Text Tradition*.

991. ————. "The Greek Source of Rinuccio's Aesop."
      Classical Philology, 29 (1934), 53-62.

      Attempts to identify the immediate source of the 1438
      translation from Greek into Latin of the life and fables
      of Aesop by Rinuccio d'Arezzo. Some Greek manuscript
      of the Vindobonensis class, perhaps a direct ancestor
      of both Rinuccio's source and the codex Palat. Gr. 269
      is suggested on the basis of omissions common to both
      traditions.

992. ————. *Studies in the Text History of the Life and
      Fables of Aesop*. Philological Monographs of the
      American Philological Association, no. 7. Haverford,
      Penn.: American Philological Association, 1936.
      ix + 240 pp.

      This monograph by one of the most important fable
      scholars of the modern day presents a somewhat contro-
      versial discussion of the text tradition of the *Vita
      Aesopi* with a bias toward the primacy of the "G" text,
      the ms 397 in the Pierpont Morgan library. Perry dates
      the archetype of the *Vita* as early as the fifth century

B.C. in part, although not reaching its present form and contents until 100 B.C.--200 A.D. The analysis continues the textual tradition of the fables, a vastly more complex problem. Four main recensions are recognized: the Augustana, the Vindobonensis, the Accursiana (the modern Vulgate Recension), and the fourth consists of paraphrases of Babrius. Extensive classification of manuscripts and detailed analysis of editions.

993. ———. "The Origin of the Epimythium." *Transactions of the American Philological Association*, 71 (1940), 391-419.

A history of the post-positional "moral tag" on classical fables finds the epimythium frequently in Phaedrus and leads Perry to the view that the epimythium is to be considered a part of the fable from the earliest times. The epimythium is descended from the promythium insofar as it is an author's moral fully generalized and was originally nothing more than an index-heading in a handbook or reference list of rhetorical features. Perry presents an excellent overview of the fable in the body of the article.

994. ———. *Aesopica: A Series of Texts Relating to Aesop or Ascribed to Him or Closely Connected with the Literary Tradition that Bears His Name*. Volume One: *Greek and Latin Texts* [all published]. Urbana, Illinois: University of Illinois Press, 1952. xvii + 765 pp.

Perry offers in this monumental collection considerably more than the fables attributed to Aesop or connected with his name. All the texts relevant to the Classical tradition of Aesop are here and more. The first part is devoted to the *Vita Aesopi*, printing in three full versions, the Greek G and W and the Latin *Lollinina*. Parts 2, 3 and 4 contain the ancient *testimonia*, *sententiae Aesopi*, and the *proverbia Aesopi*, all highly valuable, both because of their previous inaccessibility and their value for a number of problems in the literary history of the fable. The next three sections contain the corpus of Aesopic fables, 725 in total with 471 in Greek, considerably more than any other collection. Some of the fables have little claim to being Aesopic, including some obviously medieval tales, but are included because they have been associated with Aesopic collections. The result is the standard edition and

the standard for collections for some time to come.
All fables mentioned in the present bibliography are
keyed to Perry's *Aesopica* wherever possible.

995.   ——. "An Aesopic Fable in Photius." *Byzantinische*
        Zeitschrift, 46 (1953), 308-313.

        Suggests that the fable of Dionysius and the wine
        ascribed to Aesop by Photius may have been in the
        Demetrius of Phalerum collection and may have been
        accessible to him in that form. The only other attri-
        bution of the fable to Aesop occurs in the *Vita Aesopi*,
        chapter 68. Other possible analogues are listed.

996.   ——. "Babriana." *Classical Philology*, 52 (1957),
        16-23.

        Discusses new readings and emendations introduced in
        his Loeb Edition of Babrius and Phaedrus. Part of
        these are from new witnesses to the text, especially
        ms 397 in the Pierpont Morgan Library which is roughly
        a contemporary of the Athoan manuscript upon which
        alone the greater part of the Babrian tradition depends.

997.   ——. "Fable." *Studium Generale*, 12 (1959), 17-37.

        This important essay surveys various concepts of the
        fable and presents the form in its historical context
        for at least the classical forms. For Perry the only
        constant is the mechanical structure of the narrative
        which is an abstraction derived from the known existence
        of the forms. Eschews any single, all-encompassing
        definition of the fable but discusses in detail the
        forms closely associated with the fable: the simile,
        the proverb, the *chrie*, the Wellerism, *Märchen*, aetio-
        logical nature-myth, and other forms. The fable writer
        needs different factors as well, as the fable needs
        to be entertaining and interesting in content in addi-
        tion to functioning as a message carrier. The rhetorical
        use of the fables is detailed as a primary one.

998.   ——. "The Origin of the Book of Sinbad." *Fabula*,
        3 (1959), 1-94.

        Incidental to the central discussion of the text of
        Sinbad, Perry deals with the history of story-books
        in the Near East, including an extensive treatment of
        the Aesopic fables, Sumerian Wisdom literature, the
        Life of Aesop, and related materials.

999. ———. "Some Traces of Lost Medieval Story-Books."
*Humaniora: Essays in Literature, Folklore and Bib-
liography Honoring Archer Taylor on His Seventieth
Birthday.* Locust Valley, New York: Augustin, 1960,
150-160.

Sees suggestions of now-lost Greek books of stories
in the fables found in various other materials. The
codex Laurentius lvii. 30 contains four fables of unknown origin, three of which have no Aesopic analogues.
The first, P91 "Ass and his Master" (A-T 214; TMI J2413.1),
is distinct from the other four in having classical
versions. P419 "Thief and Innkeeper" (TMI K335.0.4.1),
P420 "Two Adulterers" (cf. TMI K1577), and P421 "Sailor
and Son" (TMI J1539.2) are known in their earliest
forms in this source. P585 "Sick Lion Fox and Bear"
(A-T 50; TMI B240.4, K961) is discussed in an Armenian
form and the earliest Latin version of Paulus Diaconus
suggesting a story-book intermediary.

1000. ———. "Two Fables Recovered." *Byzantinische Zeitschrift*, 54 (1961), 4-14.

Two fables mentioned in Perry's "Traces of Lost Medieval Storybooks" are recovered in full form in the cod.
1204 of the Athens National Library. P421 is given in
a full narrative form, revealing a greatly different
story line than had been reconstructed in *Aesopica*.
"Sailor and Son" is shown to contain the jest of
counting: one, two, and then adding the counted objects for a total of three. P91 "Ass and Master" is
given as a novelistic fable rather than an Aesopic
one.

1001. ———. "Demetrius of Phalerum and the Aesopic Fables."
*Transactions of the American Philological Associa-
tion*, 93 (1962), 287-346.

Demetrius of Phalerum composed what is most likely
the first European collection of Aesopic fables. Perry
reconstructs the general characteristics and date of
this collection which might have survived as late as
the tenth century or even later. A lengthy survey of
possible survivals of material from this collection
leads Perry to conclude that the Augustana in all
probability reflects the general characteristics of
the Demetrius collection. It seems clear that Demetrius
was making a collection of materials to be used as rhetorical features by writers and speakers.

1002.   ———. *Babrius and Phaedrus*. Loeb Classical Library.
         Cambridge, Mass.: Harvard University Press, 1965.
         cii + 634 pp.

    The lengthy introduction to this definitive edition
    of the fables of Babrius and Phaedrus is an historical
    survey of the fable in general from Sumer through Rome.
    The life and works of the two poets are well detailed,
    and the editions of their fables are provided with
    facing English translations. The fables are incorpora-
    ted into the larger scheme of the entire corpus of
    Aesopica as outlined in Perry's monumental *Aesopica*
    (q.v.), and an index to that larger collection is pro-
    vided. Limited bibliography but references to all
    major editions and reference works are provided.

1002.   ———. "Some Addenda to the Life of Aesop." *Byzan-
         tinische Zeitschrift*, 59 (1966), 285-304.

    Describes two additional fragments of the *Vita Aesopi*:
    the first a loose parchment leaf in Thessalonike, not
    later than the eleventh century in the W tradition.
    The second is a sixteenth-century manuscript in the
    G tradition, codex 2993 in the National Library.

1003.   ———. "The Greek Source of Some Armenian Fables and
         Certain Closely-Related Matters of Tradition." *Poly-
         chronicon: Festschrift Franz Dölger zum 75. Geburtstag*.
         Ed. Peter Wirth. Heidelberg: Carl Winter, 1966,
         418-430.

    Deals with the codex Casinensis, conv. Soppr. 627,
    a Greek manuscript from the thirteenth century in the
    Laurentian Library and containing the Westermann ver-
    sion of the *Vita Aesopi*. Perry calls attention to
    the fact that a few Armenian fables collected by Vardan
    and edited by Marr have peculiar readings in common
    with some of those in the fables of this manuscript
    and not found anywhere else. The manuscript's depen-
    dence upon earlier recensions is pointed out.

1004.   Peters, Wilhelmus Antonius Maria. *Phaedrus: Een studie
         over persoon, werk en taal van den romeinschen
         fabeldichter*. Dissertation, Nijmegen, 1946. Pub-
         lished Nijmegen: Janssen, 1946. 119 pp.

    Peters' dissertation presents an extensive analysis
    of Phaedrus and his work, especially his language and
    style. The analysis begins with the text of Phaedrus
    and the appendix, with the relationship of Phaedrus to

the Greek Aesopic corpus and with studies of his personal references and his humor. The third section deals with his language, studying his vocabulary, archaisms, Graecisms, and use of colloquial language. Statistical treatment of the pronouns, prefixes, affixes, and the like leads to an investigation of Phaedrus' stylistic peculiarities. Peters concludes that the language and style of the appendix are basically the same as the main corpus and that Phaedrus makes great use of brevity and variation and takes great care in his choice of lexicon and phrase.

1005. Petersen, Kate Oelzner. *On the Sources of the Nonne Prestes Tale.* Radcliffe College Monographs, 10. Boston: Ginn, 1898. 144 pp.

The source for Chaucer's Nun's Priest's Tale is essentially an episode from the Reynard the Fox cycle. It is not only much reworked, however, but also reworked from other sources including oral materials. Chaucer generally follows the literary version from the mock-epic, rather than the oral forms.

1006. Petit, Léon. "A propos d'une fable de La Fontaine: Quimper-Corentin lieu d'exil." *Revue d'histoire littéraire*, 51 (1951), 468-471.

This short essay deals with La Fontaine's placing of the action in his version of P291 "Ox-driver and Heracles" (TMI J1034) in Quimper in Brittany, identified as a place of exile in the seventeenth century.

1007. Petsch, Robert. "Fr. von Hagedorn und die deutsche Fabel." *Festschrift der Hamburgischen Universität: Werner von Melle zum 80. Geburtstag.* Hamburg: Augustin, 1933, 160-188.

Uses Hagedorn's fables to demonstrate a broader theory of the fable which is more conveniently and fully explained in his *Wesen und Formen der Erzählkunst* (q.v.). The goal of the fable is to illuminate the doubts and overtones of life by having ordinary things represent other things and processes, not to deceive but to make clear and to act as an intermediary between two worlds: the daily-life world and the world that lies behind. Interesting metaphysical approach to the concept of the implied reader.

1008. ————. "Zur Lehre von den ältesten Erzählformen." *Euphorion*, 35 (1934), 96-104.

Contrasts the fable (as a special representative of
the verbal forms of expression) with the graphic mode
of expression. The fable is neither sharply delineated
nor especially colorful. The contents might be rules
for daily life or generalized into commonplace occur-
rences that might need to be stressed or emphasized.

1009. ————. *Wesen und Form der Erzählkunst.* Halle/Salle,
       1934. 2nd ed. Halle/Salle, 1947. (Buchreihe der
       Deutschen Vierteljahrschrift, 20).

Presents an aesthetic appreciation of the function
of the fable and its position in the hierarchy of
narrative. Distinguishes two fabular natures: the
first is a sort of preform in the art of epic narration
but also an ambiguous layer of nearly mythic conception is to be found. Thus the fable forms a connection
between the purely entertaining forms of narration:
the *Schwank*, the joke, anecdote, and the like on the
one hand and the "Mythenmärchen" which allows a deeper
look into the nature of man on the other. The fable
also has a "Vollform" which has in common with the
"Vorform" or preform this latter function. This type
of fable is essentially a literary form and lies between the anecdote and the short story.

1010. Pfister, Friedrich. "Aesoproman und Alexanderroman."
       Philologische Wochenschrift (1923), 812–814.

Decries the uncontested acceptance of Otto Keller's
idea that the *Vita Aesopi* was dependent upon the
Alexander epic tradition. Keller gives ten points
of contact upon which he bases his opinion; Pfister
accepts here only one as valid: the appearance of
Nektanebos in both traditions, but its mention in the
Vita Aesopi is due to the relationship of the Aesopic
materials to the Achiqar tradition.

1011. Pierce, F.W. "Cervantes' Animal Fables." *Atlante*,
       3: 4 (1955), 103–115.

Analyzes the *Coloquio* as a spin-off of the fable and
beast epic in contrast to Casalduera's attempt to relate the *Coloquio* to *El Casamiento Enganoso.*

1012. Pisi, Giordana. *Fedro traduttore di Esopo.* Florence:
       La Nuova Italia, 1977. 93 pp.

After a survey of the literature on Phaedrus, Pisi
deals with the creation of a new genre with Phaedrus'

writing a book of fables as literature, all the while treating the question of how much was Phaedrus and how much was in his "Aesop." Pisi discusses a number of fables by simply comparing the oldest Greek forms with Phaedrus' versions. This somewhat suspect methodology leads to unsupported conclusions in the summary of the recasting effect. Bibliography and indices to all fables discussed.

1013. Plessow, Max. *Geschichte der Fabeldichtung in England bis zu John Gay.* Berlin: Mauer & Müller, 1905. Also *Palaestra*, no. 42. clii + 212 pp.

The lengthy introduction which precedes Plessow's edition of Bullokar's Aesop in the original curious orthography is a thorough historical survey of the fable in England through John Gay. Good synthesis of previous research.

1014. Polak, Heinrich J. "Babriarum." *Mnemosyne*, 22 (1897), 345-356.

Makes a number of suggestions with regard to emendations to the texts in the Babrian tradition and especially readings for the fourteen fables found in the ruins of Palmyra.
See: Hesseling, "On Waxen Tablets."

1015. Poll, M. "Die Fabeln von Gottlieb Conrad Pfeffel und ihre Quellen." *Strassburger Studien*, 3 (1888), 343-471.

A lengthy listing of Pfeffel's sources and possible influences, including oral tradition. Many of the compound sources are clearly overdrawn, as are the assumed literary "echoes" listed by Poll. Good analysis of the fables and their composition techniques.

1016. Polle, Friedrich. "Zu Phaedrus Fabeln." *Philologus*, 50 (1891), 650.

Textual notes to Phaedrus, one new reading and one emendation.

1017. ———. "Zu Phädrus Fabeln." *Jahrbücher für klassische Philologie*, 145 (1892), 708-713 and 147 (1893), 778.

Lexical notes to Phaedrus and a central discussion around the difficulties of Phaedrus III, 4 "Lanius et simius," P496 "Butcher and Ape." Polle believes the

one who asks the butcher about the flavor of the ape
was in fact notoriously ugly. The one person associated with the fables that fits that description was
Aesop himself.

1018. Pope, Robert. "A Sly Toad, Physiognomy and the Problem
       of Deceit: Henryson's *The Paddock and the Mous.*"
       Neophilologus, 63 (1979), 461–468.

       An investigation of Henryson's version of P384 "Mouse
       and Frog" (A-T 278; TMI J681.1) to demonstrate that
       Henryson thought of the villain of the piece as a toad
       instead of the traditional frog. Henryson stresses
       the physical reflections of moral depravity.

1019. ———. "Henryson's *The Sheep and the Dog.*" *Essays
       in Criticism*, 30 (1980), 205–214.

       An analysis of Henryson's sixth fable, P478 "Sheep,
       Dog and Wolf" (TMI B270, Q263) which not only offers
       an interesting witness to the fifteenth-century legal
       process in consistory courts but also biting social
       satire and spiritual expressions, especially in the
       moralitas.

1020. Port, Wilhelm. "Die Literatur zur griechischen und
       römischen Fabel in den Jahren 1925–1931/32."
       Jahresbreicht für Altertumswissenschaft, 24 (1933),
       83–94, and 265 (1939), 1–29.

       A continuation of the bibliographical reports,
       highly selective and generally only on Phaedrus and
       Babrius, following Heydenreich (1873–1885) and Draheim
       (1885–1924). Port expands the field of vision slightly
       to include some folklore reports and broader treat-
       ments as well as the work done in some Slavic lan-
       guages.

1021. Porter, Laurence. "Nodier and La Fontaine." *Neophilo-
       logische Mitteilungen*, 80 (1979), 390–398.

       Charles Nodier studied La Fontaine intensively and
       published editions of his *Fables*. Porter details the
       La Fontaine influence on Nodier both in style and in
       subject.

1022. Poser, Therese. *Arbeitstexte für den Unterricht:
       Fabeln.* Stuttgart: Reclam, 1976. 83 pp.

       A short introduction to the fable designated as a

selection with study aids for the secondary level but
bringing with it not only a well-thought-out selection
but also a well-presented summary of critical work on
the form. Deals with the nature of the fable, the
didactic element, form and content studies, characterization, and the fable in the twentieth century. Short
bio-bibliographical notes to each fabulist are appended.

1023. Postgate, J.P. "Textual Notes on Phaedrus." *Classical
Philology*, 13 (1918), 262-271.

Textual criticism of the received text of Phaedrus
on the evidence of medieval paraphrasts, with various
comments on the conjectures in the research that preceded Postgate.

1024. ———. "Vindicae Phaedrianne." *American Journal of
Philology*, 39 (1918), 382-392.

A commentary on the Phaedrine texts to "vindicate"
various passages strongly disputed by earlier commentators. Postgate is generally opposed to Thiele whose
changes are put down to prejudice.

1025. ———. "Phaedriana." *Classical Quarterly*, 12 (1918),
89-97 and 151-161; 13 (1919), 81-89.

Various notes on the text of Phaedrus, especially
emendations from medieval sources and readings on
analogy of medieval paraphrases. Continues with the
"novae fabulae" of Burman, Dressler, and Müller with
versified forms of the first seven fables and then
three more in the final section.

1026. ———. "Phaedrus and Seneca." *Classical Review*, 33
(1919), 19-24.

Postgate sees parallels between Seneca and Phaedrus
in subject-matter and in expression and vocabulary.
Phaedrus III, 15 shows parallel phrasing in Seneca's
De Beneficiis and a few dozen other correspondences.
There are also echoes of Phaedrine *senarii* in Seneca's
iambic lines. Postgate comments on the usefulness of
these correspondences for the editor of the fables.
The mention of Phaedrus by Martial is discussed and
Postgate identifies Quintillian's writer of fables as
Phaedrus.

1027. ————. "On Some Quantities in Phaedrus." *Hermathena*,
       42 (1920), 52-63.

       Deals with a number of textual problems Postgate
       came across while preparing his edition of Phaedrus
       (see next entry). These deal specifically with metri-
       cal problems and various emendations.

1028. ————. *Phaedri fabule Aesopiae cum Nicolai Perotti*
       prologo et decem novis fabulis. Oxford: Clarendon
       Press, 1919 [1920]. xxviii + 222 pp.

       The introduction to this edition deals with new
       readings and emendations insofar as these had not been
       dealt with in his earlier writings on Phaedriana.
       Postgate makes considerably more use of the medieval
       paraphrases in his edition than previous scholars,
       and much of the introductory materials is a justifica-
       tion of their value.

1029. Potebnia, A.A. *Iz lektsii po teorii slovesnosti: Bas-*
       nia, poslovitsa, pogovorka. Kharkov: Tipografiya
       K. Schasni, 1894. Reprint, the Hague: Mouton,
       1970. 164 pp.

       Deals with numerous problems of the fables, especial-
       ly the fable as classical and as orally transmitted
       literature. Poetic and rhetorical devices are dis-
       cussed as are the relationships among the fable and
       various other short forms, specifically the proverb.
       The classical corpus is used as a model, but the fables
       discussed are not keyed to any standard collèction.

1030. Potente, Filomena. *Il papiro Golenischeff.* Naples:
       Tomanni, 1930. 12 pp.

       Describes the Golenischeff papyrus containing frag-
       ments of the *Vita Aesopi*, relating these materials to
       the Aesop Life W tradition as found in Westermann.

1031. Prang, Helmut. *Formgeschichte der Dichtkunst.* Stutt-
       gart: Kohlhammer, 1968. Especially pp. 50-55.

       Suggests, following Leibfried, a certain connection
       between the fable and the Märchen. The fable is also
       closely related to the riddle insofar as they both
       excapsulate and disguise their meanings. Various
       mechanisms of revelation are treated. The history
       of the fable in Germany with emphasis upon the theoret-
       ical writings of the eighteenth century is given in
       capsule form.

1032. Pratt, Robert Armstrong. "Three Old French Sources
of the *Nonnes Preestes Tale*." *Speculum*, 47 (1972),
422-444 and 646-648.

The three versions are Marie de France's fable "Del
cok e del gupil," P562 "Partridge and Fox" (A-T 6 and
cf. 61A; TMI K561.1, K721) with supplementary material
from the *Roman de Renard* and the *Renart de contrefais*.
The *Roman* contributed the overall design of the tale,
and the learning and background material, as well as
the dream sequence, come from the *Renart de contrefais*.

1033. Premerstein, Anton. "Zum Codex Remensis des Phaedrus
und Querolus." *Mittheilungen des österreichischen
Vereines für Bibliothekswesen*, 1 (1897), 1-7.

On the codex Remensis which contained the late Latin
Querolus and the fables of Phaedrus and which was
destroyed by fire in 1774. Premerstein gathers together such information as can be gleaned from various
sources, especially the readings that were preserved
by Dom Jacques Claude Vincent, the librarian at St.
Remi, as well as Hervieux and Ulysse Robert.

1034. Prinz, Karl. "Der prologus zum III. Buch von Phaedrus
Fabeln." *Sitzungsbericht der Wiener Akademie der
Wissenschaften* (1906), 31-44.

The prologue to the third book is taken as proof
that Phaedrus was convicted of some crime and was
punished by the emperor.
See: de Lorenzi, *Fedro*.

1035. ———. "Zur Chronologie und Deutung der Fablen des
Phädrus." *Wiener Studien*, 43 (1922-1923), 62-71.

Prinz discusses and dismisses other theories to return to his earlier views that Phaedrus wrote books I
and II before 31 A.D. He apparently ignores most
evidence and bases his theories on lines in the third
prologue which he reads to mean that Phaedrus was
accused and convicted and perhaps punished by Caesar
Tiberius and thus the earlier books were published
before the fall of Sejanus or before 31 A.D.

1036. Pritchard, Mary Henrietta. "Fables Moral and Political: The Adaptation of the Aesopian Fable Collection
to English Social and Political Life. 1651-1722."
Dissertation, University of Western Ontario, 1976.

Studies the fable as a political weapon and provides
a finding list of motifs in fable collections from
Caxton to Croxall, 1484-1732. Treats the development
of the Aesopic fable from its classical form into an
English literary genre specifically because of its
use in political issues, accomplished by translation
of the fables into politically charged language. The
discussion centers around Ogilby's use of the form to
satirize England in the Cromwell era.

1037. Probyn, Clive. "Source for Swift's Fable of the
       Bitches." *Notes and Queries*, 15 (1968), 206.

       Swift's poem against the repeal of the Test Act has
       as its source a fable by Abstemius as translated by
       Roger L'Estrange (no. 323).

1038. Prosch, Franz. *Gotthold Ephraim Lessing, Abhandlungen
       über die Fabel mit Einleitung, Anmerkungen und Text-
       beilagen nebst Herders Aufsätzen über die Fabel.*
       Vienna: Körner, 1889. 56 pp.

       Partial editions of Lessing's and Herder's theoreti-
       cal writings on the fable with extensive commentaries
       and an introduction is the intent of this short text.
       Prosch does not consider that Lessing was influenced
       by Gottsched, rather both he and Herder were directly
       in the tradition of Aristotle and Wolff. Prosch is
       strongly influenced by Grimm's ideas of the relation-
       ship of the beast epic to the fable.

1039. Proust, Jacques. "Remarques sur la disposition par
       livres des *Fables* de La Fontaine." *De Jean Lemaire
       de Belges à Jean Giraudoux: Mélanges d'histoire et
       de critique littéraire offerts à Pierre Jourda.*
       Paris: Editions A.G. Nizet, 1970, 227-248.

       An interesting essay on the purposeful arrangement
       of the fables within the books. The conscious composi-
       tion is no accident, rather an attempt to arrange the
       fables thematically. A series of thematic linkages
       are demonstrated, with suggestions for further research
       along these lines.

1040. Provenzo, Eugene Francis. "Education and the Aesopic
       Tradition." Dissertation, Washington University,
       St. Louis, 1976. 416 pp.

       A historical presentation of the Aesopic fable as
       an educational medium in Western tradition begins a

discussion of the variety of uses to which the fable
has been put, in part to reflect varying social, political, and economic conditions. P156 "Wolf and Crane
(Heron)" (A-T 76; TMI W154.3) is used to demonstrate
changes needed by society, with the fable traced from
Indian forms through American versions. A content
analysis study and a complete bibliography conclude
this comprehensive study.

1041. Pugliarello, Mariarosaria. *Le origini della favolis-
tica classica.* Brescia: Paideia, 1973. 162 pp.

Deals with the Greco-Roman fable and the choice of
animal versus human actors early on. Treats the relationship of the myth to the fable, mythic elements
still to be found in the form, and the oriental origins
of the fable. The main body of the text consists of
individual treatments of specific animal figures: Fox,
Wolf, Dog, Lion, Eagle and Snake. Each of these is
dealt with in detail analyzing its stereotypical
characteristics.

1042. ————. "Appunti di sintassi fedriana." *Studi e
ricerche dell'Istituto di Latino*, 4 (1981), 109-
121.

Phaedrus is shown to have used archaisms, specialized
poetic language and phrases as well as vulgarisms in
order to call attention to his work. The intensity
of his concise expression is maintained by the use of
the spectacular turn of phrase.

1043. Puntoni, Vittorio. "Directorium humanae vitae alias
parabolae antiquorum sapientum." *Annali Filosofia
e filologia, Reale scuola normale superiore de
Pisa*, 4 (1884), 101-454.

An edition of the *Directorium* preceded by an introduction tracing the history and relationships of this
collection, from its Indian origins through the Greek
translation.

1044. ————. "Sopra alcune recensioni dello *Stephanites
kai Ichnelates.*" *Atti della R. Academia dei Lincei
memorie della Classe di scienze morali, storiche e
filologiche* (1886), 172-182.

Notes on his edition of the Greek translations of
the *Kalila wa Dimna*, commonly titled *Stephanites kai*

Ichnelates. Justifies various textual decisions and
manuscript relationships.
See: Papademetriou, "Studies in the Manuscript Tradition."

1045. ———. *La Favola esopica dell'aquila e della testug-
gine*. Bologna: Gamberini e Parmeggiani, 1912. 36
pp.

This essay is an extensive account of P230 "Turtle
and Eagle" (TMI J657.2, K1041) comparing the Babrian
and Avianus forms to that found in the Indian tradition especially as represented by *Kalila wa Dimna* in
its Greek translation, *Stephanites kai Ichnelates*.

1046. Quinnam, Barbara. *Fables from Incunabula to Motion
Picture Books: A Selective Bibliography*. Washington,
D.C.: The Library of Congress, 1966. 85 pp.

Contains two hundred entries representing editions
and studies of Aesopica from the *Panchatantra* through
Krylov. Summary historical prefaces are provided for
the major collections. A very small sample is represented as the listing was presented essentially for an
exhibition of fabular literature on display in the
Library of Congress.

1047. Quintino de Almeida, M. "A Propósito de una fábula
de Fedro." *Lingua & Literatura*, 4 (1975) [1977],
391-407.

In his prologue and first fable "Lupus et agnus,"
P155 "Wolf and Lamb" (A-T 111A; TMI U31), Phaedrus
is pictured as justifying both himself and his collection. Although he may bring his readers to laughter,
he will invite them to observe and to practice wisdom.

1048. Raasch, A. *Die Entwicklung des La Fontaines Bild in
Frankreich. La Fontaines Fabeln in der literarischen
Kritik von der Klassik bis zur Gegenwart*. Disser-
tation, Kiel, 1957.

A comprehensive survey of La Fontaine criticism in
France from the early eighteenth through the mid-
twentieth centuries. Notes La Fontaine quickly became
an established norm.

1049. Ragotzky, Hedda. *Gattungserneuerung und Laienunter-
weisung in Texten des Strickers*. Tübingen: Niemeyer, 1981.

Presents interpretations of Stricker's fables, P605
"Fox with Many Tricks, Cat with Only One" (A-T 105;
TMI J1662), and other motifs in an attempt to demonstrate genre lines with a broad sociological basis.
Deals effectively with relationships between the
author and his audience and various perceptions of
the moral basis of the materials.

1050. Raj, Myrtle Dorai. "An Indian Source for the Medieval
Beast Epic: *Reynard the Fox* Considered as a Deriva-
tive of the *Panchatantra*." Dissertation, University
of California, Berkeley, 1966. 192 pp.

Reynard the Fox is ultimately to be derived from the
fables of the *Panchatantra*, although it has drawn into
itself a number of wolf/fox stories of European origin.
The frame story is the key element. Chronological and
geographical considerations are brought to bear upon
the argument which includes a number of generalizations
about fable transmission as well. Motif and tale type
indices are provided.

1051. Rajna, P. "Estratti di una Raccolta di Favole." *Giornale di Filologia Romanza*, 1 (1878), 13-42.

Deals with the transmission of Avianus during the
middle ages and with various textual emendations and
suggestions.

1052. Rammelmeyer, Alfred. *Studien zur russischen Fabel im
18. Jahrhundert*. Leipzig, 1930; rpt. Nendeln, Liech-
tenstein: Kraus, 1968. 143 pp.

An even-paced, well-presented historical survey of
the Russian fable from A.P. Sumarokov through Izmajlov,
with emphasis upon stylistic considerations. The eighteenth-century Russian fable is considered to be essentially original though completely within the European
fabular context, building upon Aesop, Phaedrus, and
especially La Fontaine and Gellert. Special attention
is paid to Majkov, Knajaschnin, Ablesimov, Bogdanovitch,
Chemnitzer, Chovostov, Dmitrijev, and Lvov. Ends with
a good bibliography.

1053. Ramondt, Marie. "Der Niedergang des Aesop." *Studien
über das Lachen*. Groningen: Wolters, 1962, 89-110.

A rapid, well-argued chronology of essentially
classical fables from the pre-Aesopic Greeks through
Aesop and the putative Demetrius collection to Babrius,

with incidental references to more modern materials
to describe Aesop and his reputation, especially the
decline of his name, to the modern day.

1054.   Rand, E.K.   "A Vade Mecum of Liberal Culture in a
        Manuscript of Fleury." *Philological Quarterly*, 1
        (1922), 258-277.

        Discusses the textual history and possible methods
        of transmission for the *Codex Vossianus Latinus Q 86*
        containing the fables of Avianus (this is the basis
        for the Lachmann edition), in light of another manu-
        script, the *Codex Reginensis 1616*, which is a very
        early witness to some of the fables of Phaedrus.
        The Vossianus is determined to have been compiled
        with an educational purpose around the middle of the
        ninth century.

1055.   Randall, Lilian M.C.   "Exempla as a Source of Gothic
        Marginal Illumination." *The Art Bulletin*, 39
        (1957), 97-107.

        On the use of exempla and fables as illustration
        themes in the thirteenth century. The exemplum and
        fabular materials grow out of their use in sermons,
        and formalistic as well as functional parallels are
        discussed in addition to the iconographical details.
        Fable motif use in both sermon and text was literally
        marginal. The most common fable motif seems to have
        been P426 "Fox and Crane" (A-T 60; TMI J1565.1).
        Illustrated.

1056.   Rank, L.   "Observatiunculae ad Phaedrum." *Mnemosyne*,
        38 (1910), 261-277; 39 (1911), 51-67; 40 (1912),
        42-62.

        Various textual notes and emendations to Phaedrus,
        especially to the Burmann edition. The first article
        includes extensive commentary on the prologues; the
        second concentrates upon the fourth book and the
        Appendix.

1057.   ————.   "Nova Phaedriana." *Mnemosyne*, 45 (1917),
        93-102.

        Continues his earlier catalogue of textual notes
        and emendations, here critical to the Havet edition
        and emendations, especially to the prologue of the
        fourth book.

1058. Ranke, Kurt. "Der 'Holzerne Johannes': eine Westeuro-
päische Redaktion der Matrone von Ephesus." *Rheinisches Jahrbuch für Volkskunde*, 4 (1953), 90-114.

Suggests derivation of "Holzerne Johannes" from the
P543 "Widow and Soldier" (A-T 1510; TMI K2213.1) complex.

1059. ————. "Lügenbrücke." *Studien zur Volkskultur,
Sprache Landesgeschichte: Festschrift Mottias Zender*.
Ed. Edith Ennen and Günther Wiegelmann. Bonn: Lud-
wig Röhrscheid, 1972. 2, 868-874. Reprint: K. Ranke,
*Die Welt der Einfachen Formen: Studien zur Motiv-,
Wort- und Quellenkunde*. Berlin: de Gruyter, 1978,
261-269.

Essentially an investigation of the German proverbial
phrase, "Kommst du auch heil über die Lügenbrücke,"
but in effect an extended look at a fabular motif P707
"Knight and Mendacious Squire" (TMT X904.2.1) as found
in various forms, as in Gellert, *Fabeln und Erzählungen*,
and, earlier, in Steinhöwel's *Esopus* (whence Perry's
form), and Waldis' *Esopus*. Contains numerous other
allusions to fabular motifs, generally in the form of
Märchen, e.g. P543 "Widow and Soldier" (A-T 1510; TMI
K11.3) and others.

1060. ————. "Avianus." *Enzyklopädie des Märchens*. Berlin:
de Gruyter, 1979. 1, 1099-1105.

Adds A-T numbers and bibliographical references to
Weische's essay (q.v.).

1061. Rásonyi Nagy, L. "Das uigurische Aesop-Josipas-Frag-
ment." *Byzantinisches-neugriechisches Jahrbuch*, 7
(1930), 429-443.

Discusses the range of possibilities of secular
literature having found its way to the Near East in
addition to the theological materials. A ninth-century
fragment of the *Vita Aesopi* from Chotsho demonstrates
the thesis; with a description of the text and a facsimile.

1062. Rattunde, Eckard. *Li Proverbs au Vilain: Untersuchungen
zur romanischen Sprachdichtung des Mittelalters*.
Heidelberg: Carl Winter, 1966.

Discusses in detail the medieval French proverb and
the relationship of the fable to the proverb before an

extensive investigation of *Li Proverbs au Vilain* and
other collections.

1063.   Rava, M.M. "Su Alcune raccolte medievali di favole."
        Archivium Latinitatis Medii Aevi (Bulletin Du Cange)
        (1929-1930), 45-49.

        An investigation of the vocabulary of five medieval
        fable collections: the so-called *Fabulae Antiquae*,
        Phaedrus manuscripts, the *Romulus Vulgaris*, *Romulus
        Nilantius*, and the *Romulus Anglici*, especially by word
        count of specifically "classical" words, does not re-
        sult in numbers that conform to their relative ages
        nor do the respective vocabularies reflect the puta-
        tive eras of their composition.

1064.   Redlich, Carl Christian. "Einleitung zu Lessings Ab-
        handlungen über die Fabel." *Lessings Werke*. Berlin,
        1879, 5-16.

        In contrast to the prevailing views of Lessing's
        theory and practice of the fable, Redlich focuses upon
        the reception of the works. Reviewing previous work,
        he concludes that Lessing's fables are to be separated
        from Gellert's by type. The fable is literary, not
        folk narrative. Redlich establishes areas for both
        types.

1065.   Redonnet, Maria Luis, and Antonio Redonnet. *Fábulas
        inéditas de Juan Cruz Varela*. Buenos Aires: Edi-
        ciones Culturales Argentinas, 1978.

        A critical edition of the neo-classical fables of
        Varela, composed around 1816.

1066.   Regula, Moritz. "Les fables de Phèdre comparées avec
        les imitations de Lafontaine." Program, Hohenelbe,
        1914. 10 pp.

        Eleven fables from the Phaedrus corpus are care-
        fully compared to their La Fontaine counterparts.
        The La Fontaine changes are examined in terms of the
        place settings, language and, specifically French
        terms and processes.

1067.   ————. "Analysen dreier Stellen aus La Fontaines
        Fabeln." *Studien zu Dante und zu anderen Themen
        der romanischen Literaturen: Festschrift für Rudolf
        Palgen zu seinem 75. Geburtstag*. Graz: Universitäts-
        Buchdruckerei Styria, 1971, 161-163.

Various notes, generally determination of syntactical and lexical problems in verses in the *Fables*. Fable IV, 20 "L'Avare qui a perdu son trésor," P225 "Miser" (TMI J1061.4); XII, 5 "Le Chat et la jeune Souris"; and VIII, 2 "Le Savetier et le Financier," and the fables in question.

1068. Rehermann, Ernst Heinrich. "Erasmus Alberus." *Enzyklopädie des Märchens*. Berlin: de Gruyter, 1979. 1, 262-264.

Biographical and bibliographical sketch of Alberus and his strongly Protestant-flavored fable collection. With a motif and tale type index for the fables. See: Vander Meulen and Peter Hasubek.

1069. ―――. "Nathanael Chytraeus." *Enzyklopädie des Märchens*. Berlin: de Gruyter, 1979. 3, 25-29.

Presents a biographical overview of Nathanael Chytraeus with emphasis upon his 1571 "Hundert Fabeln aus Esopo," characterized as a result of his strong pedagogical motivations. With bibliographical notes and an index of tale types and motifs.

1070. ―――, and Ines Köhler-Zülch. "Aspekte der Gesellschafts-und Kirchenkritik in den Fabeln von Martin Luther, Nathanael Chytraeus und Burkhard Waldis." *Die Fabel: Theorie, Geschichte und Rezeption einer Gattung*. Berlin: Schmidt, 1982, 27-47.

Begins with Martin Luther's thirteen fables in search of expressions of social and church criticism and continues with the 400-fable collection of Burkhard Waldis and the "Hundert Fabeln aus Esopo" of Nathan Chytraeus. Builds upon Gundolf Schütze's study of social criticism for the earlier centuries (q.v.) and notes that Luther takes no overt position in his fables (although clearly in a pessimistic stance), while Chytraeus, though following Luther, makes some mention of social problems. Burkhard Waldis, on the other hand, not only deals with these but also joins Erasmus Alberus in a polemic against non-Protestants.

1071. Reichelt, Harry J. "The Fable in German Literary Rococo: Tradition, Development and Perfection." Dissertation, Rutgers, 1971. 440 pp.

The fable is portrayed as a characteristic expression

of the literary side of the Rococo. Surveys the problems in defining the fable in general and the specifics
of the eighteenth-century forms, with discussions of
the type from Aesop and the classical fable theory,
the German medieval and sixteenth-century fable to the
eighteenth century, when the fable becomes a subject
for theoretical treatment. Treats eighteenth-century
Germany fabulists in general, especially Hagedorn,
Lichtwer, Meyer von Kronau, Gleim, and Pfeffel. Suggests that the fable found its greatest variety in
these fabulists.

1072. Reissenberger, Karl. "Einleitung." *Reinhard Fuchs.*
       Halle: Niemeyer, 1886, 1-31.

       In the introduction to his edition of *Reinhard
       Fuchs* in the Altdeutsche Textbibliothek, Reissenberger
       builds upon the thesis of Müllenhoff that Aesopic
       fables are to be found at the basis of a number of
       episodes of the Roman de Renart cycle.

1073. Reitzenstein, R. "Ein Stück hellenistischer Klein-
       literatur." *Neugriechische Geschichtsblätter* (1904),
       309-332.

       The text of the *Apologia kerameos pros Amenopin
       Basilea* and a historical commentary on Byzantine forms
       are provided.

1074. Rey, Carlos M. "Una fábula de La Fontaine: Análisis
       métrico-estilístico." Montevideo: Universidad de
       Republica, 1956. 35 pp. Also: "Eine Fabel La Fon-
       taines. Metrisch-stilistische Analyse." *Interpre-
       tationen französischer Gedichte.* Ed. K. Wais.
       Darmstadt: Wissenschaftliche Buchgesellschaft, 1970,
       pp. 64-77.

       An essay on "L'Huître et les Plaideurs" ("The Oyster
       and the Pilgrims," La Fontaine 14, 9) in comparison
       to Boileau and in metrical and stylistic analysis.
       Word plays, syntax, and rhetorical features discussed.
       Concludes La Fontaine's metrics are very varied, and
       much attention is paid to enjambment and the "phonetics"
       effects.

1075. Rhodes, Dennis E. "A Post Incunable Edition of Aesop."
       The Library, Series 5, 14 (1959), 281-282.

       The Accio Zucco fable collection edition (*Gesamt-
       katalog* 437b), listed as Venice from an unidentified

printer, is here classed as a sixteenth-century edition, putatively done by Manfredus de Bonellis at Venice, on the basis of the wood cuts and type resemblances.

1076. Ribbeck, Otto. "Phaedrus." *Dichtung der Kaiserherrschaft. Geschichte der Römischen Dichtung.* Stuttgart: Cotta, 1892, 22 32.

General discussion of Phaedrus with his homeland given as Macedonia and his poetic accomplishments characterized as valuable with stress given to his independence with regard to his materials. The fables in the Perotti Appendix are of uncertain genuineness.

1077. Ribezzo, Francesco. *Nuovi studi sull'origine e la propagazione delle favole indoelleniche, comunemente dette esopiche.* Naples: Gianni and Figli, 1901.

A philological and folkloristic study of fables, especially the Aesopic motifs, with an emphasis upon origins, both geographical considerations and the ultimate origin of the type from other forms of folk materials. Extensive discussion of Indian materials and a comprehensive review of the theoretical materials of the nineteenth century. Sees a distinction to be made among fable types: "mythic," "cosmological," "historical," and other forms, all of (possibly) varied origins. The third section deals with the transmission mechanisms of the fable, with the fable generally being traced from India. Part four considers Greco-Indian parallels with analysis of numerous motifs.

1078. Richter, Roland. "Georg Rollenhagens Froschmeuseler: Struktur, Rhetorik und die Funktion von Sprichwort und Fabel." Dissertation, University of California, Los Angeles, 1970. Published as *Georg Rollenhagens Froschmeuseler: Ein rhetorisches Meisterstück.* Bern: Peter Lang, 1975. 139 pp.

Investigates Rollenhagen's *Froschmeuseler* (1595) by means of a determination of the rhetorical features (and thereby the structural elements) of the proverb and the fable. Not only are fables used as structural units but also as units involved in the dialectic process and, as such, part of the overall effect of the work. The *Froschmeuseler* is demonstrated to be designed according to a fixed and predetermined plan; the fables are steps and construction blocks in this

plan. They reduce generalizations to a concrete form
of action, all the while remaining abstract and sen-
tentious.

1079. Richter, Rudolf. *Lafontaine et Lamotte.* Program, El-
bogen: K.K. Staats-Realschule, 1904.

A detailed comparison of the fabular styles of La
Fontaine and La Motte, with an eye toward exegesis of
La Motte's 1719 *Discours sur la fable*, in which La
Motte demonstrates a thorough understanding of the
style of this genre of poetics and attempts a codifica-
tion of the form. The fables of La Motte demonstrate
a pure poetic nature, a suppleness, and a richness of
language even though somewhat artificial. Those of La
Fontaine, on the other hand, are closer to the (un-
defined) "natural products" of the French character.

1080. Ricklinger, Erich. *Studien zur Tierfabel von Hans
Sachs.* Dissertation, Munich, 1909; Munich: Kastner
und Caliwey, 1909.

Identifies the animal fables of Hans Sachs and discusses the general features of medieval replication
from Latin sources. The 136 *Meistergesange* and the 53
Spruchgedichte are analyzed with regard to sources,
especially Steinhöwel's "Esopus" and the Bidpai translations. The particular characteristics of the Sachsian
fable are the subject of parts two and three. No index of fables.

1081. Ridgely, Beverly S. "Astrology and Astronomy in the
Fables of La Fontaine." *Publications of the Modern
Language Association*, 80 (1965), 180-189.

Man is advised to entrust himself to Divine Provi-
dence. La Fontaine was outspoken against the Charlatains
who tried to predict the future, expressing at length
his distance from "judicial astrology" in two fables.
His version of P40 "Astrologer and the Well" (TMI
J2133.8) La Fontaine II, 13 "L'Astrologue qui se laisse
tomber dans un puits," which concludes with an extensive discourse on the impossibility of knowing the
future. Ridgely also deals with VIII, 16 "L'Horoscopii"
which contains P363 "Boy and Painted Lion" (TMI M341.2)
and a fabular motif about Aeschylus' death. VII, 18
"Un Animal dans la lune" also treated in detail.

1082. Riedel, Volker. "Phaedrus." *Lessing und die römische
Literatur.* Weimar: Böhlans, 1976, 153-179.

Examines Gotthold Ephraim Lessing's relationship to
and understanding of Phaedrus, including his preoccupation with the fable in general and the historical acceptance and reception of the fable. Lessing used
Phaedrus early on, exemplifying various points in his
"Abhandlungen" with Phaedrus fables in contrast to
those of La Fontaine. Specific examples from Lessing's
own fable production and theoretical writings are
compared to the Phaedrine materials; strong differences
in themes and emphasis are demonstrated.

1083. Riess, Jonathan Benjamin. "The Origin and Rise of
Communal Art in Perugia: A Study of the Fresco Program of 1297 in the Palazza del Popolo." Dissertation, Columbia, 1977. 341 pp.

The murals in the Sala dei Notari of the Palazzo del
Capitan del popolo in Perugia, dating from 1297, are
examined. Subjects of these materials include eleven
Aesopic fables, each discussed separately.

1084. Riesz, János. "Metamorphosen einer Fabel: La Fontaines Le Meunier, son Fils et l'Ane." *Stimmen
der Romania: Festschrift für W. Theodor Elwert zum
70. Geburtstag.* Ed. Gerhard Schmidt and Manfred
Tietz. Wiesbaden: Heymann, 1980, 343-357.

Deals with P721 "Father, Son and Donkey" (A-T 1215;
TMI J1041.2) which is situated as the first fable in
the third book, and is discussed with regard to its
antecedents, poetological elements, the structure of
the narrative, and its relation to an actual time and
event.

1085. Rigo, Georges. "Un recueil de proverbs grecs utilisé
par Erasme pour la redaction des Adagia." *Latomus*,
32 (1973), 177-184.

Erasmus used an edition of Aesop from 1505 for the
material from the fables used in the *Adagia*.

1086. Rinn, L.W. *Phèdre nouvelle édition, avec une vie de
Phèdre et des notes en français, suivie des imitations
de La Fontaine et de Florian.* Paris: Delagrave,
1887.

An early attempt to construct a life of Phaedrus
from the few incidents mentioned in his fable collection. The edition of the fables gives parallels to
the motifs in La Fontaine and other French fabulists.

1087. Riordan, John Lancaster. "The Status of Burkard
       Waldis Studies." *Modern Language Quarterly*, 2
       (1941), 279-292.

       A well-presented essay on Waldis studies (still use-
       ful as so little new material has appeared) with a
       significant amount of coverage given over to Waldis'
       Esopus, which is characterized as of great importance
       for the history of the form. Lists editions of the
       fables.

1088. Risse, Robert Gregory. "An Edition of the Commentary
       on the Fables of Avianus in Erfurt Ms., Amplon Q 21:
       The Text and Its Place in Medieval Literary Culture."
       Dissertation, Washington University, 1964. 250 pp.

       The manuscript used for this edition was chosen as
       the best representative of the group of medieval Avianus
       commentaries, some 47 in number, that cannot be re-
       solved to a single text. After statements of editorial
       principles, Avianus' position in education and the
       intellectual life of the middle ages is discussed, as
       well as the specific uses of the fable in various medi-
       eval forms and by various authors.

1089. ————. "The Augustinian Paraphrase of Isaiah xiv,
       13-14 in *Piers Plowman* and the Commentary on the
       Fables of Avianus." *Philological Quarterly*, 45
       (1966), 712-717.

       Satan's boast from Isaiah and *Piers Plowman* in para-
       phrase is also to be found in commentaries on Avianus,
       specifically on fables two and four, with the para-
       phrase found twenty-nine times. The use of the para-
       phrase is discussed in terms of the importance of
       Avianus in medieval culture.

1090. Rist, Martin. "The Fable of the Dog in the Manger in
       the Gospel of Thomas." *Iliff Review*, 25 (1968),
       13-25.

       Extensive interpretation of P702 "Dog in Manger"
       (TMI W156).

1091. Robert, Ulysse. *Les fables de Phèdre: Edition paléo-
       graphique publiée d'après le manuscrit Rosanbo.*
       Paris: Imprimerie nationale, 1893. xlvi + 188 pp.

       A word-for-word, page-for-page facsimile-type repro-
       duction of the Rosanbo manuscript of Phaedrus, or

Pithoeanus, with a history of the manuscript dated
from the 1st half of the ninth century and of uncertain
origin. The fables have no verse numberings. Finally,
the curious text "De diversis monstrorum generibus"
which is in the Pithoeanus, is also found in the
Wolfenbüttel MS 148 in conjunction again with Phaedrus.
See: Chauncey Finch, "The Morgan Manuscript of
Phaedrus."

1092. Roberts, C.H. "A Fable Recovered." *Journal of Roman
Studies*, 47 (1957), 124-125.

Discovers a version of P39 "Wise Swallow" (cf. A-T
233C; TMI J652.2) in the "Bilingual Document" published
by Sanders of 1947. Upon the identification of the
fragment as containing a fable, certain emendations
became possible.

1093. Roberts, Warren E. "Spenser's Fable of the Oak and
the Briar." *Southern Folklore Quarterly*, 14 (1950),
150-154.

Finds a closer analogue to Spenser's version of P70
"Oak and Reed" (A-T 298C; TMI J832) in the first story
of the Seven Sages of Rome romance.

1094. Robinson, B.W. "The Tehran Manuscript of *Kalila wa
Dimna*: A Reconsideration." *Oriental Art*, 4 (1958),
3-10.

On the Gulistan copy of the *Kalila wa Dimna* tradition, first shown at Burlington House in 1931 and first
assigned to the Herat school of the late fifteenth
century. The relationship of this manuscript to the
Istanbul text is discussed, and it is dated to the
third quarter of the fifteenth century, possibly very
soon after 1468. Illustrated.

1095. ————. "Price Bāysunghur and the Fables of Bidpai."
Oriental Art, 16 (1970), 1-10.

On Bāysunghur's manuscripts of the *Kalila wa Dimna*
from 1429-30 in the Topkapi Library, Istanbul, num-
bered R, 1022 and described in Karatay as nos. 864
and 867. Fables, illustrations, and scribes are well
described and identified; connections to the Gulistan
manuscript are suggested.

1096. ————. "Two Persian Manuscripts in the Library of

the Marquees of Bute: Part II." *Oriental Art*, NS,
18 (1972), 50-56.

Description and evaluation of Lord Bute's manuscript
of the *Anwār i Suhayli* ("The lights of Canopus") with
emphasis upon the miniatures which are identified as
by Sadigu Beg Afshār. With numerous illustrations.

1097. Rocher, Daniel. "Vom Wolf in den Fabeln des Strickers."
       Third International Beast Epic, Fable and Fabliau
       Colloquium, Münster, 1979 Proceedings. Ed. Jan
       Goossens and Timothy Sodmann. Köln, 1981, 330-339.

The wolf appears in six of the seventeen true fables
of Stricker, suggesting that the character might have
meant something special to Stricker. Rocher concludes
that the wolf does not always have the same meaning,
but that it was for the poet "das grosse Tier" which
represented the higher levels of society, levels which
Stricker often brought into question. The wolf is
compared to other medieval treatments of the animal and
is found to be characterized in a different manner.

1098. Rochholz, E. "Das Thiermärchen vom gegessenen Herzen."
       Zeitschrift für deutsche Philologie, 1 (1961), 181-
       198.

Approaches P583 (TMI K402) from a literary historical
point of view: first to solve the "problem" of whether
it is of "native" German or of oriental origin. Traces
it from the Fredegar Chronicle (7th century) through
the *Kaiserchronik* (ca. 1160) and the *Gesta Romanorum*
to Burkhard Waldis' *Esopus* then returns to a similar
motif from Icelandic Poetry and ultimately to Sigurd
(Siegfried) who eats the dragon's heart. All compared
to the "oriental tradition" which includes the Aesopic
fable, "Pig without a Heart."
       See: Keidel, "Die Eselherzfabel."

1099. Rodenwaldt, R. *Die deutsche Fabel in der deutschen*
       Spruchdichtung des 12. und 13. Jahrhunderts. Program,
       Berlin, 1885.

Deals with the fables found in Middle High German
"Spruchdichtung," from the eleventh through the thirteenth centuries. Treats in detail fables (source
studies and parallels as well as some literary analysis) from Spervogel, Freidank (fl. 1216-1240), Der
Marner (fl. 1230-1270) and used the Romulus tradition,

Stolle (fl. 1256), Kelin (fl. 1246-1272), and Heinrich
Frauenlob.

1100. Roerecke, H.H. "The Integrity and Symmetry of Robert
Henryson's Moral Fables." Dissertation, Pennsyl-
vania State University, 1969.

Argues that the standard order of Henryson's *Fables*
is part of the unified structure of a complete work.
The first fable is a traditional opening fable and
Henryson's "farewell" is found at the end.

1101. Rohde, Erwin. "Ein griechisches Märchen." *Rheinisches
Museum für Philologie*, 43 (1880), 303-305.

Finds proverbial sentences, an American Indian folktale, and other materials as essentially the same
motif as in P50 "Weasel and Aphrodite" (TMI J1098.2).

1102. Röhlich, Lutz. "Sprichwörtliche Redensarten aus
Volkerzählungen." *Volk, Sprache, Dichtung: Festgabe
für Kurt Wagner*. Ed. Karl Bischolff and Lutz Röhlich.
Giessen: Wilhelm Schmitz, 1960.

Discusses the relationship of proverbs to folk narratives, including fables. Proverbial materials, he
implies, might occasionally originate in fables as
well as in most other narrative forms.

1103. ————, and Wolfgang Mieder. *Sprichwort*. Stuttgart:
Metzler, 1977. 137 pp.

In its comprehensive survey of paremiology, the relationship of the proverb to the fable is touched upon,
concluding that in actuality, very little is known
about the multifaceted relationship between the two
categories. Many proverbial phrases are shortened
fables, but the fable is often dependent upon the
proverb as well. Excellent bibliographies for all
sections.

1104. Rölleke, Heinz. "Die deutsche Fabeldichtung im Umkreis
der französischen Revolution." *Die Fabel: Theorie,
Geschichte und Rezeption einer Gattung*. Ed. Peter
Hasubek. Berlin: Schmidt, 1982, 146-162.

Deals with the German fable as a reflection of the
French Revolution. Johann Heinrich Merck is discussed
as having revolutionary tendencies; Johann Wilhelm
Ludwig Gleim rejects revolutionary ideas in general

and the French Revolution in particular; Gottlieb
Pfeffel's early fables are in the tradition of the
enlightenment, and August Christian Fischer's prose
fables are concerned with numerous events and persons
from the revolutionary milieu.

1105. Romano, Benedetto. "Fedro III Prol. V. 38-50." *Bolle-
       tino di filologia classica*, 33 (1927), 309-314.

       Close examination allows attribution of the third
       prologue (and perhaps all of the collection) to the
       reign of Tiberius. Interprets the prologue as re-
       ferring to the simple removal of certain privileges,
       not a punishment.

1106. ————. "Fedro e la sua morale." *Estratto dal Annu-
       ario II del. R. Gimnasio*. "Norberto Rosa" di Susa.
       1929.

       Romano sees the persona of Phaedrus and his signifi-
       cance for his times in his fables. Apparently con-
       siders the fables to be original with Phaedrus not
       only in style but also content.

1107. Rooth, Erk. "Kleine Bemerkungen zur Mundart des Magde-
       burger Äsop." *Niederdeutsches Jahrbuch*, 82 (1959),
       81-86.

       A number of lexical items relative to Gerhard von
       Minden's fable collection.

1108. Rosen, Charles W. "Style and Morality in La Fontaine."
       Dissertation, Princeton, 1951.

       Relates the style of the narratives of the fables
       to the morals expressed and attempts to distinguish
       differences in style for differing attitudes toward
       the contents. Extensive discussion of stylistic
       consideration.
       See: Jean Biard, *The Style of La Fontaine's Fables*.

1109. Rosenzweig, Sidney. "Ascham's *Schoolmaster* and Spen-
       ser's February Eclogue." *South Atlantic Bulletin*,
       15 (1940), 103-109.

       Discusses the use of what appears to be some fables
       by Spenser and by Ascham, pointing out the verbal
       similarities between passages from the *Schoolmaster*
       and Spenser's *Eclogue*. A passage from "King Henry the
       Sixth, Part Three" is mentioned as well.

1110.   Rossbach, O.   "Zu den Metamorphosen des Apulejus."
        Philologus, 54 (1895), 135-147.

        Contains a note to P182 "Ass with Image of a God"
        (TMI J953.4) from Cod. Vat. 5086 (14th Century), 82ᵛ
        to 83ʳ.

1111.   ————.   "Der Pithoeanus des Phaedrus."   *Philologus*,
        55 (1896), 191-198.

        Discusses the most important variant readings to be
        found in the paleographic edition produced by Ulysse
        Robert.
        See: Finch, "The Morgan Manuscript of Phaedrus."

1112.   Rotondi, Giuseppe.   "Una paratrasi medievale della
        fabula 'cassite et agricole.'"   *Renditi Istituto
        Lombardi*, Ser. II, 65 (1932), 717-732.

        Rotondi publishes a medieval paraphrase of the Ennian
        table of P325 "Lark and Farmer" (A-T 93; TMI J1031)
        and its derivation.
        See: Müller, "Ennius and Äsop."

1113.   Roussel, L.   *La fable troisième du Livre Onze, commen-
        tée*.   Paris: Les Belles Lettres, 1951.   39 pp.

        Exhaustive comparative and critical commentary on
        "Le fermier, le chien et le Renard" XI, 30 in La Fon-
        taine's *Fables*.

1114.   Rovero, Laura.   "Plutarco fonte delle 'Fables Morales'
        di Philibert Guide, fabolista del Cinquecento."
        Studi Francesi, 70 (1980), 73-81.

        This article introduces the little-known poet Guide
        from Chalon-sur-Sarône (1535-1595) who translated a
        small collection of twenty-two fables with some addi-
        tions from Plutarch and published them in 1583.

1115.   Rowlands, Mary.   "The Fables of Robert Henryson."
        Dalhousie Review, 39 (1959-1960), 491-502.

        Suggests a number of historical events to which
        Henryson might be alluding in his *Fables*.

1116.   ————.   "Robert Henryson and the Scottish Courts of
        Law."   *Aberdeen University Review*, 39 (1962),
        219-226.

        Investigates Henryson's attitude toward the courts as
        seen in the fables, especially in the "Sheep and the Dog."

1117. Rozier, Ivan. "Esope chez les Berbères." *Mercure de France*, 15 (1937), 217-218.

       On a Berber version of P149 "Lion, Ass and Fox" (A-T 51; TMI J811.1).

1118. Ruben, Walter. *Das Pancatantra und seine Morallehre*. Berlin: Akademie Verlag, 1959. 305 pp.

       Despite frequent references to some imagined "class struggles" and to the fable scholars Friedrich Engels and Lenin (!), this work provides the best available introduction to the *Panchatantra*. Discusses the *Tantrākhyaya* in great detail together with Indian commentaries, a comparative study of Aesop and the *Panchatantra*. The second part is a series of essays on the general theme of the fable collection and its moral doctrines, often again described as a function of the struggle between the "exploiters" and the people. Ruben suggests that the slave became, early on in pre-Vedic mythology, a proto-martyr.

1119. Rubuo, D. Lisardo. "El Manuscrito 37 de Burgo de Osma: Una traducción (Latin) de Esope en la escuela humanistica de Feltre." *Actas del II. congreso español de estudias clásicos*. Madrid: Publicaciones de la sociedad española de estudios clásicos, 1964, 642-650.

       Discusses the 124-fable collection in the 1461 manuscript. All are in the medieval Aesopic canon though two are not found in the Chambry edition to which the fables are keyed.

1120. Runte, Roseann. "The Paradox of the Fable in 18th Century France." *Neophilologus*, 61 (1977), 510-517.

       A number of apparent paradoxes, such as the omission of the genre fable by Boileau from the *Art poétique*, which contributed to the proliferation of the forms, and the attempt to imitate the inimitable La Fontaine, trapped the eighteenth-century French fabulists. Lists the major fabulists with their output.

1121. ———. "Narrator and Reader: Keys to Irony in La Fontaine." *Australian Journal of French Studies*, 16 (1979), 389-400.

       The creation of a self-conscious narrator in a variety of roles and the implied readers are the keys to the distance between the author and his material, the author and the narrator, and the reader and the narrative in two modes: those who approve and those who do not.

1122.   ————. "Reconstruction and Deconstruction." *Papers on French Seventeenth Century Literature*, 11 (1979), 29-46.

Discusses La Fontaine's dialogue with the reader; analysis of La Fontaine's three personae: that of translator, of commentator, and that of author and contrasts these with the two personae, or potential personae: the reader as critic and as the immediate reader with whom we identify. The omniscient narrator of Aesop is the form to which the later fable will return, and that is what went wrong with the verse fable after La Fontaine. This strict adherence to form and excessive didacticism destroy the genre.

1123.   Rupp, Heinz. "Zum 'Renner' Hugos von Trimberg." *Typologia Litterarum: Festschrift für Max Wehrli*. Zurich: Atlantis, 1969, 233-259.

Hugo von Trimberg and his use of fables in his "Renner" are discussed. Hugo's popularity today is contrasted to that of his own day; the structure of the work with the fables (together with the parables and anecdotes) as functional constructional elements. Extensive treatment of themes.

1124.   Rutherford, W. Gunion. *Babrius*. Scriptores fabularum graeci no. 1. London: Macmillan, 1883. ciii + 202 pp.

The opening chapter is an interesting history of the Greek fable in which Rutherford claims that Greek fables are at least as old as Indian although there seems to be no way of settling the question. The first study builds upon Crusius by discussing the verse forms in the historical context of Latin verse although he was writing in Greek. The language of Babrius and the history of the text finish off the introduction. The edition is outfitted with extensive notes and a lexicon.

1125.   Ryan, Calvin T. "The Oldest Method in All This World." *American Childhood*, (Feb., 1949), 12-13.

Defends the telling of fables and other tales against

charges that they are not true tales. They are useful
in that the underlying truth and morality are clear
to the child.

1126. Ryan, Eileen P. "The Verse Adaptations of Avianus.
Part I: The Astensis and Its Derivatives." Dissertation, University of Illinois at Urbana, 1940.

Text and commentary on the *Apologi Aviani*, now for
the most part superseded by Küppers and Gaide.

1127. Saillard, G. *Essai sur la fable en France au xviii*^e
siècle. Toulouse: Deuard Proval, 1912. 163 pp.

An extensive, if perforce cursory, overview of the
status of the fable in eighteenth-century France.
Presents a wide-ranging view of the popularity of the
form, noting over one hundred fabulists with special
attention to those who wrote in Latin. Sees a definite
change in tone and in the morals of the fables from
the time of La Fontaine.
See: Thomas Noel, *Theories of the Fable*.

1128. Saint-Marc, Giradin M. *La Fontaine et les fabulists*.
2 vols. Paris: Michel Levy, 1867.

Details the history of the fable from Aesop through
Babrius and Phaedrus and the "oriental fable," and
discusses its relationship to the *Roman du Renard* and
the fabliaux. La Fontaine is described in historical
context, followed by a life of the poet and detailed
analysis of the fables. Volume two deals with the
human nature of the characters in the fables and a
large number of lesser-known fabulists in the seventeenth and eighteenth centuries; much of this analysis
is still of value.

1129. Salac, A. "Ad menandri iuvenilia." *Eumonia*, 4 (1960),
38-40.

On the influence of Theophrastus' school upon Menander, who is thought to have been in Athens at the
time of Demetrius as mentioned in Phaedrus V, 1 (P523
"King Demetrius and Poet Menander").

1130. Sandrovskaja, V.S. "Die byzantinischen Fabeln in der
Leningrader Handschriftensammlungen." *Probleme der
neugriechischen Literatur*, 3 (1960), 10-20.

A listing of various fables to be found in manuscripts

from the eleventh to the fifteenth centuries to be found in Leningrad.

1131. Sareil, Jean. "Les Apologues de Voltaire." *Romanic Review*, 68 (1977), 118-127.

Voltaire is described as reluctant to use the fable, perhaps because La Fontaine had been so successful with the form and because the moral had been subordinated to the story line in the La Fontaine collection. Voltaire did, however, make use of fabular material as a rhetorical feature to emphasize certain points.

1132. Sarkady, Johannes. "Aisopos der Samier." *Acta Classica. Universitatis Debreceniensis*, 4 (1968), 6-12.

The historicity of Aesop is rehearsed, with the pronouncement that Aesop is an historical personage with Herodotus as final proof. Sees a connection between the rise of democracy and Aesop's life and activity and parallels specifically with the development of the animal fable and the history of Samos.

1133. Sasaly, Edythe Rosalyn. "Shakespeare's Use of the Fable of the Belly and the Members." M.A. Thesis, Brooklyn College, 1939. 39 pp.

Short historical introduction to Shakespeare's use of P130 "Stomach and the Feet" (A-T 293; TMI J461.1), especially in *Coriolanus*.
See: Yoder, *Animal Analogy in Shakespeare*.

1134. Sassan, Hans. *De Phaedri sermone*. Dissertation, Marburg, 1911.

Various notes on textual problems associated with, but not limited to, Phaedrus and his fables. Seems unaware of most of the work accomplished in the decade before.

1135. Saylor, Charles F. "Man, Animal and the Bestial in Lucretius." *Classical Journal*, 67 (1972), 306-316.

Lucretius uses characteristics of animals "allegorically" to represent certain aspects of human behavior. Descriptions of animal warfare in *De rerum natura* stand out in strong contrast to the poet's usual direct correlation between good and bad aspects of animal and human behavior patterns.

1136.   Sbordone, Francesco. "Recensioni retoriche delle
        favole esopiane." *Rivista Indo-Greca-Italica de
        Filologia, Lingua antichità*, 16 (1932), 35-68.

        Contributions to the textual history of the Aesopic
        fables, including the fourteen fables in the Codex
        Brancatianus IV A5, published here for the first time.
        Three are in iambics, the others in prose and may be
        the oldest from the Byzantine era. The texts are
        discussed relative to their importance for the history
        of rhetoric, language, and style. The 40 fables of
        Aphthonius are also made available here with language
        comments and notes on their relationship to Aesop and
        Babrius.

1137.   ————. "Une redaction inédite de la fable du paysan
        et du rossignol." *Byzantinoslavica: Revue inter-
        nationale des Études Byzantines*, 9 (1947-1948), 177-
        181.

        On P627 "Nightingale and the Bowman" (Cf. A-T 150;
        TMI K604) as found in the manuscript Grk. Laut. Pl 59
        from the fifteenth century from Barlaam and Josaphat.

1138.   Schäfer, Martin. "Die Fabel im Dienst der Spracherzie-
        hung." *Der Deutschunterricht*, 7: 5 (1958), 69-79.
        Reprinted in *Das Prinzip der Ganzheit im Deutsch-
        unterricht*. Ed. E. Weisser. Darmstadt, 1967, pp.
        208-221.

        Reviews uses of the fable in language instruction:
        as models for reading, as units for memorization, etc.
        The fable is especially useful because of its concise-
        ness, its logical, almost transparent content and ac-
        tion, but it is not to be reduced to a mere rhetorical
        device. The morals usually of value for children.
        Suggestions include: trying to imagine being a fabu-
        list, writing fables. Includes numerous examples.

1139.   Schanz, Martin. "Sokrates als vermeintlicher Dichter:
        Ein Beitrag zur Erklärung des Phaidon." *Hermes*, 29
        (1894), 597-601.

        Discusses Plato's statement that Socrates versified
        Aesop while in prison. This is strengthened by a
        distich quoted by Diogenes Laertius. Schanz reminds
        us that Plato was a poet as well as a philosopher and
        that Socrates' verses are therefore unlikely.

1140. ———, C. Hosius, and G. Krüger. "Avianus." *Römische Literaturgeschichte*. Munich: Beck, 1935. 2, 32–35.

On the poet's name and time (suggested dates are not past the fourth century); relationship between the fables of Babrius and Avianus. Reviews the textual problems, the medieval paraphrases. Extensive bibliography.

1141. ———, C. Hosius, and G. Krüger. "Phaedrus." *Römische Literaturgeschichte*. Munich: Beck, 1935. 2, 447–456.

Summary of what is known of Phaedrus' life and a critical assessment of his life. Comprehensive bibliography though now dated.

1142. Scharf, Georg. *Die handschriftliche Überlieferung der deutschen Cyrillus-Fabeln des Ulrich von Pottenstein*. Dissertation, Breslau, 1935. 38 pp.

Deals with the later reworkings of the Cyrillian fable in the German version of Ulrich von Pottenstein. A stemma of the manuscripts is worked out and origins as well as relationships are determined.

1143. Scheiber, Alexander. "Eine Geschichte von Ilja Ehrenburg." *Fabula*, 8 (1966), 108–109.

Note to a version of P527 "Buffon and Rustic" (TMI J2232).

1144. Scheiber, Sandor. "Hermandyi Dines Jozsef Talmudkimpendiumanak meg egy keziratos pel dange." *Magyar könguszemle*, 82 (1966), 347–349.

Discusses a fable alluded to in the manuscript copy of the compendium of the Talmud by Josef Hermandyi Dienes of Budapest.

1145. Scheler, Lucien. "La persistance du motif dans l'illustration des fables d'Esope du seizième et dix-septième siècle." *Studia Bibliographica in honorem Hermann de La Fontaine Verwey*. Amsterdam: Menno Hartzberger, 1966.

Discusses the constancy of certain motifs used to illustrate various fables in a number of editions during the sixteenth and seventeenth centuries. See: Hodnett: *Francis·Barlow, First Master*.

1146. Scheps, Walter. "Chaucer's Anti-Fable: Reductio ad
       absurdum in the Nun's Priest's Tale." *Leeds Studies
       in English*, N.S. 4 (1970), 1-10.

       Lucid, concise discussion of the Nun's Priest's Tale
       with an exposition of the treatment of the relation-
       ship between human and animal characters. It is called
       an "anti-fable" because of these relationships and
       its structure wherein the fabulist and characters often
       exchange places. Especially "anti-fabular" is the
       treatment of the *moralitas*.

1147. Schick, Carla. "Studi qui primoddi della prosa greca."
       Archivo Glottologico Italiano, 40 (1955), 89-135.

       Studies on various early Ionic and Attic prose forms,
       including a number of fables from various sources
       with special attention paid to lexical and syntactical
       questions.

1148. Schirokauer, Arno. "Luther's Arbeit am Esopo." *Modern
       Language Notes*, 62 (1947), 73-84.

       Short historical survey introduces Luther fabular
       activity, shown to be a rewriting of Heinrich Stein-
       höwel's *Esopus*. The question is whether Luther uses
       the Latin or the German. Schirokauer suggests that
       Luther most likely had the bilingual version. It is
       in the morals that Luther demonstrates his independence
       from his sources; it is here his interest lies.
       Luther does not translate the fables into German but
       into "Protestantism."

1149. ———. "Die Stellung Äsops in der Literatur des
       Mittelalters." *Festschrift für Wolfgang Stammler*.
       Berlin, 1953, pp. 179-199. Reprinted in Arno
       Schirokauer. *Germanistische Studien*. Hamburg:
       Hauewedll, 1957, pp. 396-415.

       An introductory statement concerning the fable in
       sixteenth-century Germany leads to a chronological
       account of the position of *Aesopica*, rather than Aesop,
       during a few highlighted periods in the Middle Ages.
       Suggests that the change of Aesop to Esopet signals a
       use of Aesopica by "juniores," both children and those
       of lower classes. Later then, a division is made be-
       tween the scriptures and the fables, and Schirokauer
       sees a series of parallels between the two with regard
       to edition, to vagarities in popularity, and the like.

1150. Schlicht, Else. *Das lehrhafte Gleichnis im Renner des Hugo von Trimberg*. Dissertation, Giessen, 1928. 127 pp.

On the nature of the didactic element in "Der Renner"; useful for the collection of the moralistic inserts and digressions. Very little on the fables as fables. See: Grubmüller, *Meister Esopus*.

1151. Schlingmann, Carsten. *Gellert: Eine literarhistorische Revision*. Bad Homburg: Gehlen, 1967.

The section on Gellert's fables deals with the background of the fable, especially a definition of the fable in the eighteenth century, as the opposite of the "Gelengenheitsgedicht." The French influence on the German fable is treated as a prologue to Gellert's work on and in the genre. Gellert's early fables are compared to later forms and to the reworkings of those earlier fables to bring them into conformity with his new metrical forms and ideas.

1152. Schmalz, J.H. "Sprachliche Bemerkungen zum lateinischen Aesop des Romulus." *Berliner Philologische Wochenschrift* (1914), 444-447; 476-480.

Textual notes to the Georg Thiele text edition of the Romulus collection of the middle ages.

1153. Schmaus, A. "Lessings Fabeln bei Disitej Obradovič." *Zeitschrift für slawische Philologie*, 8 (1931), 1-47.

The relationship of Lessing to Obradovič is carefully examined. Obradovič's collection owes much to Phaedrus, Abstemius, and others as well as Lessing, but Lessing was the superlative fabulist for him, even though it appears that Obradovič did not know Lessing's theoretical writings on the fable. Schmaus identifies 28 Lessing fables as translated or closely paraphrased in Obradovič and considerable influence in others. Problems of style are extensively discussed with the conclusion that the fables are better in Serbian for not having been slavishly translated.

1154. Schmid, Karl. *Studien zu den Fabeln Abrahams a Sancta Clara*. Dissertation, Munich, 1928.

Defines over 150 different true fables among which are 80 animal and plant fables, of which a majority

are found in a number of versions. Discusses Abraham's use of fables in the pulpit, relationship to
his sources, proverbs in the fables, Abraham's concept
of the fable and a total listing of the fables found
in the works at Abraham a Sancta Clara.

1155. Schmidt, Peter. "Politisches Argument und moralischer
       Appell: Zur Historizität der antiken Fabel im früh-
       kaiserzeitlichen Rom." *Der Deutschunterricht*, 31: 6
       (1976), 74-88.

       Discusses P130 "Stomach and Feet" (A-T 293; TMI 461.1)
       and P44 "Frogs Ask for a King" (A-T 277; TMI J643.1) as
       examples of the political rhetorical uses to which
       fables might be put. Schmidt feels that the fable is
       generally seen as a weapon of the underdog or as an
       instrument in the "class struggle," but that in fact
       its political nature ought to be viewed as impetus to
       the development of a new genre.

1156. Schmitt, Jean C. "Les traditions folkloriques dans le
       culture médiévale: quelques réflexions de méthode."
       Archiv de Sciences Sociales des Religions, 26 (1981),
       5-20.

       Analyzes and refines methods to evaluate popular
       religion and reviews research in popular culture
       studies using recent anthropological approaches.
       Schmitt gives two case studies, providing an analysis
       of the circulation of tales, including a number of
       fables, between the learned clergy on the one side
       and the folk traditions on the other. Later thirteenth-
       century society tended to reject the oral traditional
       material, branding it simple superstition.

1157. Schnur, Harry C. *Fabeln der Antike*. München: Heimeran,
       1978. 349 pp.

       Introduction includes a comprehensive historical
       overview of the Greek and the Roman fable up to the
       time of Avianus and the Romulus paraphrases. Selec-
       tion of fables with translations. Extensive bibliog-
       raphy.

1158. ———. "*Vorwort*: Die Fabel im Mittelalter." *Latein-
       ische Fabeln des Mittelalters*. Munich: Heimeran,
       1979.

       Builds upon Schnur's *Fabeln der Antike* historical
       presentation of the classical fable to effectively

present an overview of the medieval Latin fable, repre-
sentatives of which form the collection that is the
bulk of this edition. The classical strands are
clearly delineated from the beast epic materials and
the (ultimately) Indian collections. Brings the history of the Latin fable to the sixteenth century.
With a chronological table but no bibliography. Appendices on the manuscript tradition of Romulus and the
Jewish fable and especially on P124 (A-T 57; TMI 951.2).

1159. Schönbach, Anton. "Zur Kritik Boners." *Zeitschrift
für das deutsche Altertum*, 6 (1975), 251-290.

Extensive textual and dialectical notes to Ulrich
Boner's *Edelstein* occasioned generally by previous
work. Includes comparisons to Boner's sources and
an attempt to identify the manuscript from which he
worked.

1160. Schrader, Richard James. "A Critical and Historical
Study of Robert Henryson's *Morall Fabillis*." Dissertation, Ohio State University, 1968.

A study of Henryson's fables, eight in detail, in
relationship to his sources and analogues to highlight the poet's uses of traditional material and the
relevance of Ockhamism. Henryson is presented as the
teacher of a particular form of nominalism that postulates a radical distance between man and god although
remaining essentially optimistic. The expressed moral
system allows man enough intelligence to get on in
the world. With an appendix of sources and analogues
and bibliography.

1161. ————. "Some Backgrounds of Henryson." *Studies in
Scottish Literature*, 15 (1980), 124-138.

Sources and ancillary materials to Henryson's *Morall
Fabillis* not previously noted, including Cato's
"Distichs," Aristotle, and other classical sources as
well as Henryson's contemporaries.

1162. Schröder, Edward. "Quellen und alte Parallelen zu
Boners Beispielen." *Zeitschrift für deutsches
Altertum*, 44 (1900), 420-430.

Comments on and additions to Waas' dissertation
(1897) on Boner's sources.

1163.   ————. "Der Leipziger Aesop." *Nachrichten (Göttin-*
         gen) phil.-hist. Kl. (1933), 181-192.

         Contains a fairly comprehensive description of ms
         1279 of the Leipzig University Library, first pub-
         lished in three "Schulprogrammen" at Meinigen in 1896-
         1898 by Karl Einhorn as "Mitteldeutsche Fabeln" (q.v.).
         Schröder believes he has determined the compiler of
         this fable collection was a monk at St. Thomas in
         Leipzig between 1420 and 1450, from a note in the
         manuscript.
         See: Grubmüller, *Meister Esopus.*

1164.   Schuhl, Pierre-Maxime. "Hic Rhodus, hic saltas."
         Revue Philosophique, 157 (1967), 468-469.

         References to P33 "The Braggart" (TMI J1477) in,
         inter alia, Hegel and Karl Marx and brief references
         to its applications.

1165.   ————. "Un apologue inédit. La révolte des athlètes
         olympiques." *Revue Philosophique,* 158 (1968), 393-
         394.

         On a fable discovered by the Italian Ignoto and its
         relationship to the olympic athletes.

1166.   Schültz, L.H. *Die Entstehung der Sprache und andere*
         Vorträge. Frankfurt: St. Goar, 1914. 205 pp.

         Presents, among much else, a comprehensive introduc-
         tion to the *Jatakas,* or stories of the Buddha, con-
         taining numerous animal fables as well as parables
         and legends. A number of fables are discussed in de-
         tail.

1167.   Schütze, Gundolf. *Gesellschaftskritische Tendenzen*
         in deutschen Tierfabeln des 13. bis 15. Jahrhunderts.
         Bern: Lang, 1973. 205 pp.

         Discusses the concept of the fable as a critical
         genre and sets limits to its meaning in the Middle
         Ages, followed by a very short description of the
         five major German collections from the thirteenth to
         the fifteenth centuries. A systematic analysis of 79
         fables demonstrates that each contained socio-critical
         elements, and Schütze bravely attempts to connect these
         with some of the dynamic changes in society occurring
         at the time. Various types of critiques are identi-
         fied, and a wide-ranging, somewhat overdrawn set of

conclusions ends the discussion. An extensive table
of fables and a bibliography follow.

1168. Schwab, Ute. *Der Stricker: Tierbîspel.* Tübingen:
Niemeyer, 1960. 90 pp.

The introduction to this edition of twenty-four
fables and *exempla* of Der Stricker contains a dis-
cuoon of the nine fables in the collection with
sources and parallels. All are from either Avianus
or the medieval Romulus tradition.

1169. ———, ed. *Das Tier in der Dichtung.* "Introduction."
Heidelberg: Carl Winter, 1970. 296 pp.

The introduction to this collection of essays presents the general theme of animals in literature and
the more specific ideas of "Animal-didacticism" in
medieval and modern literature and genre problems.
Anthropomorphism in the fable and other forms is presented as a possible basis for interpretation.

1170. Schwabe, L. "Phaedrus doch in Pierien geboren."
Rheinisches Museum für Philologie, 39 (1884), 476.

An answer to Wölfflin's idea that Phaedrus was not
born on the Pierian Mountain. Takes Phaedrus literally
as Phaedrus meant it to be. Other statements of
Phaedrus lead to the conclusion that he was born in
Macedonia, and on the Pierian mountain.

1171. Schwarzbaum, Haim. "Aesopic Fables in Talmudic-
Midrashic Garb." *Yeda-'Am*, 7 (1955), 54-63 [= Journal
of the Israel Folklore Society].

Deals with a number of fables found in Jewish tradition, especially P130 "Stomach and Feet" (TMI J461.1),
with parallels and potential sources discussed.

1172. ———. "International Motifs in Petrus Alphonsi's
Disciplina Clericalis." *Sefarad*, 21 (1961), 267-
299; 22 (1962), 17-59 and 321-344; 23 (1963), 54-73.

A comprehensive discussion of the narratives, including fables found in the *Disciplina Clericalis*
with parallels, sources, and motif analysis. Notes
are listed against a number of text traditions of the
Disciplina, and the fables and facetiae are keyed to
standard collections with tale type and motif index
numbers.

1173. ————. "Talmudic-Midrashic Affinities of Some Aeso-
       pic Fables." *Laographia*, 22 (1965), 466-483.

       Numerous notes of parallels and possible source
       materials for a significant number of Aesopic fables
       in Talmudic-Midrashic tradition. Deals in detail with
       P130 "Stomach and Feet" (A-T 293; TMI 461.1) and
       others.

1174. ————. "Studies in Jewish and World Folklore."
       Berlin: de Gruyter, 1968. 603 pp.

       This extraordinary display of erudition has as its
       core comparative notes to Naftoli Gross's *Ma'aselech
       un Mesholim* with an extensive introduction and appen-
       dices. This collection of 450 Yiddish folktales and
       fables was published in New York in 1955. The commen-
       tary contains notes to each piece, with the fables
       keyed to Perry and with parallels and sources given.
       Aesopica includes anecdotes from the *Vita Aesopi*, P40
       "Astrologer and the Well" (J2133.8) and the P452,
       P628. P628A complex "Wolf and Ass on Trial" (TMI
       U11.1.1), the latter demonstrating slight overzealous-
       ness in drawing parallels. Included in the appendices
       are cursory evaluations of a number of recent works
       on the fable. Most importantly, direct evidence is
       brought forward here concerning how thoroughly embedded
       in Jewish tradition the Aesopic fable form actually is.
       Added also are tables of tale-types and narrative
       motifs.

1175. ————. "The Vision of Eternal Peace in the Animal
       Kingdom (A-T 62)." *Fabula*, 10 (1969), 107-131.

       This study will become the sixth chapter of Schwarz-
       baum's *The Mishle Shu'alim (Fox fables) of Rabbi
       Berechiah ha-Nakdan: A Study in Comparative Folklore
       and Fable Lore* (q.v.) and deals with the sixth fable
       in the collection, P671 "Fox and Dove" (A-T 62; TMI
       J1421) considered here to have come from a Talmudic
       source, from Berakhot 61b narrated by Rabbi Akiba.
       The fable is popular in Midrashic literature. An at-
       tempt is made to connect P671 with P11 and P11a
       "Fisherman Pipes to Fish" (TMI J1909.1) as well as
       other fables.

1176. ————.   "The Impact of the Medieval Beast Epics upon
       the Mishle Shu'alim of Rabbi Berechiah ha-Nakdan."
       Aspects of the Medieval Animal Epic. Proceedings of

the International Conference, Louvain, May 15-17,
1975. Leuven UP, 1977, pp. 220-239.

Deals with the specific influence of various Beast
Epics upon the 119-fable collection of Rabbi Berechiah
ha-Nakdan. Although these materials are not the primary sources for the collection, Schwarzbaum suggests
that Rabbi Berechiah's thirteenth fable, P124 "Fox
and Crow" (A-T 57; TMI K334) was influenced by the
Roman de Renart, and sees Beast epic affinities in
his 52nd fable, similar to P149 "Lion, Ass and Fox"
(A-T 51; TMI J811.1), the 85th similar to P258 "Sick
Lion" (A-T 50; TMI K961) and the 99th, P625 "Fox as
Fisherman and Wolf" (A-T 2; TMI K341.2, K371.1, K1021)
and others.

1177. ————. *The Mishle Shu'alim (Fox Fables) of Rabbi
Berechiah ha-Nakdan: A Study in Comparative Folklore
and Fable Lore*. Kiron: Institute for Jewish and
Arab Folklore Research, 1979. lv + 658 pp.

Introduction contains a survey of ideas on the nature
of fables and their use in satire, oratory, and exegesis, generally from Jewish sources but with examples
from all over. Defines the fable as a fictitious fate
told for the purpose of communicating a certain idea
or truth metaphorically. A survey of the research
on the Fox Fables of Berechiah ha-Nakdan concludes the
introduction. The massive text consists of extensive
annotations to the Fox Fables. Schwarzbaum agrees
with the consensus of modern research that there is
no single source for the ha-Nakdan collection. A very
comprehensive comparative study with a wide-ranging
bibliography and indices of narrative types and of
motifs. The fables are keyed to standard collections.

1178. Scivoletto, N. "Due note filologiche." *Giornale
italiano di filologia*, 13 (1960), 356-364.

Includes a textual note on Phaedrus, I, 5-7.

1179. Scobie, Alex. "Notes on Walter Anderson's 'Märchen
vom Eselmenschen.'" *Fabula*, 15 (1971), 222-231.

Describes the Ass-romance (*Asinus Aureus*) and its
relationship to P164 "Mendicant Priests" as well as
P600 and P186 in passing.

1180. Scott, Dorothea Hayward. "Perrault and Aesop's Fables."
Children's Literature, 7 (1978), 218-225.

Describes a labyrinth in Versailles designed by
André le Nôtre in which some 39 fountains illustrate
fables described in verse by Isaac de Benserade, which
is now known only from engravings and a few statues
now in museums. Charles Perrault composed prose versions of the fabular poems and had them published in
1675.

1181. Seemann, Erich. *Hugo von Trimberg und die Fabeln
       seines Renners*. Munich: Georg D.W. Callwey, 1923.
       308 pp.

Extensive survey of the sources and classical antecedents to the fables and individual verses of the
fables, with a broad integrated look at the medieval
attitude towards fabular motifs, especially the non-
Christian elements to be found in the Aesopic tradition. Individual fables are given separate chapters,
each with bibliographical citations. With an appendix
on the *Minor Fabularis*, mentioned as a source by Hugo,
and its text.
See: Rupp, "Zum 'Renner.'"

1182. Seiler, Thomas Henry. "Devices of Brevity in the
       Narrative Poetry of Robert Henryson." Dissertation,
       University of Texas at Austin, 1975. 128 pp.

Brevity is seen as both a structural principle and
a device in Henryson. In the *Morall Fabillis of
Esope*, a number of fables are united into a whole
essentially by devices of diction.

1183. Seran, Herman Joseph. "Didactic Elements of Pancha-
       tantra Origin in Indonesian Fables and Their Social
       Values." Dissertation, University of San Carlos,
       1961.

A discussion of motifs common to Indonesian "folk"
tales and the *Panchatantra*, focusing upon the didactic
animal stories, the fables, and their application to
present-day social problems in Indonesia.

1184. Servaes, Franz-Wilhelm. "Typologie und mittellatein-
       ische Tierdichtung." *Der altsprachliche Unterricht*,
       17: 1 (1974), 17-29.

Notes toward the use of medieval literature in
schools and, in particular, toward a determination of
a typology of medieval Latin literature with animals,

especially fables and the beast epic, and the *Physio-logus* material which is found in a number of simpler prose and poetic texts.

1185. Shackleton Baily, D.R. "Aviana." *Harvard Studies in Classical Philology*, 82 (1978), 295-301.

Textual notes on two fables in Avianus.

1186. ―――. "Phaedriana." *American Journal of Philology*, 99 (1978), 451-455.

Textual notes to ten fables of Phaedrus, generally interpretative rather than paleographic.

1187. Shai, Donna. "A Kurdish-Jewish Animal Tale in Its Sociocultural Context." *Studies in Jewish Folklore*. Ed. Frank Talmage. Cambridge, Mass.: Association for Jewish Studies, 1980, 297-306.

A brief discussion of the position of the fable in the Near East and particularly among the Kurdish Jews in Israel is followed by an intensive discussion of a Kurdish version of P605 "Fox with many Tricks and Cat with One" (A-T 105; TMI J514.1). Shai traces the tale from the *Panchatantra* through the European Beast Epic, Odo of Cheriton of the thirteenth century, and La Fontaine. The Kurdish tale is discussed in the context of the beliefs and attitudes toward animals.

1188. Shakura, Catherine. "Preface." *Fables in Monosyllables by Mrs. Teachwell (Lady Ellenor Fenn)*. New York: Johnson Reprint Collection, 1970, vii-xiv.

Describes Lady Fenn's purpose in rewriting the fables into simpler forms, applying Rousseau's ideas of pedagogy for the very young.

1189. Shallers, Alvin P. "The Renart Tradition in the Literature of Medieval England." Dissertation, Wisconsin, 1971.

The Renart romance is traced in England through Odo of Cheriton and the *Vox and Wolf*, and its influence is seen in John of Sheppey, Nicole Bozon, John of Bromyard, Chaucer, and Henryson.

1190. Shea, John Stephen. "Introduction." *Bernard Mandeville: Aesop Dress'd or a Collection of Fables Writ in Familiar Verse*. Los Angeles: William Andrews Clark Memorial Library, 1966. i-xi.

Historical overview of the 1704 *Aesop Dress'd*, its
predecessor (*Fables after the Easie and Familiar Method
of Monsieur de la Fontaine*, 1703) with thirty-nine
fables, two of which are original. Each fable is
treated in some detail, contrasting with the La Fontaine original and the John Dennis translation which
appeared ten years before Mandeville.

1191.   ————. "Studies in the Verse Fable from La Fontaine
         to Gay." Dissertation, University of Minnesota,
         1967.

Sees the versified animal verse fable developing a
distinctive or a "proper" style to correspond to the
"proper" style in French by La Fontaine. Progress
towards this goal is illustrated by a study of the
fables of John Ogilby, John Dennis, Bernard Mandeville, and John Gay; the latter is ranked as the
only English fabulist of the caliber of La Fontaine.

1192.   Sheldon, E.S. "The Fable Referred to in Aliscans."
         Publications of the Modern Language Association, 18
         (1903), 335-340.

Suggests P655 "Fasting Wolf and Lamb" as the fable
referred to in verse 3053 of *Aliscans*. The fable is
known in the Marie de France collection and other
early sources.

1193.   Shell, John Ewing. "The Role of the Emblem and the
         Fable in the Didactic Literature of the Sixteenth
         Century." Dissertation, Rice University, 1972.

Investigates the widely recognized popularity of the
emblem and the fable and some of the attitudes of
which that great interest might be reflective. Attempts to explain why the two are not, in fact, more
intimately associated. Concludes that a strong relationship between fable and emblem, due in part to the
similarity of didactic function and other surface
similarities such as brevity, does not seem to be
well founded. The fable does not seem to provide
the basis for many emblems because in part the emblem and the fable seemed to appeal to different elements in the society. The emblem is of a more highly
esoteric quality and grew out of a humanistic delight
in esoteric iconography, whereas the fable was on a
more popular level. Suggests that the fable was perhaps
too strongly identified with the Lutheran movement to
be used by the Catholic emblem writers.

1194. Siegrist, Christoph. "Fabel und Lehrgedicht: Gemein-
      samkeiten und Differenzen." *Die Fabel: Theorie,*
      Geschichte und Rezeption einer Gattung. Ed. Peter
      Hasubek (q.v.). Berlin: Schmidt, 1982, 106-118.

      On the similarities and differences between the
      fable and the "Lehrgedicht" in eighteenth-century
      Germany. Suggests the two forms are based upon the
      concept of literature basic to the *Aufklärung*, that
      these forms justify their existence only insofar as
      they perform a useful, didactic function and treats
      this concept of the fable historically. The essential
      differences lie in the presentation and essential
      function. The fable is a popular fiction; the "Lehr-
      gedicht" is a philosophical, moral, or scientific
      truth not a fictional narration. The fable will sur-
      vive because of the adaptability of its intent.

1195. Sijpesteijn, P.J. "Three Papyri from the Private
      Collection of A.M. Hakkart." *Studia Papyrologica:*
      Revista española de papirologia, 6 (1967), 7-13.

      One fragment of a papyrus of the third century ap-
      parently contains a prose paraphrase of some fables
      of Babrius.

1196. Silcher, Georg. *Tierfabel, Tiermärchen und Tierepos*
      mit besonderer Berücksichtigung des Roman de Renart.
      Program, Reutlingen, 1905. 33 pp.

      Continues and essentially affirms Grimm's theory that
      the animal fable as well as the beast epic is more or
      less derived from the "Tiermärchen" with which term
      he replaces Grimm's "Tiersage," to no great effect.

1197. Silman, Tamara Isakovna. *Posobie po stilističeskomu*
      analigu nemeckoj chadozestvennoj literatury. Lenin-
      grad: Izdat "Prosvescenie," 1969. 327 pp.

      Lessing's Fables and their relationship to Lessing's
      theoretical works and their influence are discussed on
      pp. 5-23.

1198. Simon, Sándor. "Horatius és a Fabula Aesopea."
      Egyetemes Philologai Közlöny (Budapest) (1939),
      1-15.

      Discusses the satirical use of the fables found
      quoted in or alluded to in Horace in contrast to the
      Greek use of these materials. The Horatian fable is

described structurally with emphasis upon the moral,
especially P352 "Country Mouse and City Mouse" (A-T
112; TMI J211.1).

1199. Simon, Uriel. "The Fable of Jotham, Its Application
       and Narrative Framework." *Tarbiz*, 34 (1964), 1-34.

       The Jotham fable and its application are similar to
       a curse; thus the fable does not agree well with its
       application or its framework.

1200. ———. "The Poor Man's Ewe-Lamb: An Example of a
       Juridical Parable." *Biblia*, 48 (1967), 207-242.
       Also in *Bar-Ilan: Annual of Bar-Ilan University*,
       7-8 (1970), 9-37.

       The fable of the "Poor Man's Lamb" (II Sam. xii) is
       used to defend the juridical parable as a realistic
       story concerning the breaking of the law but is told
       as an example to someone who had committed a similar
       offense, in the hope that the offender would then un-
       wittingly pass judgment upon himself. The Old Testa-
       ment contains five of these juridical parables: II
       Sam, xi, 1-14; xiv, 1-20; I Kings xx, 35-43; Isaiah v,
       1-7; Jer iii, 1-5.

1201. Singer, Aaron M. "Animals in Rabbinic Teaching: The
       Fable." Dissertation, The Jewish Theological
       Seminary of America, 1979. 203 pp.

       An extensive investigation of the use of animals
       in Rabbinical teaching, especially the animal fables
       found in the Midrash and the Talmud. The rabbinical
       teachings are seen as underscoring the biblical con-
       cept of man's relationship to animals as well as demon-
       strating the biblical forms of argumentation, etc.
       Investigates the didactic approach towards nature
       and admixture of animal metaphor common to rabbinic
       fables and the special social function of the animal
       fable. With a subject heading index and Hebrew texts
       of the fables.

1202. Sinko, Th. "Literatura Tyberyanska." *Eos*, 20: 2
       (1914/15), 113-133.

       Overview of Roman Literature in the era of Tiberius:
       Phaedrus and his fables are treated in some detail
       near the end of the essay.

1203. Sironic, M. "Esopi grčka basna." *Zbornik Radora* (Zagreb) (1951), 433-443.

An attempt to relate the fables of Aesop to the actual social and political conditions of the time in more specific manner than that inherent in the limitations of the language and literature of the time.

1204. Sisam, Kenneth. *The Nun's Priest's Tale.* Oxford: Clarendon Press, 1927.

Concludes that the source used by Chaucer for the fabular material was some version deriving from the *Roman de Renart*.

1205. Slethaug, Gordon Emmett. "Thoreau's Use of the Pastoral and the Fable Traditions." Dissertation, University of Nebraska, 1968. 170 pp.

Concerned with the unity of the form and the content of Thoreau's work. *Walden* is a pastoral with the satire of the Aesopic fable tradition which explains his use of some animals as well. Structurally, *Walden* is classified as found within the rhetorical side of the fable tradition with actual fables also found embedded within the rhetorical framework, comparing man with nature in such a way as to point up his folly.

1206. Smend, Rudolf. *Alter und Herkunft des Achikar-Romans und sein Verhältnis zu Aesop.* Beihefte zur Zeitschrift für die Alttestamentliche Wissenschaft, no. 13. Giessen: Alfred Töpelmann, 1908. viii + 125 pp.

Begins with the contents of the Achikar romance, which contains a number of fables, and a comprehensive textual history. The fables are given Aesopic parallels wherever possible, and Smend suggests that a number in the Aesopic tradition might well be from Achikar fables. The relationship of Achikar to the *Vita Aesopi* is discussed, and Smend suggests that the Aesop romance is based upon the Achikar. The implications of this possibility for the Aesopic fable canon are then detailed.

1207. Smith, Angie Aleta. "Moral Outlook as Seen in Roman Fable, Proverb and Maxim." M.A. (Classics), University of Illinois, 1920. 60 pp.

The morals of the Phaedrine fable and the implied wisdom and moral system of the maxims and proverbs

found in others are contrasted in an attempt to
describe the underlying moral viewpoints of the Romans.

1208. Smith, Mahlon Ellwood. "A History of the Fable in
       English to the Death of Pope." Dissertation, Har-
       vard, 1912. 585 pp.

       A comprehensive and detailed historical survey of
       the English and Scottish fable from Lydgate and Henry-
       son to Pope. The problem of the definition of the
       fable as a genre and as a literary type is discussed
       with the fable compared to other short narrative
       types. Excellent bibliography of primary and secondary
       sources. Some parallels given to fables, but collec-
       tions are not keyed to standard Aesopica editions.

1209. ———. "The Fable and Kindred Forms." *Journal of
       English and Germanic Philology*, 14 (1915), 519-529.

       Defines fable as a short tale, obviously false, de-
       vised to impress by the symbolic representation of
       human types, lessons of expediency and morality.
       Considers the form to be essentially a *survival* of a
       form. The form is contrasted to those forms closely
       allied to it, to the typical illustrative tale, the
       allegory, the proverb, and the parable.

1210. ———. "Notes on the Rimed Fable in England." *Modern
       Language Notes*, 31 (1916), 206-216.

       One of the reasons for the lack of fable collections
       in verse from Henryson to the end of the sixteenth
       century might have been the use of the prose Aesop in
       the schools. Aesop's veneration as a poet gave place
       to the more familiar regard for him as a teller of
       moral tales.

1211. ———. "The Fable as Poetry in English Critics."
       Modern Language Notes, 32 (1917), 466-470.

       A discussion of the poetic concept of fable which
       prevailed in seventeenth-century England. Sidney and
       Bacon and their allegorical approach are well-illus-
       trated as well as the change in meaning of "fable"
       during the period, and the two distinct meanings that
       occur today, i.e., Aesopic and the more unusual ex-
       tended meaning, that of the plot or story line. The
       history of the rimed fable in England shows that even
       before its revival, there were those who were asserting
       the poetic value of the form.

1212. ————. "A Classification for Fables, Based upon the
Collection of Marie de France." *Modern Philology*,
15 (1917), 93-105.

Reviews various schemes for the classification of
fables from Aphthonius through Herder and Lessing
(the first and only one to attempt a definition at
least partially based upon important factors) and de-
vises classification scheme of three types of fables:
(1) in which actors and setting are symbolic; (2) those
in which only actors are symbolic, while the action is
that of typical human beings; and (3) those in which
the action is symbolic, but the actors consist of
human beings. Explains the ordering by means of fables
from the collection of Marie de France. Types one and
two are found there; type three is not in the collection, and there are fables in the Marie de France collection that cannot be comfortably accommodated. These
are classed as "non-fables."

1213. ————. "Aesop: A Decayed Celebrity." *Publications
of the Modern Language Association*, 46 (1931), 225-
236.

Covers various allusions to Aesop as extensions to
their existence as fables as well as allusions to the
fabulist Aesop himself. Historical accounting of the
view of Aesop as expressed by those who quote him;
from Lydgate and Henryson through Ben Jonson's interest
in the man and his fables. Aesop on the stage in the
seventeenth century highlights Aesop the character's
popularity.

1214. Smith, Richard Emmanuel. "A Study of the Correspondences between the *Roman de Renard*, Jamaican Anansi
Stories, and West African Animal Tales Collected in
Cultural Area V." Dissertation, Ohio State University, 1971. 179 pp.

Three traditions isolated in tales from Europe
(represented by the Renart tradition), Jamaica, and
West Africa. One fable in particular P426 "Fox and
Crane" (A-T 60; TMI J1561.1) is shared by all traditions, and West African primacy is presumed. A wide-
ranging number of motifs are studied with the aetio-
logical aspects highlighted.

1215. Smith, Sidney. "Notes on 'The Assyrian Tree.'" *Bulletin of the School of Oriental and African Studies*,
4 (1926/28), 69-76.

Deals with the text "Drakhti Asurik" published by
Unvala (q.v.) and cuneiform contest tales of the type
related to the Babylonian "Tamarisk and Palm," known
in the Greek tradition in Callimachus' "Laurel and
Olive," P439 "Laurel and Olive" (TMI N255.4). Smith
lists parallels and possible source texts suggesting
that the Pahlavi version in Unvala might have had
cuneiform origins rather than Arabic.
See: Lambert, *Babylonian Wisdom Literature*.

1216. Snavely, Guy Everett. "The Ysopet of Jehan de Vignay."
        Studies in Honor of A. Marshall Elliott. 2 vols.
        Baltimore: Johns Hopkins Press, 1901, 1, 347-374.

The Jehan de Vignay translation of *Mireoir Historical* is extant in forty-one manuscripts and the
fable collection is interpolated into nine of them.
Snavely publishes here a text from Ms. fr. 316 of the
Bibliothèque Nationale, the oldest and best. With
introduction, notes and bibliography of known manuscripts.

1217. ————. *The Aesopic Fables in the Mireoir Historical
        of Jehan de Vignay*. Dissertation, Johns Hopkins,
        1908. Also Baltimore: J.H. Furox, 1908.

A detailed account of Jehan de Vignay and his works,
especially the fables found in his translation of
Vincent of Beauvais' *Mireoir Historical* of the early
fourteenth century. The *Mireoir* gives a general history of the world into which Vincent had interpolated
a collection of fables. This occurs after the mention
of Aesop in early Greek history.

1218. Snell, Bruno. "Äsop und Menipp als Hofnarren." *Illi-
        nois Classical Studies*, 6 (1981), 317.

Velázquez does not use classical motifs very frequently, and it is therefore somewhat surprising to see two
large paintings by him in a single room in the Prado,
one of Aesop and one of the Cynic Menippus, both apparently the "court fool" types he was so fond of
painting. These fools were representative of truth
and cleverness.
See: Palm, "Diego Velazquez."

1219. Sobel, Eli. *Alte Neue Zeitung*. Folklore Studies,
        no. 10, Los Angeles: University of California Press,
        1958.

An annotated edition of the 54-fable collection of
Georg Rollenhagen, with an overview of the history
of the fable in Germany as a popular form, and an introduction to Rollenhagen. Rollenhagen's fables are
a mixed lot, some very common, others known only here.
Deals with the difficult problem of authorship and
the more delicate one of religious leanings. Extensive
notes; all fables keyed to the standard editions.

1220. Solá-Solé, Josep M. "De nuevo sobre el *Libro de Los
      Gatos.*" *Kentucky Romance Notes*, 19 (1972), 471-483.

      Concerns the illogical title of the Spanish transla-
      tion of Odo of Cheriton's fables, suggests *Cato*, in
      place of the usual emendation of *quentos*.

1221. Sorge, Thomas. "'Body Politic' and 'Human Body' in
      Coriolanus: Ein Beitrag zur Commonwealth-Thematik
      bei Shakespeare." *Shakespeare Jahrbuch* (Weimar),
      115 (1979), 89-97.

      On the concept of the government, the body politic,
      as a human body metaphor, including P130 "Stomach and
      Feet" (A-T 293; TMI J461.1) used by Shakespeare in
      Coriolanus.

1222. Soriano, Marc. "Histoire littéraire et folklore: La
      source oubliée de deux fables de La Fontaine."
      Revue d'Histoire Littéraire de la France, 70 (1970),
      836-860.

      Well-presented study of P572 "Kid and Wolf" (A-T 123;
      TMI J144, K1832, K1839.1) in La Fontaine and its
      sources. Differences between the La Fontaine versions
      and the Aesopic forms are discussed and compared to the
      oral versions, suggesting ultimately that La Fontaine
      influence upon folklore is here as strong as its ef-
      fects upon him. Intensive analysis of the text. Of
      special interest is the historical perspective afforded
      us by the fable.

1223. ————. "Des Contes aux Fables." *Europe*, 515 (1972),
      99-131.

      Deals with La Fontaine's version of P682 "Contrary
      Wife" (TMI T255.2) and other La Fontaine fables with
      women and compares with stories, especially *Femme
      Noyée*. More generally, the treatment of people in La
      Fontaine is analyzed, especially in the fable of the

ass with his Old Master and the story of Democritus
and the Abderites.

1224. Soudée, Madeleine Marie Guyot. "Quatre fabulists:
       Phèdre, Avianus, Marie de France et La Fontaine."
       Dissertation, George Washington University, 1977.
       285 pp.

       Sees a unifying consistency of theme and form for
       each of the four collections. Phaedrus used his fables
       for literary polemic; Avianus' collection is seen as
       a program for an individual's advance toward self-
       improvement. Marie de France is characterized as
       writing fables as court propaganda. La Fontaine's
       collection as a whole comprises a "theater of the
       world," filled with constant surprise.

1225. ———. "Le dessein d'Avianus. Nouveau critière
       d'authenticité des fables." *Echos du Monde Classique:
       Classical News and Views* (Ottawa), 22 (1978), 63-70.

       The Avianus collection as a whole forms a structure
       the design of which is revealed in the intellectual
       milieu in which they were produced. Neoplatonic,
       anti-Christian, but intellectual is the poet.

1226. ———. "Le dédicatoire des Ysopets de Marie de
       France." *Les Lettres Romanes*, 35 (1981), 183-198.

       Suggests that William Marshal may have commissioned
       the work which in turn is a call for strengthening
       oneself against falsehood and against treachery, the
       hallmarks of the quarrels between Stephen and Henry
       II.

1227. South, Helen Pennock. "The Upstart Crow." *Modern
       Philology*, 25 (1927), 83-86.

       Simple review of variants to P123 "Jackdaw and
       Crows" (TMI 951.2), P129 "Jackdaw and Pigeons" (A-T
       244; TMI J951.2) and P472 "Vainglorious Jackdaw and
       the Peacock" (A-T 244; TMI J512, J951.2).

1228. South, Malcolm Hudson. "Animal Imagery in Ben Jonson's
       Plays." Dissertation, University of Georgia, 1968.
       169 pp.

       Examines the literary use of various animal references,
       often of a fabular nature, primarily for characteriza-
       tion but also secondarily effecting plot development.

Discusses Jonson's sources of animal lore and its didactic uses.

1229. Soyter, G. "Die neugriechischen Sprichwörter in der Volksliedersammlung Werner von Haxthausens." *Byzantinisch-neugriechische Jahrbücher*, 16 (1939-1940), 171-189.

An analysis of the proverbs in a collection of modern Greek folk songs, describing many of the proverbs as having their origin in fables. With an index of proverbs and translations.

1230. Span, Shelomo. *Mishle Aesopos*. Jerusalem: The Bialik Institute, 1960.

In the afterword to this translation of Greek fables into Hebrew "Aesopos ve-Hamashal," Span gives an historical overview of the fable in Greek and Indian literature as well as a survey of the fable in European literature. Some discussion of the concept of the fable as a genre.

1231. Spanier, Sandra. "Structural Symmetry in Henryson's 'The Preaching of the Swallow.'" *Comitatus*, 10 (1979-1980), 123-127.

A note on parallel constructions and format in Henryson's version of P39 "Wise Swallow" (A-T 233c; TMI J652.2); cf. P437, 437a.

1232. Sparmberg, Paul. "Zu Steinhöwels 13. Extravagante." *Zeitschrift für deutsche Philologie*, 46 (1915), 80-83.

Sparmberg maintains that this was not originally a fable at all but a *Märchen* concerning three clever brothers. The fables listed as "Extravagantes" in Steinhöwel's collection are all of uncertain origin.

1233. ———. *Zur Geschichte der deutschen Fabel in der mittelhochdeutschen Spruchdichtung*. Dissertation, Marburg, 1918. 114 pp.

A chronological account of fabular motifs in Middle High German poetry from Herger through anonymous poems of the *Meisterlieder* manuscripts of the different centuries. Concludes for the history of the fable that one of the most noticeable aspects is the distance of these motifs to the classical forms. Marner was

the first to paraphrase Aesop. The general tendency
is to rewrite exempla from the popular tradition and
the animal epic, with a deemphasis of the moral.

1234. Speckenbach, Klaus. "Die Fabel von der Fabel: Zur
       Überlieferungsgeschichte der Fabel von Hahn und
       Perle." *Frühmittelalterliche Studien*, 12 (1978),
       178-229.

       Exhaustive study of the Phaedrine fable and especially
       P503 "Cockeral and Pearl" (TMI J1061.1), which became
       the introductory fable for many medieval collections.
       Considers the fable tradition in the Middle Ages to
       have been generally faithful to the text, although
       with the accretion of later medieval Christian-flavored
       morals, a step taken by the *Anonymous Neveleti*. Dis-
       cusses the fable in school and in sermons and discusses
       in detail the use of P503 by Marie de France, Juan
       Ruiz, Heinrich von dem Türlin, Der Stricker, Ulrich
       Boner, and others through Luther, La Fontaine to Ivan
       Krylov. Ends with a list of allusions to the fable
       and another listing of collections in which the fable
       appears.

1235. Spengel, A. "Zu den Fabeln des Phädrus." *Philologus*,
       33 (1874), 722-727.

       Working out from the posthumously collected papers
       of Fröhlich, Spengel proposes a number of wide-
       ranging textual emendations and suggestions for the
       collection of Phaedrus, some of which are original.

1236. Speroni, Charles. "I proverbi della 'Posilecheata.'"
       Folklore, 8 (1953-1954), 3-22.

       The fable-collection by Pompeo Sarnelli is studied
       with regard to the proverbs found there and their
       functions within the texts.

1237. Spiero, Ella. *Florians Fabeln in ihrem Verhältnis
       zu den Fabeln La Fontaines.* Dissertation, Berlin,
       1912. Leipzig: Fock, 1912.

       A thoroughgoing comparison of Florian and his fables
       to La Fontaine and his. The sources of Florian's
       fables are carefully investigated, followed by the
       characters in the fables by the two poets. The morals
       and general themes are compared as are poetic tech-
       nique, dramatic forms, natural description, and the
       like. The language and metrics of Florian are pre-

cisely described, and allusion is made to La Fontaine. A survey of literary criticism of the Florian fable ends the dissertation.

1238. Spiewok, Wolfgang. *Der Fuchs und der Trauben: Deutsche Tierdichtung des Mittelalters*. Wiesbaden: VMA-Verlag, 1978.

In the introduction to this collection of medieval fables, Spiewok provides an overview of the history of the fable and a general discussion of the position of the fable in the Middle Ages and its connection to the Beast Epic. An extended appendix provides short biographical introductions to the fabulists and contains a short glossary.

1239. Spitz, Hans-Jörg. "Lessings Fabeln in Prolog- und Epilogfunktion." *Sagen mit Sinne: Festschrift für Marie-Luise Dittrich zum 65. Geburtstag*. Göppingen: Kümmerle, 1976, pp. 291-327.

Discusses Lessing's fable production and especially the organization of his fables into three books of thirty fables each, with the opening and closing fable in each case serving in the office of a prologue and epilogue. Relates this structuring to Lessing's fable theory. Reprints the six fables in an appendix.

1240. Spitzer, Leo. "Die Kunst des Übergangs bei La Fontaine." *Publications of the Modern Language Association*, 53 (1938), 393-433. Reprinted in *Romanische Literaturstudien*. Tübingen, 1959, pp. 160-209.

La Fontaine does not use aesthetics in service to his moral purpose but in fact uses his morals in service to the aesthetic. Very extensive commentary with numerous examples and exhaustive stylistic analysis.

1241. Spoerri, Theophil. "Der Aufstand der Fabel." *Trivium*, 1 (1942), 31-63. Reprinted in *La Fontaine, Hundert Fabeln*. Zurich, 1965.

Calls the fable a philosophy for the disfranchised and oppressed, which demonstrates the social opposition of rich and poor so as to present the social origin of the fable and the socio-political nature of its inherent didacticism. Spoerri then jumps to La Fontaine and individual interpretations of various fables.

1242. Spölgen, J. *Ulrich Boner als Didaktiker*. Program,
       Aachen, 1888.

       Details the rediscovery of Ulrich Boner's *Edelstein*
       in the eighteenth century and especially Lessing's
       part in the identification of Boner and his sources.
       Compares the Boner fable with more modern reworkings
       and determines that teaching was the essential reason
       for the Boner fable. Stylistic considerations are
       brought to bear on the nature of the didacticism.

1243. Staege, Max. *Die Geschichte der deutschen Fabel-
       theorie*. Dissertation, Bern, 1929. Printed as
       Sprache und Dichtung, no. 44. 78 pp.

       Traces the history of theoretical occupation with
       the fable in Germany from the sixteenth through the
       twentieth centuries, including the literary and folk-
       lore dichotomy. The fable is found to have been re-
       flective of whatever age embraces it: in the service
       of the reformation in the sixteenth century and in
       the eighteenth, a practically and theoretically full-
       fledged literary genre. With bibliography but no
       index of fables.
       See: Briegel-Florig, "Geschichte."

1244. Stahl, Sandra. "Sour Grapes: Fable, Proverb, Unripe
       Fruit." *Folklore on Two Continents: Essays in Honor
       of Linda Dégh*. Ed. Nikolai Burlakoff and Carl
       Lindahl. Bloomington, Ind.: Trickster, 1980,
       160-168.

       Working from a mixed set of ideas about the fable,
       Stahl discusses the relationship of that form to the
       proverb, insightfully recognizing that the true re-
       lationship is one of association rather than of the
       necessary generation of the one by the other.

1245. Stearns, Marshall W. "A Note on Robert Henryson's
       Allusions to Religion and Law." *Modern Language
       Notes*, 59 (1944), 257-264. Expanded in Marshall
       Stearn's *Robert Henryson*. New York: Columbia Univer-
       sity Press, 1949, 14-32.

       Notes the obvious topical references in Henryson's
       Fables to events of his day. Numerous social, legal,
       and other allusions are found together with religious
       notes to Fox and Wolf as well as Sheep and Dog (P628
       "Wolf Hearing Confession" and P478 "Sheep, Dog and
       Wolf").

1246. ————. "A Note on Henryson and Lydgate." *Modern Language Notes*, 60 (1945), 101-103.

Discusses the possibility of the influence of Lydgate upon Henryson's fable collection and concludes that direct influence is to be considered unlikely.

1247. ————. "Henryson and Chaucer." *Modern Language Quarterly*, 6 (1945), 271-84. Expanded form in Marshall Stearns, *Robert Henryson*. New York: Columbia University Press, 1949, 48-69.

The original essay examines *The Testament* to demonstrate strong indebtedness to Chaucer; expanded form deals with Henryson's version of P562 "Partridge and Fox" (A-T 6; TMI K561.1, K721) compared to Chaucer's Nun's Priest's Tale so as to approach the problem of Henryson's personal attitude toward courtly love. See: MacDonald, "Henryson and Chaucer."

1248. ————. *Robert Henryson*. New York: Columbia University Press, 1949. 155 pp.

Contains seven essays on Henryson's life and works. In addition to earlier entries found here in expanded form (q.v.), new material is offered. "The Poet as Humanitarian" deals with the fables in detail, in which the poet's treatment of character is used to determine his general attitudes. Henryson denounces the nobility and corrupt clergy and derides the rising middle class. His heroes are simple folk, and he often varies them significantly from traditional characterizations to make his point. Contains appendices and a selective though extensive bibliography and an index.

1249. Stein, Ferdinand. *La Fontaines Einfluss auf die deutsche Fabeldichtung des achtzehnten Jahrhunderts*. Program, Aachen: 1888/89. 29 pp.

Attempts to put La Fontaine's influence upon the German fable in perspective; La Motte's more "rational" language appealed to the German, the direct influence of Franck's 1716 Phaedrus which heavily influenced Hunold.

1250. Steinberg, Willi. *Martin Luthers Fabeln*. Halle: Niemeyer, 1961.

A revised edition of Luther's fables with an excellent introductory essay and full apparatus. Luther is

described as fabulist, and the full text tradition of
his fragmentary collection is given.

1251. Steiner, Grundy. "Aesopic Reminiscences in the Litera-
       ture of Later Antiquity." M.A. Thesis, University
       of Illinois, 1938. 77 pp.

       Attempts to find traces of "Aesopic" fables in the
       Silver poets and literature to the fourth century.

1252. Steinschneider, M. "Zu Kalila wa-Dimna." *Zeitschrift
       der deutschen Morgenländischen Gesellschaft*, 27
       (1873), 553–565.

       The first part of this essay deals with Jakob ben
       Elasar, a previously unknown translator of the *Kalila
       wa-Dimna* into Hebrew during the twelfth century. The
       second part is concerned with the parallels to this
       collection.

1253. ————. "Ysopet Hebräisch, ein Beitrag zur Geschichte
       der Fabeln im Mittelalter." *Jahrbuch für romanische
       und englische Literatur*, N.F. 1 (1895), 362–77.

       On the position of the Hebrew fable, and especially
       the Hebrew translations of the Aesopic corpus during
       the Middle Ages.

1254. Stennik, Ju. V. "O specifike žanrovoj prirody basni."
       Russkaja Literatura: Istoriko-literaturnyj Žurnal,
       4 (1980), 106–119.

       On the evolution of the fable as a form and in con-
       tent, specifically the changes in didacticism.

1255. Stenstrom, Oscar Sten Paul. *Proverbs of the Bakongo*.
       Dissertation, Hartford Seminary, 1948. 582 pp.

       Details the use and function of proverbs among the
       Bakongo peoples with a lengthy section on the relation-
       ship of the proverb to the fable in origin and form.

1256. Stepanov, Nikolay L. *Russkaja basnja xviii i xix veka*.
       Leningrad: AN SSSR, 1949, 1–lviii.

       Surveys the Russian fable from the seventeenth
       through the nineteenth centuries in the introduction
       to this anthology. Biographical details for the
       fabulists and bibliographical references to all col-
       lections.

1257. ————. *I.A. Krylov: Zhizn i tvorchesto.* Moscow: Nauk, 1958. 467 pp.

A detailed study of Krylov as a fable writer, with special concern for the changes of Krylov's style and attitude. Stepanov notes an increasingly pessimistic bias in his fables and discusses the corresponding increase in political concern in his later fables. Krylov's last fables are essentially political satires.

1258. ————. *Ivan Krylov.* New York: Twayne, 1973. 174 pp.

Begins with a life of the fabulist and his position in the world of satire and fable. The history and tradition of the Russian fable follows together with a discussion of the fable as a genre. Suggests the Krylovian fable is about real characters and is best enjoyed read aloud. Extensive analysis of the characters in the fable. Good bibliography and fable index.

1259. Stephens, James. "Bacon's Fable-Making: A Strategy of Style." *Studies in English Literature,* 14 (1974), 111-127.

An essay ostensibly concerned with Francis Bacon's use of "fables and parables" to construct a "new myth for the modern age." The term fable is apparantly used during the course of the argument to mean Aesopic fable but generally seems to mean something quite else, usually myth or mythic motif. Stephens returns to the Aesopic type only to mean, later, something fabulous and irrational.

1260. Sternbach, Leo. "Fabularum Aesopiarum Sylloge." *Rozprawy Wydzialu filologicznego Akademii Umiejetności v Krakowie,* 21 (1894), 320-333; 23 (1894), 377-388.

Attempts to establish a series of fables as the "Sylloge Augustana," with reconstructions of the received tradition and various emendations.

1261. ————. "Lectionum Aesopiarum fasciculus." *Eos,* 1: 1 (1894), 12-30.

An attempt to establish the text of fable 150A of the "Sylloge Augustana," with help of the Paris manuscript in Suppl. Gr. 690. Published in slightly enlarged form as *Fabularum Aesopiarum Sylloge e codice Parisino Gr. Nr. 690 Suppl.* Krakau, 1894.

1262.   ————. "Lessings Anmerkungen zu den Fabeln des
        Aesops kritisch beleuchtet." *Wiener Studien*, 17
        (1895), 31-102.

   An exhaustive commentary to the Lessing annotations
   to a copy of the Codex Augustanus prepared by Frau
   Reiske in 1772. The text was used later as the basis
   for Johann Schneider's edition of Aesopic fables.
   Most of Lessing's commentary is now dated and some
   portions were incorrect. Sternbach meticulously corrects and enlarges each entry.

1263.   Sternberger, Dolf. *Figuren der Fabel*. Berlin: Suhr-
        kamp, 1950, pp. 7-24; 70-97.

   Bases his argument upon the premise that the fable
   is a moralistic genre. Especially "Über eine Fabel
   von Lessing," reprinted also in *Die Wandlung* (Heidelberg), 1 (1945), 488-500, and also in *G.E. Lessing*.
   Darmstadt: Wissenschaftliche Buchgesellschaft, 1968,
   pp. 245-259, concerning "Der Esel mit dem Löwen."

1264.   Stiefel, Arthur Ludwig. "Ein Fastnachtspiel des Hans
        Folz und seine Quelle." *Archiv für das Studium der
        neueren Sprachen und Literaturen*, 90 (1893), 1-12.

   The 13th Extravagantes fable "De patre et tribus
   filiis," P703 "Three Sons dividing an Inheritance" (A-T
   1950; TMI H507.3, K171.1) is discussed as the source
   for a Hans Folz *Fastnachtspiel*.

1265.   ————. "Über die Quellen des Fabeln, Märchen und
        Schwänke des Hans Sachs." *Hans Sachs Forschungen,
        Festschrift zum 400. Geburtstag des Dichters*. Nürn-
        berg, 1893, 33-192.

   Very extensive commentary on source studies for Hans
   Sachs' many fables, Märchen, and other pieces. Numerous
   new sources are given and many more are suggested.
   Some notes on Hans Sachs' methodology are included.

1266.   ————. "Zu den Quellen der Erasmus Alberschen Fabeln."
        Euphorion, 9 (1902), 609-621.

   Discovers a few new sources for the fable collection
   of Erasmus Alberus, as a supplement for Braune, who in
   his edition listed Martin Dorp's Latin collection as
   the main source and suggested oral tradition for seven.
   Stiefel suggests Pauli and Luther as the ultimate
   source for four fables.

1267. ————. "Zu den Quellen des Esopus von B. Waldis."
*Archiv für der Studium der neueren Sprachen und
Literaturen*, 109 (1902), 249-279.

Suggests Camerarius' *Fabulae Aesopicae* of 1538 as
another source for Waldis' collection. Waldis' use of
Camerarius is shown to be similar to his treatment of
the fables in the Martin Dorp collection already
identified as his primary source.

1268. ————. "Zu den Quellen der Fabeln und Schwänke des
Hans Sachs." *Studium der vergleichende Literaturgeschichte*, 2 (1902), 146-183.

Source study defending his previous work in the
sources of Hans Sachs (1893). Rejects the notion that
the source's prosody might have determined the style
used by Sachs. Demonstrates Sachs used the *Gesta
Romanorum* and various Chronicles and suggests Sachs
used a number of sources for individual pieces.

1269. ————. "Über den Esopus der Burkhard Waldis."
Studien zur vergleichenden Literaturgeschichte, 3
(1903), 486-495.

Cursory discussion of the Waldis 400-fable collection, followed by an investigation into the sources
not previously identified by Kurz and Tittmann.

1270. ————. "Neue Beiträge zur Quellenkunde Hans Sachs-
ischer Fabeln und Schwänke." *Studien zur vergleichenden Literaturgeschichte*, 8 (1908), 273-310.

Continues Stiefel's massive 1893 study on the
sources of Hans Sachs' fables and *Schwänke*. Suggests
numerous possible influences and quite a few clearly
overdrawn examples.

1271. ————. "Die Centum et quinquaginta fabulae des
Pantaleon Candidus und ihre Quellen." *Archiv für
das Studium der neueren Sprachen und Literaturne*,
125 (1910), 102-127.

Discusses in some detail the 152 (not 150 as titled)
fables of the Austrian Pantaleon Candidus (1540-1608),
printed in the *Deliciae poetarum Germanorum*. The
chief source (for all save 10) for the collection
was Joachim Camerarius' *Fabulae Aesopicae*.

1272. Stierle, Karlheinz. "Poesie des Unpoetischen: Über La

Fontaines Umgang mit der Fabel." *Poetica*, 1 (1967), 508-533.

Points to the fundamental underlying reality of the fable and the fact that La Fontaine takes this reality seriously but ironically. The irony, i.e., the distance the narrator takes from his material, changes the closed universe of the moral into the open horizon of reflection. Here then is the critical change: a subjective point of view on the part of the narrator in great distinction to the fable of the Middle Ages.

1273. Stinton, T.C.W. "Phaedrus and Folklore: An Old Problem Restated." *Classical Quarterly*, NS 29 (1979), 432-435.

Defends the historical-geographical approach to narrative motif diffusion to account for the various versions of Phaedrus App. 16, P544 "Two Suitors" (TMI K1371.1, N721) indicated in J.G. Henderson's article "The Homing Instinct" (q.v.). Rejects coincidence or polygenesis by archetypal patterns or genetic encoding of narrative patterns.

1274. Stockwell, David. "Aesop's Fable in Philadelphia Furniture." *Antiques*, 60 (1951), 522-525.

On fable illustrations on various pieces of furniture from a pre-revolutionary Chippendale highboy to a frieze in a mantelpiece. Speculation upon the carvers and upon the reasons for the use of the motifs.

1275. Stol, M. "De voogeshiedenis van een fabel." *Hermeneus*, 44 (1972), 49-51.

Derives Assyrian origin for P137 "Gnat and the Bull" (A-T 281 with a gnat instead of a fly; TMI J953.10). The Babrian version is traced to Near Eastern origins, as, in fact, is claimed by Babrius himself.

1276. Strahm, Hans. "Ulrich Boner's *Edelstein*: A Medieval Book of Fables from the Time of the Minnesinger." *Graphis*, 1 (April/June, 1945), 197-198.

A note on the illustrations accompanying the *Edelstein*. These are the more interesting as the book might well be the first full-length book printed in the German language (1461).

1277. Strömberg, Reinhold. *On Some Greek Proverbial Phrases.*
Göteborg: Gumperts Förlag, 1947.

A number of thematically linked Greek proverbs are
discussed in their historical and philological contexts with regard to source and meaning. Their relationship to fables is also analyzed.

1278. Sudre, Léopold. *Les Sources du Roman de Renart.*
Paris, 1892. Reprint, Geneva: Slatkine, 1974.
357 pp.

Deals with Aesopica as a possible source for the
Roman de Renart cycle. Considers some connection
between the fables and the tales to be undeniable,
but the question seems quite complex. Some fables
are clearly more closely connected to the tales than
others. After dealing with the enormous popularity
of Phaedrus and Avianus during the Middle Ages, concludes that the influence of the fables on the individual tales is indirect. Sudre deals convincingly
with a number of fables: P258 "Sick Lion, Wolf and
Fox" (A-T 50; TMI K961), P585 "Sick Lion" (TMI B240.4)
and especially P149 and P339, both versions of the
"Lion's Share" (A-T 51; TMI J811.1 and J811.1.1) as
well as P124 "Fox and the Crow" (A-T 57; TMI K334.1),
P562 "Partridge and Fox" (A-T 6; TMI K561.1, K721),
and P597 "Fox confesses his Sins to the Cock" (TMI
K2027).

1279. Suster, Guido. "Miscellanea critica." *Rivista di
filologia,* 19 (1890), 85-98.

A note on Phaedrus I, 5 defends the received reading
against a number of textual critics.

1280. Sutton, Robert Francis. "The Moral Fables of Robert
Henryson, the Scots Makar." Dissertation, University
of Massachusetts, 1975. 502 pp.

Henryson is characterized as being more didactic
and less satirical than other writers in Britain of
his period. Henryson consciously attempted to entertain while seeking moral uplift for his audience.
The *Moral Fables* is a descendant of both the Aesopic
tradition and the Bestiaries. Structure is functional
throughout, and a certain order might be seen in the
collection as a whole.

1281. Swidzinska, Haline. "I.I. Dmitriev: A Classicist and
       a Sentimentalist in the Context of the World and
       the Russian Fable." Dissertation, Pittsburgh, 1972.
       481 pp.

       This dissertation traces the evolution of the fable
       toward a literary genre with special emphasis upon the
       Russian fable and specifically the fables of I.I.
       Dmitriev. La Fontaine was successfully emulated by
       this poet in Russian, creating a style called "collo-
       quial middle style," thus paralleling a similar effect
       by the Polish fabulist I. Krasicki in his own land.

1282. Swoboda, Michael. "De Phaedro Aesopi aemulatore."
       Eos: Commentarii Societatis Philologae Polonorum,
       52 (1962), 323-336.

       Phaedrus is quite liberal with his Aesopic models
       as he adapts them to Roman tastes and fits them to
       the events of his time. Nevertheless, he is re-
       markably faithful to his predecessor in themes and
       moral content.

1283. Sydow, C.W. "Kategorien der Prosa-Volksdichtung."
       Volkskundliche Gaben John Meier zum 70. Geburtstag.
       Freiburg i. Breisgau: Waltari, 1934, 253-268.

       The fable is presented, among a number of other
       "prose folk forms," as a sub-division of the *Märchen*.
       Here the fable is classified as a monoepisodic
       Märchen.

1284. Tacke, Alfred. "Phaedriana." Dissertation, Berlin,
       1911. 52 pp.

       A commentary to the Phaedrine corpus that stands
       in strong contrast to its predecessors as it sets
       out not to emend and to provide variant readings but
       to explicate. Tacke deals especially with Thiele's
       Phaedrus commentary. Extensive treatment of each
       fable and of fable groups, generally with lexical
       and syntactical features noted. Complete bibliog-
       raphy and index of fables.

1285. Tacke, Otto. "Eine bisher unbekannte Äsopübersetzung
       aus dem 15. Jahrhundert." *Rheinisches Museum für
       Philologie des Mittelalters*, 61 (1912), 285-299.

       Publishes the forty-fable collection of the Humanist
       Leonardo Dati from ca. 1428, in Latin distichs. Dati's

manuscript source is here identified as belonging to
the Augustana Recension tradition on the basis of the
order of the fables and from a number of readings.

1286. ————. *Die Fabeln des Erzpriesters von Hita im
Rahmen mittelalterlichen Fabelliteratur.* Disserta-
tion, Breslau, 1911. Reprinted in *Romanische
Forschungen*, 31 (1912), 550-705.

An exhaustive study of the twenty-two fables from
the Aesopic tradition woven into Ruiz's *Libro de buen
amor.* Tacke identifies the fables' source as ultimately the Latin versions of Walter of England (Gualterus
Anglicus). Tacke also identifies the influence of a
particular translation of the Walter collection, the
French version known as the *Lyoner Isopet.*
See: Claybourne and Finch, "The Fables of Aesop in
Libro de buen amor."

1287. Tahovske, A.G. "Ad Phaedri versum I, i, 8." *Ziva
Antika*, 2 (1952), 78-80.

Emends the eighth line to read: "A te decurrit ad
meum os haustus liquor."

1288. Tailleaux, Dominique. "The Saga of La Fontaine or a
Certain Art of Living." Trans. Ronald Margolin.
Children's Literature, 1 (1972), 37-41.

Suggests that fables might play a role in establishing a way of life. La Fontaine's picture of a wise
man is the pre-eighteenth-century "philosophe."
Tailleaux seeks this sage in the fables and finds
characteristics of this idealized person from lines
gleaned from various places throughout the collection.

1289. Tapp, W.H. "First Chelsea Fable Painter." *Apollo*,
38 (1943), 38-42.

Jean (or Jaques) Leebre of Tournai is identified as
the first producer of the raised anchor Chelsea fable-
decorated porcelain. Includes numerous examples of
porcelain painting with scenes from tentatively identified fable collections.

1290. Taylor, Archer. "A Metaphor of the Human Body in
Literature and Tradition." *Corona: Festschrift
Samuel Singer.* Durham, N.C.: Duke University Press,
1941, 3-7.

Short study of the metaphor of the body as a house
as in P130 "Stomach and Feet" (A-T 293; TMI J461.1).
Discusses an Egyptian *Märchen* related to the metaphor
in Ecclesiasticus 12:1-7 and well-known riddles for
which the answer is the body or parts thereof.
See: Gombel, Hale.

1291.   ————. "Proverbs and Proverbial Phrases in Roger
L'Estrange, *The Fables*." *Southern Folklore Quarterly*,
26 (1962), 232-245.

A long list of the proverbs and proverbial phrases
to be found in Roger L'Estrange's edition of *Fables*.
All entries are keyed to the *Dictionary of American
Proverbs* and other standard works.

1292.   ————. "'It Is Good Fishing in Troubled (Muddy)
Waters.'" *Proverbium*, 11 (1968), 268-275.

The titular proverb is traced back to medieval Latin
versions dating from the twelfth century, but Taylor
suggests the proverb might have had its origin in
Aristophanes or in P26 "Fisherman Beats the Water"
(TMI U141).

1293.   Taylor, James L. "Animal Tales as Fabliaux." *Reading
Medieval Studies*, 3 (1977), 63-79.

Questions whether animal tales, including fables,
might have served as the basis for fabliaux. Gives
examples of a few that have.

1294.   Terzaghi, Nicola. *Per la storia della satira*. Torino,
1933.

A theory of the development of Roman satire from
the cynic diatribe. Phaedrus is discussed extensively
in an attempt to illuminate the putative connection
between the satirical writings of Horace and the
fables of Phaedrus. For these purposes, those fables
of Phaedrus without Aesopian analogues are focused
upon. The idea that Phaedrus had a specific moral
system is rejected.

1295.   Tetel, Marcel. "Giulio Cesare Croce: Canastorie or
Literary Artist." *Forum Italicum*, 4 (1970), 32-38.

In *Bertoldo e Bertoldino*, Croce stresses the idea
of paradox, expressed early on by proverbs, later
with fables. Proverbs and fables placate the king.

1296. Thaarup-Andersen, Lis. "Fiskefangstfablen in den skriftlige litteratur og folklitteraturen." *Danske Studier*, 51 (1954), 127-142.

Wide-ranging, comprehensive treatment of P625 "Wolf as Fisherman and Fox" (A-T 2; TMI K1021) in literary sources and in orally transmitted narrative.

1297. Thalheim, Hans-Günther. "Zu Lessings Fabeln." *Zur Literatur der Goethezeit*. Berlin: Rütten und Loening, 1969, 9-37. (Originally published as "Nachwort" to the 1963 Reclam edition of Lessing's fables.)

Thalheim reviews Lessing's occupation with the theory of the fable in its historical context, introducing Lessing's own fable production, in comparison with other fabulists of his day, especially Gellert. Lessing's fable theory is a consequence of and a reaction to his analysis of the activities of his contemporaries, all oriented toward the model of La Fontaine. The *Abhandlungen* are outlined and Herder's ideas on the fable are contrasted with those of Lessing. The essay ends with illuminating criticism of three of Lessing's fables.

1298. Thiel, Helmut van. "Sprichwort in Fabeln." *Antike und Abendland: Beiträge zum Verständnis der Griechen und Römer und ihres Nachlebens*, 17 (1971), 105-118.

Begins with P460 "Shadow of an Ass" (TMI J1169, K477.2) to describe the phenomenon of a proverbial phrase resulting from the familiarity of a well-known fable. The fable is characterized as an orally transmitted narrative form, even after it had become a literary form. Numerous examples of fable-motif proverbs and proverbial phrases ranging from the still current "sour grapes," from P15 "Fox and Grapes" (A-T 59; TMI J871) to a Greek proverb based upon P3 "Eagle and Beetle." Ends with a discussion of the categorization of the fable. Fables are all keyed to Perry and to other standard collections.

1299. Thiel, Josef Franz. "Das Verhältnis zwischen den Herrschenden und Beherrschten bei den Yansi (Congo) im Spiegel ihrer Fabel." *Anthropos*, 66 (1971), 485-534.

In this compelling and informative essay, certain relationships within the social life of the Yansi of

the Republic of the Congo, especially those of the
leaders and their people, are shown to have parallels
in their fables. The political chief is a leopard
and that animal plays a leading role in the Yansi
fables. The leopard is strong but it is often tricked,
an indication of the rivalry between the ruler and the
ruled. With fable texts and translations into German.

1300. Thiele, Ernst. *Luthers Fabeln nach seiner Hs und den
       Drucken.* Neudrucke deutscher Literaturwerken, no.
       76. Halle: Niemeyer, 1888. 2nd edition 1911.

A critical edition of Luther's fragmentary fable
collection, with a description of the editions and
manuscripts including Luther's autograph manuscript
(Cod. Ottob. lat. 3029) in the Vatican. Historical
accounting of the writing of the fables.
See: Willi Steinberg, *Martin Luthers Fabeln.*

1301. Thiele, Georg. *Der illustrierte lateinische Aesop
       in der Handschrift des Ademars, Codex Vossianus
       lat. oct. 15, fol. 195-205.* Leiden: A.W. Sijthoff,
       1905. 3 pl. 68 pp.

Facsimile and edition of 67 fables, 38 of which are
from the Romulus collection; 29 seem to be directly
from Phaedrus. The collection called the Anonymous
Nilanti after the first printed edition. The manuscript was compiled at least in part by Ademar of
Chabanais in the eleventh century and is most valuable
for the illustrations. The style points to Roman
origin, approximately the fourth century. Thiele
concludes that the Anonymous comes from the Romulus
tradition, which is not, however, a simple paraphrase
of the Phaedrus corpus but an independent reworking of
traditional fabular material.

1302. ————. "Die vorliterarische Fabel der Griechen."
       *Neue Jahrbücher für das klassische Altertum,
       Geschichte und deutsche Literatur und fur Pädagogik,*
       Supplement 21 (1908), 377-400.

Sees evidence of the preliterary Greek fable in the
Vita Aesopi and in various other manifestations,
including the proverb and observations in nature.
Distinguishes the "libyshe" fable from the *ainoi*,
found in classical sources. The humorous "Tierschwank"
is the source of some fables, but the *Märchen* cannot
be the source of most fables. Ends with an attempt at
sharpening genre lines for forms of the Greek fable.

1303. ————. "Phaedrus-Studien." *Hermes*, 41 (1906), 562-
592; 43 (1908), 337-372; 46 (1910), 376-392.

This series of long essays deals with Phaedriana
from all standpoints. The first sorts out the
"philosophising" fables. IV, 12: P111 "Hercules and
Pluto" (TMI J451.1); App. 5: P535 "Prometheus and
Guile"; IV, 21: P518 "Fox and Dragon" (TMI B11.6.2);
IV, 15: P515a "Prometheus"; III, 15: P506 "Dog to the
Lamb" (TMI J391.1); I, 27: P483 "Dog and Treasure"
(TMI J1061.1), all have cynical features. III, 19:
P510 "Aesop's Response" (TMI J1303) is clearly reflective of the Diogenes scene. Thiele concludes
that the Aesopic fable, as represented in the Phaedrus
collection was related to the cynics. Another group
of fables, "Götterschwänke," reinforces Thiele's ideas
that more is lost in Phaedrus than had been suspected.
The loss is attributed to Hellenistic fable reworkings.
There are at least two recensions in the Romulus tradition and this has led to many unnecessary emendations. Part three deals with P521 "Ant and the Fly"
(TMI J242.6) and the Callimachus poem P439 "Laurel
and Olive" (TMI J411.7). Models for Phaedrus and
Babrius were in prose.

1304. ————. *Der lateinische Aesop des Romulus und die
Fassungen des Phaedrus*. Heidelberg: Carl Winter,
1910. ccxxxviii + 360 pp.

A wide-ranging investigation of the medieval fable
tradition especially as it deals with the Romulus
or the prose paraphrases of Phaedrus. Presents a
comparative study of the various fable texts, for
which a "Latin Aesop" (from the fourth century) and
a Latin collection of 100 fables (fifth century) are
postulated. Deals with the Romulus corpus and its
sources, and the descent of the tradition. Discusses
the text of Phaedrus, its relationship to the Romulus
corpus, and the so-called letter of Aesop to Rufus.
The texts are the Recensio gallicana, the Recensio W
(from the Gudianus Lat. 148 in Wolfenbüttel), and the
Recensio Vetus. Ends with a glossary, various other
indices and two illustrations.

1305. ————. "Martial III, 20." *Philologus*, 70 (1911), 540-
548.

The only mention of Phaedrus before the fourth century is by Martial in a not well-preserved line "improbi

locos Phaedri." Concludes that "improbus" means
"Dreist"; "ioci" is perhaps "locos."

1306. ————. "Die Phädrus Excerpte des Kardinals Perotti."
Hermes, 46 (1911), 633-637.

On the Neapolitan manuscripts and Vatican Urb. 368
and their relationship to the Phaedrus tradition.
The Perotti appendix with its thirty fables is evaluated, generally positively.

1307. ————. "Zur libyschen Fabel." *Philologus*, 75
(1919), 227-231.

A demonstration of the pieces of evidence for the
perseverance of the so-called "libyschen" fable.
P303 "Woodcutters and the Pine" (TMI U162) finds an
echo in the Syrian *Achikar*.

1308. Thiele, Herbert. "Lehrhafte Dichtung in der Schule:
Drei Beispiele zur Erschliessung erzieherischer
Prosa." *Der Deutschunterricht*, 16: 1 (1964), 121-
127.

Deals with three forms of didactic literature including the fable, which is characterized as one of
the most steadfast elements in German elementary
school readers. Its immediate importance and its
potential for use as introductory material for in-
structional and philosophical material later on are
noted.

1309. Thoen, Paul. "*Aesopus Dorpii*: Essai sur l'Esope latin
des temps modernes." *Humanistica Lovaniensia*, 19
(1970), 214-316.

A systematic examination of the Martin Dorp Aesopic
collection (first appeared in its mature form in 1513)
with careful contrastive studies of the numerous editions. The position of the work in the sixteenth
century is well-documented and its later influence is
charted. Contains descriptions of the various forms
of the collections, of source collections, and complete bibliographical materials.

1310. ————. "Les grands recueils ésopiques Latins des xv^e
et xvie siècles et leur importance pour les let-
tératures des temps modernes." *Acta Conventus Neo-
Latini Lovaniensis: Proceedings of the First International Congress of Neo-Latin Studies*. Ed. I.
IJsweijn and E. Kessler. Munich: Fink, 1973, pp.
659-679.

This comprehensive essay deals expertly with the fable collections of the fifteenth and early sixteenth centuries, describing the collections and some of the interconnections of the Italian Humanist translation/collections and the collections of the North and demonstrating the confluence of the Renaissance and medieval traditions in Steinhöwel and later editions. Excellent bibliographical materials.

1311. Thomas, L.V. "Veillée djiwat." *Notes Africanes*, 116 (Oct. 1967), 105-109.

Six fables of the Diola, for whom fables and other folktales play a significant role in guiding social interactions. With notes to a number of stylistic and content particulars.

1312. Thompson, Norma Jean. "The Old French Fabliaux: A Classification and Definition." Dissertation, University of Southern California, 1972. 343 pp.

An examination of the *fabliaux* within French literary history. Summary of *fabliaux* criticism; ancestry of the genre related to the *exemplum* and the fable as well as to other didactic forms. Discusses various problems of definition within the genres.

1313. Thompson, Stith. *The Folktale*. New York: Holt, Rinehart and Winston, 1946. (Often reprinted.)

The fable is defined as an animal tale with an acknowledged moral purpose, and the best known of the fables are given as the literary forms, with only a few recorded from oral storytellers. Many fables are discussed as folktales of a more general nature. Excludes numerous fabular motifs and fables (e.g., those in the Reynard cycle) from the category of fable although the fable as received from the East, and particularly the Jataka forms and the new fables composed in the Renaissance, are given extensive treatment. Good indices; fables are keyed to standard collections.

1314. Thurnher, E. "Die Tierfabel aus Waffe politischer Kampfes. Zu Deutung der Fabelsprüche des Bruder Wernher." *Römische Historische Mitteilungen*, 18 (1976), 55-66.

Sees Wernher's *Sprüche* as political evaluations of the decline in morals observed by the Austrian Friar in the latter part of the thirteenth century.

1315. Tiefenbrun, Susan W. "Signs of Irony in La Fontaine's
       Fables." *Papers on French Seventeenth Century Litera-
       ture*, 11 (1979), 51-76.

       Irony is here understood as "intersections of code"
       and is studied with levels of meaning in La Fontaine's
       fables; some basic patterns of structure such as oppo-
       sition and reversal are examined.

1316. Tiemann, Barbara. "Sebastian Brant und das frühe
       Emblem in Frankreich." *Deutsche Vierteljahrschrift*,
       47 (1973), 598-644.

       A lengthy and comprehensive treatment of Sebastian
       Brant's use of illustrations in the *Narrenschiff*,
       their relationship to the emblem tradition, and the
       special relationship to the proverb, the exemplum,
       and the fable. Discusses Brant's specific relation
       to the fable, especially with regard to the didacti-
       cism, noting the surprisingly small amount of fabular
       material in the *Narrenschiff*. Lists Brant's refer-
       ences to P35 "Man and Satyr," P142 "Aged Lion and
       Fox" (A-T 50A; TMI J644.1), P179 "Ass and Gardener"
       (TMI N255.2), and P322 "Crab and his Mother" (A-T 276;
       TMI J1053, U121.1).

1317. ————. *Fabel und Emblem. Gilles Corrozet und die
       französische Renaissancefabel*. Munich: Fink, 1974.
       265 pp. + 40 ill.

       Very comprehensive treatment of Gilles Corrozet
       (1516-1568) and the relationship of the fable to the
       emblem. Insightfully recognizes the protean nature
       of the fable, developed within a larger literary
       field of production and reception in a constant ex-
       change with other forms.

1318. Tiemann, Hermann. "Wort und Bild in der Fabeltradi-
       tion bis zu La Fontaine." *Buch und Welt: Festschrift
       für Gustav Hofmann*. Ed. Hans Striedl and Joachim
       Wieder. Wiesbaden: Otto Harrassowitz, 1965, 237-260.

       The fable is important as a source for the devices
       for emblems in the sixteenth and seventeenth centuries

in part due to a centuries-long tradition of fable
illustrations. The two are importantly connected in
an internal sense as both share aspects of moralizing
metaphors. The function of both is transmission of
"Wahrheit im Sensus moralis."

1319. Tilley, A. "La Fontaine and Bidpai." *Modern Language
Review*, 34 (1939), 21-39.

Indicates the twenty or so fables that La Fontaine
drew from the Panchatantra tradition with an extensive
history of the fables of Bidpai from Sanskrit to its
European editions. La Fontaine's source was a French
translation of the *Anwār-i-Suhailī* (Lights of Canopus)
version. The translation, *Livre des Lumières*, appeared
in 1644. Ends with a commentary on a number of the
fables from this tradition.

1320. Timm, Erika. "Die Fabel vom alten Löwen in jiddis-
tischer und komparatistischer Sicht." *Zeitschrift
für deutsche Philologie*, 100 (Sonderheft, 1981),
109-170.

Discusses the oldest fable surviving in Yiddish
tradition, the fable of the "Old Lion," to demonstrate
the interaction of Hebrew and Western tradition, with
the two fused in the collection of Wallich.

1321. Tittmann, Julius. *Esopus von Burchard Waldis.* Leipzig: F.A. Brockhaus, 1882.

A partial edition of Burkhard Waldis' 1548 fable
collection with an introduction to the problem of
sources. Martin Dorp's fable collection is identified
as the primary material used.
See: Martens, *Entstehungsgeschichte*.

1322. Tobler, A. "Lateinische Beispielsammlung mit Bilder."
Zeitschrift fur römanische Philologie, 12 (1889),
57-88.

A discussion and edition of ms. 300 Hamilton, now
Berlin, with many types of tales, including fables,
e.g., P18 "Fisherman and Little Fish" (TMI J321.1)
and P70 "Oak and Reed" (A-T 298C; TMI J832).

1323. Tobler, R. "Der Schuster und der Reiche." *Archiv für
das Studium für der neueren Sprachen und Literaturen*,
117 (1906), 325-344.

Discusses La Fontaine's "Le savetier et le financier" as derived from Stobaeus' Florilegium (from the
sixth century) by way of Etienne de Bourbon, Des
Periers, and the 82nd fable of Burkhard Waldis. In
Germany Hans Sachs, Kirchhof, and Hagedorn used the
same motif; in France Lesage and Florian. Other uses
of the same motif are mentioned.

1324.   Toldo, Pietro. "Fonti e propaggini italiane della
        favole del La Fontaine." *Giornale storico della
        Letteratura Italiana*, 59 (1912), 1-46 and 749-811.

        A detailed accounting of the La Fontaine fables in
        Italy. Italian sources for a number of the fables are
        postulated, including the obvious Phaedrus. A wide-
        ranging list of parallels is included.

1325.   Toliver, Harold. "Robert Henryson: From *Moralitas* to
        Irony." *English Studies*, 46 (1965), 300-309.

        Argues that both the tale and the *moralitas* are
        necessary to a complete understanding of Henryson's
        fables in contrast to earlier criticism. In the
        moral, man is approached directly; in the fable narrative
        the approach is oblique. Both viewpoints are valuable,
        and the conscious moral adds levels of awareness and
        irony.

1326.   Tortora, L. "Recenti studi su Fedro. (1967-1974)."
        Bollettino di studi latini (Naples), 5 (1975),
        266-273.

        A survey of Phaedrus literature from 1967 to 1974,
        excluding translations and school editions.

1327.   Travis, Albert Hartman. "Improbi Iocos Phaedri."
        *Transactions of the American Philological Associa-
        tion*, 71 (1940), 579-586.

        The only mention of Phaedrus in classical times is
        by Martial in the twentieth epigram of book three in
        "improbi iocos Phaedri." The argument centers around
        the word "improbi." After a discussion of previous
        criticism, Travis decides that the meaning is essen-
        tially that used by Phaedrus himself; a term charac-
        teristic of the fable for Martial, something approach-
        ing the roguish opportunistic way of life portrayed
        by Phaedrus.

1328. Trencsenyi-Waldapfel, I. "Eine aesopische Fabel und ihre orientalischen Parallelen." *Acta Antiqua Academiae Scientiarum Hungaricae*, 7 (1959), 317-327.

Attempts to highlight the different treatment of P1 "Eagle and Fox" (TMI K2295, L315.3) by Aesop, Phaedrus, and Babrius when compared to Archilochus. The Oriental originals are the cause.

1329. ————. "Der Hund in der Krippe." *Acta Orientalia Academiae Scientarium Hungaricae*, 14 (1962), 139-143.

Note to P702 "Dog in the Manger" (TMI W153 and W156), suggesting the paroemiographic tradition can be traced back to Lucian, as is the case with the "fable" in Halm and the reconstructed Humanistic fable in Perry (from Steinhöwel). Evidence suggests the popularity of the phrase due to Lucian's coinage and not a case of Lucian using an already popular "Aesopic" fable allusion.

1330. Triesch, Manfred. "Men and Animals: James Thurber and the Conversion of a Literary Genre." *Studies in Short Fiction*, 3 (1966), 307-313.

A good overview of Thurber's fables, concluding that Thurber uses both old and new techniques in his fables; he does not teach but rather presents reality as he sees it, all the while maintaining common purpose with the classical fable.

1331. Trisk, J.M. "Gregorius de Hungaricali Broda Moravus auctor fabularum medii aevi moralium quae quadripartitus appelantur." *Listy Filologické* (Prague), N.S. 11 (1954), 37-59.

On an edition of fables falsely attributed to St. Cyril of Jerusalem.

1332. Triwedi, Mitchell D. "Source and Meaning of the Pelican Fable in El Castigo sin Venganzy." *Modern Language Notes*, 92 (1977), 326-329.

Traces the fable of the pelican hunt, in which the captured pelican tries to save its fledglings. The source is shown to be the *Hieroglyphia* by Horapollo, an early sixteenth century collection of fabular material, attempting to explain the Egyptian hieroglyphs.

1333.   Tronquat, G.   "Notule sur La Fontaine et l'astrologie."
        Dix-septième Siècle, 60 (1963), 49-59.

        La Fontaine's frequent references to various forms
        of astral influences are literally meant and are to
        be taken seriously. Virgil might be his source for
        his interest in astrology. Tronquart accepts influ-
        ence upon general temperament but stops short of allow-
        ing astral influence upon details of one's life.
        See: Ridgely, "Astrology and Astronomy."

1334.   Tschirch, Fritz. "Geschmiedetes Gitterwerk. Eine
        Lessing-Fabel als künsterische Gestalt." Mutter-
        sprache (1950), 138-144.

        Notes on "Die Eule und der Schatzgräber" by Lessing,
        with emphasis upon Lessing's stylistic peculiarities.

1335.   Tubach, Frederic. Index Exemplorum: A Handbook of
        Medieval Religious Tales. FFC, no. 204. Helsinki:
        Finnish Academy of Science and Letters, 1969.

        An index to and finding list for the medieval exempla
        tradition, including many fables. Now standard cita-
        tion index.

1336.   Turturro, Giuseppi. Una famiglia dell'Esopo italiano
        nei codici e negli incunaboli fiorentini, con la
        trascrizione di un Esopo palatino, ancora inedita,
        di altra famiglia. Bari: Leveccio, 1907.

        A list of manuscripts and incunabula with an inter-
        related Aesopic tradition with complete descriptions
        of contents and relationship, contrasted with the
        Tuppo Aesop and the Accursiana.

1337.   Tyroller, Franz. "Die Fabel von dem Mann und dem
        Vogel in ihrer Verbreitung in der Weltliteratur."
        Dissertation, Berlin E. Felber, 1912. Published as:
        Literarhistorische Forschungen, 51 (1912).   328 pp.

        Contains a report on the literature up to 1910 on
        the motif. Contains a source study of Lydgate and
        the Disciplina Clericalis versions with texts and pre-
        sents an historical overview of the motif (P627
        "Nightingale and Bowman," cf. P159 "Wolf and Sheep";
        A-T 150; TMI J21.12, K604) from Western and Eastern
        sources.

1338.   Ulbricht, Carl.   De animalium nominibus Aesopeis capita *tria.* Dissertation, Marburg, 1908. Published, Marburg: Koch, 1908. 70 pp.

This dissertation is a listing of the names of all animals found in the Aesopic fables, by occurrence in Greek (especially Babrius) first, then in Latin (Phaedrus and Avianus). The history of the works used to describe the animal is given together with a short discussion of uses outside the fabular corpus, particularly proverbs. The third chapter is an attempt to reconcile the Greek with the Latin. Appendices on the use of nouns as both substantives and adjectives and notes on the names of the young of the animals.

1339. Unrein, Otto. *De Aviani aetate.* Dissertation, Jena, 1885. 64 pp.

Unrein concludes that Avianus lived at the end of the fourth century or the beginning of the fifth century A.D. The most important evidence is Avianus' relationship to Titianus, but linguistic evidence is evaluated as well. Excellent survey of critical literature up to his time.
See: Küppers, *Die Fabeln Avians.*

1340. Unvala, J.M. "Draxt I Asurik." *Bulletin of the School of Oriental and African Studies,* 21 (1922–1923), 637–678.

Presents an edition and a translation of "The Assyrian Tree," a Pahlavi fable related to the Babylonian "Tamarisk and Palm," related in turn to Callimachus' version of P439 "Laurel and Olive" (TMI N255.4).
See: Lambert, *Babylonian Wisdom Literature.*

1341. Upadhyaya, K.D. "The Classification and Chief Characteristics of Indian (Hindi) Folk-Tales." *Fabula,* 7 (1963), 225–229.

Together with a host of other tale forms, the fable is common in India. Suggests that the tales might be classified by content, but offers nothing substantial in the way of a classification scheme.

1342. Urbas, Wilhelm. "Die Sprichwörter und ihre Enstehung." *Neue Monatschefte für Dichtkunst und Kritik,* 4 (1876), 501–513.

Concerned primarily with definitions and the complex

relationships of the proverb to other forms, including
the fable, and attempts a determination of the use of
these forms for such studies as national character.

1343. Ursing, Urban. *Studien zur griechischen Fabel*. Dis-
        sertation, Lund, 1930. ix + 111 pp.

This dissertation begins with the little-studied
codex Moscovensis 436 collection of Æsopic fables
studied essentially for its metrical and linguistic
peculiarities. The manuscript is identified as being
of the Vindobonensis family with the language classified as a Koine mixed with vulgarisms. Variant readings and indices with fables keyed to Chambry and
Halm.

1344. Vail, Curtis C.D. "Richardson's 'Aesop's Fables.'"
        *Lessing's Relation to the English Language and Litera-
        ture*. New York: Columbia University Press, 1936.
        Reprinted New York: AMS Press, 1966, 54-67.

Discusses Lessing's little-known translation of
Richardson's *Aesop's Fables* with editions of 1757,
1761, 1773, 1783, and 1806 as a further example of
Lessing's preoccupation with both English literature
and the fable in history and literature. Vail is
unable to definitely identify the original edition
though the text he describes now at Harvard is
clearly the one from which he worked. Details the
mechanics of translation and concludes that the translation is extremely competent.

1345. Vaio, John. "Babrius 143.1 Perry." *Classical Review*,
        18: 2 (1968), 149.

A short note to suggest a textual emendation to
Babrius 143, P176 "Man who Warmed a Snake" (A-T 155;
TMI W154.2).

1346. ————. "Four Notes on the Text of Babrius." *Classi-
        cal Philology*, 64 (1969), 154-161.

Textual emendations to Babrius' Prologue and to some
Babrian fables. A number of possible corrections are
offered for Babrius 130, P345 "Fox and Wolf at a Trap"
(TMI K1115.1); Babrius 142, P302 "Oak Tree and Zeus"
(TMI U162); 143, P176 "Man who Warmed a Snake" (A-T
155; TMI W154.2) and other places. The article ends
with a reconstructed text.

1347. ———. "An Alleged Paraphrase of Babrius." *Greek, Roman and Byzantine Studies*, 11 (1970), 49-52.

Maintains that, contrary to Sijpesteijn, the evidence does not support identification of the text in Papyrus Hakkert 1 as a version of P11 "Fisherman Pipes to Fish" (TMI J1909.1) as in Babrius 9. Neither Babrius nor the textual history of the fables can be dated by means of the papyrus.

1348. ———. "Aristophanes' *Wasps*: The Relevance of the Final Scenes." *Greek, Roman and Byzantine Studies*, 12 (1971), 335-351.

Discusses the relevance of the final scenes by focusing upon important motifs that serve as links. Fables are used as a specific against prosecution and to pacify victims. P3 "Eagle and Beetle" (TMI L315.7) is especially apt in this regard and is the fable which Aesop told the Delphians when falsely accused by them of theft in the *Vita Aesopi*.

1349. ———. "Babrius 110, 3-4." *Philologus*, 117 (1973), 140-141.

Textual emendations to the fourth line of Babrius 110, P330 "Dog and his Master" (TMI J1475).

1350. ———. "A New Manuscript of Babrius: Fact or Fable?" *Illinois Classical Studies*, 11 (1977), 173-183.

Discusses the evidence for the authenticity of the "L" manuscript, the companion to the Athoan codex of Babrius, purchased by the British Museum in 1859 from Minoides Mynas, and which is often called Babrius, Part II. The manuscript has been dismissed as a forgery. New manuscript material, now BN sup. gr. 1245, Mq. proposed by Dain, is apparently derived from the Vatican manuscript not an independent tradition. Vaio suggests that Mq is also a forgery.

1351. ———. "New Non-Evidence for the Name of Babrius." *Emerita*, 48 (1980), 1-3.

The Paris, gr. 2511 (P) manuscript, a close relative of Harley ms 3521 (H), which has been the source for the name Valerius Babrius, does not show any trace of *Babriou*; gives only *Baleriou*, a malformation parallel to the codex A and its *Balebriou*.

1352. Vandale, Hilaire. *Qua mente Phaeder fabellas scrip-*
       serit. Paris: E. Bouillon, 1897. iv + 113 pp.

       Discusses: the order of the fables, suggesting that
       book two was written at Rome at the time of Sejanus
       and thus the chronology of the other fables might
       be worked out; the "sense" of the fables, character-
       izing Phaedrus as a satirist; and the cause of the
       entertainment wit in the fables. An overview of the
       poet's life ends the monograph.

1353. Vander Meulen, Ross. "The Fables of Erasmus Alberus."
       Dissertation, Michigan, 1972. 183 pp.

       Deals with Alberus as one who followed Luther in
       using the fable in the service of the Reformation,
       likening the form to scripture and to Christ's use of
       Parables. Alberus' narrator might have been sug-
       gested by Luther's idea of Aesop. The digressions
       and the specifically Protestant flavor of the re-
       workings are treated extensively. The morals are
       classified and evaluated. Bibliography and fable key
       to the Braune edition.

1354. ————. "Luther's 'Betriegen zur warheit' and the
       Fables of Erasmus Alberus." *Germanic Review*, 52: 1
       (1977), 5–15.

       Vander Meulen deals with the narrator in Alberus'
       fables in this illuminating essay. The fables are
       discussed in groups demonstrating Alberus' use of de-
       ception, in the Lutherian meaning of the phrase, as a
       mechanism to insure the transference of the message.
       The message here is thoroughly Protestant in flavor.

1355. Van Dijk, J.J.A. *La Sagesse Suméro-Accadienne, Re-*
       cherches sur les Genres Littéraires des Textes
       Sapientiaux avec Choix de Textes. Leiden: Brill,
       1953.

       A comprehensive survey of the Sumerian Wisdom
       Literature and the research to mid-century. Provides
       a selection of texts, including some fables or near-
       fables.
       See: Lambert, *Babylonian Wisdom Literature.*

1356. Van Riet, Simone. "Fable et sagesse antique: D'Ibn
       al Muqaffa à Jean de La Fontaine." *Images of Man*
       in Ancient and Medieval Thought. Ed. Ferdnand

Frans Bossier. Louvain: Leuven University Press, 1976, 249-256.

The second edition of La Fontaine's fables brought a number of new fables, many of which descend ultimately from Indian sources and which have gone through a series of different cultures. The Bidpai fables are known to La Fontaine from a translation from the Arabic of Ibn al-Maqaffa, but there are other possible sources for these fables in seventeenth-century France, including the French translation of the *Stephanites kai Ichnelates* which is in turn a Greek translation of the *Kalila wa Dimna*.

1357. Varga, A. Kibédi. "L'invention de la fable. Forme et contenu selon la poétique du classicisme." *Poétique*, 25 (1976), 107-115.

Discusses the theoretical treatment of the fable in France in the sixteenth and seventeenth centuries. Discusses the invention of the fable with the maxim as one ancestor and actual events considered to be another. The poetics of classicism had to deal with the term "fable" as representing a variety of forms.

1358. Vessiot, Alexandre. *Pages de Pedagogie*. Paris: Lecene et Oudin, 1895. vi + 409 pp.

Education in numerous forms, including the fable, is investigated in detail. The fable in pedagogy is given comprehensive treatment, especially with discussion of Lessing, Florian, and La Fontaine. Mention is made of many others from classical times, Quintillian through more modern authors, in particular, Tolstoy.

1359. Vinaver, Eugene. "Le chêne et le roseau." *Modern Languages*, 42 (1961), 1-8.

A discussion of *explication* as suitable for purposes of literary studies is introduced by a satire of that method involving La Fontaine's "Le chêne et le roseau," P70 "Oak and Reed" (A-T 298 C; TMI J832) as found in a short play by Courteline.

1360. Vincent, Michael Charles. "Le Jeu du Language chez La Fontaine: Essai d'Analyse des Functions poétiques dans quelques Fables." Dissertation, Wisconsin, 1979. 249 pp.

Focuses upon the language of the *Fables* of La Fontaine, especially La Fontaine's "playing" with language, detailed by means of an analysis of six fables from the second edition, each chosen to illustrate a specific point.

1361. Vindt, Lidija. "Basnja kak literaturnyj zanr." *Poetika* (1927), 87–101. Reprinted, *Slavische Propyläen*, 104 (1970), 1–22.

Meant as an introductory chapter for a history of the Russian fable, this essay defines the fable as a complex that exists as a normative idea in literary consciousness and which is not identical with definitions proposed by canonical *poeticae*. Fabulists such as Krylov and Sumarokov form complex systems with their own semantics, their own versification schemes, and other specifics. Deals with a series of generalizations and the specifics of genre lines for individual fabulists. The fable has, in summary, "its own poetics."

1362. Vine, Guthrie. "Around the Earliest Spanish Version of Aesop's Fables." *The John Rylands Library Bulletin*, 25 (1941), 97–118.

Deals with the Spanish translation of *Aesopica* printed at Toulouse in 1488, of which the only known copy is in the John Rylands Library and which is a Spanish version of the *Esopus* of Heinrich Steinhöwel. The translation was made for Henry, Infant of Aragon.

1363. Voigt, Ernst. *Ysengrimus.* Halle/Salle: Niemeyer, 1884.

The numerous annotations and the lengthy introduction touch on the relationship of the beast epic to the Aesopic fable and identify numerous fabular motifs found in the work, especially *leo agrotans*, P585 "Sick Lion, Fox and Bear" (A–T 50; TMI B240.4).

1364. ———. *Egberts von Lüttich Fecunda Ratis.* Halle/Salle: Niemeyer, 1889. lxvi + 273 pp.

Text and extensive commentary to Egbert's collection of sentenciae, with mention of some sixteen fables.

1365. ———. "Ein unbekanntes Lehrbuch der Metrik aus dem 11. Jahrhundert." *Mitteilungen der Gesellschaft für deutsche Erziehungs- und Schulgeschichte*, 4 (1894), 149–158.

Two parchment leaves found in the wood covers of the
Würzburg manuscript of Ambrosius (Theol. fol. 26) contain fables as examples of metrical rules from a textbook on metrics. The examples are given as promythia,
followed by the corresponding fables in hexameters.

1366. Vollgraf, G. "Ad Phaedr. Append. Fab. XI." *Mnemosyne*,
42 (1914), 444.

Textual emendation suggestion to Phaedrus' "Iuno,
Venus et Galliana," P539 "Juno, Venus and the Hen"
(TMI J1908).

1367. Vollmer, Friedrich. "Beiträge zur Chronologie und
Deutung der Fabeln des Phaedrus." *Sitzungsbericht
der bayerische Akademie der Wissenschaften* (1919),
44-122.

Places Phaedrus significantly later than usual.
Vollmer suggests that the literary activity of Phaedrus
belongs to a later time than before the fall of Sejanus,
perhaps Claudius, and therefore the prologue to book III
has been understood incorrectly.

1368. Volz, Hans. "Ein Quellenbeitrag zu den Fabeln des
Erasmus Alber." *Zeitschrift für deutsche Philologie*,
(1958), 59-63.

On Erasmus Alberus' version of P640 "Soldier and
Serpent" and P640A "Dragon and Peasant" (TMI J1172.3)
and its source. Volz finds the fable with Alberus'
peculiarities in Melanchthon and in the collection of
Joachim Camerarius, Melanchthon's friend.

1369. Vonessen, F. "Die Erde als Stiefmutter: Zur Mythologie
eines Märchenmotifs." *Symbolon*, 1 (1972), 113-137.

Touches upon Babrius 35, P218 "The Ape's Twin Off-
spring" (TMI L141.1, L146.1) with the concept of the
mother Earth being the true mother of mankind. Deals
with Lucretius, Plato, and others.

1370. Vossler, Karl. *La Fontaine und sein Fabelwerk*.
Heidelberg: Carl Winter, 1919. 196 pp.

Vossler first places La Fontaine in his chronological
and political environment and discusses his education,
leading to his position as a satirist and as a humorist.
The fable is treated in detail, with an historical
survey leading up to La Fontaine and covering some of

the literary influence of the poet. The fables are
dealt with in detail and two of the appendices are
devoted to individual motifs. With bibliographical
notes.

1371. Waas, Christian. *Die Quellen der Beispiele Boners.*
Dissertation, Giessen, 1897.

Source study on Ulrich Boner's *Edelstein.* Most
fables are from the recension of Romulus although
numerous other possible and probable sources are
postulated.

1372. ————. "Quellen des Bonarius." *Zeitschrift für
deutsches Altertum,* 46 (1902), 341-359.

Extensive listings of possible sources and parallels
to Der Edelstein, the fables of Ulrich Boner.

1373. Wache, Karl. "Der Tierfabel in der Weltliteratur."
Zeitschrift für die osterreichischen Gymnasien, 69
(1919/1920), 416-439.

Essentially a listing of all sorts of *Tierdichtungen,*
including fables, from all over the world, but especially those in German and Latin for use in schools.

1374. Waddell, W.G. "Codex Alexandrinus Aesopi fabularum."
*Byzantion: Revue internationale des Etudes Byzan-
tines,* 6 (1931), 326-331.

A description of Codex 57 of the Library of the
Greek Patriarchs of Alexandria and its importance for
the textual tradition of the fables of the Greek
Prose tradition. Contains 140 fables written in two
hands. With two plates.

1375. ————. "A Plea for Aesop in the Greek Classroom."
Classical Journal, 32 (1936), 167-170.

Gives various reasons why Aesop ought to be a
suitable text for the learning of Greek just as the
Phaedrus fables have always been for Latin studies.

1376. Wadsworth, Phillip A. *Young La Fontaine: A Study of
his Artistic Growth in his Early Poetry and First
Fables.* Evanston, Ill.: Northwestern University
Press, 1952. 229 pp.

A compelling introduction to the literary activities
of La Fontaine up to and including the composition of

the first edition of the *Fables* in 1668. The last chapter is devoted to the *Fables*, including the importance of the little-known *Clymène* and the fable tradition that preceded him, especially Phaedrus and the texts contained in the *Mythologia aesopica*, which served as La Fontaine's source material if not models. The Greek fables, "Aesop," are treated differently; a separate section is also given over to La Fontaine's fable theory, including his ideas on brevity. The work ends with a discussion of the publication of the first edition and the illustrations of the fables; the conclusion deals with the aftermath of the publication and La Fontaine becoming a public figure.

1377. ————. "La Fontaine's Theories on the Fable as a Literary Form." *Rice University Studies*, 57: 2 (1971), 115-127.

La Fontaine's First Edition was essentially a new literary genre with few theoretical underpinnings. The preface contains a recounting of Phaedrine and other classical rhetorical arguments, but La Fontaine was also aware of such contemporary theorists as there were. La Fontaine does not develop, however, a full-blown theory for the verse fable.

1378. ————. "The Art of Allegory in La Fontaine's *Fables*." *French Review*, 45 (1972), 1125-1135.

The Fables are allegorical in that they contain a moral and have thus a literal meaning and a didactic element. There is also a web of allegorical allusions among the animal characters in the fables to be compared to those humans for whom they stand. Allegory is always present though usually quite subtle.

1379. ————. "Le douzième livre des *Fables*." *Cahiers de l'Association Internationale des Etudes Françaises*, 26 (1974), 103-115.

An investigation into the nature of the twelfth, the last, book in the *Fables* by La Fontaine describes contents and bibliographical details with comments upon the materials written for the pleasure and instruction of the Duke of Bourgogne.

1380. ————. "La Fontaine's Poems of Self-Appraisal." *Papers on French Seventeenth-Century Literature*, 4: 5 (1976), 57-74.

Demonstrates that La Fontaine was greatly dependent
upon models and that he tried too many paths and
missed too many goals in following, occasionally,
the wrong model in his poems and fables.

1381. ————. "La Fontaine and the Classical Ideal." *French*
Literature Studies, 7 (1980), 1-15.

Deals with the fables and a number of other works
as representative of La Fontaine's idea of classicism.
A number of La Fontaine's expressed opinions on literature and aesthetics are found in the fables as they
reflect a sense of proportion, of modesty in expression of feelings and ideas, and other aspects
of classicism. Yet La Fontaine's aesthetics were
reduced to stylistic problems.

1382. Wagner, Fritz. "Äsopika." *Enzyklopädie des Märchens*.
Ed. Kurt Ranke, et al. Berlin: de Gruyter, 1977.
1, 889-901.

Concise historical overview of the fable essentially
in Germany from the earliest collections through
Rudolf Kirsten and Helmut Arntzen. Bibliographical
notes.

1383. ————. "Babrios." *Enzyklopädie des Märchens*. Ed.
Kurt Ranke et al. Berlin: de Gruyter, 1979. I,
1123-1128.

Recounts the rediscovery of Babrius and his fables
together with a reconstruction of the history of the
fables. Appends a history of Tale Types to show the
vitality of the motifs in oral tradition. Good bibliography in the notes.

1384. ————. "Bestiarien." *Enzyklopädie des Märchens*. Ed.
Kurt Ranke et al. Berlin: de Gruyter, 1979. 2,
214-226.

An excellent concise historical survey of the European tradition of bestiaries with occasional mention
of fables. Bibliographical materials covered in the
notes.

1385. Walther, Heinrich. "Fabeln und Anekdoten im 5. und 6.
Schuljahr." *Der Deutschunterricht*, 31: 4 (1979),
19-30.

Discusses the work of Dorothea Adler and Axel Kress

and presents a practical methodological system for the use of fables in the fifth and, later, with another approach, the seventh school year. Texts and examples of leading questions, hints, and partial compositions are provided.

1386. Waltz, René. "Phèdre et La Fontaine." *L'Information Littéraire*, 6: 3 (1954), 89-97.

Attempts to demonstrate La Fontaine's enrichment of Phaedrus' motifs in his treatment. La Fontaine is considered the greatest poet of his time, and Phaedrus is hardly to be counted a great poet. Surveys Phaedrus' historical evaluation and suggests La Fontaine's opinion of the Latin fabulist. Numerous comparisons of selected passages from Phaedrus compared to the corresponding sections in La Fontaine.

1387. Warnke, Karl. *Die Fabeln der Marie de France*. Biblioteca Norman: ca. no. 6. Halle/Salle: Niemeyer, 1898. cxlvi + 447 pp.

The definitive edition of Marie de France's 102 fables preceded by an extensive introduction detailing the textual history and sources. The variant readings from all major manuscripts are given in the apparatus and a glossary is printed.

1388. ————. "Die Quellen des Esope der Marie de France." *Forschungen zur Romanischen Philologie: Festgabe für Hermann Sucher*. Halle/Salle: Niemeyer, 1900, pp. 161-284.

Comprehensive presentation of the fable collection of Marie de France, the oldest European vernacular collection. Discusses individually and in detail the sources for the fables which are based upon the collection of "Alfred" from the early 12th century. The primary source is ultimately the Romulus Nilantii tradition, and the complicated transmission into the putative "Alfred" collection. Each fable is described with regard to its position in the tradition as well as its ultimate source.

1389. Warren, S.J. "Herodot VI, 126." *Hermes*, 29 (1894), 476-478.

On an Indian fable from the Jātakas, which has apparent echoes in Herodotus' mention of a proverb.

1390. Watson, A. "Aesop's Fables." *American Artist*, 5: 9
       (1941), 18-19.

       Reproductions of three of Watson's illustrations
       for the Peter Pauper Press edition of *Aesop's Fables*,
       together with a short biography.

1391. Waugh, Butler Higgins, Jr. "The Child and the Snake:
       A-T 285, 672c and Related Forms in Europe and
       America: A Comparative Folklore Study." Disserta-
       tion, Indiana, 1960.

       In addition to the main body of the text, a study
       of A-T 285, 672c, the closely related fable P51 "Farmer
       and Snake" (A-T 285A; TMI J15) is studied so as to
       demonstrate that the tale, as exemplified by Grimm 105,
       did not proceed from the fable. The original home of
       the tale is given as Northwestern Europe, perhaps
       England.

1392. Weales, Gerald. "The World in Thurber's Fables."
       Commonweal, 55 (1957), 409-411.

       A review of James Thurber's *Further Fables for Our
       Time* and a comparison of this collection with Thurber's
       Fables for Our Times which appeared fifteen years
       earlier. The newer collection is characterized as
       bitter but with a new kind of strength when compared
       to the flippant earlier fables. Thurber's political
       fables are discussed in their historical milieu.

1393. Weddigen, Otto. *Das Wesen und die Theorie der Fabel
       und ihre Hauptvertreter in Deutschland*. Leipzig,
       1913.

       Deals essentially with Lessing, Gellert and Grimm
       only, despite the title. The theoretical writings of
       Lessing are paraphrased and then compared to those of
       Grimm, stressing in the comparison Lessing's own
       fables rather than his theoretical writings. Con-
       siders Gellert's verse fable to be continuing in the
       tradition of La Fontaine (all of which Lessing dis-
       avows) and the true carrier of the genre.

1394. Wehrli, Max. "Vom Sinn des mittelalterlichen Tierepos."
       German Life and Letters, 10 (1956), 219-228. Re-
       printed in *Mittellateinische Dichtung*. Ed. Karl
       Langosch. Darmstadt: Wissenschaftliche Buchgesell-
       schaft, 1969, 467-480.

A survey of the medieval beast epic with the fable
mentioned in passing as being associated with the form.
The beast epic is assumed to have developed essentially
from the Aesopic fable. Extensive discussion of the
medieval exponents of the genre: *Ecbasis captivi*, *Isen-*
grimus, *Reinhart Fuchs*, and other narratives.

1395. Weil, Henri. "Plusieurs fables de Babrios sur tab-
lettes de cire." *Journal des Savants* (1894), 142-152
and 320.

Notes on the third-century wax tablets containing
fragments of Babrian fables. Notes to Hesseling "On
Waxen Tablets," with emendations and suggests that
Babrius had two versions of no. 43, P74 "Stag at the
Fountain" (TMI L461).

1396. Weinreich, Otto Karl. *Fabel, Aretalogie, Novelle.*
Beiträge zu Phadrus, Petron, Martial und Apuleius.
Sitzungsbericht der Heidelberger. Heidelberger Akademie
der Wissenschaften. Philosophisch-historische Klasse,
1930-1931, 7. Abhandlung. 74 pp. Heidelberg: Winter,
1931. 75 pp. + illus.

Starts with the notion in Thiele's *Phaedrus Studien*
of the connections between Phaedrus and the *Novella*.
A number of Phaedrus fables are used to describe
the relationship, especially Phaedrus Appendix 16,
P544 "Two Suitors" (TMI K1371.1, N721), which is compared to Apuleius. The second part attributes a number of fables to Martial and the essay concludes with an
extended discussion P543 "Widow and Soldier" ("Widow
of Ephesus," TMI K2213.1).

1397. ———. "Zu Babrius 107 und Martial I, 20." *Philo-*
logus, 40 (1931), 370-372.

On P150 "Lion and Mouse" (A-T 75; TMI B371.1) as
found in Babrius 107 and possible mention of the fable
in Martial.

1398. Weis, Ludwig. "Die Tierfabel in der Volksschule."
Neue Wege zur Unterrichtsgestaltung (Berlin), 15
(1964), 254-264.

Various notes on the use of fables in elementary
and secondary education within the German school system.

1399. Weische, Alfons. "Avianus." *Enzyklopädie des Märchens.*
Berlin: de Gruyter, 1979. I, 1099-1104.

A concise survey of Avianus' life and works insofar
as these facts are known. Avianus' forty-two fables
are characterized as coming from Babrius. Bibliographical notes. The article is followed by a note
by Kurt Ranke (q.v.).

1400. Weitzmann, Kurt. "Aesopian Fable." *Ancient Book Il-
       lustration*. Cambridge: Harvard University Press,
       1959, 111-114.+ plates.

       Aesop's fables' popularity as a subject for illus-
       trations is here attributed to the popularity of the
       form itself and its "fitness to pictorialization."
       The article provides a cursory overview of picture
       cycles that demonstrate illustrated Aesop manuscripts
       in classical antiquity. Pl "Fox and Eagle" (TMI
       K2295) and P158 "Wolf and Nurse" (TMI J2066.5) are
       shown in various illustrations.
       See: Goldschmidt, "An Early Manuscript," and Hodnett.

1401. Welsch, David. *Ignacy Krasicki*. New York: Twayne,
       1969, pp. 52-57.

       Introduced by a brief survey of the history of the
       Aesopic in Poland, the chapter "Krasicki the Fabulist"
       surveys the various editions of Krasicki fables with
       regard to source material and the particular ideas
       of the author on the form. The fables are written
       to illustrate human weaknesses but use animals in
       other than their stereotypical characterizations.
       Fables and parables are treated together. With a
       useful bibliography.

1402. Werchun, Zofia Jonina. "The Influence of La Fontaine
       on Krylov." Dissertation, Northwestern, 1973. 126
       pp.

       Deals with two specific areas: the use of themes
       borrowed by Krylov from La Fontaine and an evaluation
       of those sections which can be compared. A number of
       changes are discussed although the influence of La
       Fontaine is still clearly seen. The fabular worlds
       of the two poets, though connected by important liter-
       ary ties, are nevertheless quite distinct. Krylov is
       shown to be strongly individualistic.

1403. Werner, J. *Quaestiones Babrianae*. Berlin: Calvery,
       1891. 27 pp.

       Deals with questions of authorship of a number of

fables that have survived only in prose paraphrase and problems of metrics. Babrius' nationality is briefly touched upon.

1404. Wesselski, Albert. *Erlesenes*. Prag: Gesellschaft deutscher Bücherfreunde, 1928.

Deals with short narratives, including fables, together with much else, though only incidentally with other forms.

1405. West, M.L. "The Parodos of the Agamemnon." *Classical Quarterly*, 29 (1979), 1-6.

West points out that commentators have noted Aeschylus was influenced by two Homeric Vulture similies in the Agamemnon Parados but that there is yet a third passage of early poetry, the Archilochus' epode containing Pl "Eagle and Fox" (TMI K2295, L315.3). A number of close parallels are pointed out for comparison.

1406. White, H. "A Debated Passage in Theocritus." *Hermes*, 106 (1978), 250-251.

A disputed passage, Theocritus I, 46 ff. is explained by a similar circumstance in Babrius 86, P24 "Fox with Swollen Belly" (A-T 41; K1022.1).

1407. White, P.F. "Rewriting Fables." *English Language Teaching*, 29: 2 (1975), 129-134.

Suggests four criteria or levels for adapting and rewriting fables for English as a Second Language classes: vocabulary, structure and phonology, cultural appropriateness, and "skills of living."

1408. White, Robert Ogden. "The Importance of Verse Fables in Swift's Poetic Achievement: 'In Proper Terms to Write a Fable.'" Dissertation, Boston University, 1976. 572 pp.

A far-reaching study of the use of Jonathan Swift's verse fables, especially his special combination of imitative and innovative style in his Aesopic adaptations. Investigation of Swift's fable style suggests various methods for analyzing Swift's other material. The dialogue within a fable imitates popular speech, whether used by animal or human actors. The fables are studied in their historical context, and connections

are drawn between the themes of some of the fables
and those of Swift's more famous works.

1409. Whitesell, Frederick R. "Fables in Medieval Exempla."
       Journal of English and Germanic Philology, 46 (1947),
       348-366.

       A somewhat confused introductory statement on the
       nature of the fable and exempla tradition is followed
       by a very useful catalog and finding list of fables
       found within exempla collections and together with
       exempla in other texts. 311 fables were found in
       medieval exempla collections, some frequently.

1410. Widmayer, Jayne A. "Hemingway's Hemingway Parodies:
       The Hypocritical Griffon and the Dumb Ox." *Studies
       in Short Fiction* (1969), 433-438.

       Deals with Hemingway's "The Good Lion" and "The
       Faithful Bull," published in 1951 as satiric attacks
       on pretension and affectations. "The Good Lion" is a
       parody of the way the Hemingway hero acts, "The Faith-
       ful Bull" parodies the motivations of the Hemingway
       hero.

1411. Wiechers, Anton. *Aesop in Delphi*. Dissertation,
       Köln, 1959. And Beiträge zur klassischen Philologie,
       no. 2. Meisenheim/Glan: Hain, 1961. 51 pp.

       A description of the tale of Aesop's death at Delphi
       as related in *Vita G* and in *Vita W*, as well as in
       Herodotus. An analogy is drawn to the idea of the
       pharmkos ritual and to other purification rites in
       Greek religion. A connection is made to the mytho-
       logical tradition of the death of Neoptolemes at
       Delphi; concludes that the two traditions run parallel.

1412. Wienert, Walter. *Die Typen der griechisch-römischen
       Fabel mit einer Einleitung über das Wesen der Fabel*.
       FFC, no. 56. Helsinki: Finnish Academy, 1925.

       A rewrite of Wienert's dissertation for Giessen, on
       the pattern of Aarne attempts a work preparatory to a
       comparative study and history of the fable. Begins
       with nature of the fable in which he defines the fable
       as a narration of a concrete action, from which a
       generalized truth or truism can be gleaned by means
       of active mental activity on the part of the hearer.
       This can be allegorical or metaphysical or a simple
       generalization. Contains a good overview of the litera-

ture on the theoretical basis for the fable up to his time. The main body of the text is concerned with a classification scheme for the Aesopic type of fables, according to main groupings: the *Erzählungstypen*, in which the fables are classified according to *Märchen-fabeln*, with many sub-divisions; *Sagen* and *Legendenfabel*, *Novellenfabeln* and anecdotal fables, according to their similarity to those types, which are not well-defined. The *Märchen* becomes essentially a fable by means of didactic content; the *Sage* and the *Novelle* by a form of generalization. The other main classification system is according to *Sinntypen* or to 57 different themes expressed by fables. The work ends with a register of fables according to *Erzählungstyp* and to *Sinntyp*. The essay on the nature of the fable still has value; the classification scheme has found no followers.

1413. Wierschin, Martin. "Einfache Formen bei Stricker? Zu Strickers Tierbispel und seinen kurzen Verserzählungen." *Werk—Typ—Situation*. *Festschrift Hugo Kuhn*. Ed. Ingeborg Glier et al. Stuttgart: Matzler, 1969, 118-136.

Modifies Jolles' system to include the *bîspel*, although staying with literary production rather than Jolles' archetypical forms, so as to discuss Der Stricker's fables in contrast to other *einfache Formen*.

1414. Wikander, Stig. "Från indisk djurfabel till isländsk saga." Vetenskaps-Societeten i Lund. *Arsbok* (1964), 87-114.

Postulates from faint traces an Arabic fable in Saxo Grammaticus and in the *Gautreks Saga* of Iceland. The path of transmission would be from the *Kalila and Dimna* Arabic tradition as literary influences upon Northern Europe through the medium of the Humanism, especially the French Coast Humanism of the 12th century. Baldo's *Novus Aesopus*, the Latin Paraphrase of *Kalila*, is the most likely immediate transmittor.

1415. Wilisch, Erich. "Spuren altkorinthischer Dichtung ausser Eumelos." *Jahrbucher für classische Philologie*, 27 (1881), 161-169.

Discusses the relationship of Aesop to Corinth; through Socrates' versification of Aesop and proverbial study a connection to the Corinthians is established.

The etymology of the name is also associated with
Corinthian Greek.

1416. Wilke, Christian Hartung. "Fabel als Instrument der
Aufklärung." *Basis: Jahrbuch für deutsche Gegenwarts-
literatur*, 2 (1971), 71-102.

A concise overview of German fable research during
the 1960's, with incisive (though overdrawn in part)
thoughts on the modern fable which leads Wilke to the
eighteenth century, especially Pfeffel and Lessing,
and then back to the modern fabulists Arntzen, Schnurre,
Schütt, and others. The idea of a resurgence of the
fable as an independent form in the modern day is un-
thinkable, but the ironic fable and fragments continue.

1417. Wilkinson, James V.S. *The Lights of Canopus, Anvār i
Suhailī*. London: The Studio, 1929. 53 pp.

Description of Add. 18.579 in the British Museum
with a precis of the fables in a historical overview.
Fourteen miniature illustrations accompany the stories
in this Mogul manuscript.

1418. Williams, Gordon. "Dogs and Leather." *Classical Review*, 9 (1959), 97-100.

Discusses P135 "Famished Dogs" (TMI J1791.3.2) in
connection with Greek proverbs linking dogs with an
insatiable appetite for leather.

1419. Williams, Perry A. "La Fontaine in Haitian Creole: A
Study of Cric? Crac! by Georges Sylvain." Dissertation, Fordham, 1973. 71 pp.

A study of Sylvain's *Cric? Crac!* (1901), a thirty-
one fable collection of Haitian Creole versions of La
Fontaine fables, to determine the purpose, technique,
and the language of the work. Sylvain reworked an
earlier Martiniquan version of La Fontaine, using
various techniques to recreate and imitate the oral
narratives of Haiti. The language is an idealized
representation of a rural western Haitian dialect.

1420. Williams, Ronald J. "The Literary History of a Mesopotamian Fable." *The Phoenix*, 10 (1956), 70-77.

A Mesopotamian fable "Serpent and Eagle" loosely
connected to P1 "Eagle and Fox" (TMI K2295; L315.3)
is traced from the Akkadian legend of Etana (preserved

in three recensions, Old Babylonian, Middle Assyrian, and Neo-Assyrian) through Archilochus, "Aesop," Aristophanes, Phaedrus, Babrius, and the *Panchatantra* as well as Syriac versions, medieval Greek forms, Armenian, and Marie de France's Old French and the Mishle Shu'alim's Hebrew.

1421. ————. "The Fable in the Ancient Near East." *A Stubborn Faith: Papers on Old Testament and Related Subjects Presented to Honor W.A. Irwin.* Dallas: Southern Methodist University Press, 1956, 3-26.

Points out that the fable with both animal and plant actors can be placed at least one thousand years earlier than Aesop (roughly sixth century, B.C.) and much earlier than the Indian fables as found in the *Panchatantra,* which Williams dates to roughly the fourth century A.D. Gives a significant number of Babylonian and Egyptian texts and bibliographical references.

1422. Wilson, Robert H. "The Poggiana in Caxton's *Esope.*" *Philological Quarterly,* 30 (1951), 348-352.

Discusses the thirteen tales and fables from Poggio Braccolini in Caxton's *Esope,* which was translated into English from Julien Macho's French version of Heinrich Steinhöwel's *Esopus.* Discusses especially the additions to this section apparently made by Caxton.
See: Lenaghan, *Caxton's Aesop.*

1423. Wilson, R.M. *The Lost Literature of Medieval England.* 2nd ed. London: Methuen, 1970.

Discusses shreds of evidence for now-lost fable collections (pp. 124-127). Reference is made to the lost collection of Walter of England which served as the basis for Marie de France and gives three isolated examples of survivals before Caxton's printing of the Steinhöwel collection.

1424. Windfuhr, Manfred. "Nachwort." *Deutsche Fabeln des 18. Jahrhunderts.* Stuttgart: Reclam, 1965.

Discusses in overview the form and function of the fable in Germany during the eighteenth century. With numerous examples from representative fabulists from Triller to Heinse, roughly from 1740-1790, a period during which scarcely a German writer did not at least attempt the fable form.

1425. Winkler, Emil. "Das Kunstproblem der Tierdichtung,
       besonders der Tierfabel." *Hauptfragen der Romanistik:*
       Festschrift für Phillip August Becker. Heidelberg:
       Winter, 1922, pp. 280-306.

       Argues for an emphasis upon artistic and psychological
       studies of medieval literature in place of the source
       studies that had been the hallmark of earlier work.
       Investigates the underlying mechanics of the anthropo-
       morphism of the animal fable, the extent of the process,
       and the aesthetics of such a literary technique. Dis-
       cusses prejudices for and against certain animals as
       conditioning elements, investigating Lessing's re-
       search in this area. A survey of studies of reality
       in the fable ends the essay.

1426. Winterfeld, Paul. "Zu Avianus." *Rheinisches Museum*
       für Philologie, 57 (1902), 167-168.

       Suggests that Lachmann's dating of Avianus ought to
       be put down. Earliest possible date seems to be the
       second half of the fourth century because of the
       metrics the poet used.

1427. Wirth, Peter. "Eine bislang unbekannte griechische
       Fabel." *Wiener Studien*, 75 (1962), 161-162.

       Texts of "Strogthion kai Ixeytes" a fable not in the
       Aesopian texts from Byzantine authors but found in full
       form in the historian Gregorus and in shorter form in
       Kantakuzenos.

1428. Witt, Karl. "Heinrich Harries. Ein schleswig-holst-
       einer Fabeldichter der Aufklärungszeit." *Neue*
       Heimat, 57 (1950), 90-92.

       A note on the life of Harries and brief mention of
       a few of his fables.

1429. Witzel, Maurus. "Ein Stück sumerischer Weisheit."
       Orientalia, 17 (1948), 1-16.

       Text and commentary on a fragmentary Sumerian fable
       concerning fish and birds who take a dispute to Enki
       for judgment.

1430. Wolf, Herbert. "Erzähltradition in homelititschen
       Quellen." *Volkserzählung und Reformation: Ein Hand-*
       buch zur Tradierung und Funktion von Erzählstoffen
       und Erzählliteratur im Protestantismus. Ed. Wolfgang
       Brückner. Berlin: Schmidt, 1974, 705-756.

A comprehensive survey of the use of traditional narrative materials, especially in sixteenth-century sermons, including a large number of fables and other *Aesopica*. This material is discussed in regard to rhetorical functions. Points out the lack of formal training and a comprehensive, theoretical framework connecting the numerous protestant preachers and suggests the use of traditional materials is a natural consequence. The problems of classifying the wide range of materials used are enumerated as are the various genres represented. The fable is described as extremely popular in the pulpit although not without its critics. The fable in Luther, Herberger, Cober, Schnapp, and others is studied in detail.

1431. ————. "Fabeln." *Martin Luther*. Stuttgart: J.B. Metzler, 1980, 145-149.

Good survey of previous research on and overview of Luther's fable activity as part of an overall treatment of Luther from the point of view of philology. Luther's attitude toward the fable as genre and his use of the form points to his emphasis upon the moral content and the epimythium, especially after 1528 when the value of the fable as a learning tool is stressed. A short bibliographical note ends the chapter.

1432. Wolfe, Bernard. "Uncle Remus and the Malevolent Rabbit." *Commentary*, 8 (1949), 31-41.

Curiously describes the Uncle Remus stories as sublimated, thinly disguised manifestations of "hate by the Negro." Chandler Harris was a psychopath and the proof that there could be no African origin for the tales is that the conditions of slavery did not exist there. The tales are more likely to derive from the *Roman de Renard* and the Easter Bunny.

1433. Wolff, Ludwig. "Zum zeitlichen Ansatz der Äsopdichtung Gerhards von Minden." *Jahrbuch des Vereins für niederdeutsche Sprachforschung*, 97 (1974), 113-115.

Suggests ca. 1270 as the most likely date for the 125-fable collection by Gerhard von Minden.

1434. Wölfflin, Eduard. "Die Epoden des Archilochus." *Rheinisches Museum*, 39 (1884), 156-157.

Archilochus' fables might be an integral part of his

satire. Also maintains that the homeland of Phaedrus
could not be "Perien"; rather one might only say he was
born on a mountain.

1435.   Wooller, Susan Jacqueline. "Lupus in Fabula: The Wolf
        in Medieval German Fables." Dissertation, McGill,
        1976.

An investigation of German medieval wolf fables, the
most numerous type. The majority of these first appear after the year 1000. The fables are analyzed and
classified with source studies and sociological implications.

1436.   Wotke, K. "Beiträge zu Babrius." *Wiener Studien*, 15:
        2 (1895), 301-305.

Suggests that the second Prologue after fable 107 can
be traced back to a manuscript in which the fables were
not arranged alphabetically.

1437.   Woznowski, Wactaw. *Bajka w literaturze poskiego oświe-
        cenia*. Universitus Iagellonica Acta scientiarum
        Litterarumque, 340. Jagiello University Press,
        1975. 186 pp.

The fable was an important genre in Polish literature, just as in other European literature. This interest was not confined to production but also involved
theoretical work. Lessing's work in the fable, for
example, was known in Poland at the beginning of the
nineteenth century. This monograph investigates the
work of Piramowicz, Trapczynski, Czerski, and Niemce-
wicz and traces the development of the fable generally
as a function of the reception of the La Fontaine
fable, especially in the case of Krasicki, who consciously imitated the French poet.

1438.   Wray, William. "The English Fable: 1650-1800." Dis-
        sertation, Yale, 1950.

Outlines and evaluates the rise and fall of the
fable as a literary genre in England through the close
of the eighteenth century. The fables of Ogilby,
L'Estrange, Swift, Gay (considered the best of English
fabulists), Gray, Smart, and others are examined. Good
bibliographical and indexing materials.
See: Noel, *Theories of the Fable*.

1439. Wünsche, August. "Die Pflanzenfabel in der neueren
       deutschen Literatur." *Zeitschrift für deutschen
       Unterricht*, 16 (1902), 20-44 and 77-110. Collected
       and expanded into *Die Pflanzenfabel in der Welt-
       literatur*. Leipzig: Akademischer Verlag, 1905.
       184 pp.

       A comprehensive survey of plant fables as a sub-
       category of the Aesopic type from Indian and classical
       literature through nineteenth-century German litera-
       ture, with most of the work actually concerned with
       the German forms. The commentary consists generally
       of source studies and listings of parallels. No index
       and the fables cited are not keyed to standard collec-
       tions.

1440. Yarmolinsky, Avrahm. "Aesop in Russia: A Spencer
       Accession." *Bulletin of the New York Public Library*,
       58 (1954), 2-5.

       Describes the *Zhitie ostroumnavo Esopa* ("The Life of
       Sharpwitted Aesop") acquired by the Spencer collection.
       The sixteen-page text is apparently a paraphrase of
       the *Vita Aesopi* in the Planudean tradition although
       not composed by Planudes as Yarmolinsky incorrectly
       indicates here. Engravings and translation are care-
       fully delineated.

1441. Yates, Donald Neal. "The Cock and the Fox Episodes of
       Isengrimus, Attributed to Simon of Ghent: A Literary
       and Historical Study." Dissertation, North Carolina,
       Chapel Hill, 1969. 202 pp.

       Two episodes of *Isengrimus* are versions of P562
       "Partridge and Fox" (A-T 60, cf. 61A; TMI K561.1,
       K721) and P671 "Fox and Dove" (A-T 62; TMI J1421) and
       these are related to historical events concerning Al-
       visus, the Bishop of Arras. The literary forms are
       traced carefully from antiquity through the twelfth
       century with analogues in Ademar, Alcuin, Marie de
       France, and numerous other sources and parallels.
       The insertion of these fables into a mock-epic is
       likened to the development of Arthurian materials.
       The author is determined to be most likely Simon of
       Ghent.

1442. Yoder, Audry. *Animal Analogy in Shakespeare's Charac-
       ter Portrayal*. New York: Columbia University Press,
       1947.

Following Baldwin, Yoder believes that the ultimate
source of virtually all of Shakespeare's fables and
allusions to fable characters is the Latin collection
of Joachim Camerarius and adds to Baldwin's lists of
fables and fable fragments identified previously from
that source. Yoder then lists other references to
animals to determine typical characterizations,
demonstrating that the poet generally follows the
classical tradition. The very functional appendices
are listings of animal references, notes to editions
of Aesop since Shakespeare, and forms of the Aesopic
fables alluded to or quoted by Shakespeare. Extensive bibliography.

1443. Zacher, J. "Zu Boner." *Zeitschrift für deutsche
       Philologie*, 11 (1880), 336-343.

       Presents versions of three fabular motifs, including
       P543 "Widow and Soldier" (A-T 1510; TMI K2213.1), from
       the library at Wernigerode. These materials are
       closely connected to the Ulrich Boner fable tradition.
       The manuscript is described and the three texts are
       reprinted with parallels listed.

1444. Zahlten, Emil. *Sprichwort und Redensart in den Fast-
       nachtspielen des Hans Sachs*. Dissertation, Hamburg,
       1921. 144 pp.

       Lists and discusses hundreds of proverbs and pro-
       verbial phrases found in the work of Hans Sachs, in-
       cluding a number of fabular origin. The relationship
       of proverbs to fables is discussed in the context of
       Hans Sachs having used well over one hundred fables in
       his writing.

1445. Zajaczkowski, Ananjusz. "Turecka wersja baiki ezopwei
       o zonie i smierci." *Pamietnik Literacki*, 29 (1932),
       465-475.

       Discusses a Turkish translation and parallel versions
       to P60 "Old Man and Death" (TMI C11) and mentions other
       fabular motifs.

1446. Zander, Karl M. *De generibus et libris paraphrasium
       Phaedrianarum*. Lund: Royal Society, 1897. 42 pp.

       Especially careful analysis of the Phaedrine para-
       phrases of the Middle Ages. Presents no firm conclu-
       sions but points out numerous potential areas for re-

search. Excellent summaries of research through the nineteenth century.

1447.   ————. *Phaedrus solutus vel Phaedri fabulae novae xxx.* Lund: G. Gleerup, 1921. xcii + 71 pp.

Reconstruction of thirty Phaedrine fables, based essentially upon Ademar's illustrated manuscript. The Introduction deals with the establishment of the text and the criteria used in evaluating the tradition, all of which is a de facto commentary on Thiele, *Der lateinische Aesop.* Zander determines that the Romulus tradition is based upon at least two separate collections: one from the third century and the other from the fifth or early sixth. Annotations to the individual fables contain generally linguistic comments as the prose versions are printed on the left, the reconstructed verse forms on facing right-hand sides on the page. Zander is convinced of their authenticity, citing extensive stylistic evidence.

1447A. Zeitz, Heinrich. *Die Fragmente des Äsopromans in Papyrushandschriften.* Dissertation, Giessen, 1935. vi + 40 pp.

Partial publication of the dissertation includes the fragments from five papyri and some commentary. The comprehensive history of the material and its integration into the history of the *Vita Aesopi* followed in his "Der Äsoproman und seine Geschichte" (q.v.).
See: Perry, *Studies in the Text History.*

1448.   ————. "Der Äsoproman und seine Geschichte." *Aegyptus,* 16 (1936), 225-256.

Deals with the fragments found in various papyri concerning the text of the *Vita Aesopi,* but goes beyond those fragments toward an understanding of the history and tradition of the *Äsoproman.* Individual episodes are discussed in detail and the overall history is attempted. Herodotus is the oldest witness to the historicity of Aesop. The stay in Samos and his death at the hands of the Delphians are the oldest parts of the legends, and fables were attached to the Vita at its earliest stages. In addition to these elements, Aesop was early on associated with the "Seven Wise Ones" and there was an extensive oral tradition, possibly influenced by the oral tradition of Diogenes. The *Vita Aesopi,* as we have it in whatever version, is a relatively late work.

1449. Zeydel, Edwin H. "Betrachtungen über die *Ecbasis Cap-*
       tivi." *Mittellateinisches Jahrbuch*, 2 (1965), 102-
       110.

       This essay consists of a number of relatively un-
       related notes on the *Ecbasis Captivi* including the
       leo agrotans, P258 "Sick Lion, Wolf and Fox" (A-T 50;
       TMI B240.4, K961) motif which is discussed in terms
       of parallel uses and possible sources.

1450. Zielinski, Theo. "Das Wiesel als Braut." *Rheinisches*
       Museum für Philologie, 44 (1889), 156-157.

       A note on P50 "Weasel and Aphrodite" (TMI J1908.2)
       which is to be traced to the *Panchatantra*. Zielinski
       queries the use of the weasel and suggests that a
       near pun helped in the choice of animal character.

1451. Zimmermann, R.C.W. "Die Zeit des Babrio." *Blätter*
       für das Bayerische Gymnasial-Schulwesen, 59 (1933),
       310-318.

       Babrius is identified as a Syrian on the basis of
       statements in his collection favorable to Syria, and
       is dated at the beginning of the first century A.D.

1452. ———. "Zu Phaedrus." *Berliner Philologische*
       Wochenschrift, 54 (1934), 476-480.

       Suggests Phaedrus was falsely imprisoned on the
       basis of a curious reading of lines 38-50 of the third
       prologue. Various other aspects of Phaedrus' life and
       the chronology of the fables are discussed.

1453. Zirn, Anton. "Stoffe und Motive bei Hans Sachs in
       seinen Fabeln und Schwänken." Dissertation, Würzburg,
       1924. 202 pp.

       Listings of various themes and motifs in the fables
       of Hans Sachs as found in the Goetze-Drescher six-
       volume edition of Sachs' *Fabeln und Schwänke*. Zirn's
       work presents a difficult organizational system with
       numerous sub-categories. Most entries are single
       entries and are not related to other motif classifica-
       tion schemes.

1454. Zivojinović Massuka, Velimir. "Jedra studija o Lessing-
       ovim basnama u Dositeja Obradovica." *Misao. God.*,
       13 (1931), 285-286 and 379-380.

       Two notes on the presence of Lessing's fables in

Dositei Obradorić and on Schmaus' essay on the relationship of the two.

1455. Zoppi, Giovanni Battista. *La Morale della favole:*
Tempi antichi e medioevo. Milan: L.F. Cogliati,
1903. 264 pp.

Discusses the idea of the fable and its relationship to allegory with an introduction to the idea of
literature with morals. The "oriental" fable is outlined, leading to a discussion of the Aesopic type
which is treated historically. The limits of the
morals and various forms of the morals in fables from
India, Greece, and Rome are contrasted. The morals
and the influence of Christianity lead to a discussion
of various medieval collections from Marie de France
to John of Capua. The morals in the fable collections
are not always representative of the society in which
they are found.

1456. Zwierlein, Otto. "Der Codex Pithoeanus des Phaedrus
in der Pierpont Morgan Library." *Rheinisches Museum*
für Philologie, 113 (1970), 91-93.

An announcement that the Codex Pithoeanus of the
Phaedrine fables, dating from the ninth century and
until 1965 in the possession of the Marquis of Rosanbo,
is now in the Pierpont Morgan Library in New York.
Numerous textual emendations to the only previously
known copy of this manuscript, the 1893 copy made by
Roberts, are offered.

1457. Zwitzers, A.E. *Einiges über das Wesen der Fabel mit*
besonderer Berücksichtigung der Auffassung Lessings.
Emden, 1893. 16 pp.

Proceeds from Jacob Grimm's theory of the fable as
originating from the beast epic and, with a misunder-
standing of Lessing and polemic against Gervinus,
presents a scientifically exact set of observations
from nature as though this were in accord with Lessing's
view of the fable and the characters to be found in the
narratives.

NAME AND SUBJECT INDEX

The following index contains the names of fabulists and subjects treated in the works cited in the body of the bibliography. Individual fables are found in the fable index which follows.

INDEX OF FABLES

The following index lists those fables which are the subject of extended discussion in the works listed in the bibliography by Perry number, as found in that author's *Aesopica*. Other fables are ordered alphabetically by collection after these listings.

Other Fables:

TALE TYPE INDEX

The following index is a listing of those types which are the subject of extended or otherwise significant discussion within the works cited in the bibliography. The numbers correspond to those in Antti Aarne and Stith Thompson, *The Types of the Folktale: A Classification and Bibliography* (Helsinki: Academia scientiarum Fennica, 1964). These A-T numbers are followed by the Perry fable numbers and then by the Thompson Motif Index numbers in parentheses, wherever these are applicable. Entry numbers from the bibliography end the citations.

1	(TMI K341.2, K1026). 119, 660
2	(P625, "Wolf and Fox"; TMI K1021). 650, 728, 1176, 1296
6	(P562, P562A "Partridge and Fox"; TMI K561.1, K721). 366, 452, 608, 649, 815, 816, 945, 1032, 1247, 1278, 1441
31	(P9 "Fox and Goat in the Well"; TMI K652). 954
32	(P593 "Fox and Wolf in the Well"; TMI K651). 366, 389, 452, 725, 831
34	(P669 "Fox and Shadow of the Moon"; TMI J1791.3). 366
34A	(P133 "Dog with Meat and His Shadow"; TMI J1791). 24, 271, 297, 452, 638, 712
41	(P24 "Fox with Swollen Belly"; TMI K1027.1). 452, 498, 1406
47B	(P187 "Physician Wolf"; TMI K551.18, K566). 74, 646
47C	(P693 "Unlucky Wolf, Fox and Mule"; TMI K566, K1955). 74, 350, 728
47E	(P638 "Ass with Privilege"; TMI J1608, K55.1.18). 650, 690
50	(P142 "Fox and Old Lion"; TMI J644.1). 23, 48, 59, 1316. (P258 "Sick Lion, Wolf and Fox"; TMI K961). 340, 452, 519, 668, 1176, 1276, 1449. (P336 "Sick Lion, Fox and Stag"; TMI K402.3, K813). 23, 232, 675. (P585 "Sick Lion, Fox and Bear"; TMI B240.4). 668, 928, 999, 1278, 1363
51	(P149 "Lion's Share; TMI J811.1). 18, 143, 204, 290, 428, 712, 1117, 1176, 1278. (P339 "Lion and Ass,